THE SPECTACLE of DEATH

Kristin Boudreau

THE SPECTACLE of DEATH

Populist Literary Responses to American Capital Cases

Prometheus Books

59 John Glenn Drive
Amherst, New York 14228-2197

Published 2006 by Prometheus Books

Inquiries should be addressed to
Prometheus Books
59 John Glenn Drive
Amherst, New York 14228–2197
VOICE: 716–691–0133, ext. 207
FAX: 716–564–2711
WWW.PROMETHEUSBOOKS.COM

10 09 08 07 06   5 4 3 2 1

Library of Congress Cataloging-in-Publication Data

Boudreau, Kristin, 1965–
    The spectacle of death : populist literary responses to American capital cases / Kristin Boudreau.
        p. cm.
    Includes bibliographical references and index.
    ISBN 1–59102–403–X (pbk. : alk. paper)
    1. Popular literature—United States—History and criticism. 2. Capital punishment in literature. 3. Executions and executioners in literature. 4. American literature—19th century—History and criticism. 5. American literature—20th century—History and criticism. 6. Capital punishment—United States—Public opinion. 7. Capital punishment in popular culture—United States. 8. Public opinion—United States. I. Title.

PS169.P64B68 2006
810.9'3554—dc22

                                                                                        2005038056

Printed in the United States of America on acid-free paper

For Kes

CONTENTS

Acknowledgments 9

Preface 11

Theoretical Introduction to Execution Literature:
Early American Criminal Narratives, the Power of Reading,
and the Problem of Public Sentiments 19

Chapter One
Rewriting the Fall River Murder:
A Factory Town Turns to Sentimental Narratives 37

Chapter Two
The Haymarket Anarchist Trial of 1886 67

Chapter Three
Wisdom, Justice, and Moderation Abandoned: The Lynching of Leo Frank 105

Chapter Four
No Other Remedy: Community Awakening and the Lynching of Emmett Till 129

Chapter Five
Witnesses to an Execution: Norman Mailer's Spectacle of Death 163

Chapter Six
The Sweetheart of Death Row:
Karla Faye Tucker and the Problem of Public Sentiments   187

Conclusion
Artful Uprisings: The Campaign against Capital Punishment   207

Notes   225

Bibliography   269

Index   281

ACKNOWLEDGMENTS

I n the years since I began writing this book, I have spent a lot of time away from home in libraries and historical societies. I am grateful for the many research grants that have enabled me to travel. The University of Georgia provided funding from a variety of sources: the Sarah Moss Foundation, the UGA Research Foundation, and the UGA Center for Humanities and Arts. Interlibrary loan staff at Trinity University and the University of Georgia cheerfully and promptly responded to all my requests, and I thank them as well. I have been fortunate to visit the fine archives at Harvard University's Houghton Library, the John Hay Library at Brown University, the Fall River (Massachusetts) Historical Society, the American Antiquarian Society, the Rhode Island Historical Society, the William Bremen Jewish Heritage Museum in Atlanta, the Robert W. Woodruff Library at Emory University, the Newberry Library in Chicago, and the Chicago Historical Society.

I am also grateful for permission to reproduce work here that originally appeared elsewhere: the introduction was first published in *Early American Literature;* part of chapter one appeared in *ESQ: A Journal of the American Renaissance*; and part of chapter two appeared in *American Literature*. For permission to quote from its archives, I thank the Houghton Library at Harvard University. Thanks are also due to the following libraries and individuals for permission to reproduce their images: The John Hay Library at Brown University, the *Ligue Internationale Contre le Racism et l'Antisemitisme*, the Chicago Historical Society, *Newsweek*, and Kevin Kallaugher. Christopher Metress was extremely generous in sharing his research into the Emmett Till case. Susan Rosenbaum, Frances Kerr, and Jana Argersinger were discerning readers of parts of this book, and it is a better book because of them. At the University of Georgia I have enjoyed the friendship and confidence of Anne Williams, Doug Anderson, and Adam Parkes, who encouraged me in this project from the beginning; at home in Syracuse, Gordon Boudreau followed its fate as only a parent can; and here in Athens, Kes Roberts keeps me from brooding too long over books and newspapers. This book owes much to all of them. Above all, I am grateful to my brother Vince Boudreau for the many absorbing conversations we've had over the years about populist political movements. I wish this book bore more traces of the heights one reaches when talking to him about a favorite subject, or revealed him here as the cherished example of wisdom and enthusiasm that he's always been.

Finally, in the month before I finished this manuscript I had the great fortune of participating in a National Endowment for the Humanities seminar on Ralph Waldo Emerson, directed by Russell Goodman at the University of New Mexico. It has been a pleasure to wrap up this project with the example of Russell and my other Emersonian friends uppermost in my mind: their faith that many people do still read, that words can strike the chain that darkly binds us, and that when we give voice to the rules of love and justice, our words are current in all countries. It is an Emersonian exhortation, finally, that guides this book: "Speak what you think now in hard words."[1]

PREFACE

I f, as Plato believed, "there is an old quarrel between philosophy and poetry,"[1] it is also true that in the modern age the political realm has had good reason to quarrel with poetry and with imaginative literature more generally. Plato was suspicious of poetry because he understood its immense power in shaping cultural beliefs, and he considered that philosophers were in a better position to discern and to teach the proper attitudes toward ethics and politics. If in Plato's day poetry and philosophy competed for the just human soul, in our own day we might say that justice is being contested by politicians and imaginative writers. In ancient Greece, poetry was not printed and read in silence; it was performed in public spaces, like a contemporary play or rock concert. Just as ancient poets turned, dangerously, to public assemblies in order to stir up the human soul, some of the most troublesome literature of the days since Plato has relied on a mass readership, sometimes assembled together in (real or virtual) public spaces. The peril of such literary assemblies is nowhere more apparent than when the literature is written in response to controversies like capital trials and executions.

A contemporary example will illustrate this point. When the former prostitute, drug user, and pickax murderer Karla Faye Tucker was put to death by lethal injection in Texas in 1998, her execution provoked angry lamentations from around the globe. Tucker had been sentenced to die for a brutal murder; she did not deny that she had committed it. Still, with few exceptions, the many people who had followed her story in the press—a story of violence, incarceration, penitence, and redemption—found themselves identifying with the penitent criminal and wishing that her execution might be averted. When it was not, they wrote angry and sorrowful entries on a Web site devoted to the memory of this fallen woman.

Tucker was a remarkable death-row inmate because she inspired widespread pity, admiration, and tenderness, even among Americans who generally supported the death penalty and hardly noticed when a criminal was put to death. But if she seemed exceptional in 1998, her story would have been utterly predictable to anyone living in colonial America, where women were frequently executed for theft, infanticide, and other crimes, and where their executions (which were conducted in public, usually in the presence of an enormous crowd) often inspired this kind of outrage against the government. Some of the outrage survives in the form of literary expressions that might be seen as a primitive ancestor to the World Wide Web. In cheap and hastily produced broadsides, meant for immediate consumption in the wake of a public execution, ordinary Americans expressed their feelings in verse while their neighbors eagerly bought these publications, read them aloud, and circulated them to other readers. Because some of these ephemeral publications still survive, we know that a woman in Tucker's position was a familiar figure for American colonists, who were often confronted by and asked to judge the fallen woman standing before them. The close connection between executions, the sentiments of ordinary individuals, and popular literature is the subject of this book.

The nineteenth-century novelist Nathaniel Hawthorne understood these connections and dramatized the conflict between law and public sentiments. Public executions had been mostly abolished by Hawthorne's day, but he continued to recognize the troubling effect of law on public sentiments and public sentiments on law. How should a capital offender be treated, and can law withstand the conflicting feelings of the public? Hawthorne's 1850 romance, *The Scarlet Letter*, opens with a discussion about a capital crime and the decision to forego the customary death sentence in favor of a more lenient one. Adultery was a capital offense in the Massachusetts Bay Colony, the setting for Hawthorne's novel, but the magistrates' task of determining a just punishment for Hester Prynne is complicated by the fact that they do not know whether Hester's husband, missing for two years, is still alive. If he is dead, the woman is guilty of the lesser crime of fornication, a crime that does not require her execution. Hawthorne's Massachusetts magistrates clearly worry over this important distinction, but they also take advantage of the discretionary latitude allowed them in determining Hester's punishment. As one New Englander explains in this early scene, "Our Massachusetts magistracy, bethinking themselves that this woman is youthful and fair, and doubtless strongly tempted to her fall . . . have not been bold to put in force the extremity of our righteous law against her."[2] Swayed by "their great mercy and tenderness of heart," these leaders settle upon a lesser punishment for the unhappy Hester Prynne.[3] She is to stand for three hours upon the scaffold and to wear the scarlet letter, "a mark of shame upon her bosom," for the rest of her life.[4]

Though Hester regards the punishment as worse than death, her judges are clearly interested in rehabilitating as well as disciplining the wayward woman. When they urge her to confess and name the father of her child, they are calling for "a proof and consequence" of her earnest repentance[5]—and they intimate that such proof "may avail to take the scarlet letter off [her] breast."[6] Indeed, the magistrates have clearly agonized over the dilemma of how to treat this woman; having "laid their heads together in vain" to discover her partner in crime, they have also discussed sentencing options.[7] Their deliberations have concluded before the novel begins; like the adultery itself, this private debate among the magistrates takes place beyond the narrative.

But we do observe a parallel discussion that transpires among the colonists, ordinary people—primarily women—who have no official say in Hester Prynne's punishment. These women are characterized by a "boldness and rotundity of speech" and they express unequivocal opinions about the proper punishment for Hester.[8] Many of them dispute the official sentence handed down by the magistrates. One argues that "we women, being of mature age and church-members in good repute, should have the handling of such malefactresses as this Hester Prynne"; in such a case, the criminal would not "come off with such a sentence as the worshipful magistrates have awarded."[9] One calls for a more painful and permanent mark of shame: "At the very least, they should have put the brand of a hot iron on Hester Prynne's forehead."[10] Another calls for deeper humiliation: "I'll bestow a rag of mine own rheumatic flannel, to make a fitter" letter.[11] Yet another reminds her companions that the law calls for execution. "This woman has brought shame upon us all, and ought to die. Is there not law for it? Truly there is, both in the Scripture and the statute-book."[12] Other opinions are also offered—from a young woman who recognizes that Hester is suffering acutely, and from a man who rejects the idea that virtue depends upon the deterrent effects of punishment. The debate is interrupted by the public spectacle that ensues when the governor and clergymen, standing on the balcony of the meetinghouse, address Hester in front of her townspeople.

These two discussions—in the marketplace and on the balcony, among ordinary colonists and among their leaders—are separate but related. While the townspeople have no say in Hester's punishment, they are called upon to witness and participate in it, because the punitive effects of Hester's public shame depend upon the spectators who judge her. Hester imagines her punishment in corporeal terms: she feels "the heavy weight of a thousand unrelenting eyes"[13] and claims that the letter is "too deeply branded" to be removed.[14] The scarlet letter would have no penal value if it weren't for the many spectators who see it as "a living sermon against sin."[15] Hawthorne understood that official punishment was not entirely detached from public opinion—that, as Thomas Jefferson had written, the just power of any government is derived from the consent of the governed, and that the debates of private citizens over public policy were a necessary part of American society. Hawthorne's seventeenth-century marketplace resembles Jürgen Habermas's public sphere, which emerged in the eighteenth century as a place where private opinion was "purified through critical discussion . . . to constitute a true opinion."[16] Such public opinion "could compel lawmakers to legitimize themselves."[17] While ordinary subjects might not always have an official say in a criminal's sentence, they certainly play a role in seeing that their government imposed punishment fairly.

Hawthorne's novel, though set in colonial Massachusetts, is clearly the work of a nineteenth-century democrat, for in urging its readers to consider the interplay between public opinion and official judicial sentencing, *The Scarlet Letter* insists on the importance of reading, debating, and judging to the establishment and preservation of communal standards of justice. Hawthorne also understood that the political effects of reading communities could be secured by means of fictional texts, which brought spatially distant subjects together in what Benedict Anderson calls "imagined communities."[18] Though Hester Prynne was a fictitious character, her story was a composite of several capital cases that had confronted the first leaders of the Massachusetts Bay Colony.[19] More important, her story prompted readers to consider issues of justice, rebellion, and consent that were critical to nineteenth-century American culture. In drawing on historical fact to animate his fiction, Hawthorne resembled the many writers in American literary history who have used literary forms to dramatize actual capital cases.

The permeable boundary between fact and fiction, between civic activity and art, and between Hawthorne's marketplace and the balcony—between, that is, public opinion and the judicial system—is the subject of this book, which considers some of the most prominent American capital cases that generated debate among ordinary citizens. While Hester Prynne's townspeople (like their real seventeenth-century counterparts) had no access to the printing press, their discussions resemble the kinds of debates that would later be carried out in pamphlets, broadsides, poems, and novels, many of them hastily written, as well as in even more ephemeral literary forms like songs, speeches, and plays. I am using a flexible definition of "literary" here: although many of the authors of the texts I examine preferred using the forms favored by imaginative writers—poems, songs, plays, and novels—they did not especially care about their reputations as literary artists but were more concerned with reaching an immediate audience and persuading that audience to take some particular stand on a specific capital case. Most of the authors I examine would not have objected to being labeled propagandists. They used their access to the press in the way Habermas describes: in order to foster a rational-critical debate that would either approve of official decisions or subject such decisions to the authority of what they saw as reasonable citizen opinion. They saw imaginative literature as one potent means of fostering such a debate.

My introduction lays out the theoretical groundwork for this study, describing the emergence of gallows literature in the American colonies and the unruly political effects it could have on private readers. As I examine the complicated role of public sentiments in enforcing public order—and the threat to that order when witnesses to the rule of law identify more closely with the condemned criminal than with the law that requires execution—I demonstrate the important role that popular literary texts played in stirring up sentiment against the state when a charismatic convict was being put to death. Eighteenth-century debates about the value of fiction indicate that political leaders were well aware of this dangerous potential. The frequent public executions in early America enable us to consider the problems that public executions posed for the colonies and new republic. Political leaders called on the public to witness and endorse state-sponsored executions even as they feared that generous minds who witnessed such executions might turn against the state. Benjamin Rush's 1787 warning against public punishments cautioned that executions and other forms of punishment could provoke dangerous sympathy for the condemned criminal, pitting law-abiding subjects against their government. The 1797 execution of John Young and the ephemeral literature it inspired suggest that this fear was well founded. The chapters that follow explore the ways that public sentiments continued to prove dangerous throughout the history of America's long experiment with the death penalty.

Chapter 1 examines the 1833 capital trial of the Reverend Ephraim K. Avery, accused of murdering a factory worker near Fall River, Massachusetts. Avery's official trial was paralleled in the public sphere by a trial of words that, featuring Avery and his victim, set the Methodist Church against the textile factory owners and operatives. Although Avery's courtroom trial ended in an acquittal, the outraged citizens who believed he was guilty found a kind of surrogate justice in the marketplace, which issued a sentence of exile, obscurity, and poverty for the itinerant preacher and a charge of corruption against the court system.

Chapter 2 investigates the 1887 execution of the Chicago Haymarket anarchists, whose murder trial placed them at the center of a confrontation between labor and capital. The anarchists exploited the permeable boundary between marketplace and courtroom, using their defense as a means of echoing and inspiring the parallel trial that was taking place in the public sphere. Though their trial ended in conviction— and, for five of them, death—they managed to stimulate a well-orchestrated populist uprising that affected labor relations for years after their execution.

While the Haymarket case dramatizes the ways that the official realm informs and is informed by the public sphere, the boundary between these two arenas is nowhere more clear than in the case of lynchings, where citizens in the public sphere, feeling that official culture is unresponsive to them, take the law into their own hands and execute their own extralegal justice.

Chapter 3 considers the case of Leo Frank, who stood trial in 1914 for the murder of a factory worker under his supervision. A Northern Jew who supervised impoverished Southern workers, many of them the daughters of destitute rural whites, Frank was fighting not only a murder charge but also smoldering resentments about the Civil War. Frank's trial ended in a conviction and death sentence. A strong propaganda effort that emanated from New York targeted the realm of official justice and resulted in executive clemency, but its failure to take into account the public sphere ended tragically for Frank, who was lynched by a mob of the very Southerners whom his publicity campaign had overlooked.

The lesson for Frank's supporters came too late, when they realized that their misdirected protests had been responsible for Frank's death and resolved not to compound their error by protesting the lynching. The case of Emmett Till, explored in chapter 4, draws on the lessons of the Frank incident to tell a different story. A black Chicago youth who visited Mississippi at exactly the wrong time—the summer before the 1954 Brown desegregation decision was to take effect in Southern schools—Till was lynched for allegedly whistling at a white woman. His murderers were acquitted, but Till's defenders, who represented a worldwide audience, were determined to find unofficial justice if the courtroom failed to provide official justice. As David Halberstam has noted, the Till lynching became the first media event of the Civil Rights movement, as writers and reporters exploited the printed page and the newly popular medium of television to publicize the injustice of Till's murder and to do what Frank's defenders had neglected: to overcome the prejudices of ordinary Southerners.

Chapter 5, concerning the trial and execution of Gary Gilmore, is my only sustained exploration of what might be considered highbrow literature. Here I examine in detail Norman Mailer's 1979 novel, *The Executioner's Song*. Though Mailer, unlike many of the writers I examine here, is indeed concerned with his lasting literary reputation, his book resembles many of the other texts under consideration here in that its form—substituting what Mailer called "photographic realism" for the traditional narrator—closely resembles the welter of competing and sometimes consenting voices of the public sphere, voices dramatized in the marketplace scene of *The Scarlet Letter* as well as in the literary products of the other cases under consideration here. The petty, almost mundane murders that initiate Gilmore's trip to death row recede in importance as the novel takes up the political debates surrounding Gilmore's 1977 execution, the first since the Supreme Court allowed the resumption of executions after a ten-year hiatus.

The story of Karla Faye Tucker's 1998 execution, told in chapter 6, reveals the ways that Mailer's late-twentieth-century novel resembles the conditions surrounding capital punishment in the American colonies. A public discussion very like the one that Mailer depicted in his experimental form in 1979 appeared spontaneously on the Internet during the months leading up to and following Tucker's death by lethal injection. In the years between the Gilmore and Tucker executions, the Internet had made the world virtually smaller, allowing ordinary people to feel as if they were standing in Hawthorne's colonial marketplace and discussing (often in real time) public events taking place before their eyes. The attractive appearance and gentle demeanor of Tucker, a born-again Christian who repudiated her violent life and seemed sincerely to repent of her gruesome crime, drew a large and passionate following and reminded the world of the danger of public executions: as Benjamin Rush had cautioned in 1787, "generous minds" who witness a state-sponsored execution may come to sympathize with the condemned criminal and turn against the state responsible for her execution.

The final chapter discusses the campaign against capital punishment in the United States that accelerated during the last years of the twentieth century and the beginning of the twenty-first. Like the propagandists I have been considering throughout this study, contemporary writers, musicians, actors, and other artists are actively using the literary arts to bring about a discussion in the public sphere that they hope will have some influence over the official policies of capital punishment. This final chapter moves away from specific capital cases in order to explore the conversation about the death penalty itself that is happening right now in the artistic marketplace.

Today's opponents of capital punishment like to point out that in the lottery of death—the selection of whom, among all those convicted of capital crimes, our judicial system chooses to die for their crimes—the crime itself is much less significant a factor than other variables: where the crime was committed, which lawyer is selected to represent the defendant, how much money the defending attorney receives for his or her work. The cases I examine suggest that in the most prominent capital cases, the crime itself is often a minor factor in public discussions about justice. The seven Haymarket anarchists, launching their defense, insisted on making their trial a forum for discussing the abuses of capital upon labor rather than the specific crime of murder for which they stood trial. In doing so, they made explicit what all of the cases in this study reveal: that their murder trial was not primarily about the crimes listed on the bill of indictment, but was more explosively about other, more threatening social problems. In the 1833 Avery trial, the 1887 Haymarket trial, and the 1914 Frank trial, the problem was the conflict between impoverished laborers and those who held social and economic power in a changing economy—the Methodist Church, large corporations, and Northern capitalists. In the trial of Emmett Till's lynchers, the problem was again a clash between old and new social systems, this time rural Southern segregationalists and Northerners who represented federal intervention in the Southern way of life. In Gilmore's case, the question was the death penalty itself and whether this one individual who clearly wished to die was entitled to set a deadly precedent for other inmates simply because he was tired of life in prison. In Tucker's case, the question focused on the role of state-sponsored punishments: are they meant only to satisfy public and private vengeance, or is rehabilitation part of the process? And what is the purpose of official clemency? My consideration of these different capital cases reveals that while official courtroom trials attempt (and often fail) to exclude these broader issues, the unofficial trials that take place in the public world of the printed page openly invite just such debates.

While this book explores particular prominent capital cases throughout American history, it is finally an investigation into the role of literary efforts in the public sphere to have some impact upon the formal worlds of the balcony and the courtroom. Although in theory a free society offers all literate members the chance to debate public matters in the newspapers, in truth very few citizens have access to this medium, and as we shall see, when feeling angry and disempowered they often turn to the popular literary forms more immediately available to them. A number of literary critics, from Jane Tompkins to Gregg Crane, have made claims about the power of literature to "redefine the social order."[20] Arguments about the cultural work of literature presuppose the power of writers to shape the world around them rather than merely to reflect the values of the culture and the discourses that they inhabit. My examination of this series of capital cases and the literary responses they generated leads me to question the extent of literary influence on readers and on the world beyond the public sphere. Assuming that literature can foster the kind of populist debate that Jürgen Habermas envisioned (and that Plato feared), assuming even that literature can inspire subjects to accept the moral conclusions presented by writers, how far, and under what conditions, can the changes brought about in the public sphere affect the operations of the official realms of government? If literary texts can transform the minds of private readers, what are the legal and judicial effects of such a transformation? How much can we really claim for the political effects of literature? The case histories I explore in the following pages suggest both the possibilities and the limits of literary pressure on the judicial system.

THEORETICAL INTRODUCTION TO EXECUTION LITERATURE

Early American Criminal Narratives, the Power of Reading, and the Problem of Public Sentiments

I n 1787, Benjamin Rush delivered an address to a political society gathered at the home of Benjamin Franklin in Philadelphia. In that talk, "An Enquiry into the Effects of Public Punishments Upon Criminals, and Upon Society," Rush cautioned members of the Society for Promoting Political Enquiries that public punishments were dangerous to the social and legal authority of the new nation. For Rush, irrepressible human sentiments all but guaranteed that public punishments would turn spectators against the institutions responsible for the punishments:

> By an immutable law of our nature, distress of all kinds, when *seen*, produces sympathy, and a disposition to relieve it. This sympathy, in generous minds, is not lessened by the distress being the offspring of crimes: on the contrary, even the crimes themselves are often palliated by the reflection that they were unfortunate consequences of extreme poverty—of seducing company—or of the want of a virtuous education, from the loss or negligence of parents in early life. Now, as the distress which the criminals suffer, is the effect of a law of the state, which cannot be resisted, the sympathy of the spectator is rendered abortive, and returns empty to the bosom in which it was awakened.[1]

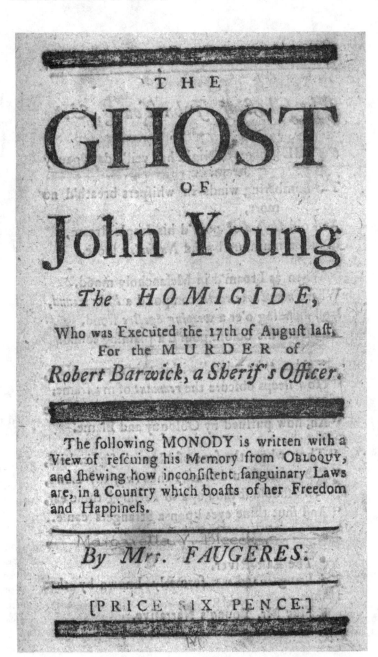

Frontispiece to Margaretta Faugeres's poem,
"The Ghost of John Young" (1797). Courtesy of
the John Hay Library at Brown University.

Rush's term for the effect of such occasions, "abortive" sympathy, implies the miscarriage of an otherwise proper and salubrious sentiment. For Rush as for other founders of the republic, natural sentiments like sympathy played an active role in the dispensation and preservation of law and order. While recent critical attention to nineteenth-century sentimental fiction and poetry has perhaps tempted many of us to understand the conventions of sympathy as derived from Romantic impulses, such limited scrutiny of sympathy ignores the important engagements of sentiments by eighteenth-century social theorists.[2] Statesmen of the early republic, like their European counterparts, understood that sympathy with existing conditions could enhance the power of the government to maintain its laws. Deriving their conclusions from the moral philosophy of Adam Smith, David Hume, and Francis Hutcheson, they understood that social order is maintained by a natural impulse of fellow-feeling, which, when violated by the unjust treatment of one individual, could provoke the wrath and disorder of the populace.[3] As Elizabeth Cady Stanton noted in the nineteenth century and Ida B. Wells in the twentieth, law has no power when it is at odds with public sentiments.[4] The idea was familiar to Benjamin Rush, Benjamin Franklin, and Thomas Jefferson, influential leaders of the early republic who sought to affirm the forms of social control not merely in the public but in the private, sentimental realm.

For Rush, then, appropriate sensibilities, or personal sympathies with proper objects, were crucial for the political health of the new nation. Rush depended upon a natural, indissoluble human sentiment of compassion to bind all citizens in a stable social order based on common sensibilities. These natural principles provide the cornerstone for liberal society, bringing otherwise diverse individuals together in the imaginative contact of sympathy. By imagining the feelings of others, citizens manage to overcome whatever differences appear to separate them when they look objectively at themselves and their social surroundings. But since sympathy with different objects would provoke different actions and impulses, Rush sought to forge the strongest sympathies between the people and the values of the government. Thus citizens would be prompted toward legally and socially acceptable actions not only by their fears of retribution, but also by their innate sensibilities.[5]

As part of their commitment to the founding of a new nation, Rush and Jefferson found themselves engaged in the project of educating people to exercise proper sensibilities. Both agreed that in a healthy citizenry, all members are emotionally alive to the suffering of others and are consequently willing to help alleviate that suffering. Although the inculcation of virtuous behavior may take place within a range of arenas, nowhere was the undertaking more apparent than in the literary realm, where individuals could be drawn toward or repelled from particular conduct depending on their private responses to strong characters and narrators. And nowhere was the question of moral influence more contested than in discussions of novels.[6] Both Jefferson and Rush understood the grave power of literature, but they were unable to lead their fellow citizens toward an unambiguous conclusion about the value of that power. Jefferson was himself deeply divided about the genre. At times he regarded the influence of fiction positively, contending that the reading of novels would enable people to practice their sensibilities even in the absence of actual sentimental stimuli. If, as he once wrote, "every thing is useful which contributes to fix in us the principles and practices of virtue,"[7] it was not important to distinguish between the civic effects of fictional and real events. In a famous letter, Jefferson advises Robert Skipwith not to overlook novels when compiling his library:

> Now every emotion of this kind is an exercise of our virtuous dispositions; and dispositions of the mind, like limbs of the body, acquire strength by exercise. But exercise produces habit; and in the instance of which we speak, the exercise being of the moral feelings, produces a habit of thinking and acting virtuously.[8]

At other times, however, and in different contexts, Jefferson was less sanguine about the influence of fiction. Calling it a "poison" that "infects the mind," he once charged novels with exiling reason: "The result is a bloated imagination, sickly judgment, and disgust towards all the real businesses of life." Still, some novels could redeem themselves: "some few modeling their narratives, although fictitious, on the incidents of real life, have been able to make them interesting and useful vehicles of a sound morality."[9]

While Rush agreed with Jefferson's goals, he considered that the emotions generated by fiction were without exception destructive to the inculcation of public sensibilities. Though compassion, according to Rush, was natural, it could be depleted by a reader's encounters with melodramatic fictional scenes and thus unavailable when the society most required it. In a 1787 address to the Young Ladies' Academy in Philadelphia, Rush warned his audience against novel reading:

> Let it not be said, that the tales of distress, which fill modern novels, have a tendency to soften the female hearts into acts of humanity. The fact is the reverse of this. The abortive sympathy which is excited by the recital of imaginary distress, blunts the heart to that which is real; and, hence, we sometimes see instances of young ladies, who weep away a whole forenoon over the criminal sorrows of a fictitious Charlotte or Werter, turning with disdain at three o'clock from the sight of a beggar, who solicits in feeble accents or signs, a small portion only of the crumbs which fall from their fathers' tables.[10]

Again Rush uses this term, "abortive sympathy," which he had summoned four months earlier in order to insist that to be useful, sympathies must have a designated recipient and be followed by a particular course of action. In this case, sympathy ought to be enlisted in behalf of charity in order to perform the work of the government both in assisting a fellow citizen and in thereby ensuring social stability. The woman who merely weeps over a fictional character has lost her chance to offer her charity, and thus her consent, to the actual social order.

While the discussion between Rush and Jefferson may seem a precursor to later arguments that pit television, computer games, and other products of popular culture against more high-brow forms of learning, I am drawn to this contest over the novel because it raises important questions regarding the power of private sympathies to undermine official authority. Whereas one might, like Jefferson, wish to recruit the novel for its aid in training the sensibilities of the public, the private experience of novel reading might in fact thwart that very aim, moving readers in directions very different from institutionally sanctioned responses. Emotional threats to authority were introduced in the new world long before the novel, and they predated the republic itself. Nor are the problems raised by fiction confined to novels and readers. The anxieties about social authority revealed in the founding fathers' concerns were in fact brewing long before the revolution, not in the form of novels but in public executions, which were meant to consolidate and affirm a general condemnation of sin and crime but which, like the novel and the narratives that accompanied many executions, may well have undermined that very intent.

As I will demonstrate in a brief discussion of these executions and the immensely popular gallows literature that developed in the colonies, early American execution literature resembled the eighteenth-century novel in its often contradictory aims, and the popularity of such reading material among the masses all but ensured a turn of public sympathies away from church and state.

As many historians have noted, the rituals of execution day in colonial America guaranteed an immense public spectacle, one that began on the Sunday before the execution with a church service and a sermon aimed at interpreting the event and generating public interest. A number of sermons, for example, took as their text the words of the penitent thief crucified with Christ: "Lord, remember me when thou comest into thy Kingdom" (Luke 23:42).[11] The day of execution itself often began with a sermon and procession to the gallows, where the crowd usually observed a few final words from a leading minister, followed by the criminal's last words and then the execution itself. The event was usually preceded and followed by an assortment of printed ephemera meant to further protract the occasion: broadside publications often provided a brief narrative of the criminal's life, along with the execution sermon and sometimes a poem commemorating the event.[12]

In early colonial days, when Puritan ministers still wielded significant social and legal authority, these rituals seemed calculated to keep public sentiments in line with official church teachings. Although church authority would soon weaken, the first execution-day materials, like all the earliest colonial publications, were entirely controlled by the clergy. As John Tebbel notes, New World publishing began partly as an attempt to secure piety and religious training in the colonies. Settlers of Massachusetts Bay

> were practical men who understood that the settlements they had established with
> such difficulty must be held together by the exertion of authority, ecclesiastical and
> civil. The printing press was plainly the best extension of authority, confirming the
> propagandizing at once, as the Church had already done in Mexico. Control of the
> information from it was the best insurance that authority could not be challenged.[13]

The religious and social power exerted by keepers of the press was immense. Literacy in New England was almost universal, and as long as publications were confined to religious material, the clergy could ensure a measure of conformity among the settlers. In controlling the output of colonial printers, religious leaders were able to consolidate their authority over their congregations. By publishing their works, they added to the textual authority they already enjoyed as they interpreted scripture for literate but not learned parishioners.

Still, Rush's insight—that public spectacles of misery might turn hearts in the wrong direction—was no less true for the clerically governed colonial America, though these problems were much less likely to have been debated in the public sphere. The absence of public debate, however, should not mislead us into thinking that public punishments did not pose grave threats to religious leaders. A remarkable number of sermons begin with lengthy justifications of execution, like the one that held the attention of townspeople in Portsmouth, New Hampshire. Nobody had been put to death in that province until the year 1740, when a dead infant was discovered in a well. A search for the mother revealed that two women had recently delivered and destroyed their infants, though both insisted that the corpse was not that of their offspring. The case drew widespread public attention for several reasons: the first execution in the province was a double one, involving women rather than men, and the evidence which led to the executions implied the presence of a third, undiscovered capital offender in New Hampshire. When William Shurtleff's execution sermon was published in Boston that year, it included a preface, "To the Christian Reader," that sought to clarify the law whereby the destruction of an illegitimate child was considered a capital offense. "The women that were lately executed at *Portsmouth*," the publisher announced, "were condemn'd by a Law, which I think proper to recite, . . . that it may be better known in all the families that shall have the following sermon."[14] This preface, of course, was meant to educate the people of New Hampshire and to fortify the law by its widespread dissemination, just as the executions of the two criminals were meant to announce public censure of infanticide. And yet these very acts of judicial authority underscore their precarious status: by beginning with a recitation of the law, the publisher seems to suggest that he would like to forestall a public outcry against a double execution. The executions—at which the condemned criminals were typically invited to address their townspeople in words of faith and penitence—may well have inspired mixed feelings in the breasts of observers, feelings of indignation toward both the crime and the punishment. Although we do not have evidence of the public response to these early executions, we can infer from the degree of defensiveness in the official sermons that lawmakers and clergymen were concerned about misplaced sympathies.

A sermon published two years earlier in Connecticut seems even more clearly set against the public sympathies that Rush feared. In 1738 Eliphalet Adams attended the execution of Katherine Garret, a Pequot Indian woman also convicted of infanticide. His execution sermon uses the text of Proverbs 28:17, "A man that doth Violence to the blood of any person, shall flee to the Pit, Let no man stay him."

Adams's sermon, like Shurtleff's, was meant to remind his community that pity should not interfere with justice and that social and religious stability demands swift and impartial punishment. "For this Reason," Adams warned, "Government hath been *Instituted* and Laws have been provided, that Injuries may Either be prevented or redressed and Societies may be kept in tolerable peace and order. For there would be no Living in any Safety, if there were no Restraints, laid upon peoples [sic] Evil Inclinations."[15] The role of "the Ministers of Justice, those publick *Avengers of Blood*," is to bring criminals "with all Convenient hast[e]" to justice. These ministers, moreover, merely serve the public, who are therefore obliged to assist in the prosecution of justice. Adams dwells significantly on the exhortation, "Let no man stay him," advising that sympathy for the criminal should not interfere with the law:

> Every one in their Place should Discountenance the Violence that hath been done and rise up as with a general Consent to testify against it; They should Contribute what is in their Power and lend an hand towards the bringing of such offenders unto Justice; If it were in their power to stop the prosecution, defeat the process or Elude the Sentence, they must not do it; For such Offenders as these have forfeited their Claim to the protection of mankind and must now be driven from among men.[16]

In this warning, Adams plainly struggles between dangerous bonds of sentiment and the more proper bonds of justice; even in performing deeds which constitute the forfeiture of a place in human society, criminals still maintain ties of affection either with loved ones or with those who might for other reasons sympathize. These and other sermons suggest that even as clergymen were attempting to reaffirm their authority by appealing to communal notions of morality and justice, their authority was endangered by the sympathies of a public inclined, at least in part, to identify with the criminal whose past had been revealed to them.

The sermons of both Adams and Shurtleff underscore simultaneously how crucial audience sympathy was to the public denunciation of sin and how dangerous it could be to the authority of those who decried and punished capital crimes. Many sermons, including theirs, begin with exhortations to the people to witness the executions not out of curiosity but because of some "better principle."[17] That principle depends upon a moderate degree of sympathy properly directed. Both preachers caution their audiences against uncompassionate conduct toward the unfortunate spectacle. Adams warns, "Let none be so Barbarous as to Insult her in this *Day of her Calamity*, But let Every ones [sic] Compassions be moved as far as you have Interest in Heaven, Improve [sic] it Earnestly on her account, to draw down a Blessing upon her if possible, in her last Moments; her Condition *Cryes to you* for this, her Melancholy Appearance and beseeching Air may even Extort it from You."[18] Shurtleff likewise announces that the two condemned women "are most certainly fit and proper Objects of your Pity: Behold them then with a becoming Compassion and Concern: And let it be our united Cry to our great LORD and Saviour, that he would *remember them now he is in his Kingdom*."[19] Though widespread contempt for the sinners on display may have served to clarify the boundaries between proper and improper behavior, Adams and Shurtleff insist that there are equally compelling reasons for understanding the resemblances between law-abiding people and those condemned to die. As Shurtleff suggests, his parishioners should "consider, *who it is that maketh you to differ*, and admire and adore his distinguishing Grace."[20] A certain degree of identification with the malefactor, in other words, helps to remind the people of the dangers of temptation and cautions them to be ever vigilant for sinful impulses in their own souls. To sympathize with the condemned criminal is to understand that the devil lays snares for us all.

On the other hand, Adams understood that sympathy, once awakened, could have disastrous consequences, and so he devoted much of his sermon to the topic of appropriate and inappropriate expressions of fellow-feeling. "It may well be expected," he wrote, "that Natural Affection will greatly work at such a time and Interest will have a strong Influence, but neither should prevail against the honour of God, the rules of Justice, and the safety of Society."[21] Though his particular topic was the prosecution of justice through honest testimony, his warning may be considered more generally, for all who—witnessing such a spectacle of grief as a public execution—turn against the laws of the land. It was important for social cohesion in the colonies not only that witnesses testified honestly against an accused criminal, but that in their minds they did not blame God, justice, or society for the outcome of the trial. The governors, justices, and clergymen owed much of their authority to the people's belief that they all shared the same values.

For this reason, rather than repressing irrepressible compassion, Adams advised his congregation how to use it. "Whatever pity, whatever good will any man may be inclin'd to shew to such kind of Malefactors, Let it be in other ways than this [helping criminals to escape], In Instructing, advising & Counselling of them for the good of their Souls, praying for them, Encouraging them to fly to and hope in God's Mercy, And (when they have truly repented & thrown themselves at God's feet) in chearing and bearing them up against the fears of Death."[22]

The twenty-five pages that Adams devotes to the topic of sympathy before he launches a more conventional sermon suggest that the problem of public sympathy was already apparent in 1738. Though unconventional, his discourse is not at odds with more familiar execution-day practices. The careful orchestration of these activities, even down to the often formulaic expression of penitence on the part of the condemned, was calculated to steer public sympathies in the proper direction: toward the community itself, victimized by the breach of law and morality but able to regain its soundness in the conviction, reformation, and public execution of the criminal. The narratives published alongside these events, likewise formulaic, were meant as part of that same process of communal fortification. As Daniel E. Williams has noted, the printed materials resembled the execution itself in their efforts to "mark the borders of acceptable behavior and thus reinforce the collective social identity."[23] The brief narratives recounting the lives of the criminals gave significant attention to the stages of moral decline, the crime, and the work of local clergymen to gain the criminal's penitence and conversion. To read a number of these accounts is to understand how ritualized the process soon became, down to the discrete stages of the narration. One young mother's declaration reveals her awareness of convention: "as it may be necessary, so doubtless it will be expected of me, that I give the World a particular account of that great Sin, with the aggravations of it, which has brought me to this Shameful Death."[24] The earliest narratives, introduced to the public by such prominent clergymen as Samuel Danforth and Increase and Cotton Mather, were often brief and highly uniform in structure and content.[25] A typical early account, for example, begins abruptly: "I am a Miserable Sinner; and I have Justly Provoked the Holy God to leave me unto that Folly of my own Heart, for which I am now Condemned to Dy [sic]."[26] The conventions usually included a brief confession of the sin along with statements of penitence, entreaties for forgiveness from all injured parties, expressions of hope for eternal salvation, thanks to God and his ministers for the opportunity to repent, and various warnings to the living. Exhortations to obedience usually played an important role in the last statement of a dying malefactor: to parents and masters to discipline their charges and raise them religiously; to servants and children to obey their masters and parents; to young people to beware the ways of idleness and wickedness; and often to tavern keepers, that they "do not let Persons have too much Drink," as one criminal put it, "being that by those Means they become in a great Measure chargeable with the Sins which others commit when depriv'd of their Senses thereby."[27] Such narratives—which focused on the wages of sin and the promises of redemption—sought to unite the community in an affirmation of law and righteousness. So powerful was the force of convention, in fact, that when John Ury was executed in New York in 1741 for a part he insistently denied in "the late Negro-Conspiracy," he nevertheless played the expected role for the public. While denying his guilt in the particular crime, he offered himself up to his fellow citizens as a spectacle of sinful man preparing to meet his Maker:

> And now a Word of Advice to you, Spectators: Behold me launching into Eternity; seriously, solemnly view me; and ask yourselves seriously, How stands the Case with me? Die I must, am I prepared to meet my Lord, when the Midnight-Cry is echoed forth? Shall I then have the Wedding-Garment on? O Sinners! trifle no longer! Consider Life hangs on a Thread; here to-day, and gone to-morrow. Forsake your Sins, ere you be forsaken for ever.[28]

As a man who claimed to be innocent of the crime for which he was convicted but guilty of many other sins, Ury aptly represented the people watching him. In doing so, moreover, he underscored the criminal's willingness to play a fictional and highly theatrical role. If he thereby offered his life to the social authority of the colonial judicial system, he also undermined the social requirements of executions by blurring the distinctions between fiction and justice.

Indeed, it would be a mistake to conclude from the power of these execution-day conventions, even over a man whose claims to innocence might have impelled him to resist lending his voice to the entire process, that clerical authority in the colonies was unwavering, that Rush's anxieties applied only to a democracy, where individual rights sometimes took precedence over the good of the whole. There is significant evidence, on the contrary, that the most successfully staged scenes of penitence may in fact have worked against clerical and judicial authority. When Esther Rodgers was executed in 1701 for the murder of her infant child, she proved an ideal spectacle for the gathering crowds and for those who would return to the scene in its printed form. John Rogers, the pastor at Ipswich, published the account of her life and execution, choosing a title that suggested his optimistic interpretation of the event: *Death the Certain Wages of Sin to the Impenitent; Life the Future Reward of Grace to the Penitent.*[29] Although several pages are devoted to her life and crime, most of the publication is given over to the process of her conversion, including accounts of her conversations with the several ministers who visited her.

The publication concludes with this description of Rodgers's death:

> THE manner of her Entertaining DEATH, was even astonishing to a Multitude of Spectators, (being as was judged Four or Five Thousand People at least) with that Composure of Spirit, Cheerfulness of Countenance, pleasantness of Speech, and a sort of Complaisantness in Carriage towards the Ministers who were assistant to her, with their Prayers and Counsils, that even melted the hearts of all that were within seeing or hearing, into Tears of affection, with greatest wonder and admiration. Her undaunted Courage and unshaken Confidence she modestly enough expressed, yet stedfastly held unto the end. So that he must needs want Faith for himself, that wants Charity for such an one.[30]

The apparently affecting scene of Rodgers's last moments posed no danger to the agents of her execution—the ministers and justices—because Rodgers accepted her fate and embraced her death. Sympathy with the condemned, in other words, would result in a thorough acceptance of her convictions, including the belief that her execution was just. But the author's claim that thousands of spectators melted in "tears of affection" might have given pause to those who staged public executions. If Rodgers appealed to the sympathies of her audience by means of her countenance, speech, and carriage, other gifted actors, as I will show, were able to do the same but toward a more troubling end.

I do not mean to imply that all dying conversions were insincere. Whatever the degree of sincerity, however, it is clear from all accounts that the behavior of a dying sinner was staged, from the numerous conversations with ministers, often reprinted, to the walk to the gallows and dying words and conduct. The historical record cannot offer much insight into the true state of mind of these criminals, since the ministers responsible for the publication of gallows literature had a clear interest in believing in and representing the "true" redemption of convicted criminals. But whatever the convictions of the dying criminal, his or her actions and even words were highly formulaic and predictable.

When we turn from the mere presence of a condemned criminal to his or her narrative and dying words, addressed to the community of spectators and often written in plaintive and penitent terms, we can see how these texts threatened the very project they were meant to endorse. For one thing, the more successfully the penitent sinner staged the scene of repentance and saintliness, the more likely the world might be to identify with the dying spectacle, to consider the plight of the (reformed) sinner and to overlook the sin. The criminal narrative, in fact, combines the two elements that Rush found most damaging to public sympathies: the public execution and the novel.[31] Even if the execution were not featured in the narrative, the fate of the subject was clear to all readers, many of whom had attended the actual execution. The narrative, moreover, offered private details unavailable to spectators of the execution, details of personality and background that may have forged the kinds of sentimental alliances with readers that Rush feared from novels.[32] Sometimes these stories were told from the first person or otherwise narrated from a point of view not readily identifiable as that of the judge, the minister, or some other agent of the law. These narratives, meant to shape public sentiments in order to support the institutions of law, government, church, and family, threatened at the same time to seduce readers away from the desired response: a limited identification with the condemned—just enough to suggest the dangers sin posed to all present—and a loyalty to the standards of law and morality that upheld the community. As Rush later warned, sympathies can and do wander.

The case of John Young, executed in 1797 for the murder of a sheriff's deputy, dramatizes the damaging social effects of misplaced sympathies. Like Esther Rodgers, the articulate and compliant Young proved himself a worthy candidate for redemption. So eagerly did Young embrace the efforts of the Reverend Christopher Flanagan, in fact, that he wrote the hymn that was sung at his own execution and printed in his narrative and confession.[33] Flanagan reflects the likely impression that Young made on the crowds of spectators when he describes Young's leave-taking of his fellow prisoners: "As he came through the Prison, some of the genteeler Debtors came and took their last farewell of him with affected hearts, and gushing eyes, which greatly affected him."[34] Nor, according to Flanagan, were Young's admirers confined to other prisoners. "However dissipated he might have lived, however aggravated the crime might have been that was the cause of his shameful death, it must appear evident to every impartial mind, he died a subject of Divine Mercy and Favor."[35]

To Flanagan, Young seemed "spiritually alive to God, so that not only resignation to his fate was evident, but a constant chearfulness and serenity which is the result of a mind at peace with God, and all mankind."[36] If Young's demeanor affected his spectators so deeply, how might we expect readers to respond to the detailed autobiography of this articulate man? Young's narrative, published on the day of his execution in New York, presents a character in keeping with the one Flanagan describes. Unlike many criminal narratives, which assign a certain measure of blame to careless parents and unholy upbringings, Young confines his story to immediate events, pointing out his generosity as he does so. "It needs not then," he begins, "that I speak of my parents and relations, who or what they are, is of little moment to the Public, thus silent, they will avoid the taunts of unfeeling men. I shall therefore touch not on the transactions of my life at an early period."[37]

Though he frames his narrative in the recent past, Young focuses less expansively on his conversion and penitence than on the events leading up to the crime, and in so doing he stretches the conventions of the early American criminal narrative. Notwithstanding his apparently deep regret for the murder, he offers a detailed account of his motives and state of mind leading to the crime. Whether true or false, his story seems calculated to stir up massive indignation at his conviction. According to his story, Young was a poor publisher of sheet music in Philadelphia who traveled to New York and entered into a business deal with a notary public, Daniel Thew. Thew soon swindled Young and arranged for his arrest. During the following weeks, Young was harassed by creditors and corrupt agents of the law, including a deputy sheriff who, Young claimed, staged an arrest in order to collect a bribe, and a lawyer who purchased an imaginary debt of Young's. Repeatedly imprisoned, unable to pay off his legitimate debts, and plagued by spurious debts, Young finally shot a deputy sheriff in a fit of pique: "distress'd in mind, harrass'd with my cares, and the dread of again being confined operated at this moment to determine me not to go to Gaol."[38]

What is unique about the narrative, but not surprising in a genre that by 1797 had escaped the conventions originally meant to harness public feelings, are the many authorial asides, meant to shore up audience support for the criminal's sense of outrage:

> Thus it is Debtors are abused, thus it is, in a State who boast their protection of the subject and their detestation of despotic sway, permit their administrators of Justice to twist an arbitrary construction of the Laws, to countenance these hirelings to distress the honest tho' unfortunate Citizens it requires more than mortal fortitude to resist punishing such mortals, who regard more extortion, than the administration of Justice.[39]

When the agents of justice cannot be trusted to carry out their charges honestly, when legal institutions cannot intervene in the acts of corrupt representatives, then the individual is nearly warranted, Young suggests, in taking the law into his own hands. Young's narrative, published just ten years after the Constitutional Convention, could barely avoid striking a chord with those citizens who worried that their new government might eventually resemble the old, and that true heroism in an unjust society consisted in breaking all of its laws whether just or not. Young might, in fact, be seen as a precursor to that great American hero, Henry David Thoreau, who fifty-two years later announced that "Under a government which imprisons any unjustly, the true place for a just man is also in prison."[40] In describing the corruption of lawyers and sheriffs, Young exclaims, "Shame, shame on such practices, practices that disgrace the name of civilization, which every honest mind must revolt at, and which I am sorry to say, is too much countenanced by those whose duty as well as inclination should teach to punish more than encourage such infamy."[41] In his narrative, Young appeals to the sympathies of all citizens who may incline toward respect for the individual and resentment for an oppressive government. Since the American Revolution was less than a generation old, the terms of his story may have stirred up uncomfortable consequences for the new government.[42]

By the time of Young's execution, of course, a popular movement to abolish capital punishment was well underway. As Louis Masur has demonstrated, the combined forces of European Enlightenment and postrevolutionary beliefs in republicanism and liberal theology impelled many Americans to oppose executions in favor of incarceration, a response that seemed more in keeping with the values of a republic.[43] Certainly the growing opposition to capital punishment influenced the way that all executions, including Young's, were received, and likewise, Young's execution and narrative no doubt fueled that movement. If there were not more at stake in this episode than social reform, then we might consider that Young's narrative represents the evolution of the criminal narrative, a development that fitted the genre in its eighteenth-century guise to a more enlightened social milieu. But Young's narrative does not simply argue against executions. Given the revelations of corruption, it threatens much more than a public policy on the verge of abolition; Young's publication indicts the very integrity of the new nation and thus threatens the authority of government itself.

Nor were Young's execution and narrative the only ones in the New World to stir up such sympathy and indignation. To be sure, in the force of his appeal to the masses Young was not absolutely typical. (Like today, many condemned criminals aroused nothing but feelings of contempt and vengeance.) Still, Young resembled many criminals who represented to the people the excesses of political authority. Although spectators in the early days of the colonies might not have felt free to declaim publicly against the process of execution, let alone to sabotage it, I have been suggesting that the sympathies of the crowds who watched were always volatile and unpredictable and could easily pour out against the agents of execution, whatever measures were taken to steer those sentiments in more compliant ways. Young's execution was hardly the first to incite such dangerous sentiments.[44]

Although we can only speculate about how Young's spectators received his story, there is some historical evidence to suggest that his execution did indeed threaten the social order. A newspaper account of the execution notes that the New York sheriff was relieved by the orderly conduct of the crowd, for he had anticipated some resistance:

> The sheriff of the city, on account of some anonymous letters which he had received, having expressed to the executive an apprehension of a rescue, a detachment of the militia were under arms on the occasion—The magistrates of the city were also attending at a house adjacent to the place of execution—But though the crowd of spectators was immense; not the smallest symptom of any disturbance appeared.[45]

Although prison escapes were frequent and rumors of escape may have been predictable had the condemned man been a member of a gang of thieves, a threat of this kind was remarkable in a case like Young's.[46] Poor and alone, he could have expected assistance and loyalty only from people who were enraged by his story and his treatment by legal and judicial authorities.

But while the execution went smoothly, the impression that Young left on Americans was more troubling. Later that year, a Mrs. Margaretta Faugeres published a poem, "The Ghost of John Young." Unlike most execution-day poems, which were meant to sensationalize or commemorate the event, usually by following in the conventions of the sermon and personal narrative with warnings to the living, this poem was more clearly opposed both to the usual standards of execution literature and, more dangerously, to the society responsible for Young's execution. A note on the title page tells all: "The following MONODY is written with a View of rescuing his Memory from OBLOQUY, and shewing how inconsistent sanguinary Laws are, in a Country which boasts of her Freedom and Happiness."[47] It might of course be argued that by 1797 the public sentiment toward executions was changing, especially in a republic that defined itself in opposition to British tyranny. But it is very possible that this was a more private matter, a matter of personal sympathies. Young's particular account of himself and other published descriptions of his conduct may well have combined to turn public sentiment not against the law breaker, erected in front of the people as an example of improper conduct, but against the lawmakers who conspired to put him there. The precise target is not merely a particular law—which may, of course, be reformed—but an entire government, represented here as tyrannical and heartless.

The differences between Faugeres's poem and others of the genre are immediately evident. Though conventionally didactic, her poem takes issue not with the crime but with the punishment. Its tone, too, is far different from other gallows literature. Inspired not by rationalism or piety but by the melancholy and reflective mood of Romanticism, the poem opens with a solitary wanderer:

> The glooms of Night had veil'd day's gaudy beam,
> The slumbering winds in whispers breath'd no more,
> And old Haspedoc pour'd his ample stream,
> In sullen murmurs by sad Nassau's shore.
> When as I roam'd in Melancholy mood,
> Where *new broke earth* compos'd a *little mound*,
> Lo! bending o'er a *weeping Spectre* stood,
> And from his bosom pour'd a plaining sound.

That the speaker is presented in "Melancholy mood" even before encountering Young's ghost suggests the turn from issues of the public good toward private concerns and reflections; this Romantic preoccupation seems destined, as it does in Wordsworth's *Lyrical Ballads*, published the following year, to offer individual sympathy uncontaminated by the formulaic attitudes of criminal literature.[48] Although the imagery, mood, and verse form of this poem recall the earlier graveyard poets, the politicized position of this sympathetic speaker clearly anticipates the use to which Wordsworth puts sentiment in his subsequent lyrics. In the British Romantic tradition inaugurated by Wordsworth in 1798, in fact, sympathy is not incidental but central to the recitation of a life's story. As Wordsworth writes in his 1802 preface, "it will be the wish of the Poet to bring his feelings near to those of the persons whose feelings he describes, nay, for short spaces of time perhaps, to let himself slip into an entire delusion, and even confound and identify his own feeling with theirs."[49] Conventional criminal narratives depended upon readers' limited identification with the criminal. Often incorporated into the sermons of a church official, moreover, these narratives never confounded the criminal's feelings and behavior with those of the clergyman, who instead maintained a dignified distance from the condemned. One might object that Wordsworth's poetic policy of identification should not be compared with the intents of execution sermons, since this earlier genre openly addressed religious, political, and judicial concerns. But Faugeres's poem clearly descends from the American tradition of gallows literature, and its similarities with Wordsworth's "sympathetic" ballads suggests how far gallows literature could deviate from the intent of those who invented the genre.

Like Wordsworth, Faugeres seems to confound her identity with that of the dead John Young. Her poem gives voice to Young's ghost, whose complaints are motivated by the need to correct the historical record:

"Alas," he cried, "within this narrow place,
"How sleeps obscure the *remnant* of my frame,
"How *marr'd* how *mangled* ere it fill'd this space
"Ah, how pursued by Obloquy and Blame."

The ghost, like the actual Young in his narrative, asserts that his conviction was based in part on the perjury of several witnesses and the readiness of the court to believe them.

But while the poem seems motivated by private sympathy for the dead man rather than cooperation with the works of publishers, ministers, and judges in securing the social order, this apparently private origin does not mean that the poem has no political role. On the contrary, the primary thrust of the poem is outrage at the society that executed John Young. Thus the ghost offers a monologue calculated to turn public sentiment against capital punishment:

"Yes, I a Murderer was by *rage* propell'd,
"And I have heard the last the harsh decree,
But, if the *Maniac* is a Murderer held,
Say *cool deliberate actors, what are ye?* . . .
"Shame on the Country where such laws prevail,
"Savage as those of rude and barbarous lands,
"Where *Power* from *Justice* wrests the trembling feale,
"And cooly dips in human gore his hands."

The new nation, only twenty-one years old (and thus, like the criminal himself, officially of age and liable to adult punishment) is here condemned in terms meant to enlist public support for a convicted felon. Ten years after Benjamin Rush's warning about public punishments, Faugeres proves the validity of his worries. Her understanding of the murder does not mitigate her outrage at the execution. In fact, she raises the specter of an unfair trial in order to imply that Young may not have been entirely guilty. Nor, as an individual, did Faugeres have any power to alleviate Young's distress. Instead, her sympathy, stirred up by Young's narrative, Reverend Flanagan's description, and possibly the sight of the actual execution, had nothing productive to do. Rush may well have underestimated the threat of misguided sympathies. For him, if the "law of the state . . . cannot be resisted, the sympathy of the spectator is rendered abortive, and returns empty to the bosom in which it was awakened." Faugeres demonstrates that resistance can take many forms. If she cannot actually haul the man off the gallows and thus avert his untimely death, she can resurrect him in a fictional guise in order to continue his lament and stir up further resistance. If sentiments, as Rush well knew, could have powerful productive consequences, they could also wreak havoc on the orderly conduct of a nation's citizens.

Although it is not my aim here to trace organized opposition to capital punishment to the spectacle of public executions or to the literary narratives that coincided with these events, the example of John Young offers a powerful suggestion that Rush may have been right: that collective political action begins not as a set of abstract principles, but as a series of unanticipated and certainly unwanted, private, and sentimental responses to a gut-wrenching public event. In any case, though "abortive" sympathies perhaps prompted prison reform, they also posed the graver threat to the republic, that of turning the hearts of private citizens against the public leaders and against the very principles of their country. While rational opposition may have been in the minds of those who systematically fought capital punishment, other vehement objections were probably motivated by the spontaneous overflow of powerful emotions.

As Michel Foucault has demonstrated in his now-famous discussion of the penal system, the past two hundred years have witnessed an apparent shift in the objective of punitive operations from the body to the soul. "The expiation that once rained down upon the body," he writes, "must be replaced by a punishment that acts in depth on the heart, the thoughts, the will, the inclinations."[50] For Foucault and others who have been influenced by his work, the arenas of medicine, psychology, sociology, and law have internalized, softened, and transformed official responses to criminality, which had once been addressed publicly and bodily. Although Foucault indicates that ultimately even these affective realms are corporeal as well, he ignores the possibility that the reverse is likewise true. In redirecting attention from the site of the criminal to the sentiments of the spectator who witnesses his or her punishment and reformation, I am suggesting that even where the body of the malefactor has been the apparent locus of punishment, the thoughts, allegiances, and sympathies of the public called to witness the execution and later to read the words of the condemned criminal—these things which Foucault designates as "soul"—have always been a more thoroughgoing concern of lawmakers than Foucault perhaps allows. As the apparent failure of two hundred years of penal reform has demonstrated, it is a difficult thing to manipulate the soul, whether that entails overcoming years of environmental conditioning or merely appealing to proper rather than improper sympathies. Early American ministers and judges, like today's psychologists, sociologists, and parole officers, had both compelling reasons for wanting to police public sensibilities and enormous difficulties doing so. It was only a matter of years before the clergy lost its monopoly on criminal narratives. The development of the genre from the brief lives published in the seventeenth century to the lengthier, more detailed, and novelistic life stories of the eighteenth, from the clearly delineated moral positions to the more complicated and dramatic appeals for sympathy that took place in this ostensibly private encounter between reader and character, suggests a number of ways in which criminal narratives turned against the institution that invented them, swayed by sentiments that could not be brought under official control. In the centuries that followed, down to our own day, gallows literature has continued to stir up feelings that are dangerous to the social order. Though we have developed elaborate mechanisms to force compliance upon the body, marvelous machines of torture and, more recently, contraptions for ending life humanely, the discipline of the soul is a much more difficult matter. The following chapters explore some of the most celebrated cases of outraged and, at times, unruly literary responses to capital crimes and executions.

**Lithograph of Sarah Maria
Cornell, from *A Brief and Impartial
Narrative of the Life of Sarah Maria
Cornell* (New York: G. Williams,
n.d.). Courtesy of the John Hay
Library at Brown University.**

Chapter One

REWRITING THE FALL RIVER MURDER

A Factory Town Turns to
Sentimental Narratives

T he 1832 murder of a female factory worker and the subsequent trial of a
Methodist minister for the crime provoked anxieties not only about seeking justice for the murder but also about protecting the competing interests of factories, the
family, and the Methodist Church. The debate that broke out in the public sphere, as we
shall see, was an unabashedly populist one, and it drew on the conventions of popular
literary forms, particularly the melodramatic sentimental novel, in order to establish a
logic that distinguished itself from what many saw as the elitist values of the courtroom.

I. THE DEATH OF SARAH CORNELL

On the morning of December 21, 1832, John Durfee, a farmer in Tiverton, Rhode
Island, discovered the frozen body of a young woman hanging from a stake on his
property. Durfee sought the assistance of several neighboring farmers to cut down her
body, then he summoned the coroner to the scene. As a crowd of onlookers gathered,
the victim was identified as Sarah Maria Cornell, a factory mill worker from nearby

Fall River, Massachusetts. While her body was taken into his house, John Durfee went to the boarding house where Cornell had lived, in order to find clothes for her burial. What he found there would arrest the attention not only of this quiet New England farming town, but also, eventually, of all New England. In Cornell's trunk were several unsigned letters and a note from the dead woman that implicated a prominent minister in her murder. Thus began one of the most fascinating and controversial murder cases of the century, one that would still be remembered fifty years later.

Convening on the day after the alarming discovery, a jury determined that the dead woman was pregnant and announced its verdict, "that they believe the said Sarah M. Cornell committed suicide by hanging herself upon a stake in said stackyard, and was influenced to commit the crime by the wicked conduct of a married man, which we gather from Dr. Wilbur, together with the contents of three letters found in the trunk of the said Sarah M. Cornell."[1] The anonymous letters seemed to have been written by the father of Cornell's unborn child.

Dr. Thomas Wilbur, one of the examining physicians, was already familiar with the deceased, having several times been consulted by Cornell during the early stages of her pregnancy. Wilbur testified that Cornell had identified the father of her unborn child as Ephraim K. Avery, a married Methodist minister from Bristol, Rhode Island. Since the jury's verdict pointed to no criminal mischief, however, the body was buried on the Durfee farm, near the Durfee family graves, and the case was closed.

The matter did not rest for long. From the beginning, citizens of Tiverton and Fall River were dissatisfied with the official verdict. The women responsible for laying out the body had observed dark bruises along Cornell's back, abdomen, thighs, and shoulder blades, including marks that resembled handprints. One witness "thought very harsh means had been used upon her" and another declared that "*rash violence* had been used upon her."[2] Another witness claimed to have heard screams on the night of the murder.[3] Still others, Cornell's coworkers at the cotton mill, insisted that the woman had been cheerful on the night of her death as she made preparations for her future; she paid one factory girl to buy her an apron, asked another to wind some yarn for her to knit, and requested help in getting her loom fixed.[4] None of these signs pointed to suicide.

A series of town meetings held in Fall River resulted in the formation of a committee to investigate the crime and a subscription to defray the expenses of the prosecution. Suspicion turned abruptly toward the Reverend Avery because of the note Cornell had left in her bandbox: "If I am missing," she wrote, "inquire of Rev. Mr. Avery, Bristol. He will know where I am gone. S.M. Cornell. Dec. 20th."[5] At this time, a second inquest was conducted, the body was exhumed and reexamined, and the jury reversed its earlier determination, finding this time reason to suspect foul play. Avery was arrested, examined for fourteen days, and finally acquitted because of insufficient "probable cause to suspect him guilty."[6]

Again the citizens of Tiverton and Fall River were incensed. On January 8, after Avery's acquittal, seven hundred people attended a meeting in Fall River, and a meeting the following day attracted six hundred.[7] These citizens complained that

Avery's examination had taken place in his own town of Bristol, rather than in Tiverton where the crime had been committed. Combined with his prominent position as a notable Methodist preacher, this choice of location all but guaranteed Avery's acquittal. Two days after the examination, a meeting among citizens of Fall River and Tiverton determined that the Fall River investigation committee should procure another warrant against Avery. By the time the warrant was issued on January 14, 1833, Avery was nowhere to be found. He was tracked down in the New Hampshire town of Rindge and returned to Rhode Island, where he stood trial in May.[8]

The trial took place in Newport, where all parties vainly hoped for an unbiased hearing of this crime that had stirred excitement all over the Northeast. The selection of the jury occupied two days; 122 potential jurors were examined before twelve could be found who had not already formed an unwavering opinion about the notorious case.[9] The trial itself commenced on May 9 and drew capacity crowds. Public interest was so intense that the court ordered that "such gentlemen as might be in Court for the purpose of taking notes were prohibited from causing the same to be published, until after the verdict of the jury should be rendered."[10] The admonition was necessary, since the trial was covered extensively not only in New England but also in the New York and Philadelphia presses. Still, trial proceedings were sometimes leaked to the newspapers and published. On May 23, the *Boston Morning Press* began running summaries of the evidence presented at trial; other newspapers reprinted the reports, until the judge discovered the violation and barred the reporter from his courtroom.

Predictably, the trial was lengthy. As the counsel for the defense explained in his summation, "No trial for a capital felony, since the first settlement of the country, has ever so long engaged the attention of a jury."[11] The trial consumed twenty-seven and one-half days, sixty-eight prosecution witnesses, and 128 defense witnesses. The Methodist Church was largely responsible for Avery's defense; church leaders helped to collect a nearly endless parade of witnesses and to defray the substantial court costs. The prosecution was enabled by citizens of local factory towns, especially Fall River and Tiverton. On the evening of June 1, after the prosecution's closing arguments and the judge's brief instructions, the jury retired to consider the evidence. After deliberating overnight, the jury returned its verdict of not guilty.

II. A DARK CLOUD OF SUSPICION

An explosion of public indignation followed. Journalists and editors busied themselves preparing responses to the verdict—some of them reexamining the evidence, gathering further facts, introducing evidence not suitable for court, and assigning blame for what they considered a politically motivated trial and verdict. Others, who supported Avery or the court system, insisted that the outcome had been justly arrived at and should be allowed to stand. As one editorial noted two months after the trial, "The Avery trial continues to excite an intense interest in the country, and the minds of men are yet fiercely agitated. Thousands hesitate not to denounce the

Methodist as the murderer and the jury as accomplices in his escape."[12] For nearly a year, newspapers and other publishers actively engaged in an often irate public debate about the crime, the trial, and the conduct of the two sides of the trial.

Debates were greatly facilitated by the abundant sources of information in circulation. An almost unprecedented number of trial transcripts were published during and soon after the trial. In addition to two pamphlet reports of Avery's initial examination, held at Bristol in January, more than half a dozen different (and variously accurate) transcripts of the Newport trial were circulated during the weeks following the trial. These included a substantial effort by Richard Hildreth, a "legal gentleman" of Boston, whose 143-page trial report claims to be a "full, fair, and impartial account" of the legal investigation, without also being an exact transcript. "The examinations of the witnesses," the author notes, "and particularly the cross-examinations, ran to such a length, that, were they reported verbatim, they would fill a large volume."[13] Benjamin F. Hallett's *Full Report* of the trial consumes 191 pages, while the unnamed author of *The Correct, Full and Impartial Report of the Trial* takes 178 pages to "present an accurate and full Report of a trial which has occupied a very large space of the public mind for the last four months."[14] An anonymous trial report published in New York (*The Trial at Large*) is a briefer fifty-one pages. Hallett also published several other pamphlets: the medical testimony of Drs. Channing and Turner; a supplement to the original trial transcript, *Avery's Trial*; and the *Arguments of Counsel in the Close of the Trial*, featuring the full closing statements of both attorneys. That same year, a booklet was published containing lithographic facsimiles of the letters admitted into evidence. David Kasserman observes that this publication, "Theoretically a neutral document designed to let the public compare the handwriting, . . . included a helpful list of points of comparison by which readers could convince themselves that Avery was the author of the disputed letters."[15] All of these publications apparently aimed at allowing private citizens to make up their own minds as to the fairness of the verdict. As one editor wrote immediately following the trial, "The evidence . . . produced when Mr. Avery was on trial for his life, and when both parties made the greatest exertions to bring forward every species of testimony bearing on the case,—must be that on which the public must mainly rely in forming their opinion of his guilt or innocence."[16]

In addition to the proliferation of editorials designed to influence public opinion on this issue, a number of other deeply partisan documents were published. Soon after the Newport trial, the Methodist Conference held its own inquiry into the matter. Without hearing new witnesses or considering new evidence, the conference reexamined the materials brought before the legal tribunal and declared the minister not only not guilty, but free from all suspicion of guilt on both the fornication and murder charges. A flurry of outraged editorials followed. "Admit," wrote one angry writer,

> that the verdict of the jury shows that the evidence was not sufficient to convict him of murder—still the testimony leaves a dark cloud of suspicion upon his character, which no number of compurgators of his innocence can remove. . . . Their vote cannot and ought not to have any influence on the public mind, in opposition to the impression produced by a perusal of the trial.[17]

Many readers resented these attempts by the Methodist Conference not only to secure an acquittal in the official trial, but to shape public sentiments following that acquittal. "Granting the verdict honest and the conviction of Avery's innocence unequivocal," wrote another editor, "it was certainly most unwise at once to reinstate him as a Christian minister, and apparently to command the world to proclaim him a guiltless martyr."[18]

The evidence of this folly was not long in emerging. Two venomous series of editorials began appearing soon after the trial, both anonymously authored and apparently provoked by the Methodist Conference. "Proteus" introduced his editorials in the *Newport Rhode Island Republican* in June, and soon after a series by "Aristides" appeared in the *Providence Republican Herald*. As Aristides argued in his first number,

> The public feels itself injured, common justice and common decorum, religion and morality, feel themselves outraged, not so much by the acquittal of Avery in a legal point of view, as by the bold and daring manifesto of the Methodist Conference, which acquits Avery even of suspicion, which all know to be incorrect, thrusts him into the pulpit as a public teacher of religion, who should be free from the very appearance of evil, and virtually recommends him as a man of unimpeachable integrity and purity of character.[19]

In spite of his intent to condemn the Methodist Church, Aristides did not confine himself to criticism of that body but sifted over the court testimony, even introducing some of his own, and laid it all before the public while drawing his own often fiery conclusions. Eighteen numbers were published in all. In September, after the editors of the *Republican Herald* were inundated with requests for back issues, the full series was published in a pamphlet, titled *Strictures on the Case of Ephraim K. Avery*. Catharine Williams, who was prompted by rage over clerical excesses to write her account of the murder trial, noted that if "Ecclesiastical Councils should take the place of Courts of Justice, and become the law of the land," then trial transcripts will "be condemned to be burnt by the common hangman and their authors to some modern 'Inquisition.'"[20] In self-defense, Avery announced that he would soon publish a rebuttal, aimed at clearing both himself and his fellow Methodist ministers. Before he had a chance, however, to publish his *Vindication of the Result of the Trial of Rev. Ephraim K. Avery* (which did not appear until February 1834), he found himself the victim of a hoax. A new document purporting to be written by Avery—the *Explanation of the Circumstances Connected with the Death of Sarah Maria Cornell*—argued that the woman's death had been accidental; as "Avery" explained, he had only meant to abort his child ("this being the only means I could imagine for preventing a disclosure which must have ultimately ruined my character, my family, and the cause of Christ in that neighborhood"), but he killed its mother in the process and subsequently covered his tracks by hanging Cornell's body.[21]

Though the public found different ways of expressing its disgust, the consensus among all but Avery's most ardent defenders was that the Methodist church had overstepped its authority and outraged public feeling by absolving the minister of all guilt. As Proteus argued, public rage is hardly a shameful emotion. "The passion of anger," he noted,

> was not implanted in the mind merely by an oversight of nature; like all other strong passions, it is liable to great abuse, but is eminently useful and commendable when properly directed and restrained. Its legitimate direction is against criminals of every grade. . . . Man is made capable of violent resentment, that he may redress his wrongs, with promptness, when redress is rational.[22]

Left to express their injuries, private citizens could only rehearse the details of the court case and declare the minister clearly guilty. This they did with a vengeance, in an endless stream of publications.

Though we can never know precisely how individual citizens responded to this ongoing saturation in the newspapers of details, facts, and discussion about the case, we do have some clues that the Avery trial absorbed many people, for whom constant discussion provided a means of expressing their rage. For one thing, no less than three plays were written in response to the episode. In September, a play opened in Newport called *The Factory Girl; or, the Fall River Murder*.[23] According to the local press, this sold-out play was "rapturously received" and the audience "highly gratified."[24] Another, written by Mary Carr Clarke, was published in New York in 1833.[25] Finally, in late August, the seedy Richmond Hill Theater in New York opened with *Sarah Maria Cornell; or, the Fall River Murder*. All three plays vilified Avery and cast his victim as a pious and gentle young woman. Although the texts of two of them seem to be no longer extant, one theater historian calls the New York drama "lurid enough to attract overflowing audiences" during an otherwise dismal commercial season for the artistically irredeemable theater.[26] The disapproving reviews in the *New York Mirror* apparently did nothing to discourage hoards of theater-goers, who perhaps wished to see a kind of justice done. As the *Mirror* argued:

> Now, although it must unavoidably happen, in some cases, that juries will arrive at incorrect conclusions regarding the guilt or innocence of accused persons, yet, as a general rule, it would be the most dangerous absurdity which ever had a place in the long catalogue of human errors, to maintain, that the opinions of individuals or parties should be paramount to the solemn decision of twelve sworn men, founded on evidence carefully submitted to them, compared and collated during a patient investigation, and elucidated by the assistance of counsel, and the charge of a responsible judge. If, then, it is received as a general rule, that the decision of a jury, in regard to guilt or innocence, shall be conclusive, those who violate this rule are guilty of an offense which no community should, for a moment, sanction. If it is sanctioned, no reputation is safe.[27]

This writer's censure of both the play and the people who patronized it seems inadvertently but precisely to explain the play's popularity. Why else, after all, would crowds of people flock to a play that had apparently no literary or dramatic merit, than because they could gather as an alternative jury, an assembly of like-minded citizens who rejected the verdict of a legal tribunal and sought, instead, to affirm their belief that Avery was guilty?

A second review in the *Mirror* noted only that continued crowds at the theater speak "volumes for the moral sense of the community."[28] This terse comment suggests (albeit ironically) that the continued public obsession with the case can best be understood as a moral response to what people considered a morally intolerable outcome. Audiences reacted enthusiastically to works that were critical of the trial, the suspect, or the Methodist Church. The favorable general response to the plays is a case in point. Catharine Williams's book, which appeared late in 1833, is another; it was so popular that it went into a second printing in 1834. Williams attempted to reexamine the trial, offering a narrative that would admit the kind of evidence excluded from an official trial and endeavoring, insofar as possible, to allow the dead woman to speak through her own letters. Private individuals, moreover, did more than buy, read, and discuss these works. As Williams notes, Cornell's gravesite on the Durfee property became the pilgrimage destination of thousands of people who had been moved by the story of her death. "Few have visited that spot without tears," Williams remarks.[29] Angry mobs assembled and effigies of Avery were displayed and burned on numerous occasions after the trial when the minister attempted to preach.[30] Dozens of anonymous poems appeared in newspapers and broadsides, demonizing the minister, venturing outraged sentiments, and cautioning young women against the wiles of charismatic preachers. These broadsides sold rapidly. Perhaps the strangest of all the individual responses to this public preoccupation with the Avery case took place on June 23, 1833, just weeks after the trial had ended. In Concord, New Hampshire, an eighteen-year-old servant, Abraham Prescott, beat his mistress to death and then sat down to read the Avery trial report. His defense—that he had been maddened by all the talk of the Avery trial, which had been constant conversation for months in his employers' household—did not keep him from being executed in 1836.[31] But it did express the widespread public fascination with this crime and its outcome, which many ordinary citizens considered a miscarriage of justice. As members of a democracy, they wished to arrive at their own verdict. Though the jury's decision was legally binding, the citizenry availed themselves of a venue for debate made possible by the publishing industry and their own literacy, assembling in a literary marketplace in which they could both ensure that Avery did not enjoy the full freedom of an innocent man and pledge that his victim would not be forgotten.

For its part, the defense team—by summoning a procession of witnesses and by appealing to the jury's uncertainty in a capital case involving a prominent defendant—managed to avoid conviction, which would almost surely have meant Avery's execution. But they could not protect the minister from being pilloried in the press, jeered by congregations, and threatened by mobs in the streets.[32] In the following pages, I will examine this unofficial trial, whose verdict condemned Avery to a life of fear and flight. After trying to win back public acceptance, the minister finally fled to Ohio, where he lived obscurely as a farmer and died in 1869.

III. "A CLASS INDISPENSABLE TO THE INDUSTRY OF THE COUNTRY"

William C. McLoughlin has argued that the Avery case captured the American imagination because it represented the social and political upheavals confronting a nation undergoing rapid industrialization.[33] The audacity of Methodism, a populist religion that found an influential place in Jacksonian America, was exemplified by this married minister who allegedly seduced a young factory worker, deprived her of a place in his church by defaming her throughout New England, then killed her and successfully defended himself in court. "As small-town agricultural life gave way to the anonymous factory life of the new mill towns," McLoughlin writes, "this murder seemed to portend the worst; deranged times would lead to deranged behavior."[34] Cornell, McLoughlin notes, was a rural girl from a Congregationalist family when she left home to work in the factories, where she converted to Methodism.[35] She thus represented the replacement of old values and institutions with new ones.

Regardless of its outcome, the case would force this changing society to confront significant social issues regarding the place of unmarried women and the authority of two relatively new institutions: the textile industry and the Methodist Church. Of course, the popularity of Methodism depended in large part upon the acquittal of the defendant, who had been supported publicly by his church. Likewise, the strength of the textile industry required that parents feel confident that their daughters would be safe working in a factory, perhaps hundreds of miles away from home; Avery's conviction would send a message that the despoilers and murderers of factory workers would not go unpunished.

Single women, after all, played a substantial role in the prosperity of factory towns. Fall River was one of many New England manufactory towns that owed their livelihoods to the textile industry. According to local historians, "its soil was not particularly fertile, and its terrain made transportation difficult. Its harbor was adequate for local trade but did not attract much shipping; it was shallow and exposed to westerly winds. Fall River's shipping was less important than that of the neighboring towns of Assonet and Taunton."[36]

By 1839 textile factories had expanded so dramatically that "more than one sixth, or 1,105" inhabitants of Fall River "were employed in the ten cotton and one woolen mills in the town."[37] Thus the town depended heavily on the factories, which in turn needed cheap female labor to run successfully. Factory labor was so meagerly rewarded "that several members of a family had to work in a mill to make ends meet."[38] Given the low pay, factories were largely staffed either by young women whose income would supplement what their fathers or brothers earned, or by those who were excited by the prospect of working in the new factories. And because one town was seldom adequate to the labor needs of a factory, the workforce came from surrounding towns and states and from abroad, particularly England, Ireland, and Scotland.[39] An advertisement for the sale of the Troy Mill in 1827 promised that "the surrounding country abounds in such kinds of labourers as are wanted in the manufacturing business."[40]

The cheapest available sources of labor were single women, and many of these came from remote places.[41] A critical natural resource, young women might become scarce if their families could not satisfy themselves that their sisters and daughters would be well protected in these industrial settings. The economic stability of the factories, and consequently of the factory towns, depended on the security of factory workers, especially unmarried women. Rural families must be assured that the textile industry would all but guarantee the safety and chastity of their daughters. Regulations throughout factory towns insisted on the same kind of behavior that would be expected of well-bred young women at home: many textile mills required regular church attendance somewhere, and "boarding house rules were innumerable and covered every smallest corner of the operatives' lives," according to John Coolidge, a historian of the Lowell factories, which were typical of other factories throughout New England.[42] While factory work was not overly arduous during the early years of these mills,[43] a paternalistic system of surveillance kept close watch on the workers, particularly women.[44]

Although some critics of the mills complained that factory work disqualified women for marriage,[45] others argued strongly for the wholesome influence of factory life.[46] When the Reverend William Scoresby of Yorkshire visited Lowell in 1844, he concluded that the female factory workers of that city nearly lived up to their widespread reputation for purity and industry. Scoresby's visit verified the opinion of a Lowell physician, Dr. Bartlett, who argued that "the great preponderance of influence" on the factory workers "is enlightening, elevating and improving—not darkening, debasing, and deteriorating."[47] Quoting Bartlett with approval, Scoresby marveled that this manufactory town managed to overcome the great vulnerability of young women, who, "as strangers from the country, separated from their natural protectors, and left almost entirely to their own discretion and moral self-dependence, . . . [are] singularly exposed to risk and temptation."[48] The reason for the success of this social experiment, he concluded, was "the watchful consideration and moral care, for the young women, taken by their employers and others."[49] Noting that boardinghouse superintendents and factory owners and overseers all took equal part in the supervision of single women, Scoresby again cites Bartlett: "'The moral police,' he says, 'of all the establishments is vigilant, active, and rigid. While industry and good conduct are respected and rewarded, no violations of the excellent and judicious rules of the corporation, and no improper or suspicious conduct meet with any indulgence or toleration.'"[50] Though they were far from their own families, the women employed in New England factories found themselves living and working under conditions that deliberately replicated the middle-class family structure. Scoresby notes that "some, probably very many, of the principle proprietors of the factories of Lowell, are men highly distinguished among their countrymen for piety and benevolence,—and who, therefore, exercise a watchful and beneficial influence over the moral tone of the operatives they employ."[51] In the case of Fall River, where Cornell worked, the family model was more than a replica; the factories had been established, and the town controlled by a few closely knit families who devoted themselves to the fiscal, civic, and moral responsibilities that fell to prominent businessmen.[52]

For young, unmarried women like Sarah Cornell, then, life in a factory town provided an interim stage between childhood, passed in the parents' home, and the typical adult existence of marriage and motherhood.[53] The factory, superintended by benevolent paternal figures, constituted a surrogate family, one where a young woman could find refuge, security, and limited economic independence while she awaited marriage. Boarding houses extended this family structure to a woman's living quarters. The entire arrangement, including labor, leisure, and habitation, resembled the ideal pattern of domestic life in a young woman's own family.

Not surprisingly, then, the citizens of Fall River thought of Sarah Cornell as one of their own, and their interest in the investigation and trial was analogous to that of the victim's own family. When the Methodist Church refused to give Cornell a decent burial, the Durfee family stepped in to volunteer their land, while a Congregationalist minister performed the funeral rites. Citizens of Fall River and Tiverton raised funds to assist the investigation and prosecution of Avery. Their outrage when they felt that the victim would not receive justice was no less than that of a bereaved family.

It is hard to distinguish real familial regard for the victim from the propaganda we might expect from an industrial town under fire. Residents of Fall River undoubtedly felt paternalistic concern for Cornell and a measure of responsibility for her demise. But they also surely feared that the infamous episode would send a message to far-off families of mill workers that factories could not protect their employees. Their interest in the trial was twofold: to secure a conviction in order to avenge the woman's death, and to prove to the world that factories insisted upon piety and respectability in return for the protection they extended to their employees.

Two literary responses to the Cornell murder trial demonstrate the authors' commitment to this second purpose, a commitment exemplified by their depictions of mill life. Early in *Fall River: an Authentic Narrative*, Catharine Williams recalls a vivid memory of her visit to one of the factories. Entering "one of the weaving rooms . . . , where the noise was very distracting arising from a vast number of looms going at once," Williams noted that "the machinery suddenly stopped, and a strain of music arose simultaneously from every part of the room, in such perfect concord that I at first thought it a chime of bells. My conductor smiled when I asked him if it was not, and pointed to the girls, who each kept their station until they had sung the tune through."[54] This image betokens more than musical concord: the factory workers represent an almost prelapsarian scene of carefree labor. They are orderly, cheerful, and industrious, and inspire confidence in the benevolent system of factory labor.

The second act of Clarke's play also invokes the harmony of factory life, again presented as an ideal domestic economy. Here again the female laborers sing at their looms, only the playwright supplies her audience with cheerful lyrics as well: "And as the wind blows," the weavers sing, "So the mill goes— / Say who are so happy, / So happy, as we."[55] The ensuing conversation between Sarah and her employer,

Mr. Thornhill, serves several purposes. First, it indicates Sarah's pleasure at having employment in the textile factory. "Ah, sir," she tells Thornhill, "it is industry makes me gay. When I have no work I am so sad and low-spirited. Oh, dear me, what would we poor girls do if it was not for the institution of manufactories?—how could we live?"[56] The point, it seems, is that marriage is not always an immediate option for young women whose parents can no longer afford to keep them at home. Textile factories, offering these women rewarding and pleasurable work, fill the void left open by an inadequate supply of eligible bachelors.

Clarke's theatrical polemic also reminds the audience that the support of young factory workers like Sarah depends upon a long line of others, from cotton suppliers to consumers. Thornhill gives Sarah a brief lesson in macroeconomics, one that Clarke clearly intended for her theater audience as well. "Thank the American system of domestic industry" for steady work and regular wages, Thornhill tells Sarah, "as it is that alone which enables me to give employment to my working people, whose services are as essential to me as my employment is to them." As the economic lesson sinks in, Sarah observes that "we look up to you for our means of subsistence while you depend on every one to purchase our work." Thornhill agrees and elaborates: "If I cannot get cotton, your work would cease. This is the great care on my mind, and if I can't dispose of my goods, I should be compelled to shut up the factory. . . . Thus you see, Sarah, I am in a sense dependent on the world as much as you are on me."[57] While appealing to Americans to support the work of New England textile factories, Clarke also assures them that their patronage supports a necessary and benevolent social institution, perhaps the only one available to unmarried women.

Finally, Clarke also obliquely indicates that a tragedy like the murder of a factory hand has consequences for the entire system. Thornhill instructs Sarah to see her work as part of a larger economic machine: "Society, Sarah, is a vast chain: one link depends on the other, and an injury to one of them may be felt by the whole."[58] Though the dramatic Sarah has not yet met her fate, Clarke's audiences would certainly have caught the allusion to Cornell's death and the further "injury" of an acquittal. While Clarke could not correct these irreversible injuries, she could and did endeavor to repair the damage to Cornell's reputation and that of the entire culture of textile factories.

Given the image that factory towns wished to project, it should come as no surprise that the deceased woman's character was a dramatic focal point of the trial and subsequent discussions of her life. The question of Cornell's character came to represent the ability of factories to provide an acceptable alternative to marriage for those women who could not or did not wish to marry, an alternative that would reproduce as far as possible the home and replace parental protection with the protection of the factory and its owners. Thus we see that specific discussions of the case often echoed the general defenses of factory life for women with which we are already familiar.

Cornell was nearly thirty years old and still unmarried when she died. Though she never gave up hope of one day having a family of her own, she was relatively old to be unmarried and dependent for protection on someone other than a husband.

Her failure to marry was significant enough for both her defenders and detractors to mention. As the defense attorney argued, Cornell had contemplated suicide because of "the disease that had preyed upon her mind—disappointment in marriage."[59] Williams, on the other hand, muses on a different outcome than Cornell's tragic end:

> How different her fate would have been could she have been settled in life and tied to the duties of wife and mother, we cannot say, but the probability is she would have made a very respectable figure in society, and a much better wife than ordinary, owing to the natural docility of her disposition, her perfect habitual good nature, and forbearance and forgiveness.[60]

In both of these accounts, Cornell's failure to marry comes to represent one significant cause of her demise. What might seem an advantage for the factory that offered her employment—her single status, her need to earn a living on her own, her freedom from family duties, which would prevent her from working long hours—posed a heightened risk for the woman herself. It would be in the factory's best interest to turn Cornell's marital status into a neutral fact if not a character strength. This they could do by presenting her as an honest, generous, and admirable young woman whose labor in the factory provided an apprenticeship that would eventually prepare her for the roles of wife and mother.

The prosecution, on the other hand, sought to depict Cornell as a depraved coquette, one whose word could not be trusted—a woman capable of attempting blackmail on an innocent Methodist minister and, failing that, of committing suicide merely to frame him. The defense closed its case by explaining that the limits of female corruption are unimaginable:

> That there is a charm, a refinement, a delicacy in the female sex, superior to man, no civilized community has ever doubted. It is female character, when pure and unstained, which contributes to the embellishment and refinement of society in the highest degree, but in the same proportion as woman, when chaste and pure, excels the other sex, by just so much, when profligate, does she sink below them; and if you were to seek for some of the vilest monsters in wickedness and depravity, you would find them in the female form.[61]

The defense tried to inspire the jury with unqualified horror for this woman, so that they would neither identify with her nor think that her death was especially regrettable. As one of Williams's unnamed sources said, "he did not think such a drab worth having a trial about!"[62]

While the prosecution understood that it would not do to represent this unmarried, pregnant woman as sinless—"her life," said Albert Greene in his summation, "was one of transgression and remorse—of sensual indulgence, and religious enthusiasm—of piety and passion"[63]—others writing after the trial were not constrained by fears of a courtroom rebuttal. Some, like Aristides, admitted that "her character for chastity [was] ad"[64] but acknowledged only that single character flaw. Her nature, he argued, was subject to the control of *one* powerful appetite, without sufficient strength, fortitude or prudence to control its fury. But it exhibits also those feelings of shame, that nice sense of discrimination of what constitutes female honor, and that acuteness of suffering under its loss, that no female, the subject of hardened depravity, ever yet experienced, or ever can.[65]

Like this journalist, others, including Catharine Williams, shifted focus from Cornell's sexual transgressions to other aspects of her character: her generosity, piety, and charity. Williams, who conducted hundreds of interviews with residents of Fall River and other factory towns where Cornell had worked, explained that

> Various anecdotes . . . have been related to the author respecting the charity, kindness of heart and gentle disposition of S.M. Cornell: but they would swell this volume beyond the bounds allotted to a work of this kind. Suffice it to say, that from all accounts, it appears her hand was ever open to the suffering poor, according to her slender means; . . . that she was kind to the sick and afflicted; and retained a most affectionate regard towards her relatives, through the whole of her long absence from them.[66]

Williams rehabilitates her subject's battered reputation by noting how good, honorable people had been affected by Cornell. "In the respectable house where she boarded, . . . she was much beloved, having won their regard by the gentleness of her manners and the apparent amiability of her temper."[67] In death, Cornell inspired similar people with feelings of sympathy and tenderness. When the Methodist Church—Cornell's own church—refused to provide for her burial, John Durfee offered his land for her burial place. "And without any fear of contamination," Williams notes, Durfee "gave orders to have a grave prepared for her near his own family."[68] Perhaps Williams's strongest evidence for the respectability of her tragic subject comes from common people, the hundreds of pilgrims who visit Cornell's grave: "It is in vain that the friends of Avery endeavour to place that unfortunate being beneath even the pity of the virtuous. Her own sex feel she was a woman, and as such entitled to their sympathies, the other, more generally inclined to compassionate female frailty, pity her with undissembled sorrow."[69]

Other defenders, like the anonymous author who had known Cornell when she was younger, insisted that the "grave ought to be permitted to protect its victims"; cruelty alone could justify mentioning "every guilty act . . . [that might] be dragged fourth [sic] to light, to fix odium and shame and stigma on the memory of the poor ill-fated girl."[70]

Perhaps the most exaggerated character reference is found in the opening scene of Clarke's melodrama. Sarah, worried about the meaning of a "dreadful dream," is reluctant to reveal its content to her friends, who might "despise me if I tell." But her coworkers assure her of their high regard: "What! hate you for a dream? impossible!" says one; "Sarah, we know, is good, virtuous and industrious." Another explains, "I could not hate you if I would. Don't you remember last winter, when I was sick a whole week, how you did my work and your own too—kept my place for me, and brought my wages to mother every Saturday night." The other girls add to this testimony of Sarah's generosity, as if Cornell were already on trial for her good name. The entire play constitutes a defense of the virtuous young victim of Methodist conspiracy.[71]

Both in the court and in the public domain, those who worked for the prosecution of Ephraim Avery demonstrated their deep interest not only in Sarah Cornell but also in that essential resource she represented, the female factory operative. The arguments and preoccupations of the trial were startlingly similar to those of editorials, histories, and fictional retellings of the case. As the prosecuting attorney argued in his opening statement, the deceased was a "'Factory girl,' but she was one of that class of women and children of which we have 7000 usefully and honorably employed in the 150 Cotton Mills in this State; a class indispensable to the industry of the country and whose rights, therefore, the interest of the community require should be protected and their wrongs avenged."[72] The stakes for Fall River and similar manufacturing communities, clearly, were high: to prosecute Avery successfully was to guarantee that the textile industry would continue unimpaired by this crime.

As we have seen, the prosecution did not win its case. We might wonder about the consequences for the cotton manufactories and the towns that depended upon their success. McLoughlin contends that the trial brought into relief people's ambivalence about industrial development. Because factory towns offered anonymity but "no close-knit community to keep tabs on everyone," progress was "a double-edged sword. It promised prosperity, cheaper mass-produced goods, a higher standard of living for all but it required uprooting the old, stable ways of small-town rural life."[73] If the published debates over Avery's trial offer any hint of such uncertainty, they do so only in the most oblique way, speaking with a confidence about factory life that could only have come from writers who were themselves the products of an industrial ideology. In defending that ideology, the hundreds of ordinary citizens who discussed the case in print not only deprived Avery of his influential position as a regular preacher, but drove him from New England and rescued the reputation of Sarah Cornell, who came to serve as the most representative factory girl in all of New England. As if they understood the threats to factory life but refused to acknowledge them, the legions of writers who defended Cornell in print employed her as the heroine of an idealized representation of factory life, one that drew heavily on the conventions of sentimental novels. In their accounts, the textile factory was nearly synonymous with pre-industrial domestic life, and Sarah Cornell presided as the embattled protagonist of that world.

IV. "YOUNG MAIDENS ALL A WARNING TAKE"

As a narrative, the Avery case mirrored the stories of seduction and death so often told in the earliest American novels. Seduction novels, arguably the most popular literary form in early nineteenth-century America, were replete with stories of young women whose own families could not safeguard their chastity. The American interest in the genre suggests the paradoxical role of chastity in early republican life; it was deemed both necessary to the character of a woman and the society she represented, and a fragile commodity nearly impossible for paternalistic institutions to protect. When he drew toward the close of his case, the prosecuting attorney sounded like a stock character of seduction novels, the benevolent matron who issues sexual advice to the heroine; he defined a woman's reputation as a "jewel which, once lost, can never be restored, and without which woman becomes an outcast from society."[74]

The attorneys were not the only ones whose accounts of the case followed the typical pattern of seduction novels, where the innocent woman is torn away from her home by the false rake. In many of the popular stories of Cornell's life, the factory provided the ideal domestic setting from which the young woman was lured. As her despoiler, Avery acted as a mere representative of a larger institution, the Methodist Church, repeatedly cast as the dominant seducer of poor working women.

The tragedy of Cornell's seduction was made more poignant to her readers by the fact that the benevolent factory had been her second home, a virtual replacement for a family life that had failed terribly. Like those of the tragic figures in many seduction novels, Cornell's family history involved the pain of an earlier unwise union. Her mother, an educated young woman from a wealthy family, "carefully brought up and accustomed only to the best society," formed an "unfortunate attachment" to James Cornell, a man employed in her father's factory. Against her father's wishes she married Cornell, who according to Williams had been planning to live on his father-in-law's money.[75] When those funds dried up, Cornell

> carried his wife and children to her father's house, and leaving them, quit the country, and relieved himself forever from the task of supporting a woman whom he had probably married without the least sentiment of affection whatever, and abandoning the children in their helpless infancy, whom the laws of God, and the laws of the land both required him to support.[76]

The four children were separated and brought up in the homes of relatives. Sarah lived with her mother until the age of eleven, when she was sent to an aunt; at fifteen she was apprenticed to a tailor.[77]

While Cornell was not exactly an orphan, she often saw herself as set adrift from her family, as we can see in her plaintive letters home. Williams's history of Fall River includes sixteen letters that Sarah wrote between 1819 and 1832, most of them addressed to her mother and sister. Those letters alternate between resignation to her solitude —"I should be pleased could we all meet once more," she writes in 1822, "but I don't expect we ever shall"[78]—and passionate insistence on keeping her strained family ties intact. "I wish," she writes her mother in 1825, "you would send me word by William if you have heard from James, and where he is, that I may know where to write to."[79] Repeatedly she tried to make plans for a brief reunion with her family, though her factory work often proved prohibitive. As she suggested on one occasion, "If I thought you and Lucretia would be at home, I should come that way and spend one night with you."[80] On another she wrote, "I want to see Mother and if any of you desire to see me—write and let me know and I will try to come and spend a few days with you before long."[81] Her apparent despair over her frail family connections escalated as Cornell got older. In 1827, at the age of twenty-five, she wrote, "Dear Mother if you have any regard for me do write if it is only two lines."[82] In 1829 she sounded more desperate: "It seems a long time since I have heard from you," she told her mother, "and I almost begin to think you have forgotten me or you would have written before this. I have written two letters and sent two papers since I have resided in this place [Lowell], and not received a line from any of you. I hope you will consider I am a stranger in a strange land, exposed to sickness and death."[83] One of her most stirring letters, from Lowell, is dated 1830:

> MY DEAR MOTHER—After waiting for more than eight long months for an answer to a letter that I wrote you last spring, I once more take up my pen to address you. You wrote me then you were going to visit your friends at Norwich, and that you would write me immediately on your return, but as I have never received a line from that time, I have concluded that you were either sick or dead, for it appears to me if you were in the land of the living and possess a parent's feelings you would have written before this. When I last wrote to you that if the Lord spared my life and health I should visit Connecticut in August last past. A long time I waited for your return from Norwich, thinking you would write and let me know, but at length concluded it was neither your wish nor that of my brother and sister that I should visit Killingly—but enough of this—I will cease to trouble your minds with such painful feelings. Not a day has rolled over my head since I left you but what I have thought of home, and the dear friends I have left many miles from this.[84]

Though Sarah Cornell had been first abandoned by her father and then driven away from her mother and siblings by economic difficulties, she apparently yearned for the domestic affections, stability, and security that she had been denied in her young life. It should come as no surprise that the textile industry, modeled on the ideal family structure, should attract a young woman who craved a family of her own. Catharine Williams's explanation for Cornell's fall from chastity is just as useful in explaining her devotion to factory work: "It seemed as though her affections sought constantly for some object upon which to repose themselves, for something to lavish that tenderness upon with which her heart was overflowing."[85]

The main difficulty with Cornell's factory life—the one contradiction with its claims to replicate domesticity and the cause of Cornell's demise cited most often by her defenders and detractors alike—was the itinerant lifestyle it forced upon her. Cornell was aware of her family's alarm regarding her nomadic existence. "I received a letter from mother about four months since," she writes her sister, "in which she mentioned she thought I was a moving planet, but I would tell my dear mother that I do not think I have moved much for two years past."[86] Though on that occasion Cornell defended her rootlessness by comparing herself to the Methodist clergy—"she must remember that I am connected with a people that do not believe in tarrying in any one place longer than a year or two years at most at any one time"—in truth Cornell longed to settle down, and her many dislocations were caused largely by economic difficulties inherent to her trade. In 1824 she seems to have found a home in Slatersville, Rhode Island, where she was employed when she announced to her mother that "the year past has been the happiest of my life. I have lived in this village almost nineteen months, and have boarded in a very respectable family."[87] The next year she wrote of her expectations "to spend my days in Slatersville. I dont want great riches nor honours—but a humble plain decent and comfortable living will suit me best."[88] On another occasion she worried about another departure: "Sometimes when I think of leaving Slatersville, it strikes a dread upon me."[89] A fire at the Slatersville factory in early 1826 compelled her to leave that "place highly favoured by God."[90] By 1830 she had found another home. "I have been in Lowell so long," she tells her mother, "that I should feel lonesome anywhere else."[91]

Other reasons for her frequent relocations involved more personal matters—namely, her damaged reputation. Although Cornell often moved because of malicious rumors that followed her to her many new homes, it is also apparent that her itinerant life might have provoked some of those rumors. Williams sadly points to "that baneful disposition to rove, to keep moving from place to place," as "the ruin of so many," including Cornell.[92] While Williams does not try to refute the many rumors of deceit and sexual licentiousness introduced as fact at Avery's trial, she does note that such tales took greater hold because Cornell had no permanent home. "Poor unfortunate being! she did not realize the danger of changing neighborhoods so often, nor know that it was safest for people to stay where they are best known, and where slanderers make out to live upon one old story for a thousand years, but transport it into a new neighborhood and ten thousand will immediately be added to it."[93] For Cornell's defenders in print, the problem was not factory life itself, which as we have seen provided her with a surrogate family when her own was chronically unavailable, but the conditions requiring her to move so frequently from one factory town to another.

Still, the public accounts of Sarah Cornell's life repeatedly assert that her employers, coworkers, and landlords supplied her with a place in an honorable and orderly domestic world, that same world we have seen promised by the advertisements issued by factories and their advocates. Though Cornell did not live with a pair of respectable and doting parents like the heroine of a typical seduction novel, the popular accounts of her life insistently depicted the textile industry as surrogate parents, represented by employers at the cotton factories who stepped in and befriended Cornell when her own family had all but abandoned her.

Both Williams and Clarke portray the factory as a beneficent influence, the village in its shadow as an orderly and pious place. Williams's industrial landscape is almost pastoral: "the thriving city exhibits the appearance of industry and application and enterprise, [and] the rural landscape teems with sights and sounds of human happiness."[94] Industry and religion coexist in this landscape, where "it is evident . . . from the number of houses of worship, schools, &c. that the moral and religious education of the rising generation is not neglected."[95] In Clarke's account, piety is displayed not by the scheming Methodist ministers, but by Mr. Thornhill, Cornell's boss at the factory. He is the one who professes his faith in "a supreme power that governs all, and to him alone we ought to look for comfort, support, and happiness."[96] But his is not passive faith; Thornhill also serves as a magistrate and is thereby entrusted with the public good. When he hears of a Methodist camp meeting, he considers that his "presence may be requisite to keep the peace."[97] Indeed it is: although he arrives too late to forestall Sarah's rape at the hands of Avery, Thornhill interrupts a scene of theft, deception, and sexual chaos. His speech to the assembled people clearly establishes his role as moral, legal, and parental authority figure. "A precious set of saints you all are," he scolds the ministers. "But by the virtue of the laws, I dismiss this assemblage of persons. Men, take your wives and daughters from this scene of fanaticism, and hypocrisy. Come, Sarah, you are from my manufactory therefore entitled to my protection."[98]

In the conventional seduction novel, frivolous amusements present the primary threat to the parental authority embodied by Thornhill. Sarah Cornell, according to one account, resembled other susceptible women in her attachment to "gay and lively company." At age sixteen, she became "fond of visiting with her female companions scenes of innocent amusement and pleasure."[99] Innocent in themselves, these scenes distracted Sarah from more sober pursuits and left her a prey to those who sought to capitalize on her capacity for spontaneous pleasure. Like many authors of cautionary tales for young women, Cornell's defenders all agree that her impulsiveness contributed to her demise. But in Cornell's case, her downfall was secured by a religious enthusiasm sweeping the nation, one that victimized passionate women like herself. Williams argues that the great religious revival of her day fed on "general excitement" and "a great deal of self-deception. The quick feelings and sanguine temperament of S. M. Cornell were calculated to mislead her, and it was not long before she rushed with the multitude to the altar of baptism."[100] The author of the *Brief and Impartial Narrative* says that "with a temperament naturally ardent, and a high flow of spirits, it is not surprising that she should be wrought up to a high degree of feeling and excitement . . . but there is a line where religion and piety terminates and enthusiasm begins, and it is supposed that Maria overstepped this line and wandered away into the mazy and unexplored regions of religious fanaticism."[101]

For these and other authors, Methodism not only failed to protect Cornell from the consequences of a mind too little given to sober thought; it actively recruited young women like her, playing to their immature and passionate natures, and providing a succession of camp meetings in which to exploit their ardency. In this role, camp meetings supplanted the usual culprit, the theater, in the narratives of those who wanted explanations for Cornell's seduction and death. Both Clarke and Williams compare the camp meeting to the theater, finding at best no difference between them, and at worst a greater culpability among Methodist preachers. In Clarke's play, a sanctimonious mother condemns the "playhouse" as "the devil's tabernacle, where all who visit get into the high road to destruction."[102] This statement undoubtedly provoked knowing smiles among Clarke's own audience, who may have believed that their own highest motive for attending her play was righteous outrage at the outcome of the Avery trial. Clarke builds upon her joke when Mrs. Houseman, almost immediately after indicting the theater, announces her intention to attend the next camp meeting. Her niece, Tabby, is mature enough to deplore these meetings, where "the men and women all [lie] higglety-pigglety on straw in tents"; her ingenuous daughter Mary reminds her mother of the last such meeting, where one of the preachers, Mr. Muffit, "squeezed you one night till you were almost dead."[103] Williams's comparison is more somber but makes the same point. The camp meeting, she insists, is

> A thing much more to be dreaded than even theatrical entertainments, inasmuch as it goes under the name of religion; whereas the former is called by all sorts of evil names that can serve to warn people. When people go to the theatre they know where they are going. They go with their eyes open. They know it is at best but a profane entertainment, and they go against the warnings of the pious of all denominations. But when they go to a Camp ground, they do not know of the dangers that lurk there and menace them at every step . . .[104]

One of the most frequently quoted condemnations of these camp meetings came from the dead woman herself. Cornell's statement to her friend, Lucy Hathaway, was admitted at Avery's initial examination and again at the trial, and it soon became part of the public domain. Hathaway testified that Cornell had been "unwell since the camp meeting at Thompson, and spoke of her illness as having originated there."[105] Cornell's incriminating statement was that, though she had once been an active participant of camp meetings, "she would never go to one again,—she had seen there things to disgust her, between a church member and a minister, and that minister a married man."[106] Cornell's statement was repeated and embellished in many subsequent narratives.

The popular account that emerged during and after the trial depicted Cornell as a virtuous but naive young woman whose respectable domestic existence, superintended by the factories where she worked and the boardinghouses where she lived, was powerless against the subtle deceptions of the Methodist Church. Whereas factory life was orderly and benevolent, Methodist camp life was licentious and chaotic. In contrast to the well-regulated factory that we have seen portrayed in the descriptions of factory life, camps appeared wild and uncontrolled. Williams asks: "Who can contend that this free intermingling of society is not dangerous, this tumbling and falling about not indecent. That the familiar habit of life practiced there is not full of temptation; to prove this would be to prove that the persons who frequent them are not made of flesh and blood."[107]

Perhaps one reason for these stark representations is that readers of Cornell's story were already familiar with the conventions of seduction novels, conventions that easily accommodated both factory owners and Methodists to the recognizable categories of protectors and villains. For another explanation we would have to consider the threat that Methodism posed to family life. Whereas Congregationalism, a well-established religion in New England and the one in which Cornell had been raised, represented permanence and hierarchy, Methodism was a relatively new religion, it required an itinerant lifestyle of its clergy, and it seemed to have appealed to lonely individuals rather than solid families. Indeed, several of Cornell's letters to her family indicate that her religious affiliation posed a threat to both her familial relations and her employment. In December 1825 she writes her mother that she has been "making calculations all the fall of coming up" for a visit with her mother, "but I am disappointed I have lost so much time, I have been out sick a week—and last Saturday I went to Douglass to quarterly meeting—and Mr. Osterhold is not very willing I should stay out of the factory so soon again."[108] In 1827 she writes her mother, "I have been expecting all summer to visit you this month on my tour to Ashford camp meeting—and had engaged a passage in the stage, but I found it would be so expensive—and I could stay so short a time—that I concluded to give it up—and go to Lunenburg with my Boston brethren."[109] The following year she writes, "I wish it was so that I could come and go with you [to Norwich], but I do not think it will be possible, as I have lately given five dollars for the purpose of erecting a new Methodist meeting house in this town, which is to be built by sub-scription."[110] Evidently, the Methodist Church competed with both families and employers for their members' time, money, and loyalty. Nor did the fictionalized accounts fail to recognize how Methodist ministers preyed on the scanty resources of poor working factory girls. When the greedy ministers in Clarke's play enter the factory in order to hawk Bibles to the textile workers, Sarah scolds them for their deception: "Will selling bibles and tracts at an extravagant price to poor girls, and cheat[ing] them into the purchase, fill your pockets or save your soul best."[111]

V. "NO VERDICT CAN THE MONSTER CLEAR"

The unofficial trial that took place in the press sounded a steady complaint: the religious body that had claimed to protect Cornell had in fact ruined her. This point is conveyed clumsily by Clarke's character, the Reverend Averio (whose Italianized surname plainly indicates his role as villain). As he is about to seduce her, Averio speaks in paternalistic terms. "Sarah, as an orphan, you have a powerful claim on my sympathy," he tells her, thereby reminding his audience, if not himself, that Sarah's isolation ought to have entitled her to protection, above all, from the church to which she belonged.[112] When Williams begins her narrative, she strikes a conventional chord, expressing her hope that Cornell's story will serve "as a salutary and timely warning to young women in the same situation in life"; the warning includes a caution "against that idolatrous regard for ministers, for preachers of the gospel, which at the present day is a scandal to the cause of Christianity."[113] Avery's fellow ministers complained that "Vigorous and unceasing efforts have been made" since the acquittal "to blacken the character of his brethren and the New England Conference, as though they were leagued with a seducer and murderer."[114] Their accusation was hardly exaggerated; Clarke's play makes the charge of conspiracy among preachers as explicitly as possible when Averio, anticipating a successful camp meeting, explains "the main object of our camp-meetings" to his fellow ministers: "Here on our own ground alone the dear little creatures' hearts will melt at our preaching—the singing soothes even pride, and at the lonely midnight hour, when only the silver moon and twinkling stars are witnesses to our spiritual conversation, we mould them to our will, and are divinely bless'd. This is my mode of conversion."[115] While some of his brothers prefer to wrest money and jewelry from their converts, all commit themselves to helping each other attain their particular profane desires. As Brother Jenks says, "This is likely to be a profitable meeting; the ground is spacious and romantic; charming shrubbery, plenty of bushes, and I hope for a variety of fine girls to admire them with us."[116] His peers nod lustily and keep tabs on each other's accomplishments. One asks Averio, "did you convert [Sarah]?—ha, ha, ha!"; to which Averio replies, "No, but I intend that this meeting."[117]

Such literary treatments capitalized on the fact that in spite of the acquittal, Avery's trial had left much doubt about the defendant's innocence. Aristides announced that "their verdict to the contrary notwithstanding," the jury "have . . . expressed their belief of his guilt. Nor are they singular in this respect: for Chief Justice Eddy, who presided on the trial, has said, since that trial, that he had very little, if any, more doubt of the guilt of Ephraim K. Avery, THAN OF HIS OWN EXISTENCE."[118]

Unlike this official verdict, the ruling in the popular press couldn't have been less equivocal. Though Clarke's Averio demurs before killing his mistress, saying, "Oh! this is too much; I cannot murder her," he steadies his resolve. "Syren. You shall die," he tells her as he fastens his hands on her throat.[119] One anonymous broadside poem has Avery say, "fair maid now learn your doom, / I'll ne'er convey you further, / But in this lonesome dreary place, / I quickly will you murder."[120] Another poem, written to the tune of "The Star-Spangled Banner," depicts Cornell's murder in graphic, enraged detail:

> Those hands that in her's had been tenderly laid,
> Like paws of the tiger, now fiercely did clutch her;
> Those hands he had raised o'er the vows that he made,
> Now wallowed in blood, they were those of her butcher.
> Thou demon, go prowl where kindred fiends howl,
> All mankind despise thee, thou monster most foul.[121]

According to another anonymous poem, Cornell's "lovely locks with rage he tore, / And strewed the ground with hair, / Then to a stack her form he bore, / And hung the body there."[122] Though the author of the *Brief and Impartial Narrative* declines to depict the crime, he leaves little doubt of his conviction that Avery was the killer, warning that "the most secret actions of mortal man cannot be concealed" from the eyes of God, who will one day call the defendant before a second, "more awful tribunal."[123] Williams, too, reluctant to open herself to libel charges, refrains from depicting the murder in her narrative. But she inserts two poems. The first, her own, comes no closer to an accusation than in its final couplet: "No verdict can the monster clear / Who dies a hypocrite must wake to weep."[124] The other, whose author is only identified as "an old lady over eighty years of age," does not hesitate to accuse the minister of murder: "He killed the mother and the child, / What a wicked man was he; / The devil helped him all the while, / How wicked he must be."[125]

These and other populist arguments, appearing in the wake of the court verdict, all agreed that the public tribunal had different standards and values than the judicial court. Those who wished for a general indictment in the public domain merely repeated what the defense attorney had argued to the jury to secure an acquittal. When Jeremiah Mason summed up for the prisoner, he reminded the jury of the difference between their task and that of those who passed judgment in the press. While the public, he warned, may believe many stories about Avery's conduct, "we are not now before that tribunal. You gentlemen, are bound by legal evidence."[126] "Nothing but legal proof, given here at the Bar," he continued, "shall reach the defendant. Conviction shall not follow mere probability. Legal proof, judicial certainty, are one thing—common belief, ordinary suspicion, are another thing; and it is very important that these be not confounded."[127]

And indeed, the public did not confound the two. Aristides was not alone in distinguishing between a courtroom acquittal and the bar of public opinion. "I was satisfied with the verdict of the jury," he announced, "and have reason to think the public, generally, were."[128] But jury findings, he reasoned, should not "enchain [people's] thoughts, prevent the action of reason, deprive them of the right of private judgment, or seal their lips to bar the utterance of their honest conviction. All this they have the right to do."[129]

One of the most commonly cited reasons for the difference between these two courts was the conviction that the trial had been overdetermined by a powerful Methodist influence. Had they been convinced that the trial had produced accurate, truthful testimony, then perhaps the public would have been more inclined to accept the verdict. But ordinary citizens reading press reports, editorials, and anecdotal accounts of the trial were convinced that imperious defense attorneys wielding subtle deceptions had overmastered the common sense of the jury. Williams was typical in her contention that "the counsel for the prisoner had sketched out a romance, not to be equalled by any thing we know or read of Spanish or Italian vengeance, and dressing it up in a most ingenious manner, presented it to the attention of the Jury."[130] The opening and closing arguments were not the only part of the trial that had been fictionalized, according to the angry public. As they reconsidered the case, New Englanders repeatedly raised the more damning charge of witness tampering. Williams describes in detail the efforts to confound witnesses and compel them to change their testimony in order to save the life of a prominent minister.[131] As late as 1877, an anonymous author delivers as uncontested truth the claim that the defense had paid off witnesses to provide alibis for Avery:

> Something must be done to rebut the strong evidence of his guilt, and to offset the strenuous efforts being made by the citizens of Fall River to have justice done. The country was scoured in search of witnesses not over scrupulous or nice, who would swear to any story that might be taught them. Money was raised to defray the expenses of the trial, to employ the best legal talent, to buy and to bribe.[132]

What had begun as a widespread suspicion of witness tampering eventually turned to virtual certainty, and an insulted public, perhaps willing to accept Avery's legal acquittal, nevertheless insisted on explaining how in their opinion it had been achieved. Another frequently sounded complaint, perhaps more dangerous than the charge of criminality in this particular trial, was the claim that in general legal tribunals were fundamentally flawed. Given the restrictions upon certain kinds of evidence and the manner in which it could be presented, many critics maintained that judicial deliberations precluded the time-tested human modes of deciding moral questions. As Aristides argued, courtroom attorneys can "tak[e] advantage of legal quibbles and technicalities"; Avery "has received all the advantages and benefits that such a course could ensure to any man."[133]

If these popular accounts of the crime and trial have anything in common, it is their tenacious demand for a different trial with different standards. Perhaps many critics of the trial took their cue from the prosecuting attorney, whose own argument to the jury at times sounded a populist note. In his summation, Albert Greene tried to discredit the medical testimony for the defense by pitting it against common sense. "For my own part," he told the jury, "I profess to know but little about the science upon which so much learned testimony has been given in this trial; but I would sooner trust to the EYES of four sensible, experienced women, to ascertain the real state of the facts, than to the theories of a whole college of physicians."[134] By admitting his own medical ignorance, Greene encouraged the jury to identify with him as he demystified the professional arcana admitted in the trial and reassured his audience that common sense could be trusted in such a case. Though he did not win the trial, his argument was echoed in the press. Aristides pointed out that "the medical witnesses seem to have said very little indeed, on their own responsibility, most of their testimony having been drawn from books, and that there is very little dependence to be placed on them, in a case of this description, several of them readily and frankly admit."[135] That the technical language of expert witnesses clouded the jury's judgment was a common complaint.

The deliberations of reasonable people could be tainted not only by obscure testimony but indeed by the entire judicial process. Catharine Williams begins her narrative by explaining its usefulness as an alternative to the published trial reports. "As to the trial," she writes, "it does not treat of things in their proper order, nor cannot: and in the next place, none but what is called legal evidence is admissible."[136] Williams retries the case in her book, offering exactly this previously inadmissible evidence as to both the defendant's and the victim's characters.[137] One lengthy apparent digression in her book—the transcripts of all but one of Cornell's extant letters to her family—is no digression at all, but rather precisely the sort of pertinent evidence about Cornell's character that would be omitted from a courtroom trial. Whereas "those who wished to make her appear a monster of wickedness, have continually said all that is possible to say against any individual, and said it . . . from a place *where she cannot answer them back again*," in Williams's own text, "it is . . . no more than fair that [Cornell's] letters should speak for her."[138]

These popular accounts claimed to suspend the rules of courtroom conduct in favor of a less technical, more humane, reasonable, and legitimate way of judging character and conduct. As Aristides argues, "we have [Avery] now at the bar of reason and common sense; and shall therefore pursue the track they appear to point out."[139] Aristides, acknowledging that in court the burden of proof rests with the prosecution, maintains that the public standard is higher. "I know," he writes, "the law did not require of him to prove this statement in court. It was incumbent upon the prosecutor to prove it false. But public opinion requires the proof of him, and without that proof, public opinion will not acquit him. Justice, reason, common sense and the cause of religion require it of him."[140] Turning their anger over an unjust courtroom proceeding into an active attempt to retry the case in the public domain, these writers appealed to their readers to join in the process.

VI. THE TRAGIC FIGURE OF SARAH CORNELL

When Aristides reprinted his *Strictures on the Case of Ephraim K. Avery* as a single volume, he appended an epigraph from Shakespeare, Claudius's private confession: "My offence is rank—it smells to Heaven." He was not alone in suggesting literary parallels between the Avery case and familiar fictions. Clarke's Sarah at times speaks like a low-brow Hamlet, as when she discloses her feeling of melancholy. "Would that I could shake off this distressing feeling and be myself again," she sighs. "But in vain. Superstitious apprehension of impending evil hangs on my spirits and damps all energy. The *blues* have got complete possession of my mind, and unless I can expel them by singing, I shall be miserable all day."[141] Williams opens her narrative with an echo of Romantic scenes. Sounding vaguely as if she were describing her own *Lyrical Ballads*, she predicts that

> the traveller in future ages, as he wends his way through the delightful village we have been describing, shall point to the lowly grave on the side of yonder hill, and say, "even here, has the curse been felt—even here, has murder stalked abroad, amidst scenes of nature's loveliness, calculated to warm the coldest heart with gratitude towards that good and glorious Being who clothes the fields in plenty and bids the landscape smile."[142]

Years later, when Cornell's story had been revisited, it was published in a lurid and sensational form, its title suggesting the drama of tragedy: *The Terrible Hay-Stack Murder: Life and Trial of the Rev. Ephraim K. Avery, for the Murder of the Young and Beautiful Miss Sarah M. Cornell, a Factory Girl of Fall River, Mass.* This edition, published in 1877, is accompanied by dramatic illustrations depicting pivotal scenes from the story: "The Meeting of Rev. E. K. Avery and his Victim"; "The witness described a 'ministerial-looking gentleman who took tea at her house, on the night in question.' Was it Avery in disguise?"; "The unsuspecting girl was strangled by the scoundrel ere she became aware of his cruel intention," and so on.

The many literary adaptations of the case, including both allusions to and wholesale appropriations of familiar literary forms, suggest just how completely the authors of these published accounts intended to depart from the protocol of official courtroom narrative. As Williams argues in her preface, "A narrative . . . that would embrace the facts, without any of the odious details in the trial, is highly necessary, if public curiosity on the subject is lawful: and who shall say that it is not?"[143] The omission of "odious details," primarily medical testimony about Cornell's fetus, was not the only emendation in these accounts. They are just as significant for the additions supplied by sentimental narrative conventions, which more starkly distinguish these stories from the report given by the prosecution than any other single feature.

The anonymous *Brief and Impartial Narrative of the Life of Sarah Maria Cornell* may be brief, but its frontispiece belies any authorial claims to impartiality. The most prominent feature of that page is a lithograph of Cornell, clearly an attractive woman, whose character is depicted in lieu of the author's name in this series of lines printed beneath her image:

Written By One, Who,
Early knew her—when her mind
    "Untainted then by art,
Was noble, just, humane and kind
And virtue warm'd her heart—
    —But, ah! The cruel spoiler came!"

Evidently intending to introduce the case by appealing to his reader's sympathies, the anonymous author of this pamphlet presents Cornell as the beautiful heroine of a sentimental novel. Though we know her fate before we begin reading (for anyone still unfamiliar with Cornell's story, the author supplies a subtitle: *Who was found dead [suspended by the neck, and suspected to have been murdered] near Fall River, Mass. December 22, 1832*), we are meant to identify her as a virtuous woman whose tragedy is our own loss.

Other accounts, too, capitalized on what Poe identified as that most poetic subject, the death of a beautiful woman. In Clarke's play, the dead Cornell is treated much as Shakespeare depicts the dead Ophelia. When the body is discovered, Mrs. Houseman reminds us that Cornell is more than mere evidence in a murder trial. "Poor Sarah!" she wails, "my husband intended you should have been his daughter-in-law, (weeps), I am sorry for your untimely and dreadful death—from my house, as a daughter, she shall be buried."[144] This speech rescues Cornell's character from the damage done at Avery's trial, and it provides audiences a chance to express themselves alongside these gushing characters. As the body is carried off on a bier, the women follow, weeping. Clarke's play ends not with the arrest of Avery but with a different kind of justice. As the funeral procession begins, Mr. Houseman "solemnly" utters the final words of the play. "We are met," he tells his neighbors, "on a melancholy occasion; but though a stranger to me, the ill-fated victim of seduction and barbarity, shall receive every testimony of pity and respect we can show her.—See! the poor remains of an admired beauty comes."[145]

Such reflections on an untimely death animated others as well with sentimental and poetic reflections. Williams describes her first approach to "that lowly grave," where the mystery of darkness (occasioned by a lunar eclipse and thoughts of Cornell's death) pressed upon her, inspiring a poem. That poem, which Williams initially published in the *Fall River Monitor* and then inserted in her book, begins with a heartfelt meditation on the dead woman: "And here thou makest thy lonely bed, / Thou poor forlorn and injured one; / Here rests thy aching head— / Marked by a nameless stone."[146]

Lest we think that Cornell's story stirs only idle women, weakened by a surplus of melodramatic novels, Williams inserts a dramatized version of Cornell's first encounter with Dr. Wilbur in order to show that even when living, Cornell aroused compassionate people with a lively regard for her case. When the fallen Cornell seeks a diagnosis, the good doctor is immediately touched: "the air of extreme dejection that she wore, caught his eye, and in a moment interested him in behalf of the unknown sufferer."[147] "Endeavor[ing] to penetrate so deep a grief and ascertain the cause of this visit," he asks her if she is married and triggers profuse weeping.[148] After Cornell's death, the doctor is haunted by the contrast between this beautiful young woman and the corpse he is called to examine: "'That terrible look,' said the doctor, 'was present with me for months, and often in the dead of night has appeared to my imagination with such force as to awake me, and I can scarcely think of it now without a chill.'"[149]

Although Williams inserts this episode in order to convince readers of foul play, she also intends, in the tradition of sentimental literature, to awaken in their minds a lively sense of her heroine's suffering. If the court proceeding erred on the side of arcane details meant to befuddle otherwise sensible people, these popular reconsiderations of the case all endeavored to highlight the romantic, emotional elements of Cornell's tale.[150] Appealing to their readers' feelings as well as to their intellects, authors like Williams and Clarke led the attempt to turn Cornell into a melodramatic heroine.

In the many literary treatments of her life, the scene of seduction is critical in representing Cornell as a sentimental heroine. We have seen how Cornell's life resembled the plot of a seduction novel. If we look briefly at a pivotal scene in her biography, we will understand how her defenders attempted to ensure a sympathetic reading of her life. The woman's fall from virtue is central to the seduction novel, though it may seem out of place in a reconsideration of courtroom evidence in a murder case. And yet Clarke, Williams, and a host of anonymous poets all give it significant weight in their accounts. In each episode, the author highlights the fallen woman's sense of shame. Clarke's Sarah weeps during her soliloquy: "Oh, what a miserable wretch have I made myself! Now I know what ails me; a mother—an unmarried mother—whither can I fly to conceal my guilty head, and to whom look for redress? Every door will close against me, and the finger of scorn will be pointed at me everywhere."[151] In this scene Cornell's shame redeems her even as it proves excessive, for her landlady, the respectable and charitable Mrs. Patton, comforts her, as if thereby guiding the audience to temper their judgment. "You are not the first of your sex, by numbers, who has been deceived," Mrs. Patton assures Sarah, "nor you won't be the last: so cheer up; my door will never close on you for this error."[152] Williams likewise offers a respectable witness to Sarah's shame. Dr. Wilbur is struck with "pity and admiration" for his patient. "He looked upon her as one of the most unfortunate women, but could not despise her as he might have done in other circumstances."[153] Cornell's anonymous biographer instructs us that "many an innocent and accomplished female, . . . having lost possession of herself, has been left abandoned by her more than barbarous betrayer." As evidence, the author "begs liberty to acquaint his readers with an affecting scene, which he was but a short time since an eye-witness to." Present in court on a day of sentencing, the author's "compassion was excited and my feelings highly interested" by the appearance of a beautiful but inconsolable young woman, brought to the bar on charges of theft. "While many of the spectators, fixed upon her a look of contempt, and pointed the finger of scorn, my feelings were those of compassion; for I viewed her as an interesting object, and thought I could perceive in her conduct, marks of contrition and true penitence."[154] The curious and sympathetic author learns the woman's history: like many others before her, she had been "lost and undone, her character ruined, and her family divested of a lovely ornament, and their bosoms torn with grief, by the base arts of a villain."[155] By emphasizing the aftermath of a sexual fall, these authors represented Cornell in a manner that was familiar to readers of seduction novels, even while they took advantage of conventional literary means to trigger emotional responses on behalf of their subject. By presenting a compassionate and virtuous witness to the woman's shame, moreover, they modeled for their readers the ideal response to Cornell's seduction. The point was clear: in contrast to the defamation aimed at the dead woman in court, the superior reaction to her biography called for compassion and pity.[156]

Though feelings could not reverse the jury's verdict, they were immensely valued by a populace that felt itself ignored and insulted by the courtroom proceedings. Some anonymous broadside poems called for the death of Avery. "But blood for blood aloud doth cry, / All murderers surely ought to die," argues one.[157] Another exhorts readers to "Hang him, hang him on a tree, / Tie round the clove-hitch knot; / And there for ever let him be, / And never be forgot."[158] Other broadsides were more temperate, urging readers simply to remember the case. "The Death of Sarah M. Cornell," for instance, ends with a sentiment that seems to represent other literary efforts to commemorate Cornell's story:

> Come all young men and maidens too,
> Residing at Fall river,
> Maria Cornell's cruel death,
> May you remember ever.
> She 'twas as 'twere but yesterday
> Among your happy number,
> By perjury she unreveng'd,
> Now lies in death's cold slumber.

The chance for revenge had been lost when Avery was acquitted in June. But, as these lines suggest, a kind of justice could be granted the dead woman by those who read her story, entered into her sufferings, and "remember[ed] ever" the tale. In their many published accounts of the episode, ordinary citizens attempted to restore natural human sentiment to a case that had in court been stripped of its emotional content, thereby achieving a crude kind of justice (if not for Avery, then for his victim) in the public domain.

VII. THE JUDGMENT OF A NATION'S VOICE

While Avery's critics were retrying his case in the public arena, his advocates leveled charges of double jeopardy. His "secret persecutors," according to one publication, "resolved to do that in another way which they had failed to accomplish by legal process,—namely, to destroy his character and standing in society," thereby nullifying the verdict of the jury.[159] But Avery's critics and Cornell's supporters, and indeed all people who were outraged by the trial, vigorously defended their right to speak out on the case. Aristides, incensed at suggestions that the verdict closed the case to all discussion, contended that "the right of judgment, and the freedom of opinion respecting the conduct of their servants, [is] a right among the last that a free people will relinquish, legal verdicts to the contrary notwithstanding."[160] Eschewing any special privilege as a journalist, he claimed "the right of an American freeman, in canvassing a subject open to public investigation."[161]

According to these published statements, the real trial was only beginning. Taking seriously the defense attorney's distinction between a legal court and the court of public opinion, many writers, after rehearsing the evidence against Avery, submitted it to their readers, as if to allow the entire nation to take part in a second, no less critical, deliberation regarding his guilt. Williams noted that although the official trial transcripts were available to anyone who wished to read them, "there are many, probably, . . . who have never read the trial and never will, and some who will not even permit that document to come into their houses"; these other printed reports, therefore, offered the relevant evidence "without going into the whole revolting particulars."[162] Writers on both sides of the debate called on their readers to "read, try, judge and determine for yourselves."[163] Avery's Methodist colleagues introduced their *Vindication* with the hope that "the reader will give it his serious attention, and decide the case of Mr. Avery in the fear of God."[164] But they ended it more firmly, with a command:

> The reader has now gone through this long and laborious case, and is required to render his verdict. It is hoped that no one will excuse himself on account of its length, or the difficulties in which it is involved. . . . [B]y all that is just, humane, and sacred, you are bound to decide one way or the other—either that the Rev. E. K. Avery is GUILTY, or that he is NOT GUILTY of the crime of murdering S. M. Cornell."[165]

In his final instructions, Judge Eddy had exhorted the jury to "proceed in the grave duty now incumbent upon you, with coolness, caution, candor, and deliberation."[166]

In his own summation, Wilbur Fisk, one of the Methodist ministers charged with defending Avery in print, issued as strong a challenge and laid as heavy an obligation upon his readers, intimating that they, by reading the *Vindication*, had incurred a duty that they could not refuse.

Whatever their particular opinions regarding Avery's guilt or innocence, these writers all shared an assumption that literacy and the availability of printed information on the Avery case imposed a responsibility on citizens akin to that borne by the jury; such was the burden of being a citizen in a democracy. In Mary Carr Clarke's play, after Cornell's body is discovered and suspicion falls on Reverend Avery, Mr. Thornhill predicts that the suspect will receive justice one way or another. "The law shall investigate the case," he observes, "and if that cannot bring the perpetrator to his merits, the judgment of a nation's voice shall rest on him."[167] Thornhill's comment, to be sure, is no neutral observation about democracies; Clarke, convinced of Avery's guilt, wrote the play after his acquittal. Still, in Thornhill she invented a character who represents law, order, and morality, one who refuses to see these values thwarted even if they are not upheld in a court of law. Thornhill seems to speak for many law-abiding citizens, frustrated by the failure of due process, wary of mob violence, and yet determined to find justice somehow.

It mattered tremendously to those who encouraged open debate that they not be accused of stirring mass violence. Public excitement, they argued, was understandable and legal. "I suppose the truth is," wrote Harvey Herndon, the man responsible for finding and arresting Avery in New Hampshire, "the people in the village of Fall River are not radically different from others, but that they have something of that curiosity, which in a case of this kind, can be satisfied in no other way, than by the sight of the man accused."[168] Aristides went further. While claiming that "the public have never thirsted for the blood of Avery,"[169] he also argued that anyone who "would not have broken out in a burst of honest indignation" after the trial and Methodist Conference "would scarcely deserve the name of civilized."[170] In this argument he drew on a powerful historical precedent, Thomas Paine's *Common Sense*, which claims that an outraged response to tyranny is the birthright of a democratic people.[171] The court case, these writers argued, had settled only the legal question. The people themselves must decide the case of Avery's reputation and his place in their society. In the printed aftermath of the trial, ordinary citizens seized their own day in court. By turns angry and insulted, usually thorough and always earnest, they succeeded in overturning the jury's verdict. This public tribunal ultimately had more force than the official result of the trial, for it not only discredited the Methodist Church, which would need years to recover, and banished Avery from the pulpit and public life, but it reaffirmed the people's commitment to collective debates.

"The Execution" (lithograph, F. J. Schulte & Co., Chicago, 1889).
Courtesy of the Chicago Historical Society. ICHI-03675.

Chapter Two

THE HAYMARKET ANARCHIST TRIAL OF 1886

Both sides of the debate over the Haymarket anarchist trial took advantage of print media in order to propagate their message to the American public. While corporations were allied with mainstream newspapers, the labor movement depended on populist literary forms, particularly songs and poems, to solidify and inspire communities gathered to protest the Haymarket case.

I. THE MEETING, THE BOMB, AND THE TRIAL

On November 11, 1887, four men were hanged at the Cook County Jail for their role in the Chicago Haymarket bombing a year and a half earlier. The execution of August Spies, Albert Parsons, Adolph Fischer, and George Engel and the previous day's suicide of Louis Lingg were the dramatic culmination of a chaotic period of labor agitation in Chicago. While some labor advocates hoped to reform capitalism by unionizing and by seeking the legislation that would limit the workday to eight hours and otherwise improve labor conditions, others, including the men tried and hanged in

Chicago, contended that capitalism was an exploitive system that could not be reformed and must be abolished. Alternately designated as socialists and anarchists, these activists had predicted class uprisings against the monstrosities of capitalism. Meanwhile, many newspapers and leaders in the business and religious communities had denounced all labor unionists as foreign savages "who mean to sweep through modern society with the disastrous fury of a cyclone, tearing up, over-turning, and mingling in a common ruin, government, and law, everything which lies at the basis of civilization . . . in the most advanced nations of the earth to-day."[1]

The executions and the lifetime prison sentences of the three remaining anarchists, Michael Schwab, Oscar Neebe, and Samuel Fielden, officially closed a chapter in American labor and criminal history that began on the evening of May 4, 1886.[2] A bomb exploded that night at a labor rally held near Chicago's Haymarket Square, turning a peaceable demonstration for labor reform into what Timothy L. Parrish has called "an eighteen-month-long national riot."[3] The rally had been organized on short notice to protest the previous day's police violence against striking workers. Entire families attended, listening to speeches by some of Chicago's most popular labor activists. The meeting was interrupted by the arrival of the Chicago police force, who ordered the crowd to disperse. Someone whose identity has never been established threw a dynamite bomb into the lines of policemen, and rioting immediately erupted. By the time it ended, seven policemen were dead and countless civilians were dead or injured.

The ensuing police investigation and trial focused aggressively on radical labor activists and eventually resulted in the indictment of eight of Chicago's most prominent labor speakers, writers, and organizers. By virtually all accounts, there was no evidence that any of them had thrown the bomb. Although three of the men arrested—August Spies, Albert Parsons, and Samuel Fielden—had been featured speakers at the Haymarket meeting, the others had not been present. Fielden, a former preacher and a noted labor speaker, had been the last to address the Haymarket meeting that night, though his speech was not inflammatory. Spies and Parsons were editors of two small but influential anarchist newspapers. Michael Schwab and Adolph Fischer, Spies's coworkers at the German labor newspaper, the *Arbeiter-Zeitung*, were also arrested. The sixth and seventh defendants, George Engel and Oscar Neebe, were socialists; nothing else was ever proven against them. Only the final defendant, Louis Lingg, seemed a plausible suspect, an anarchist who had made a great many dynamite bombs. Until the time of the trial, however, few of the other men had ever met Lingg and none could be connected to his preparations for violence. If there was no evidence linking the eight men to a Haymarket plot, they did share a deep resistance to the capitalist order of the day, and it seems that this was what drew police scrutiny their way.

The trial and execution were heavily reported in the press and widely followed by an attentive public, among whom no clear consensus emerged. While the daily press was nearly unanimous in designating the eight defendants—and many other labor agitators—"foreign savages," "venomous reptiles," and "incendiary scum" from the "lowest stratum found in humanity's foundation,"[4] others saw them as earnest laborers who were "stung with a sense of injustice" when they considered the relations between capital and labor,[5] men who found "the prisons always open to receive them, but the courts of justice . . . practically closed to them."[6] As for the Haymarket meeting itself, the mainstream press spoke with one voice in describing the meeting as an "unscrupulous cold-blooded massacre,"[7] and popular images like one that appeared in *Harper's* helped to propagate this myth.[8] But the mayor, who had been present at the meeting, others who had been involved in the labor struggle, and those who cared to read firsthand accounts of the event—including, eventually, the Illinois governor who pardoned the surviving anarchists—maintained that the meeting had been peaceable until the police troops arrived to foment violence.[9] On the other hand, even among those who worked for clemency and believed the condemned men innocent of the May 4 violence, many regarded them as dangerous radicals. Others who supported labor reform, including the celebrated labor leader Samuel Gompers, refused initially to speak out against what they considered an unfair trial because they worried that the labor movement would suffer if it were identified too closely with the anarchists. The philosopher William James, generally committed to an Emersonian belief that individuals could transform the world, refused to sign a petition opposing the executions, though even his wife and brother-in-law urged him to do so.[10] The only conclusion that everyone shared was that Chicago had suffered a tragedy that would leave its stain upon the city. Two days after the executions, the Reverend H. W. Thomas delivered a sermon in which he argued that no event since the Civil War had "produced such profound and long-continued interest and excitement as have been felt over the Haymarket tragedy in this city."[11]

Although the Haymarket affair, like the Avery trial, was fraught with social and economic issues reaching well beyond the actual murder case, it differed from the Fall River trial in the international attention it attracted. On the day of the verdict, the *Chicago Daily News* announced that "Chicago is the central point toward which the eyes of the world are directed."[12] Although the *Boston Transcript* claimed that with its "history of rapid and unparalleled growth," Chicago was "hardly an American city," other journalists clamored for Chicago to set an example and later praised the city for the guilty verdict. Chicago "deserves the thanks and the gratitude of every community in the country," wrote the *New York Sun*; the *Brooklyn Eagle* predicted that the "precedent will be faithfully observed."[13] The Haymarket case was understood to have widespread implications because the incident took place in a climate already hostile to labor struggles, in which Chicago and other American cities stood poised for a violent outbreak. Because Chicago was one of the fastest-growing American cities, because industrial workers were heavily concentrated in its large factories, and because foreign laborers flowed rapidly into that wildly expanding city, Chicago became the center of labor unrest for the rest of the nation. Although prior to the explosion the tide of public sentiments had been turning in favor of the eight-hour workday, violent confrontations between strikers and capitalists (represented by both the police and the Pinkerton Detective Agency) were increasing.

Three days before Haymarket, the *Chicago Mail* prophesied violence and named two of the men who would later be hanged for the Haymarket explosion: "There are two dangerous ruffians at large in this city; two skulking cowards who are trying to create trouble. One of them is named Parsons; the other is named Spies. . . . Mark them for today. . . . Make an example of them if trouble does occur."[14] Both the labor leaders and those who feared them saw large-scale political consequences in the events of the labor struggle, and when the bomb exploded in the Haymarket, it represented much more than the single murder for which the men stood trial. The prosecuting attorney seemed to voice an acknowledged truth when he concluded his case by telling the jurors, "your verdict . . . will make history."[15]

Another difference between Haymarket and the Fall River trial had to do with the imbalance of power between the two sides, the result of industrial expansion and the unprecedented growth of capital during the postwar years. Unlike the Fall River case, which pitted two evenly matched institutions against each other, the Haymarket trial brought together the combined force of immense capital and a mighty newspaper empire against a relatively powerless—though well organized—working class. The Methodist Church was a feeble force compared to Chicago industrialists such as Marshall Field, Philip Armour, George Pullman, Cyrus McCormick, and the newspaper editors they influenced, while the Haymarket anarchists had no such allies as the factory towns to defend them.

The public debate surrounding the Haymarket bomb, the trial, and the executions reached fever heat in part because the explosion confirmed what many opponents of labor reform believed to be the foreign and incendiary origins of the labor movement. Carl Smith notes that even prior to Haymarket, opponents of organized labor deliberately conflated "immigrants, tramps, union organizers, and communists together as enemies of public order whose activities must be answered with force."[16] Desiring to better their conditions by organizing, striking, and calling for a shortened workday, labor activists were repeatedly accused of laziness, lawlessness, and un-American values. "Criminals and outlaws at home," the *New York Commercial Advertiser* called them, these European immigrants were understood to have landed in a peaceful new world only to stir up formerly contented workers.[17]

These critics of labor were right about one thing: labor activists in Chicago tended to be European immigrants. As Chicago industrialized after the Civil War, as skilled work disappeared and factory jobs multiplied, a ready supply of European immigrants appeared to fill these positions. Labor-saving machinery had not improved the life of the worker, however; it meant weary toil for those fortunate enough to work and unemployment for the remaining masses. The immigrants who had come looking for a promised land found conditions often worse than those they had fled, and they carried with them socialist notions that prompted them to speak out against what they called wage slavery. The composition of the Haymarket defendants was representative of the labor movement in Chicago: of the eight convicted men, only Albert Parsons was unambiguously American.[18]

Middle- and upper-class Americans therefore considered labor activity to be the result of ill-bred foreign ingrates who enjoyed employment and American freedoms without paying for them with loyalty to American traditions. As one editorial contended, "The Anarchists are foreigners. They have no property interests in this country, and therefore have nothing to lose in the depression of labor and the consequent paralysis of business, which is the sequence of the practical operation of their anarchical ideas."[19] Writing soon after Haymarket, Paul C. Hull charged that Chicago, as "the central distributing point for all the vast European immigration that has sought the United States for the last decade," abounded in "the only human material from which social peace in America has anything to fear. . . . [B]orne along [by a stream of immigration] are the scum and dregs of countries where despotism has made paupers and tyranny has bred conspirators."[20] Although the ultimate villains in these accounts were the tyrannical governments of Europe, Americans transferred much of their hostility to the victims of that tyranny, the "scum and dregs" who failed to distinguish between despotic and benevolent governments.

John Higham notes that nativism originated with the labor turmoil of the 1880s.[21] In part such xenophobia sprang from the conviction that all labor agitation was essentially un-American. In Henry Clews's tautology, "Strikes may have been justifiable in other nations but they are not justifiable in our country. The Almighty has made this country for the oppressed of other nations, and therefore this is the land of refuge . . . and the hand of the laboring man should not be raised against it."[22] Opponents of labor organizations claimed that they exercised over their members "a despotism more arbitrary, absolute and relentless than any hitherto known in this country." If working men "would ask for better rewards of service, not with a threat of strike and violence, in case of refusal, but with a strong assurance of more earnest and faithful service, and patience to wait for justice, they would soon discover the immeasurable superiority of law and order over conspiracy and violence."[23] In these accounts, unionization and other defenses of labor were seen as underhanded attacks on democracy: "we who seek this country as our home, because of its advantages and the superior facilities for obtaining a livelihood or of amassing wealth," wrote one critic, "can be guilty of no baser act than to endeavor to sow the seeds of discord and confusion among the peaceful and well-organized brotherhood in this land of freedom and prosperity."[24] Clearly the mainstream press regarded organized labor activities as inimical to the American way. And if strikes, boycotts, and unions were un-American, that feeling was confirmed by the international composition of most labor organizations.

Thus when the dynamite exploded at the Haymarket, the lines were already sharply drawn between workers who were outraged at the previous day's act of police brutality, and middle- and upper-class Americans who read the scene as just another episode involving foreign malcontents trying to stage a revolution. The men who would later be convicted for the explosion had been speaking throughout Chicago during a week of strikes. On May 3, August Spies, addressing a nearby union meeting, was called to the McCormick Harvester Works, where the police were firing upon the mostly unarmed crowd. The violence he witnessed there provoked him to call a protest meeting the following evening in Haymarket Square. As Spies later wrote in his autobiography, "All I could see was that about 150 men, women and small boys were chased by as many or more policemen who emptied their revolvers in rapid succession upon the fleeing and screaming 'mob.'"[25]

Others cast these labor troubles in a vastly different light, however: "The present state of this city, and indeed of the whole country, is one of anxiety and alarm," wrote Charles Carroll Bonney. "We have seen production largely suspended; trade and transportation crippled; violence and intimidation preventing thousands of men who want to work, from earning wages; crime threatening ruin, shedding blood, and destroying human life."[26] According to this and other representations of the labor trouble, the United States was a nation whose productivity meant enviable jobs for anyone willing to throw his or her lot in with other contented American citizens. When workers turned disgruntled, and when violence erupted, it was the work of foreign incendiaries fomenting unnatural resentments rather than that of workers discovering and rebelling against an inequitable system. Whatever the cause, all agreed that the effect was crippling. The *Illustrated Graphic News* of May 15 announced that "[t]he wide extent of territory over which the labor troubles have exerted such a paralyzing influence, during the Spring months has been the source of gloomy forebodings to many minds, and predictions have been frequently indulged, that the country is on the brink of a social revolution."[27] The many daily press reports, determined to cast the eight defendants as bloodthirsty and lawless aliens, also strove to identify the labor and socialist movements as threats to national security.

Were they rabble or martyrs, traitors or patriots? During the eighteen months between their arrests and their executions, the five who died and the three who remained in prison became the focus of a struggle for the interpretation of the Haymarket tragedy. Often the arguments went to the heart of the question about character. What did it mean that these men were atheists? Were they, as Reverend Frederick Noble maintained, merely the modern-day counterparts of the old-time villain, manifesting "the same dishonesty, the same malignity, the same disdain of God, and the same cruel indifference to human welfare"?[28] Or were they rather, as Parsons argued, committed to the idea that "There is but one God—Humanity. Any other kind of religion is a mockery, a delusion and a snare"?[29] Were these shiftless men who "never did an honest hour's work in their lives,"[30] cowards who never expected to be arrested and who "like dumb, obedient beasts bowed in submission" when the verdict was announced,[31] or were they "intelligent and brave men, who never whimpered nor once showed the pallid flag of fear"?[32]

Although newspaper coverage was starkly one-sided, debates were aided by the fact that the words and images of these eloquent men were readily available for public consideration. The photographs of the accused taken at the Cook County Jail became the source for numerous newspaper and broadside illustrations.[33] Spies and Parsons were well known in Chicago before the Haymarket explosion, and all eight men achieved international reputations during their trial and appeals. The trial was reported in detail by the daily press and thrown open to spectators during the closing statements. As Smith notes, the defendants used the trial as a public forum explaining their political ideologies.[34] The words of these eloquent men, moreover, became widely available in a variety of sources. During the trial, Spies and Parsons were asked to recreate their speeches from the night of May 4, and these were reported in the daily papers. The *Chicago Times* described the "spell-bound audience of spectators, an amazed jury, and a surprised judge" who witnessed the performances. "If the jury, the court, and the audience have been entertained since the trial began," the *Times* reported, "they were entertained by the chief agitator of the Chicago Anarchists [Parsons]. He pulled out of his pocket a bundle of notes, and began at the jury in tones which betokened that the speaker was primed for the finest speech of his life."[35] The men had a second, more dramatic chance to speak after the verdict was announced, when the judge asked them to give cause why sentence should not be passed. These three days of courtroom speeches culminated in Albert Parsons's two-day address, consuming two hours on October 8 and six hours on October 9. These speeches established the condemned men as defiant, courageous, sympathetic, and principled, and they exposed the trial as a process governed by wealth and political power, a hopeless formality for poor but honest men.

The supporters of the anarchists understood the power of their words, for these speeches were placed before the public almost immediately as *The Accused and the Accusers*. Although the title ostensibly refers to the defendants and the prosecution, it also suggests that the accused had good reason to censure America's economic and judicial systems. As the author of an anonymous pamphlet later wrote, these speeches "will rank in history as the most terrible indictment of legal authorities and their methods ever formulated."[36] The impulse to publish their words was most pressing while the anarchists were still alive and had a chance to win public support. In his history of the anarchist trial, Dyer Lum writes that while "many and diverse have been the reports circulated" regarding the anarchists' opinions, "Happily, their own expressions are a matter of record, and they can, as they should, be placed before the public."[37] When Joseph Buchanan, the editor for the *Chicago Labor Enquirer*, was invited to interview the anarchists for the *Chicago News*, he considered the advantages of publishing "an ungarbled expression of their views, [as] it might help their cases."[38]

For this reason, too, the condemned men wrote their autobiographies and published them in the *Chicago Knights of Labor* in 1886 and 1887 because, the editor wrote, to do so "may have some influence in deciding the fate of these men."[39] Their words did have a powerful impact on readers, partly because, whatever one's own position on labor reform, socialism, and anarchism, the Haymarket defendants were acknowledged by almost everyone who met them to be charismatic. Even Judge Gary, who presided over the corrupt and overdetermined trial, admitted that the anarchists "fascinated, apparently, those with whom they came in contact."[40] The wife of the anarchists' lawyer was one such person. "Like every one I knew," she wrote, "I felt a horror for the tragic events of that eventful night. . . . But one day one came to speak for that side which so long had been unheard,—the accused,—and I found out that, as to everything, there are two sides to this. When I learned the facts I became assured in my own mind that the wrong men had been arrested."[41] Emma Goldman was another onlooker who was deeply moved by the anarchist case; on the morning after the executions, she wrote, "I woke as from a long illness . . . I had a distinct sensation that something new and wonderful had been born in my soul. A great ideal, a burning faith, a determination to dedicate myself to the memory of my martyred comrades, to make their cause my own, to make known to the world their beautiful lives and heroic deaths."[42]

Why were these men's stories so moving? For one thing, even an objective reading of their lives reveals that their efforts on behalf of the working poor were indeed heroic. Parsons's autobiography tells how he incurred the hate of his former Confederate comrades when he supported the Thirteenth, Fourteenth, and Fifteenth Amendments securing the rights of African Americans, and how he later lost his job with the *Chicago Times* for advocating unionization.[43] "My enemies in the southern states," he wrote, "consisted of those who oppressed the black slave. My enemies in the north are among those who would perpetuate the slavery of the wage workers."[44] Oscar Neebe narrated in his courtroom speech how he had seen "that the bakers in this city were treated like dogs . . . and I helped to organize them. . . . The men are now working ten hours a day instead of fourteen and sixteen hours, and instead of being compelled to eat slops like the dogs, and sleep on the stairways or in the barn, they can sleep and work whenever they please."[45] George Engel explained to the court that he "took part in politics with the earnestness of a good citizen" but soon learned that the ballot was corrupt and decided that "the working classes would never bring about a form of society guaranteeing work, bread, and a happy life by means of the ballot."[46]

These episodes, predating the Haymarket, must be found in the anarchists's writings, but other courageous deeds took place squarely in the public eye. When Parsons, having escaped Chicago during the preliminary arrests, voluntarily returned to that city to stand trial, his appearance stirred admiration and changed many people's minds about his guilt. In his autobiography he explained that his principles, rather than faith in the court system, compelled him to return and stand beside his comrades even though "ample means were offered me to carry me safely to distant parts of the earth, if I chose to go."[47] In 1887, while Parsons was awaiting execution for his decision, Dyer Lum wrote that "[h]onor demanded it and he has not yet given one expression of regret."[48] After the US Supreme Court denied their request for a new trial, moreover, both Parsons and Spies refused to petition the governor for clemency, steadfastly maintaining their innocence. In his *Appeal to the People of America*, Parsons explained, "I am prepared to die. I am ready, if need be, to lay down my life for my rights and the rights of my fellow men. But I object to being killed on false or unproved accusations. Therefore I cannot countenance or accept the effort of those who would endeavor to procure a commutation of my sentence to imprisonment in the penitentiary."[49] Meanwhile, Parsons's wife, thrown into prison for distributing her husband's *Appeal to the People of America*, was said to have "excited the pity and admiration of the whole country."[50]

Though Spies and Parsons were among the most eloquent of the Haymarket anarchists, they were not the only ones to stand boldly behind their convictions. As Fischer wrote in his autobiography, "When I left my native country, my dear father (who died since) advised me to always utter fearlessly whatever I might hold to be the truth, and I have followed his advice faithfully."[51] "If the ruling class thinks that by executing us," he averred in his courtroom speech, ". . . they can crush out Anarchy, they will be badly mistaken, because the Anarchist loves his principles better than his life. An Anarchist is always ready to die for his principles."[52] Perhaps the most stunning of all the courtroom utterances came from Louis Lingg, who would later defy the hangman by blowing himself up with dynamite in his jail cell. He mocked the court, observing that to a man condemned for exercising his First Amendment rights, the "liberty of . . . a final speech" seemed a meager and ironic concession. After explaining anarchism and the social conditions that had brought him to his beliefs, Lingg warned the court that "the hundreds and thousands to whom I have spoken will remember my words." And his last words to the court were nothing if not memorable: "I despise you. I despise your order, your laws, your force-propped authority. Hang me for it!"[53]

For all of their defiance, these men also struck many readers and spectators as "men of broad feelings of humanity, [whose] . . . lives have been consecrated to the betterment of their fellow-men."[54] As Smith notes, the anarchists argued that they adopted their beliefs and actions in defense of the family, and "even the hostile press marveled at the touching domestic scenes in the courtroom and jail, where the children of the accused came to visit and sat in their laps as the proceedings unfolded."[55] In a sermon preached after the executions, the Reverend John Kimball explained that

> At the very time of the outbreak they were surrounded by thousands of workmen who were out on a strike for the eight-hour rule and smarting under a sense of injustice and wrong. Their sympathies were aroused, their moral natures maddened by what they saw; and it was in behalf of these men, rather than for themselves, that they conspired, so far as they did, to denounce the government and the state of society that would tolerate such outrages, that they met together.[56]

In spite of the newspaper distortions, then, it is not surprising that readers who perused the firsthand accounts of these men should find much to admire. Even the noted criminal anthropologist Cesare Lombroso, looking for physiognomical evidence of criminal behavior in the men, had to concede that these men, dying "with their ideal on their lips," were "not common criminals." The "altruistic turn" of their defiant behavior "commands our admiration and arouses our just pity."[57]

The eloquence and passion of the anarchists might not have been a sufficient threat to the press's efforts to depict them as traitors had they not also been able to draw from a ready vocabulary for their beliefs, one that was familiar to all patriotic Americans. Even though the *New York Mail and Express* claimed that the men had "no sympathy with the ideas through which Americans have made this country what it is,"[58] the defendants were well versed in the history of both American and European revolutions, and their speeches were replete with references to American heroes. When Spies and Parsons were sent to the 1883 Pittsburgh Congress of Socialists, they drew up a manifesto, which begins with the claim in *The Declaration of Independence* that the people have a right and duty to throw off a despotic government. Again and again the anarchists invoked Jefferson and other revolutionary leaders. "Our forefathers have not only told us that against despots force is justifiable, because it is the only means" the manifesto contended, "but they themselves have set the immortal example."[59] Captain Black reiterated this analogy in his introduction to the autobiographies when he explained the division of people into two classes, "Conservatives and progressists [sic], subjects and rebels. The one class yielding unfaltering obedience to the existing conditions of society, desire the preservation of the accustomed government, while the other class, with vision opened to the defects and inequalities marking the interrelation of men, long for a better order, and by this innert yearning of the spirit are often driven into open rebellion."[60] In his courtroom speech, Spies ranked himself with Jefferson, Paine, and Emerson in predicting that "the state where one class dominates over and lives upon the labor of another class, and calls this order . . . is doomed to die."[61] If the founding fathers were alive in 1886, he assured the court, "they, too, would undoubtedly be characterized as 'wild Socialists.'"[62]

Jefferson was not the only founding father to be repeatedly invoked. In their assertions that no true man will passively endure the indignities of capitalism, the anarchists echoed the rallying cries of Thomas Paine more than a hundred years earlier, when he had appealed to the legacy of fathers, insisting that "the heart that feels not now is dead; the blood of his children will curse his cowardice, who shrinks back at a time when a little might have saved the whole, and made *them* happy."[63] In the broadside circular advertising the Haymarket meeting, August Spies reminded his readers of this revolutionary legacy. "If you are men, if you are the sons of your grand sires, who have shed their blood to free you, then you will rise in your might, Hercules, and destroy the hideous monster that seeks to destroy you. To arms we call you, to arms!"[64] In a calmer moment, Parsons wrote, again echoing Paine's two most famous books, that "Reason and common sense, based upon natural law, takes the place of statute law, with its compulsion and arbitrary rules."[65]

If the anarchists turned to the American Revolution for their principles, they also sought models from the European revolutions of 1789, 1848, and 1871. Although, as Bruce C. Nelson argues, their socialism was hardly consistent, they all shared a romantic attraction to these European uprisings.[66] Oscar Neebe, to be sure, hoped that "such times" as the French Revolution "may never come again," for in those days, "when laws had been stretched like rubber, . . . the rubber stretched too long, and broke—a result which cost a good many State's attorneys and a good many honorable men their necks." Socialists like himself "do everything in [their] power to prevent" the return of bloody revolution, he maintained, "such as reducing the hours of labor and increasing wages. But . . . capitalists won't allow this to be done . . . [They] won't let the toilers live a decent life."[67] While some regretted the inevitable bloodshed and others looked forward to it, all eight men saw that revolution had come to seem inevitable, and while they fought for their lives on the grounds of historical precedent, they eventually looked to their martyrdom as inspiration for the coming revolution.

Working within a more recent American context, the anarchists and their supporters also drew on the ideas of both the Civil War and those American intellectuals—most notably Thoreau and Emerson—whose commitment to intellectual independence helped to encourage the abolition of slavery. When Louis Lingg announced to the court, "I do not recognize your law, jumbled together as it is by the nobodies of by-gone centuries,"[68] he was echoing Emerson, whose 1836 *Nature* opens with a call to be forward-looking rather than to "grope among the dry bones of the past."[69] He was also reiterating one of the most frequent claims of these anarchists: that anarchism was not an absence of all law, but a rejection of unnatural statute law in favor of a higher, natural law. "We do not object to all laws," argued Parsons, "the law which is in accordance with nature is good." But "just laws—natural laws—are not made, they are discovered."[70] These claims could be found in Emerson, who wrote of the young mind discovering scientific and moral laws in the natural world. They could also be found in more political literature, like Thoreau's "Resistance to Civil Government" and Stowe's *Uncle Tom's Cabin*, which appeal to a higher moral law when human laws call for injustice. When, only weeks before the executions, William Salter defended the anarchists to Chicago's Society for Ethical Culture, he claimed that his love of country did not deafen him to the "higher law than that which may be laid down by magistrates and courts."[71]

And the anarchists, like Thoreau, felt only contempt and pity for the person who, perceiving moral discrepancies between human and natural laws, still persisted in being an obedient subject. "The law-abiding citizen," Parsons argued, "especially if he is called upon to do something under a law that enslaves him, is an uncomplaining slave to the power that governs him."[72] The anarchists refused to be what Spies, echoing Thoreau, called "human bees."[73] Instead, as their defense attorney observed, they sacrificed their comfort for a higher moral cause. Accomplished men, "each could have far better served his own selfish interests by adapting himself to the existing order of society and seeking his own advancement in service of capital."[74] But instead not only did they refuse, with Thoreau, to be "the agent of injustice to another,"[75] but they actively sought to eradicate the injustice they observed. Seeing his fellow workers wretched, Michael Schwab explained, he realized that "for an honest and honorable man only one course was left, and I became an opponent to the order of things, and was soon called an anarchist."[76] George Engel observed that "he who speaks for the workingman today must hang. And why? Because this republic is not governed by people who have obtained their offices honestly."[77] Like Thoreau, these men took righteous pride in being outlaws from unjust systems, recalling that under despotic governments, "the true place for a just man is also a prison."[78] The anarchists found themselves to be living under the conditions Thoreau described in 1849, when he wrote that "the proper place today, the only place which Massachusetts has provided for her freer and less desponding spirits, is in her prisons, to be put out and locked out of the State by her own act, as they have already put themselves out by their principles."[79] "Can anyone feel respect for a government that accords rights only to the privileged classes and none to the workers?" Engel asked the court, explaining the contempt for law that he shared with his co-defendants.[80] And though many rejoiced in the executions, a great many vocal opponents maintained the analogy between these men and America's cultural heroes; as one preacher noted several days after the executions, "It is never the sober, industrious, law-abiding citizens who inaugurate the steps of the world's progress but, as Emerson says, the wild, restless, law-breaking spirits,—these, the despised of the State, that are the darlings of humanity."[81]

Though they all steadfastly maintained their innocence of the bomb-throwing, the anarchists were unapologetic for the threat they posed in their words and their deeds to the capitalist system of their day. And in this regard they came to be associated with John Brown, who by 1886 represented supremely heroic devotion to a moral cause. Although State Attorney Grinnell compared the anarchist movement with the Confederate firing upon Fort Sumter,[82] the defense attorney summed up by suggesting that "John Brown and his attack on Harper's Ferry may be compared to the Socialists' attack on modern evils."[83] Though they did not themselves court the comparison with Brown, the anarchists did convey the parallel between their work and the war to abolish slavery. Samuel Fielden noted that as a boy in Lancashire he was moved by the lectures of fugitive slaves and by his reading of *Uncle Tom's Cabin*; when the war broke out he became "an enthusiastic champion among my fellows of the cause of the north," even though his town suffered terribly from the lack of cotton.[84] "The propertied class of England, in sympathy with the slaveholders of the South, I know, would have interfered in order to prevent the cementing of the Union and the success of the North," he told the court. "But the . . . intelligent operatives of Lancashire, one of whom I was when a child, were the friends of the North, and they cheerfully and patiently bore with all the starvation which they suffered through the terrible struggle."[85] If they did not deliberately propagate violence as Brown had done in his day, still the anarchists believed—and their defenders believed with them—that like Brown they were at the vanguard of a moral change in American society, and if they must pay with their lives for that change, their words and deeds would one day be vindicated. As George Engel told the court, "We see from the history of this country that the first colonists won their liberty only through force; that through force slavery was abolished, and just as the man who agitated against slavery in this country had to ascend the gallows, so also must we."[86] The Reverend Kimball reiterated this sentiment in his Hartford sermon just two days after the execution:

> Thirty years ago John Brown went down into Virginia to free the negro, as rash and foolish an undertaking, and as truly a conspiracy, as the assaults of the Anarchists on society at this later day. He, too, was tried and hung, and all the virtuous newspapers of the land, and all the sober, law-abiding citizens, talked of it and rejoiced

in it precisely as they have over these recent executions—get their files and see if it is not so—yet in less than three years afterwards five hundred thousand men were marching, under the nation's banner, south to do the same law-breaking work to the song and inspiration of the old man's name.[87]

If the government was determined to execute these men, as it had earlier executed John Brown, it would betray its best principles, the anarchists repeatedly told their audiences. "The nineteenth century commits the crime of killing its best friend," warned Sam Fielden. "It will live to repent of it."[88]

II. THE PROPAGANDA CAMPAIGN AND PUBLIC DEBATES

The century did live to repent of the executions, in part because of the zealous efforts of the convicted men and their friends to change public opinion both before and after the executions. Even before the Haymarket explosion, working-class Chicagoans had been well organized and proud of their ability to propagate their social messages. In addition to the many printed sources available to them, Chicago's labor movement coalesced around mass meetings and community events such as plays and speeches and picnics. The German-American labor movement built community by incorporating the German cultural traditions of music and theater into political activities.[89] Thus a commemoration of the 1871 Paris Commune, held in Chicago in 1883, included a poem in memory of Karl Marx written by Michael Schwab, later a Haymarket defendant, and a play, *The Proletarian's Daughter*, depicting German immigrants in the United States. Among the amateur actors in that play were three future Haymarket defendants: Schwab, Spies, and Neebe.[90] Such occasions both offered communal activities and "direct[ed] the acknowledged need of workers for entertainment and diversion into the channels provided by the culture of the labor movement."[91] After the Haymarket, when the movement threw itself into saving the condemned men's lives, these rallies continued but with a more specific agenda. One of the very few Haymarket poems to be published prior to the executions, Arthur Cheesewright's "A Shout of Protest," was sung at rallies, entreating people to "save our noble brothers! / Raise your voices loud and high! / Noble men who lived for others, / Cannot, will not, must not die!"[92]

Of course the most public form of oral propaganda was the trial itself. As Smith notes, the anarchists and their lawyers disagreed over the kind of defense they should mount; while the lawyers believed they should focus on defending their clients against the specific murder charge, "the accused apparently wanted to turn the trial into a public forum in which they would explain their whole ideology."[93] The prosecutor took up their challenge, contending in his closing statement that "[l]aw is on trial. Anarchy is on trial."[94] And the accused, ironically reversing the charges, maintained that "their accusers were committing precisely the kind of criminal act of which they stood wrongly indicted. Elected officials, the police, the prosecution, the judge, and the newspapers—all in service of a capitalist elite out to reassert its immoral power—had conspired against them as part of a larger class war and in order to cover their own role in creating the current disorders."[95]

The anarchists demonstrated this point relentlessly in their courtroom speeches and again in a barrage of printed texts that emerged in the aftermath of the trial. The Chicago labor community was well organized, and the Haymarket defendants had ready access to printing presses, resources they used fully. It was no accident that Spies and Parsons, the two most prominent Haymarket defendants, were also editors of the most successful radical newspapers. Because newspaper offices had access to printing presses, they were able to publish broadsides like the "Revenge Circular" Spies's staff printed to announce the Haymarket meeting, and they were able to work on public sentiments after the arrests.

One of their primary agendas was to use the notoriety of the Haymarket case to promulgate their ideas about socialism, anarchism, capitalism, and the inadequacy of the vote. They pointed out that the socialist towns of Europe were the most prosperous towns,[96] whereas under capitalism, the worker's condition often "become[s] so desperate that life [is] no longer desirable and death [has] no terrors."[97] They described the condition of workers in industrialized factories: "It is simply impossible to work as many hours with machines as without them," argued Michael Schwab. "Without machines the workman stops here a minute, there a minute; goes slower now and then, and is careful not to overwork himself. The machine alters this. It does not stop for a minute, or run a little slower; it takes no considerations whatever. On it rattles, never tiring, never resting, and the workman is dragged along."[98] They explained their opposition to the ballot, characterizing it as "a double-edged sword, a most dangerous weapon. It makes the wage slave believe that he is a free man, while his enemies use that illusion most effectively to his deception and enslavement."[99] Finally, the accused men defended anarchism against the caricatures of the press and the prosecution, instructing "the stupid mass [who] imagined that 'Anarchists' must be something very bad,"[100] that "Anarchy is a state of society, in which the only government is reason; a state of society in which all human beings do right for the simple reason that it is right, and hate wrong because it is wrong. In such a society, no laws, no compulsion will be necessary."[101] Recasting themselves not as bloodthirsty criminals but as men of broad compassion who had lost faith in the American democratic process, they appealed to their audience to consider their philosophies in the light of the stark economic disparity they saw everywhere. "Accompany me to the quarters of the wealth creators in this city," urged August Spies. "Go with me to the half-starved miners of the Hocking Valley. Look at the pariahs in the Monongahela Valley, and many other mining districts in this country, or pass along the railroads of that great and most law-abiding citizen, Jay Gould. And then tell me whether this order has in it any moral principle for which it should be preserved."[102] Samuel Fielden seemed to speak for all his comrades when he concluded his autobiography by encouraging his readers to "calmly and dispassionately consider those facts."[103]

Together with their associates on the outside, the imprisoned men staged an intense propaganda assault from all directions. It is evident that they did not consider "propaganda" a pejorative term. When Lucy Parsons, the widow of Albert Parsons, published and sold ten thousand copies of the men's courtroom speeches in 1911, she characterized the speeches as "the greatest piece of propaganda literature extant; and when circulated among organized labor are bound to bear fruit."[104] These courtroom speeches were first published in book form in 1886, in time to persuade people that the still-living men were innocent of murder. Dyer Lum, moving from New York to Chicago in order to bring the *Alarm* back into print after its editor was imprisoned, revised the anarchists' autobiographies and had them serially printed in the *Chicago Knights of Labor* in late 1886. In the fall of 1887, just weeks before the executions, Lum published his own summary of the trial, condensing the testimony but "omitting nothing essential to the case. The testimony is taken from the official record prepared by counsel for the Supreme Court, not from the newspaper reports."[105] Meanwhile, Lucy Parsons worked tirelessly for a retrial. Though enemies called her speeches "defiant and incendiary utterances,"[106] others admired her courage and determination; in a single day she sold five thousand copies of M. M. Trumbull's pamphlet, *Was it a Fair Trial?*, and she was arrested for selling on the streets copies of her husband's *Appeal to the People of America*. When the *Alarm* began to temper its editorials, Adolph Fischer is said to have complained to Lizzie Holmes, Parsons's assistant on the newspaper, "You people are not doing anything." Holmes explained that she didn't want to hurt the men's case, but Fischer retorted, "the battle is right now."[107]

In spite of the daily newspapers, which relentlessly pursued their tendentious and hostile coverage of the anarchists and the labor movement, the defendants' commitment to propagating their message had a profound effect on public discussions. Beyond the most immediate concerns—the trial and, later, the intense and well-organized clemency movement—the debates that gusted around the Haymarket case vigorously took up the troubling and pressing contemporary concerns of anarchism, socialism, labor troubles, and the social organization of the industrialized nation. The specific legal issues were, of course, the most pressing concern for citizens who wanted either to prevent or to accelerate the executions. For many, public confidence in the court system was at stake in this case. Henry Adams voiced the misgivings of many when he wrote, "if justice frequently miscarries, men regard court as a lottery in which they take their chances."[108] The more people read about the case, the more uneasy many of them became that "this was a political trial and a class execution."[109] Hoping to forestall an unjust execution once the Illinois Supreme Court ruled against a new trial, citizens met, passed resolutions, and presented their views in print. William Salter argued that "there is no more sacred thought than that of justice. . . . But our courts are not infallible, nor does a divinity hedge and attend them in such a sense that their every verdict must be submissively received."[110]

Anarchism and socialism, of course, became central topics in these debates. Although anarchist newspapers like *Liberty* declared that none of the convicted men was a true anarchist, that anarchism and socialism were incompatible, still the case brought to prominence both stereotypes and considered discussions of these two movements. In their courtroom speeches and autobiographies, the eight defendants explained their philosophies and the circumstances that led them to adopt socialism, atheism, and anarchism. In his introduction to the autobiographies, Captain Black observed that "much will be found in this book to be considered in determining these questions—questions which each must answer for himself."[111] Were the anarchists' schemes practicable and warranted? William Salter maintained that anarchy was a social ill requiring a cure, that the way to cure anarchy was to "instruct our working people."[112] Others responded more hysterically to the threat of anarchism; the Reverend Noble, equating it with mob rule, argued that "[m]oral and religious training is not the short cut to the suppression of the mob. For that—guns."[113] Cautioning his readers against such hysteria, the Reverend J. L. Spalding argued that "the common sense of the people has not taken the outbreak in Chicago as seriously as a mere newspaper reader might be led to believe, although it must be confessed that we Americans still sadly lack repose and self-possession, and are easily startled by sensational alarms."[114] Spalding was correct about such alarms; although public sentiment was turning in favor of clemency or a retrial during the fall of 1887, after the discovery of dynamite in Louis Lingg's cell on November 6 it became nearly impossible to get new signatures for the clemency petitions, for "in the minds of the public all the condemned were associated and all were anarchists and bombers, and this act of Lingg seemed proof of this."[115]

Closely aligned with the topic of anarchism was that of free speech. Eugene Debs, confessing himself "unalterably opposed to the teachings of anarchists," nevertheless insisted on guarding "with ceaseless vigilance free speech and a free press. . . . [T]he bare mention that teaching certain doctrines, or holding to certain opinions of government, we care not how monstrous, are worthy of the death penalty, if it does not thrill the American mind with alarm, then it must be confessed that the American mind has reached a point on the road to despotism far more alarming than any of the insane harangues made by the Chicago cranks."[116] Henry Adams suggested that "it is because the poor have a just complaint against the existing order of society that men who talk murder and riot are able to gather a tolerant audience; but should the police authorities undertake to suppress the speakers, there is reason to fear that this bare tolerance would warm into genuine sympathy."[117] Trumbull reminded his readers that the practice of executing men for their words was "a vicious and dangerous principle expelled from England many years ago."[118] Others, of course, so frightened by the specter of the bloodthirsty anarchist promulgated by the daily press, believed that no abridgment of the First Amendment was too extreme a precaution.

Discussions about the labor movement were much more nuanced, though of course these, too, differed according to the forum. Most labor newspapers initially disavowed all sympathy with anarchism, noting that progress toward the eight-hour workday had been compromised by the Haymarket explosion. Other labor newspapers

—most notably the *Labor Enquirer*, whose publisher moved the paper from Denver to Chicago in early 1887—took up the cause of the condemned men as part of the larger labor movement. The *Workmen's Advocate*, writing several days after the executions, suggested that all wage laborers should be outraged by the hangings, though it might take some time for them to feel properly: "Even from a capitalist standpoint, the execution of these men is a fearful blunder. From a moral standpoint it is a crime. The working people . . . in time . . . will render *their* final decision."[119] Everywhere it seemed the public was taking the first steps toward a general discussion of the labor question, even in more mainstream publications; the Reverend Walter Rauschenbusch did not speak for the church alone when he observed that "the explosion of a dynamite bomb has set us thinking. All have been turning our attention to social questions as never before."[120] C. C. Bonney first delivered his discourse on capital and labor in Chicago and later published it "at the instance and expense of law-abiding citizens, who believe that its circulation among the masses will promote the best interests of both Labor and Capital."[121] And this moving statement issued at the Baptist Congress in November 1886 suggests a sincere attempt to understand the legitimate grievances at the heart of the Haymarket case. "Beneath the clamor of the anarchists and the demands of the socialists," mused P. S. Noxom, "and slowly working through the discontent of the great mass of laborers into clearness of idea and definiteness of speech, is the strong aspiration of sober and earnest thought, of necessity, ill instructed and often misguided, for a larger manhood, a freer life, and a higher realization of noble and reasonable hopes."[122]

Among the discussions that emerged in the aftermath of Haymarket were groping attempts from religious leaders to come to terms with their neglected relations with the poor. Lewis Wheelock notes that although the daily press "were inclined to publish only those sermons and clerical opinions which assumed an intransigently condemnatory attitude," preachers tended to take a "more moderate tone" than was generally reported.[123] Those who did adopt a rabid tone probably took their information from the daily press. Whatever their positions, all were agreed that the church was an appropriate place to discuss social questions relevant to the Haymarket case. "It is entirely proper to discuss, on Sunday and in the churches, the evils of anarchy, and the means by which an enduring peace between capital and labor may be secured," Bonney argued.[124] But if the churches passed judgment on the anarchist movement, the reverse was also true; August Spies invited American clergymen to "let us know how much you have accomplished so far by your moral lecturing toward ameliorating the condition of those wretched beings who through bitter want have been driven to crime and desperation."[125] There is good evidence that his words found a genuine response, if the Methodist General Conference of 1888 is any evidence. That year, the address of the bishops took as its topic "The Labor Problem":

There is a spiritual side to this question which we cannot disregard. It is primarily the old question of the relation of the Church to the masses, especially to the poor.

Are they drifting away from us? Have we lost our love for them, or the aggressive spirit which carries the Gospel to their homes and hearts? Have we forgotten our mission as we have increased in wealth? . . . If we have given too much attention to the rich, or cherished too much regard for social position, or have in any wise neglected the poor, we have departed from the spirit of our calling.[126]

Whether they took place in the press, the pulpit, or the meetinghouse, these discussions all shared a desire to come to terms with the composition of a rapidly changing society. Not everyone agreed that America was troubled. The *Nation* tried to stifle discussion by blaming the Haymarket on the very debates that grew out of the episode, arguing that "every professor, and preacher, and philanthropist . . . who tells crowds of ignorant and poor men that there is something wrong in the present constitution of society without showing what the wrong is and how it is to be remedied" shares in the "blood-guiltiness of this diabolical Anarchist agitation."[127] But if, as Carl Smith argues, the prosecution and its allies tried to establish "that society as constituted was in reality stable and sound,"[128] others maintained that it needed at least some elementary reforms. While we can punish anarchy, Salter argued, "we cannot so easily put down the thoughts in men's minds. . . . There is only one way to put down an idea: not by laws, not by soldiery or police, but substituting a larger, juster, truer idea in its place."[129] If anarchism was a misguided philosophy, Americans needed to resolve the social dilemmas that had given rise to the desire to overthrow all statutes. "What we need," contended the Reverend Kimball, "is to direct the energies of such men, full of grand humanitarian enthusiasms, into helpful channels to cure the evils of which they complain, not keep the evils and kill the complainers."[130] Whatever their positions on the place of anarchism in American society, the justification of violent overthrow of governments, or the proper limitations on the First Amendment, opponents of the Haymarket verdict all agreed that society and its laws should be plastic and evolving, not ossified in tradition and institutions. M. M. Trumbull was speaking of more than the Haymarket verdict when he predicted, "When reason and courage return to the people of Illinois, that judgment will be reversed, and the terrified magistrates who pronounced it and sustained it will be sentenced to an immortality of derision. It will be reversed as emphatically as the Dred Scott judgment was reversed; as righteousness in due time shall reverse a thousand more."[131]

The anarchists themselves predicted that a future reversal in judgment was the best they could expect. For a time, to be sure, they hoped that their efforts would stem the tide of public opinion against them and enable them to undergo a second, fairer trial. And for a time it looked as if that might happen. But eventually they came to see that their cause was hopeless, that the only good they could do was to change people's minds about the conditions of labor and capital and to prepare the way for a different popular verdict sometime after their deaths. They looked to the celebrity of their case to attract attention more widespread than they had ever enjoyed as mere socialists and labor agitators. As August Spies predicted, "the contemplated murder of eight men, whose only crime is that they have dared to speak the truth, may open the eyes of these suffering millions; may wake them up."[132] Sam

Fielden speculated that each man, speaking his mind in open court, "may, having failed to convince the jury that has tried him, convince the great jury that will sit upon his case when he is gone, that he is not guilty. I expect to succeed in convincing the latter, though I have failed in the former."[133]

The great jury of the people was swayed not only by the anarchists themselves but by the countless others moved to petition on their behalf. Karl Marx's daughter, Eleanor Marx-Aveling, was visiting Chicago shortly after the Haymarket trial when she read about the case. Developing a "fixed conviction" that the men were "doomed not by law but by revenge," she spent the next fourteen months "haranguing all who would listen in Radical clubs and elsewhere," exhorting her audience to protest against an inequitable sentence.[134] William Dean Howells, who had been moved by a reading of the trial transcript, read everything he could find by the anarchists and tried his best "to avert the cruellest wrong that ever threatened our fame as a nation."[135] Ernst Schmidt founded a legal defense organization to raise money to ensure a fair trial, later noting that he gathered small contributions from every state and territory in the Union as well as from all over Europe and Asia. Hoping to get a second trial, Schmidt published a broadside asking for contributions, pointing out not only that a second trial would cost at least $15,000, probably more, but also that the prosecution "is practically unlimited in its pecuniary resources, and . . . moreover, does not shrink from using this machinery for purposes unprecedented in the annals of criminal trials."[136] Once the state and federal Supreme Courts refused the men's petitions for a new trial, Schmidt turned his energies toward an amnesty campaign. "We wanted to present [the governor] with definite proof of a universally sincere desire for his executive clemency," Schmidt later wrote. "And we got it! Huge stacks of petitions asking for leniency began piling up in Springfield and Chicago, signed by thousands of organized workingmen of America, England, Germany and France; also by members of the French Chamber of Deputies and of the Paris Municipal Council. Among individual petitioners were the prominent British freethinker Annie Besant, George Bernard Shaw, William Morris and countless others who felt that a monstrous atrocity was about to take place."[137] Protests took place all over Europe, and not just among labor unions. Only days before the executions, three hundred people convened in Springfield in order to plead clemency in person. Even Judge Gary and State Attorney Grinnell finally asked the governor to commute the sentences of Fielden and Schwab.[138] One of the members of the original grand jury later admitted to being sorry about the verdict and became one of the most active members of the pardon campaign.[139] As Governor John Altgeld later explained, moreover, "there was so strong a protest movement of people, especially in organized labor, appalled by the judicial misconduct, that after the Supreme Court affirmance Governor Oglesby sent word that he would commute the sentences of Albert Parsons, August Spies, Samuel Fielden, and Michael Schwab if Chicago's leading businessmen would request it."[140] Though they did not request it—Marshall Field lodged a strenuous objection to clemency—Oglesby did commute the sentences of Fielden and Schwab at the last minute.

Printed material was speedily issued in order to convince others to join the clemency movement. Less than a month before the executions, Leon Lewis published his pamphlet, *The Facts Concerning the Eight Condemned Leaders*, in order to inform readers of the details of a corrupt investigation and trial and to "invoke the aid of all good men and women everywhere in scattering these pages, in the hope and belief that they may contribute essentially towards sparing our beloved country—still beloved, with all her terrible prostitutions and debasements—the unutterable shame and disgrace of this fiendish 'contrived murder.'"[141] Edward and Eleanor Aveling published a pamphlet stating "the chief facts of the case, so that any one fighting the cause of the men in Chicago may be armed with these facts."[142] Ernst Schmidt's clemency broadside perhaps put the case most passionately and explained why so many people within and without the labor movement wished so vehemently to prevent these executions: "If the law shall be a terror to the guilty only, but a shield to the innocent; if you would not see men sacrificed upon the altar of class-hatred and prejudice, a judgment executed without a *deliberate* and *impartial* investigation and consideration of the facts; if you would help wipe out a dark spot in the history of our people and our country; then lend us your assistance to secure that end."[143]

As we have seen, the nation was not spared the disgrace of the deaths of five of these men, but their executions did have the effect of further spreading their words. As August Spies warned while he was standing at the scaffold, "There will come a time when our silence will be more powerful than the voices you strangle today!" And indeed, the legacy of these men—anything but silent—triumphed over what Howells called the "unjust and evil deed" of the executions.[144] As one posthumous pamphlet observed, "An imposing mass of literature, principally from the pens of our strangled heroes, has found its way throughout the entire country . . . spreading information as to the aims and objects of these martyrs of the Proletariat; and why they were murdered."[145] A memorial pamphlet printed in 1912 announced that "the best vindication which the workers in general, and you, reader, in particular, can make, is to take note of the teaching and the ideals of these men who worked, suffered, and died for the emancipation of Labour, the abolition of poverty, and the happiness of mankind."[146]

Both opponents and supporters of the anarchists considered the possibility that the executions of these men might have powerful consequences, might, as one not entirely hostile source put it, "dignify a crazy cause with martyrs."[147] Some professed not to care about this effect. The Reverend Noble, for instance, claimed to "know of no cause more in need of martyrs. Let them have a few as speedily as may be."[148] Noble's blithe attitude, however, could not conceal the ambivalence that even enemies of the anarchists felt at the prospect of their deaths, for even before the November 11 execution, the world was talking of these men as if they were martyrs.

Though the condemned men never referred to themselves explicitly as sacrificial lambs, they did predict the powerful effects their deaths would have on the laboring masses. Lingg, as we have seen, wished to die in order to influence others from beyond the grave. "The more the believers in just causes are persecuted, the quicker will their ideas be realized," Fischer maintained. The "barbaric verdict" has "done more for the furtherance of Anarchism than the convicted could have accomplished in a generation."[149] Parsons asked the prosecution whether they believed they would have "settled the case when [they] are carrying [his] lifeless bones to the potter's field."[150] In these and other graphic references to their own deaths, the anarchists repeatedly invoked the spectacle of the enraged and mourning masses carrying on the work of anarchism, socialism, and labor reform after their executions. And in so doing, they placed themselves in a tradition of other martyred evangelists. "If death is the penalty for proclaiming the truth," Spies told the court, "then I will proudly and defiantly pay the costly price! Call your hangman! Truth crucified in Socrates, in Christ, in Giordano Bruno, in Huss, in Galileo, still lives—they and others whose number is legion have preceded us on this path. We are ready to follow!"[151]

As Spies's speech suggests, the anarchists' martyrdom was made more powerful by their boldness to the end. Although the daily press, antagonistic all along, still insisted that "there was nothing heroic about the end of these wretched men and no amount of imagination could invest it with a tragic glamour," still many journalists noted the men's "wonderful nerve" at the last.[152] Lingg, blowing himself up with dynamite on the day before the executions, inspired horror across the world (and speculations as to his sanity) but also grim admiration from his followers. *Freedom* reported that Lingg "died, as he had lived, defying the law and its valets." The newspaper also quoted a letter from Lingg's aunt: "'whatever happens—even the worst— show no weakness before those wretches.' And he showed none.'"[153] And though many socialist, anarchist, and labor newspapers later complained about the cowardice of the laborers who let the executions transpire without an effort to disrupt them, there is evidence that an insurrection planned for the day of the execution did not come to pass because the condemned men themselves did not sanction it.[154] When they walked to their deaths, finally, they did so calmly, no doubt aware that their compliance at the end only enhanced their heroic stature.

III. ELEGIES FOR THE HAYMARKET ANARCHISTS

By some standards the anarchists' propaganda campaign was successful. Two days after the executions, the Reverend John C. Kimball preached to a Hartford congregation that though "the newspapers may try to belittle them and laugh them down," the anarchists "are the very ore out of which the poets and balladists of all ages have wrought the lines of song which have shaped the world's onward way."[155] And in the subsequent months, labor, socialist, and other alternative newspapers swelled with elegiac poems and songs written in memory of the Haymarket anarchists. Because the elegies appeared in political newspapers rather than in books or literary journals, and because they were highly specific occasional poems, most of them have been neglected by later generations. Rather than the formal features traditionally associated with literary merit, what characterizes these poems is an informed, passionate, and moral engagement with some of the most pressing social questions of the day, when the problems of labor, immigration, and radical politics seemed to threaten a second civil war.

Dana Gioia has lamented the decline of poetry's role within mainstream American cultural and intellectual life. With smaller audiences and a more tentative sense of a shared cultural tradition than in former times, Gioia argues, poetry has retreated from its earlier cultural engagement into private, even egotistical, lyric forms, thereby losing much of its social relevance.[156] While many poets and critics regret that poetry is hardly read today outside of small academic circles, there was a time, as Gioia notes, when poetry had a much larger audience. Daily newspapers regularly printed and reviewed poems, poets assumed that their work would be read by a wide and discerning audience, and they were more confident than today of their power to address the masses on topics of broad social concern. The poets who responded to the Haymarket executions provide a striking example of how the popular press once brought poetry to a large and passionate audience who looked to poets to help foster discussions of public affairs. As my consideration of the cultural engagement of these now forgotten but, in their day, starkly significant elegies will confirm, an earlier generation of poets and readers once believed earnestly that poetry could shape the world. In their insistence on the relevance of poetry, they forged a discourse community that saw little separation between poetic language and determined action.

Although mourning for the anarchists took many forms, both written and unwritten, the dozens of poems that appeared in newspapers after November 11 all share a strong sense of their relevance. Indeed, these poems were widely read, probably discussed, and even performed on public occasions. One anonymous poem, for instance, was read at the funeral of the Haymarket anarchists and then published in the *Chicago Labor-Enquirer*. Others, set to the tune of popular songs, could be and probably were sung at labor rallies. With a clear sense of an actual (rather than idealized) audience in mind, these poets wrote with the conviction that the social impact of their verse would be more important than their literary reputations. Many of the elegies published during the months following the executions appeared anonymously, as if the poets wished to become the voices of the people rather than use the occasion to foreground their own sensibilities and to announce, like traditional elegists, their choice of a literary vocation.[157] Many of these poets may have chosen anonymity to avoid police scrutiny during the Red Scare that followed the Haymarket violence, but it is also true that what Clark D. Halker calls the "song-poem" was an unabashedly populist genre drawn largely from the oral ballad tradition, and its authors were scarcely concerned with literary fame.[158] Unlike the leftist poets of a later generation, these poets were not principally writers, did not look to their publications for their livelihoods, and had little "craft consciousness"; it probably never occurred to them, or to the editors of the labor newspapers that published them, that they might develop into what Daniel Aaron calls a "Shakespeare in overalls."[159] Even those Haymarket elegists who signed their poems were not primarily poets.

They were mostly wage laborers who either subscribed to or read labor newspapers and were moved by the executions to express their grief and anger in verse, thereby joining a larger political community. Rather than hoping to be anthologized or to win poetry awards, they assumed that their work would be read, circulated, shared, and performed in public places. And as members of a political community, they shared many of the same values and opinions.

Editors of labor or socialist publications did not insist on the distinction between literary and political magazines, as would Walt Carmen, the editor of the *New Masses* in the next century.[160] Although these earlier editors were frequently annoyed by the number of literary submissions they received (Halker notes that Terence Powderly once complained that the headquarters of the Knights of Labor were "deluged" with poems submitted by workers),[161] they printed just about every poem submitted, regardless of its literary quality. Halker estimates that several thousand song-poems were published by the labor press between the years of 1865 and 1895.[162] Given the daily press's hostility to labor in the 1880s it is unlikely that mainstream publications would have printed even general prolabor poems; and they would have particularly avoided encomiums to the Haymarket anarchists, who, after all, had been convicted in a court of law, however prejudiced the trial. So the Haymarket elegists looked to the labor press to print their poems, which usually represented the feelings of many wage laborers who had followed the Haymarket case.

The poems functioned primarily to consolidate ostensibly widespread sentiments among the masses and even move the working poor toward some kind of political action. The recitation of poetry at labor gatherings was one way of transforming feeling into activism. Halker has thoroughly described the context of these poems—both the culture that inspired them and the uses to which they may have been put. American wage laborers regularly participated in what he calls "movement culture," which encouraged a class consciousness embodying the ideology, customs, and traditions of the labor movement. Not only in their official documents (labor newspapers and organizational declarations) but also in their social gatherings, reading groups, concerts, meetings, lectures, demonstrations, and potluck suppers, workers gave voice to, shared, and strengthened their working-class identity. The vitality of the labor movement, according to Halker, "owed much to its cultural dimension."[163] Communal activities whose focus was the labor movement enabled even women and children to take part in recreation that promoted solidarity and afforded new opportunities to educate and recruit members.

Whatever the apparent content of these activities, their form was deeply political and rooted in a mass movement. "Workers," notes Halker,

> overcame some of the obstacles that had fragmented them in the past. They forged a movement against wholesale domination by industrial capitalism and formulated a formidable critique of the new order. In the process, the divide between capitalists and workers became more politicized, and a movement culture emerged to promulgate workers' vision for the future of America.[164]

The poems that emerged from this movement culture derived their form from an awareness of this mass audience. Not formally innovative, most of the Haymarket elegies use iambic meter and either blank verse or regular rhyme schemes. Many eschew imagery, employing a plain style reminiscent of Wordsworth's everyday speech. Others draw on conventional Christian or classical imagery to depict the heroism of their subjects. But we might understand this very traditionalism as radical in its unabashedly populist form. In their popular idiom, that is, these poems announce themselves as emerging from a grass-roots movement rather than from the idiosyncratic imagination of individual poets. Perhaps because they identified themselves as solidly working class, many of these poets adopted a vernacular voice that might be compared to the emerging voice of realism found in American novels. "Paddy Miles's Sentiments," for example, is spoken in the voice of a worker who chides the Knights of Labor for failing to defend the Haymarket anarchists:

> You're pretty knights, now ain't you?
> Knights ever undismayed!
> Why, if a newspaper calls you names
> You break for the woods afraid.
> And you joined the howl with your enemies
> And all cowards north and south,
> Trampling the laws to kill five men
> For a-shooting off at the mouth.[165]

Whether or not this attack on the Knights of Labor stirred debate among readers,[166] it is clearly written in a populist idiom that, if not for its rhymes, might have been directly transcribed from a bar-room debate.

Other poems used the ballad form to tell the Haymarket story in the emotional voice of labor-movement partisans, while still others employed a more elevated poetic diction borrowed from Christian and classical literature. What they all shared, however, was an open endorsement of the popular press as a means of promulgating a poetic culture and their sense that even an ephemeral medium like the newspaper could be used to forge a place in history. Whether they signed their names or remained anonymous, the Haymarket elegists all sensed that they were part of a historical movement that would help to determine how the Haymarket story was remembered by future generations. Pitting themselves against the "artificial and arbitrary means" of historiography employed by "despots and tyrants,"[167] these poets assumed an intelligent, politically engaged, and inquisitive audience, and they fitted their political poetics to a variety of popular forms. What they neglected in formal innovation they recovered in the social boldness of their content and in the conditions of their circulation.

The sentiments expressed in the fringe publications that issued these poems suggest that the charisma, eloquence, and bravery of the anarchists had infected the masses with what Edgar Lee Masters calls the "narcotic of strange idealism,"[168] and the elegists sought to spread that idealism to those who had not yet embraced it and to keep it alive for those who had. In naming the anarchists "the first martyrs in the cause of industrial freedom," Eugene Debs urged that "the halter" be seen as "the symbol of redemption."[169] Many poems commemorating the anarchists appealed to Christian typology, transposing it onto a contemporary scene and reiterating the message that the anarchists had died for something noble. The unidentified person, for example, who gave the anarchists' defense attorney a poem to read at the funeral seemed to believe that these men had transformed the gallows into "a holy-place," as John Brown had done for his contemporaries.[170] More than one poet wondered whether Waldheim, the cemetery where they were buried, would not "a Golgotha become."[171] The many poetic and visual scenes of the men at the scaffold suggest that the admirers of the dead men agreed with Lydia Platt Richards: "The gallows, now, like christian cross, behold, / Emblem of freedom, wrought in burnished gold!"[172] Many labor poets used the traditional material of Christian eschatology, revitalizing it with elements from their own historical moment. Furthermore, they seized for themselves the task of interpreting the Haymarket events. By imagining a future age that would revere the anarchists as martyrs, these poets recuperated the tragedy in an account of compensatory suffering.

For a number of poets, however, the status of these men as martyrs whose sacrifices would one day be recognized by the formerly indifferent world offered little consolation. The outpouring of elegiac poems to appear in print after the executions attests to the depths of grief felt by those who found expression for their feelings in fringe publications like labor newspapers and broadsides. One poem urged the Haymarket widow Lucy Parsons to give way to her grief for her dead husband:

> We would not bid thee not to weep,
> Nor stifle human feelings deep;
> Thy tears will moisten freedom's flower
> And nourish it in trying hour.[173]

Another begins:

> Bitter and sad is the strain I sing,
> And my heart is filled with sorrow,
> For what can the dismal future bring
> But a dark and dreary morrow.
> Five of the bravest ever born
> Have been slain spite all our pleading,
> And the thinking men of the nation mourn,
> And their hearts are torn and bleeding.[174]

The plain style of this poem—the largely monosyllabic opening line, with its somber, dirgelike pulses; the simple and predictable rhymes, as if acknowledging the inappropriateness of a more ornate form; and the repetition of "and," as if the speaker can merely pile up his woes—conveys a numbing, overwhelming grief.

Although the speaker alludes to a former "pleading"—presumably arguments on behalf of the anarchists—he ends these lines not with ideas but with the image of a maimed body. His present grief has turned "thinking men" into wounded viscera and dissolved his commentary on the political scene into primal woe.

In this and other Haymarket poems, the elegiac note eclipses all political considerations; unlike much of the propaganda issued prior to the executions, these grieving authors could not surmount their sense of bereavement to deliver a political statement. They instead wrote pure dirges. Even the passage of time did not diminish the sense of loss for many mourners. One poem commemorating the tenth anniversary declares, "November's chilly days have come / To open up the old-time wound."[175] It is easy to dismiss these poems as naive and insignificant, especially when compared to the later work of leftist poets whose literary careers were actively fostered by communist writers and editors. We do not know whether these elegists were unfamiliar with literary conventions or whether they simply refused to adhere to them, preferring a populist form that could be understood and embraced by the masses. To be sure, they sometimes had difficulty managing their preferred forms, and perhaps more experimentation would have been beyond their abilities. But whether naive or defiant, these poets' departure from long-established literary conventions enabled them to chart a new path for the elegy. Unaware that the elegy typically ended with some form of consolation, or unable to contain their anger and grief within the comforts of literary convention, most of the Haymarket poets published elegies that lingered on this "old-time wound" of November 11 without offering cheering sentiments.

In their refusal of consolation, the Haymarket elegists force us to reconsider customary accounts of the function of elegiac poetry. A number of recent critics have noted that "drastic social circumstances"—like modern war, AIDS, the Holocaust, and now, we might suppose, the collapse of the World Trade Center and the wars that have followed in its wake—distance the modern elegy from earlier norms of consolation, where nature and religion offered balms for the grieving poet.[176] Jahan Ramazani argues that "the modern elegist tends not to achieve but to resist consolation, not to override but to sustain anger, not to heal but to reopen the wounds of loss."[177] Most literary historians, however, do not acknowledge the deeply political aims, the sustained anger, and the rejection of consolation expressed in much earlier elegies.[178] Whether or not the Haymarket elegists fully understood that consolation "reins in emotion,"[179] they surely saw that traditional elegiac consolation was an "ambivalent ideal";[180] they refused to be easily comforted because they wished to put their grief to political use rather than transcend it. Unlike most deaths, the deaths of the anarchists were attributable to a specific, identifiable, and unjust agent, and the Haymarket elegists sought to remind the world that the people's grief was the direct result of the malevolent agents of a despotic social system. They therefore wished their grief to remain "unresolved, violent, and ambivalent."[181] And they drew on the physicality of poetic rhythms to elicit and exploit the deep feelings provoked by the executions.

A few poets were unable to escape the conventions of traditional elegy, of course, where grief finds its compensation;[182] these poets consoled themselves by imagining future justice in another world. The anonymous author of "Victoria" anticipates eternal justice beyond human efforts:

> The prosecutor's voice,
> Which rang so boldly at the mob's command,
> Will one day fail him, when he stands before
> The bar of too impartial fate, and hears
> The sentence ringing in his craven ears.[183]

The dead anarchists, writes another, "shall in safety and in peace / Await the just result of time—." This poet places his confidence only in

> The one just judge, who sits unswayed,
> Unmoved of passion, hate, or greed.
> To whom the lowliest may plead,
> And wait the judgment unafraid.[184]

Halker argues that most song-poets of the labor movement found religion an "invaluable" aid to interpreting the world, transforming religion "from an inert cultural inheritance into a crucial part of the labor movement and the crusade for humanity."[185] This may be true. Certainly religious emblems and beliefs figure prominently in many of the Haymarket poems.

But the vast majority refuse to allow Christian belief to distract them from the worldly struggles still at hand. Recalling the words of the dead men, for example, Fayette Munson reminds her readers of the human efforts still required for true justice:

> Oh! ye brave but burdened millions,
> Know ye not the time is here
> That bespeaks the world's redemption
> From her sorrows, pains and fears![186]

Munson is not writing of the hereafter but looking forward, as the anarchists themselves had done, to human revolution, to the day when labor would not "languish / in the greedy grasp of men." For such work to take place, mourners need to be reminded of their grief and their grievance. One important function of the Haymarket elegies, then, was to chafe the people's wounds.

As we might expect of elegies devoted to the pathos of death, one dominant element in many of these poems is the note of sentimentality, drawn primarily from domestic scenes. Men and women alike mention the tears of the dead men's wives and children. The graves of the heroes, writes one, are "bedewed with our fair women's tears."[187] Another urges a Haymarket widow to "weep, thou loved and loving wife."[188] The anonymous "The Price of Freedom" was written to the tune of

"Annie Laurie," which Albert Parsons was said to have sung in the jail at midnight on the eve of his execution.[189] Parsons is the speaker of this poem, and while he observes that "the hours are speeding by," his thoughts turn to his grieving family:

> To-night my babes are crouching
> By their weeping mother's side,
> For this country's sake their father
> Leaves his children and his bride.

Domestic affections also inform poets' depictions of the hanging itself:

> Thoughts of home, of friends, of loved ones
> Flash like lightning through the brain,
> Yet it only serves to strengthen
> Brave hearts, born to suffer pain.[190]

While one can see the political efficacy of rubbing raw the people's wounds with repeated rehearsals of the heart-searing details of these men's last hours, such sentimentality also threatened to undermine the political efforts of the Haymarket elegies, for it naturalized the Haymarket tragedy by putting its historically specific suffering into universal human terms. Dyer Lum seems to have recognized the conflict between sentiment and politics, which he dramatizes in a poem devoted to Adolph Fischer's last night. In prison on the eve of his execution, the condemned man imagines his wife ("I see in sorrow bowed one head caressed / So lovingly in other days before") until his soul is recalled "to higher thoughts, unto the noble Cause."[191] Lum's elegy invokes sentiment only to eschew it in favor of a higher ideal: "thoughts" rather than "sorrow." And though the anarchists were masters of propaganda, they too understood the limits of sentimentality. There is evidence that while they predicted that deep mourning would greet their deaths, they wished to discourage what they understood as sentimental, apolitical elegies. Parsons wrote "Last Words" in part to check this pointless response to his execution. "Come not to my grave with your mournings," he wrote,

> With your lamentations and tears,
> With your sad feelings and fears! . . .
> Poor creatures! Afraid of the darkness.[192]

Though a fair number of the poems that emerged after the executions were sentimental dirges like the ones I have been considering, far more of them recalled the politically motivated propaganda campaigns of the previous months and expressed impatience with mere sentimentality.[193] Robert Reitzel takes himself and others to task for their tame responses to the Haymarket executions: "We blink back tears, without a sound, / Not good for anything else."[194]

Voltairine de Cleyre observes that the masses are overcome with dangerous wrath:

Angry thy heart, O People,
And its bleeding
Fire-tipped with rising hate![195]

As these and other poems indicate, mixed in with the elegiac tone was an implacable note of fury, evident even in the titles of many poems: "The Blood-Stained Banner of the West," "Murder Most Foul," "The Hurricane," and "Columbia's Shame."[196] Many of these poems issued warnings of reprisals to come; as one poet admonished, "vengeance mad" will seek "retribution" for the executions.[197] While some poet-mourners clearly took comfort in traditional elegiac sentiments, many others were trying to express a rage that found a ready echo in other hearts. With its visceral rhythms, poetry (and particularly the song-poem) was the perfect vehicle for such expression. The labor newspapers were full of such poems.

And these newspapers did not shy away from poems that issued vitriolic attacks against the agents of the executions, alternately identified as capitalists, courts, newspapers, and police. One poet characterized the state as a "child of superstition," a "worthless churl that breed'st class of drones, / Emblem of hate and fear, grinder of human bones."[198] Another, depicting the anarchists as agents of enlightenment who "spoke the free and open truth," turned furiously on capitalists:

But when the cruel, man-devouring class
Had barely heard the Truth thus spoken free,
It seized its bloodstained knife in deadly grasp
And plunged into this monstrous butchery.[199]

Here the poet saturates his abstractions about class warfare with the bodily imagery of hand-to-hand combat, his iambic pentameter infusing his tirade with tragic dignity.

If rage, like grief, dominated many of the poems written in response to the Haymarket executions, these angry poems were also highly specific in their attacks. Frances Bingham's lament isolates a particular complaint, repeated by many poets, that the alleged friends of labor failed to defend—and often actively opposed or ridiculed—the Haymarket defendants:

O, Humanity strange and cruel!
For those who have loved it best,
Those names like a priceless jewel
It should wear upon its breast,
It covers with foul derision,
And rends and casts away;
Blind to the heavenly vision,
To its prophets deaf alway.[200]

Although they had plenty of blame to disburse to the enemies of labor, many who wrote of the anarchists after their executions were most disappointed in the people who should have understood these men as their dearest friends and recognized how nobly "our martyrs their torment endure[d], / For the hope of the helpless, the cause of the poor!"[201] This charge is made more explicit in other poems, where "the workmen loudly shout" for the anarchists' crucifixion.[202] The provocative "Paddy Miles's Sentiments" is unusual among Haymarket poems because it appears to divide rather than unite the labor movement. But it resembles other post–November 11 poems in its profoundly political message and its angry tone.

The poets who responded to the Haymarket executions were not slow to point out the larger implications of an apathetic and cowardly people. Reminding readers that the state is nothing more than its citizenry, these poets charged the nation's political and social leaders, its cultural and economic elite, and its masses of workers with cowardly behavior that would shame their nation and even the labor movement and would outlive all the individual participants. The executions of 1887 signified a permanent blight on American history and a betrayal of the nation's republican ideals, as a number of poets noted. The following warning, for example, was published a month before the executions:

> America! beneath thy banded flag
> Of old it was thy boast that men were free,
> To think, to speak, to meet, to come, to go.
> What meaneth then the gibbet and the gag
> Held up to Labour's sons who would not see
> Fair Freedom but a mask—a hollow show?[203]

After the executions, many poets returned to the contradiction between American values and the judicial murders. One poet asks: "Was it for this we sent out / Liberty's cry from our shore?"[204] Another wonders: "Are they of whiter clay who murder through the law, / Than he who hurled the bomb—when he rank injustice saw?"[205] These writers did not reject the nation's republican legacy, but they saw that recent events gave the lie to the claims of freedom enshrined in founding texts, in the flag, and in the national reputation enjoyed at home and abroad. They used this particular incident to reiterate a lesson often repeated by labor leaders—the deep contradiction between American republican principles and the reality of capitalism. As one poet writes:

> That glorious instrument of rights,
> Our Constitution, wisdom-framed,
> By this judicial crime defamed
> Is toppling from its lofty heights![206]

This frequent accusation from the working class here gains visibility and force when illustrated by the high-profile multiple executions in Chicago.

If one thing can be said of the poetic outpouring that followed the November 11 executions, however, it is that the many people who responded through elegiac verse to this international event did so in an attempt to change the course of history, to call attention to the nation's shame in order to see that it would not be repeated. Even less explicitly political dirges had their place in maintaining the movement culture; by offering simple laments, these poems reminded readers that the values of the working class were increasingly at odds with those of mainstream American society. But these comparatively simple poems were well outnumbered by others that situated the writer's grief within a larger social context. Even the many poems that appealed to the heroism of the anarchists at the moment of their deaths were not stripped of political specificity. Poems like "At the Tomb" recreate the scene at the scaffold but also refer to the wider context of the trial and national debate:

> Wearing their robes of white,
> As saints or martyrs might,
> Calmly, in conscious right,
> Faced they the world.[207]

Although the timelessness of white-robed saints might threaten to eclipse the historical specificity of this scene, the threat is contained in the second couplet. There the allusion to "conscious right" pitted against the world invokes the months-long battle fought in the courts and the press for the interpretation of these men's lives and deeds. Other poems, ostensibly celebrating the bravery of the men on the eve of their executions, also argue that the state stands poised to do battle with those who struggle for freedom. One describes Parsons's last night listening to the sounds of the scaffold being built in the jail yard: "calm, self-poised, whom naught can now dismay, / With pity smiles at Caesar's strokes, as strokes of / time creep on apace."[208] Aware, no doubt, that Caesar would tell his own version of this story, the poet who memorialized the anarchists' last night in jail reduces Caesar's function, here, to the dogged effort of thwarting the cause of freedom. The iambic dignity of the "self-poised" anarchist stands in sharp contrast to the implied sounds of the philistine hammer.

A number of poems tell a remarkably similar story about the men's last, private hours in jail. Whatever their intent, these poems all transform oral reports into ballad-like histories that first appeared in newspapers and would later be recounted at public gatherings. Many elegies refer to the widely admired and circulated story that the men sang the French national anthem on their last night in jail:

> Shrank the gaolers in amaze as there rang the 'Marseillaise,'
> How it throbbed exultant thro' the gloomy cell;
> For they stood, prepared to die, with both kindling cheek and eye,
> So their blood were shed for Freedom, all was well.[209]

Other poems repeat the men's famous, public last words in more than merely sentimental gestures. The two lines most quoted in elegiac poems are Parsons's and Spies's final statements, referring to First Amendment rights. Spies warned that "The time will come when our silence will be more powerful than the voices you strangle today." Parsons's last words were a request that "the voice of the people be heard," but the trap door was sprung before he finished his sentence. Many poets reproached the state for this act:

> Let the Voice of the People be heard!
> O—You strangled it with your rope!
> Denied the last dying word,
> While your Trap and your Gallows spoke![210]

Here is another:

> Then spake the Texan, staunch and true,
> "Oh let the people's voice be heard,"
> That was the last he ever said;
> The trap was sprung, no voice demurred,
> The people's voice was never heard.[211]

These poems do not try to conceal their bitterness that the almost sacred convention of the state-sponsored execution—the right to say a few final words—was flagrantly violated in Parsons's case. The unexpected repetition of "heard" in the final line here expresses the speaker's disbelief. As for Spies's words, they became the chorus of more than one song, and they were rearranged in numerous poems, such as this one, as if to verify his prophecy: "'Our silence,' cried their stoic chief, / 'More potent is than spoken word!'"[212]

In transforming newspaper accounts into elegies, in recirculating rumor as ballad, in describing the conduct of the condemned men as they faced their deaths, these poets told the history of Haymarket in what Spies called "the voice of the people": an oral, poetic history of this pivotal episode in the labor movement. When we recover and reassemble these forgotten elegies, placing them in the context of the first conventional histories of the event, those that could be read in the mainstream newspapers, we vividly recognize Emma Goldman's distinction between the "artificial and arbitrary means" of telling history available to those in power, and the grassroots history that "perpetuates itself from generation to generation."[213] Surely the Haymarket elegists saw their project in these terms as well, for their poems are replete with organic metaphors to insist that the anarchists' ideas would live on in the lives of those they had touched. Again and again these poets use the figure of the planted seed to insist that their heroes have not died but have merely sown their spirit in the hearts of the restless masses that carry on their work. Sentiments like the following are typical:

> The blood of martyrs is a seed
> That blossoms to its kind . . .
> And every drop is one step more
> To freeing all mankind.[214]

Many poets took up this idea that the martyrs' blood was a seed that would germinate in time: "The gory seed has living merit, / And animates those hearts as well."[215] In "The Gods and the People," de Cleyre contends:

> But a thousand voices rise
> Where the words of the martyr fell;
> The seed springs fast to the Skies
> Watered deep from that bloody well![216]

Here and elsewhere, these poems reveal a degree of self-consciousness about the function of poetry, oration, and music within the culture movement, as well as an awareness that these very poems would be a part of that process. The "thousand voices ris[ing]" included, as I have been arguing, the hundreds of poems that appeared in broadsides and labor newspapers and that erupted spontaneously at meetings and rallies. Those who mourned the anarchists in verse would not have placed such faith in the lasting influence of an ephemeral medium like the fringe newspaper if they did not believe that their poetry would enjoy a life beyond the printed page.

One form that these new thoughts were to take was clearly a resumption of the political activism demonstrated by the anarchists, this time popularized in poetry. Among their many functions, more than a few poems took on the task of retelling the history of the Haymarket case from the beginning of the labor agitation to the executions of the anarchists, using the familiar ballad form to narrate the events, and issuing polemics along the way. One poet asks,

> Doth Freedom dwell where ruthless kings of gain
> Like stealthy vampires, still on Labour feed—
> ... Then what of Labour's hope—the will to be
> Equal, Fraternal, knowing want nor greed—[217]

As in this poem, defenders of the anarchists reexamined the showdown between labor and capital, depicting labor reformers as heroic defenders of universal human rights. As for the enemies of labor, many poets ruthlessly attacked both the police and the Pinkerton detectives, who represented industry in its standoff against labor—and who, many believed, were responsible for the Haymarket riot. Both organizations, argues one poet, were "armed hirelings, / Keeping guard o'er labor's friends."[218] Perhaps the most vitriolic attack came from the anonymous author of "The Road to Freedom." The police, this poet wrote,

> are appointed for their weight
> In beer-blown, porcine flesh and bone;
> No other fitness need they own,
> No other human gift or trait.
> Their value is their breadth of girth;
> Superfluous is intellect,

> While mercy is a prime defect,
> And judgment is of little worth.
> They are recruited from the most
> Degraded ruffians unconfined;
> They are the lowest of their kind,
> Unfit to hold so grave a post.

While condemning the bestial nature of the police, this speaker maintains his own dignity in a controlled rhythm distinct from the grimy and chaotic content of his verse. Whatever the literary quality of the poem, it draws on its discourse community's bitterness and humor, vernacular voice, and shared values to unify the working class.

Nor were such attacks merely ad hominem slanders. Most of the poets who joined the political fray did so by means of specific references to the Haymarket case, and their animosity toward the police came directly out of their knowledge of the Chicago police department's activities during the riot and subsequent investigation. The ballad form was well suited to reiterate a familiar story to those who had followed it or to tell it for the first time to the uninitiated. In either case, these ballad-like poems served to instruct the masses and to unite them in a sense of outrage. As one poet wrote of the criminal investigation into the bombing,

> when the proper culprit fled
> They found a means to serve their ends;
> The guilt was fastened on the friends
> Who strove to sweeten Labor's bread.[219]

Likewise, the many poetic attacks on the judge, prosecutor, and jury, though full of fury, nevertheless are informed by the details of the case available in pamphlets, broadsides, and labor newspapers. Many poets condemn both "The judge, who dared not name the better cause / And mete out justice" and

> Each forsworn juror, who was not the man
> To oppose the maddened populace's cry
> For vengeance and refuse to sacrifice
> Innocent men for guilty.[220]

Others blamed these men not only for their cowardice but for the graver fault of corruption: "The shameless perjurers, bought and sold, / . . . swore away their victims' lives."[221]

When apportioning blame, these poets also recognized and noted the responsibility of what one poet calls the "spaniel press which lives and thrives / On men's misfortunes manifold."[222] The clemency movement, so nearly successful, revealed the power of the daily press to turn sentiments against the condemned men. When the "poisoned presses scream[ed]" for blood,[223] a rapacious public and the elected officials who represented them eagerly concurred. As one poet tells the story,

The balances, which for a little time
Hung trembling hitherward and fro,
Held at the close so ponderous a load
Of passion and mad fear that justice weighed
But lightly and went up.[224]

Many poets lamented that these elected officials were cowards:

Not one of all the tools of place,
The purchased puppets of the State,
Would lift his voice to stay their fate,
Or rise superior to his race.[225]

But some poets also acknowledged the responsibility of the daily newspapers in securing the executions. Promulgating their own messages in socialist and labor newspapers, these poets freely criticized the powerful mainstream dailies and attempted, as they did so, to point out the vast differences between the working class and the powerful few who edited and controlled the nation's most influential newspapers.

Many poets also believed that their role was not merely to retell the story of the Haymarket anarchists and to commemorate what they had done but to continue their unfinished work in the variety of ways offered by the cultural life of the labor movement. They understood that the struggle for justice, though it had suffered a devastating setback in the executions, would be ongoing. Some were pessimistic about their chances. As one poet writes, "this tragedy, this nameless deed, / Proves justice sleeps."[226] But others were more hopeful; one poet asks: "And did ye think thereby to strangle truth? / To gibbet justice with a hempen rope?"[227] For most of these inspired poets, justice was not dead, only latent, to be roused again by the people's rage. They saw that the obligation of poetry was to inspire people with feelings that would move them to action. In the words of one poet, "within each beating heart, / Justice shall its vigil keep."[228]

Despite their diverse reactions to the Haymarket tragedy, the poets shared a desire to turn the men's lives into inspiration, to "pierce our listless souls with [their] endeavor."[229] And in this regard, many Haymarket poems prove that the elegy need not avoid social commentary, for they turned the elegiac mode into exhortation, transformed apolitical sentimentality into calls for direct action, and strengthened the emotional and ideological bonds that defined and invigorated their community. Unlike the picture of the nineteenth-century elegist drawn by most literary historians,[230] these poets refused to offer consolation; the sentimentality that accepts easy consolation, they understood, was inimical to political reform. The encouragement expressed in the following poem was typical:

Where they lead let us follow; they fight in the van,
For the honour of labour, the freedom of man;
Shall we fail of the faith which those strangled ones preach?
By their silence a thousand times stronger than speech?[231]

If the anarchists, according to one poet, taught "the working people to sharpen their weapons for the struggle,"[232] these poets wrote in order to keep the blades keen.

There are good reasons that these elegies have been neglected by later generations. Their functions were highly specific and thus their value was only temporary. For the most part, they were written for readers who were thoroughly familiar with the events of the Haymarket case and who shared the poets' sense of outrage over the executions. Although some of the Haymarket elegies are eloquent and moving, most are not, comparatively speaking, original. Rather than expressing an unusual poetic sensibility, they reiterate shared sentiments, visit the same scenes, even use the same tropes. As I have noted, the Haymarket poets had little interest in developing their literary careers, in helping shape a canon of working-class literature, or in debating the function of art in the political movement or the effects of politics on art. Nor were they primarily interested in original expression or form. Their poems resemble other highly ritualized utterances whose merits are to be found in their predictability. Repeating a familiar narrative in accessible language, appealing to their readers through the medium of labor and socialist newspapers, and even sometimes presenting new words to a familiar tune, these poems worked to popularize already widespread sentiments and to transform them into more difficult political reform.

And yet as Cary Nelson has convincingly argued, "texts that were widely read or influential need to retain an active place in our sense of literary history, whether or not we happen, at present, to judge them to be of high quality."[233] The value of these poems is to be found not in their powerful appeals to timeless human values but in their active and effective cultural intervention. Of course, as Michael Denning has argued, we can never know the political effects of a poem except through individual reports, and these are few.[234] But if it's impossible to determine how these poems were read, we do know that the labor movement actively and deliberately promoted the public and private uses of poetry. Halker and Denning both chronicle the efforts of this nineteenth-century movement to use propaganda for the recruitment and encouragement of its members.[235] Denning describes the attempts of labor editors to replace the habitual reading material of the working poor (what one worker calls "mental trash") with proletarian, even revolutionary literature—and the fears of establishment figures that this literature would lead to social and political disintegration.[236] We know that the poems I have been considering here were part of an ambitious attempt to teach readers about class oppression, to remind them of their grievances against the government and industrial capitalists, to reinforce the bonds of class solidarity, and to inspire workers with an urge to fight for social and economic change. The populist form of these poems and their sites of publication were instrumental in the cultivation of class solidarity.

Often anonymous, almost always candidly amateur, these poets represent the "people at large" rather than a particular poetic genius.[237] They understood poetry as a popular rather than elitist form that could be reiterated at social and political gatherings, sung to familiar tunes, and thereby used to draw and mobilize crowds. Through the medium of poetry these writers continued the work of the anarchists and labor leaders, deploying a relentless propaganda assault in order to encourage community involvement in the important issues of the day. In their poetry they demonstrated the truth of Nelson's claim for poetic discourse: that it can be "capable not merely of talking about but actually of substantially deciding basic social and political issues."[238]

Poetry, though, functions in a more than discursive way, as I have been arguing. At its most rhythmic and passionate, it has an almost martial quality, which these poets appreciated. At labor events of all kinds, such poems would have been used to promote the ongoing life of the labor struggle.

Although it might be too much to claim that the Haymarket elegists transformed an essentially private genre into a more political one, their poems demonstrate that the political elegy—which refuses consolation in order to emphasize the dehumanizing conditions of modern life—has a longer history than Ramazani and others have acknowledged. Whatever the political content of canonized elegies from the nineteenth century, these more popular and ephemeral representatives of the genre indicate that many now-forgotten poets took a form that often depicts private grief and infused it with a sense of shared catastrophe, making it do the work of speeches and labor rallies. The value of these poems is to be found not in their enduring literary status but, like that of the ephemeral publications in which they appeared, in the functions they performed while they were in circulation. Although anecdotal evidence has its limitations, we might consider the fact that Emma Goldman dated her life as an anarchist from the Haymarket executions. She came to understand these men's stories and their ideals from what she read and heard about them. Goldman asserts that the memory of true "pioneers . . . perpetuates itself from generation to generation."[239] Surely poems and songs—recited, sung, or otherwise circulated—were part of this self-perpetuating memory.

The poetic responses of ordinary citizens to the Haymarket executions should remind us of Jürgen Habermas's insight into bourgeois society: the state's authority, he argued, is monitored by informed critical discussions among the people, who follow political events in the press and "compel public authority to legitimate itself before public opinion."[240] Although elegies might not at first seem to qualify as the kind of public debate Habermas had in mind, the elegiac culture that developed in the wake of the Haymarket executions was politically engaged. In Esther Schor's words, it was a culture in which "feeling flowers into action and action is nourished by feeling."[241] In this context, poets exploited powerful feelings before the moment of tranquil recollection, choosing instead to harness rage and grief in a communal setting in order to turn these feelings into political action. In writing poems that were meant to be read, recited, sung, and circulated, the Haymarket elegists followed the anarchists themselves in seeking to transform official legal, political, and labor culture. That they turned to poetry to do so suggests a faith in the cultural relevance of verse that seems to have been largely lost in our own time.

Today, as poets are struggling with ways of representing public tragedy, as ordinary people are turning once again to poets for meaningful language about loss, and as the custodians of poetry are searching for ways to recover poetry's lost cultural relevance, the Haymarket elegies might be able to tell us something about both the poetic possibilities of cultural turmoil and the social value of poetry. If poetic value cannot easily be found in a single, conventional poem, perhaps we should seek meaning in a wave of poetic responses to a single tragedy. So many of the Haymarket elegies, for instance, are modest in their own claims to immortality—publishing in ephemeral venues under the cloak of anonymity—while hazarding bold claims for their own version of history and for the progressive power of poetry. Robert Pinsky, the former US poet laureate, has done more than perhaps any other modern poet to revitalize poetry for the masses, calling for public readings of recent and classic poetry. And it seems to me entirely appropriate that he does this by acknowledging the same ephemeral, communal, even bodily aspects of poetry that the Haymarket elegists appreciated. Stressing the bodily element of poetry read aloud—what Gioia calls its "vulgar vitality"—Pinsky argues that "our evolution as an animal . . . evolved rhythmic language as a means of transmitting vital information across the generations."[242] The Haymarket elegists did more than simply refuse consolation: they insisted on the primal passion of anger, they enforced it with predictable rhythms and rhymes, and they encouraged its repetition in public spaces where the voice of a multitude could add its own physical strength.

The highly charged language of the Haymarket elegies can best be appreciated if we bear in mind the circumstances of their publication and their dissemination in the public sphere, where the consumers of this poetry learned to utter their private grief through publicly shared poems and songs and then to turn it into communal political action. It is easy to imagine, for instance, that the following poem, predicting the triumph of anarchism, was sung at many a labor rally:

> They the martyr's blood who sow yet must meet a ruthless foe,
> Not for ever will the workers starve and die;
> And the tyrant's brutal jeers shall give place to craven fears
> When the Red Flag floats in triumph 'gainst the sky![243]

The rising rhythms of this poem—not unlike "The Battle Hymn of the Republic"—draw on the martial meters of inspirational rally songs. If the note of triumph sounds odd in an elegy that cannot take consolation in conventional pieties, we should remember that the Haymarket anarchists and their followers understood that social change would transpire only when the populace lost faith that industrialists and lawmakers would willingly grant the demands of the working poor. Only when public outrage peaked would the people be moved to open revolt, and an outrageous multiple execution—what even so prominent and respectable a man as the novelist William Dean Howells referred to as an "atrocious and irreparable wrong"—might have provided the best chance for such a revolt.[244] The infectious rhythms of this poem might easily move audiences with the pleasurable mix of rage, grief, and the contagion of shared poetic energy.

Chapter Three

WISDOM, JUSTICE, AND MODERATION ABANDONED

The Lynching of Leo Frank

Like all extralegal executions, the lynching of Leo Frank exposed the distance between official law and public feelings about justice. When Frank was sentenced to death in 1913 for the murder of a factory girl, he and his allies worked hard within the appeals process to have his sentence commuted to life in prison. They underestimated the importance of appealing to the general public, however. Though they were successful in their campaign for clemency, they neglected the feelings of ordinary Georgians, while the opposing side took advantage of popular literary forms to sway public opinion against Frank.

I. THE MURDER OF MARY PHAGAN AND THE LYNCHING OF LEO FRANK

The murder of Mary Phagan, like the Haymarket explosion, might have provided an occasion for a national discussion about unfair labor practices had the parties involved been inclined to politicize the murder. In April 1913, fourteen-year-old Mary Phagan was found strangled to death in the basement of the Atlanta Pencil

Editorial cartoon,
New York World,
August 18, 1915.

Factory, where she had worked for a weekly wage of $3.60.[1] At that time, Georgia was the only state to allow ten-year-old children to work eleven-hour days.[2] The details of factory life that emerged during the investigation and murder trial would appall those who followed the case. It was difficult to ascertain, for instance, which blood stains on the factory floors were connected to the murder, because mutilations in the factory machinery were frequent and unremarkable. The nation still had not passed an eight-hour-work-day law, and Mary Phagan, like many young women employed in Georgia factories, typically worked twelve hours a day, six days a week, for five cents an hour.[3] Labor reform was slow to arrive in the deep South: twenty-six years after the Haymarket executions, labor conditions were still deplorable in Georgia.

Under different circumstances this murder case might have taken up the topic of labor conditions, and it might have given way to a widespread and successful effort at labor reform. The girl who died was young and attractive, but her family's economic circumstances forced her to work long hours in an urban factory rather than live the life of an earlier generation of farmers' daughters. She therefore represented the ways that the traditional rural family was being undermined by a changing Southern economy, and her youth and beauty touched a nerve more dramatically than would have been possible by citing even overwhelming statistics about unsafe labor conditions.[4] Like Sarah Cornell nearly a hundred years before her, Mary Phagan was typical of the many young women who were indispensable to the success of the factories where they worked: they sacrificed tradition and family in order to facilitate the industrialization of their regions.[5] And there is much evidence to suggest not only that the working poor of Atlanta were discouraged by labor conditions but that they may also have had allies among the educated and powerful. On the very day of Phagan's murder, in fact, the *Atlanta Constitution* carried a front-page story of the Southern Sociological Congress's attack on child labor; fifteen hundred people attended the convention in Atlanta to hear of the time "when child labor will be done away with, when every little tot shall have its quota of sunlight and happiness—of its hours of play and recreation."[6] The Hearst-owned *Atlanta Georgian*, moreover, was in the midst of an ongoing crusade against factory owners, particularly their habit of overworking and underpaying child laborers.[7]

Clearly, though Atlanta's expanding economy relied heavily on female and child labor, it was by no means secure in its exploitation of that labor; the murder of Mary Phagan might easily have exploded into a public debate over unfair labor practices. That the case neither resolved nor even raised the issue of labor grievances is part of the story of the uses to which Mary Phagan's murder was put by everyone involved: by the impoverished factory workers who saw themselves as represented by the dead girl, by the factory superintendent who was tried and convicted for her murder, by the Solicitor General who represented the people in the murder trial, and by the many different individuals and organizations that sought to publicize the case. As we shall see, the stifling of debate over labor reform in this case is yet another chapter in the story of how public debates are framed.

For a short while it looked as though the crime might follow the predictable trajectory of Southern justice: the victim was a white girl, suspicions were aroused that she had been raped as well as murdered, and the initial suspects were both black men. From the beginning there was much talk in Atlanta of a possible lynching. On the day the murder was reported, the *Atlanta Journal* ran a headline that read, "'God's Vengeance will Strike Brute Who Killed Her,' Says Grandfather of Mary Phagan."[8] Two days after the murder, the Atlanta business community protested the constant issuance of sensational newspaper extras, claiming that "the community is being aroused to a dangerous degree by them, and . . . they may bring extremely unfortunate conditions."[9] Upon the arrest of the first black suspect, Newt Lee, a janitor at the pencil factory, there was immediate talk of a lynching and the state militia was notified to be in readiness.[10] Once Lee was cleared of the crime, suspicion fastened upon a second black man, Jim Conley, who ran errands at the factory. Throughout the case, which continued unresolved for two and a half years, Conley was maligned in the press and at trial as shiftless, debased, and untrustworthy. One of the trial lawyers denounced Conley as a "dirty, filthy, black, drunken, lying nigger."[11] Even respectable dailies like the *New York Times* followed suit, calling Conley a "black monster."[12] The prosecution, which would soon forge an alliance with Conley for the sake of securing a conviction, never went so far as to say he was a respectable character. But abruptly the investigation changed direction when Conley turned state's evidence and the prosecution went after the twenty-nine-year-old superintendent of the factory, Leo Frank.

Partly because he was the last person known to have seen Phagan alive and partly because he was manifestly nervous during police interviews, Leo Frank, a New York Jew who had lived in Atlanta for only five years, emerged as the leading suspect and was arrested and brought to trial. After a prolonged and sensational jury trial, in which the courthouse was packed, the testimony at times ran to extremes of sexual luridness and racist stereotypes, the newspapers freely reported each day's proceedings, and the judge had difficulty quelling the frequent outbursts from courtroom spectators (most of them hostile to the defendant), Frank was convicted and sentenced to death. The defense immediately appealed on the grounds of police misconduct, witness intimidation, and the extreme influence of public sentiment upon the jury. Calling the courtroom proceeding "a farce and not in any way a trial," Frank's attorneys on appeal maintained that "the temper of the public mind was such that it invaded the court room and invaded the streets and made itself manifest at every turn the jury made; and it was just as impossible for this jury to escape the effects of this public feeling as if they had been turned loose and had been permitted to mingle with the people."[13] Although Frank never received a new trial, a public campaign eventually resulted in the commutation of his sentence to life imprisonment. Georgia's outgoing governor, John M. Slaton, hoped that eventually passions would subside sufficiently for Frank to receive a fairer trial. But that opportunity never arrived: in August 1915, just two months after Frank was moved to the state prison in Milledgeville to begin his life sentence, he was forcibly removed from the prison, driven seven hours to Marietta, and hanged from a tree.

II. THE WEALTHY JEW AND THE POOR WHITE GIRL

How shall we understand this case? Was it a simple case of anti-Semitism, as Leonard Dinnerstein has alleged?[14] An unfortunate coincidence for Frank, who happened to be falsely accused of murder at a time when the number of unsolved crimes in Atlanta had the public clamoring for a conviction of any sort, while local Atlanta papers, competing with the newly arrived Hearst newspaper, were engaged in a war for readership that prompted irresponsible and sensational journalism?[15] Given the many political contexts that informed this murder case—the relations between labor and capital, the growing pains of a rapidly changing economy, the influence of immigration on community identity, the racial and regional differences between the main characters in this drama—why did some of these issues all but disappear in discussions of the case, while others rose to prominence? In many ways the context of Mary Phagan's murder was similar to that of the Haymarket affair: it involved a confrontation between poorly paid wage laborers and the capitalists who employed them, it took place against the backdrop of a bitter strike, and it pitted racially different recent arrivals to the United States against white Protestants whose families had long been established in the region. And yet, as we shall see, in the telling of the case the politics of race and class were weirdly disguised as apolitical, historically vague—in short, as having little to do with a changing twentieth-century economy and everything to do with a script dating back to Reconstruction.

If, as with the other murder trials we have been investigating, the Frank case involved more than the specific charge of murder written on the bill of indictment, then an examination of the crime, the trial, and the aftermath might tell us something about the particular preoccupations of those who narrated the event for public consumption. In the economically unstable New South, for example, it is noteworthy that a discussion of labor conditions was conspicuously absent from most local accounts of the case, even while the nearby Fulton Bag and Cotton Mill was engaged in a bitter strike. In some ways the Leo Frank trial provides an exception to the pattern we have been observing, in that it almost deliberately evaded the explicitly political. But of course even the evasion of politics is a political gesture: here it constitutes only one of the specific uses to which the parties involved put both the murder of Mary Phagan and the system of justice, legal and illegal, that focused on Leo Frank.

What did it mean, for instance, that neither African American suspect was lynched? Though we might at first be tempted to conclude that the escape of Newt Lee and Jim Conley from the hangman's noose meant something new about racial politics in the New South, we should tread cautiously. Georgia nearly led the union for the number of lynchings in 1913, where, as elsewhere in the United States, most lynching victims were black men. In 1915, the year of Frank's murder, twenty-one others were lynched in Georgia, all of them African Americans.[16] As many critics of Georgia law pointed out after Leo Frank's lynching, the state hardly lived up to its motto, "Wisdom, Justice and Moderation." Lynching was a typical Georgia response to crime, especially when the suspects were black men. We must look carefully for an explanation as to why Jim Conley was not lynched. The prosecution maintained that Conley escaped this fate for the same reason that his testimony held up under the "skillful intellect" and the "brainy eloquence" of the Frank defense team's cross-examination: because he was telling the truth about Frank's lascivious practices with the young women who worked in the factory, about Frank's repeated attempts to seduce Mary Phagan, and about the subsequent murder to conceal his bad character.[17] Frank's defenders and even some of his onetime enemies—most notably, Mary Phagan's family minister—contended that Conley had escaped the lynch mob for symbolic reasons alone, because "one . . . negro would be poor atonement for the life of this innocent girl."[18] As Harold Ross later reported, "The crime was an abnormal one; it outshadowed all previous ones. The police realized the truth which determined their whole future course of action: The murder of Mary Phagan must be paid for with blood. And a Negro's blood would not suffice."[19] Although one of the murder ballads that circulated in Atlanta tells of the lynching of the unnamed janitor ("The sheriff he was a wise good man, / He never flicked a hair; / He let them string that janitor up / And left him hanging there"),[20] white hostility turned from Newt Lee and Jim Conley to Leo Frank. To understand this unpredictable turn of events, we need to consider the insight into lynching provided by social historians: that when on occasion "African Americans who might have been seen to be in the wrong by prevailing racist standards, and thus vulnerable to mob violence," happened somehow to escape the lynch mob, the reasons must be sought in the ways that "whites constructed and understood the incidents."[21]

At the center of Atlanta's understanding of the crime and investigation was the contention that Leo Frank was a wealthy Jew. As superintendent of the factory, Frank provoked immediate mistrust on the part of local factory workers when he hired a lawyer and a Pinkerton detective to inquire into the crime. Although such a move might seem reasonable for the supervisor of the place where Phagan was found murdered, it raised strong doubts among the impoverished factory workers of Atlanta. For one thing, as we have seen in the Haymarket case, the Pinkerton Detective Agency was notorious for its role in anti-union activities from the 1870s on; since workers at Atlanta's Fulton Bag and Cotton Mill also encountered this detective agency during their 1913 strike, when management refused to let them organize a union, the people of Mary Phagan's community were already deeply suspicious of the Pinkertons. To hire any private detective, moreover, would have looked strange to Frank's employees and their families. As Gene Wiggins explains, "These were suspicious actions to a class of people who usually pleaded guilty even when innocent because they could not hire lawyers and did not believe free ones would help."[22] In the words of Tom Watson, one of Frank's most vicious enemies, Frank's allies "pussy-footed to the strongest team of lawyers in Atlanta, and secretly employed them to defend Leo Frank" even before he was accused of any wrongdoing.[23] Watson's damning interpretation seems to have resonated strongly with many poor Georgians. Whatever the defense did to rebut these charges, they remained convincing in the minds of many.[24]

As Griffin notes, the operative forces in cases of lynching were perceptions, not realities, and in Frank's case the perception was widespread in Atlanta that wealthy Jews controlled Frank's judicial treatment. Poor laborers in Georgia came to believe that Jews owned most of the world's wealth, particularly as a defense fund for Frank was established and advertised. The B'nai Brith of Atlanta took out an advertisement—against the strong objections of Joseph Dewey Gortatowsky, an orthodox Jew and managing editor of the *Atlanta Constitution*—alleging that Frank was being prosecuted because of his religion and appealing to readers to donate money for his defense. With these funds, Frank's friends hired the high-priced legal team of Rosser and Arnold, perhaps the most famous criminal defense lawyers in the South.[25] Reports spread that Jews were determined to have Frank acquitted, regardless of his guilt or innocence,[26] and that a fund of $40,000 had been raised.[27]

The truth of the matter was that Frank was not an extraordinarily wealthy man. His father, he explained to the court, was an invalid and his parents were "people of very limited means."[28] But to the impoverished factory workers, many of whom had once been modestly successful farmers and who resented the middle-class lifestyle of this Northern Jew, Frank represented wealth and privilege. A Cornell graduate whose family had sent him to Europe to learn the pencil manufacturing business, he seemed to have access to spheres of influence that eluded them, and the prosecution played on this perception, claiming that "the only thing to the discredit of the police department" during its investigation of the Phagan murder was that, deterred by "the glamour that surrounds wealth and influence," the police "were intimidated and afraid because of the influence that was back of [Frank], to consign him to a cell like they did Lee and Conley, and it took them a little while to arrive at the point where they had the nerve and courage to face the situation and put him where he ought to be."[29]

Hardly glamorous in his wealth, Frank nevertheless earned significantly more than the people who worked under him. As Lindemann observes, Frank "supervised the work of nearly a hundred women in the pencil factory, many in their early teens. . . . Frank's own pay, at 180 dollars a week (to which was added his share of the profits), vastly exceeded Mary Phagan's, at 12 cents an hour, or her father's at the mills (20 cents an hour, perhaps $10 for a normal work week)."[30]

More significant than his actual economic power, however, was the symbolism of Frank's position as the supervisor of a factory that employed the daughters and wives of impoverished farmers. As MacLean explains, Mary Phagan was the descendent of a Piedmont farm family that had lost its land after the Civil War, falling into tenancy and eventually wage labor.[31] "Having started factory work at a very young age to help support her widowed mother and five siblings, Phagan also personified the bitter dilemma of the region's emerging industrial proletariat, forced to rely on children's wages to make ends meet."[32] While parents and particularly fathers were losing their ability to support their children at home, they were being symbolically replaced by factory superintendents and owners who made their livings off the labor of these children.

Frank seems to have represented the power of capitalism in the minds of Atlanta's working poor. Lindemann observes that "Frank appears to have been in a position of much latent tension and symbolism. . . . Frank was a hard-driving, efficient, nononsense supervisor. The potential symbolism of his position . . . is all too obvious. . . . Leo Frank was a representative of Yankee capitalism in a southern city, with row upon row of southern women, often the daughters and wives of ruined farmers."[33] Whereas Jim Conley and Newt Lee might have appeared fitting targets for an angry mob, it seems likely that they were spared because they did not share this symbolic status with Frank. Melnick convincingly speculates that Jim Conley was eventually rejected as a scapegoat because he did not run the National Pencil Company factory, did not hand out pay, did not monitor employees, and thus was not responsible for the exploitation of child labor at the factory.[34] Whatever Frank's actual earning power, his role as an agent of and witness to the daily exploitation of Atlanta's working poor marked him as a capitalist, and his Northern, Jewish roots did not help. Burton Rascoe, writing for the *Chicago Tribune* in 1914, claimed that unlike African Americans, who were not typically allowed to run businesses in the deep South, Jews in the South were often seen as "aggressive business competitors" and thus were "thoroughly hated, from economic jealousy as well as from religious prejudice."[35] Whether this economic jealousy was warranted is not really the point; the point is rather that as a Jew Frank could hardly escape being characterized as a rich and powerful man, one whose own economic success depended on the exploitation of his factory workers.

What Governor Slaton later described as the courtroom audience's "deep resentment toward Frank" during the trial was no doubt partly a response to the symbolism
on stage during that trial.[36] On Frank's side was a team of "the ablest lawyers in the
country," as Solicitor Hugh Dorsey remarked to the jury. On the other were Dorsey and
Mary Phagan's impoverished mother. The trial, Dorsey told the jury, was "extraordinary because of the prominence, learning, ability, standing of counsel pitted against
me."[37] Many courtroom spectators feared that Mary Phagan and her family would not
receive justice, that Leo Frank might well buy his way out of a conviction.

III. THE DRAMA OF RECONSTRUCTION

In addition to their perceptions of Frank as a wealthy racial outsider, Atlantans bris-
tled over the question of justice because Frank, as a Northerner, reminded them of
their still-vivid resentments about Reconstruction. During the early years of the new
century, as during Reconstruction itself, Southern development depended upon the
presence of Northern capital. As Burton Rascoe recalled in his review of the Frank
case, Northern manufacturers were relatively new to Atlanta:

> In 1907, a delegation of Atlanta businessmen came to New York seeking to interest
> Northern capital in the advantages of Atlanta for the location of manufacturing con-
> cerns. Among these advantages were cited the low wage scale obtaining in the
> South, the plenitude of women and children who were willing to work for small pay,
> the low tax rate of Atlanta, the low cost of land for building sites, the low costs for
> materials and construction, and the facilities of Atlanta for the distribution of prod-
> ucts in an undeveloped consumer area.[38]

Atlanta was perhaps the most conspicuous site of successful industrialization in the
South and the host for two cotton expositions, in 1881 and 1895.[39] But successful
Southern industrialization depended on reconciliation and cooperation with the
North. Although Rascoe's description of Atlanta's economy would surely have
looked appealing from the perspective of a Northern manufacturing firm looking to
establish new factories, the advantages being advertised to Northern firms—the low
wage scale in the South, the number of women and children willing to work for poor
pay, and the low cost of Southern land—all pointed to an impoverished community
desperate to make ends meet at any cost. The consequences of Southern industrialization, as we shall see in the Frank case, were inflamed animosities between North
and South. As Melnick argues, the expansion of Southern industrialization depended
on the labor of women and children, and Frank came to pay the price of Southern
industrialization, where "'aliens' were coming to exert power over white women and
African American men—a power that previously had been a special privilege
enjoyed only by southern white men."[40]

When Burton Rascoe recalled the case in 1947 he noted that "[a]ll the ancient
animosities between the North and South, which had lain dormant since the Civil

War, were aroused and inflamed to white heat in an orgy of name-calling, charges, counter-charges and recriminations, nearly all of it irrelevant to the real issue."[41] A look at contemporaneous press reports bears him out. The unfortunate timing of Mary Phagan's death on Confederate Memorial Day was too enticing a detail to be disregarded. Atlantans were clearly disposed to regard Phagan's murder as a symbol of Southern dispossession. As Marouf Hasian Jr. argues, Phagan's funeral rituals were orchestrated to highlight a fading Southern grandeur. "Only days after Phagan's murder, thousands of Georgians participated in cultural rituals that illustrated their reaffirmation of faith in Southern values. Many citizens marched in organized funeral processions, and millions more read about Phagan's membership in the First Christian Bible School, her rural Georgia home, and her love of the annual Confederate Memorial Day parade.... Some wrote editorials and talked about the ways in which their own daughters had suffered."[42] The *Atlanta Georgian* published retouched photos of Mary Phagan, idealizing her in the style of a Gibson Girl. As the *Georgian* reporter Herbert Asbury later remarked, "the *Georgian* devoted three pages to the mystery.... We had pictures, in somber but artistic layouts, on every page—pictures of the murdered girl, of her father, her mother, her grandfather, sisters, uncles, aunts and cousins; pictures of her birthplace in Marietta, of her home in Atlanta, of the pencil factory.... Our paper was, in modern parlance, a wow."[43] Nor was the public reluctant to respond to the *Georgian*'s jingoistic coverage: On the day that Frank's guilty verdict was announced, the *Atlanta Constitution* reported that "one aged man, whose wrinkled face and empty sleeve proclaimed service in the days of civil strife," concluded that the news of the verdict was "kinder like 'Dixie' ringing out in a place where you ain't known."[44]

It should not be surprising that this ordinary bystander understood the Frank case in larger historical terms, for the prosecution, alluding to regional tensions enduring since the Civil War, had been playing upon the coincidence of Phagan's death falling on Confederate Memorial Day to inflame the jury and anyone who witnessed or read about the trial. When Solicitor Dorsey introduced into evidence an unremarkable letter that Frank had written to his uncle on the day of Phagan's murder, a letter primarily devoted to the financial concerns of the pencil factory but also containing brief personal remarks, he wrought upon the feelings of the courtroom by reminding them that Frank was a Northerner who cared nothing for Southern traditions. The letter read, in part: "It is too short a time since you left for anything startling to have developed down here.... Today was yontiff [holiday] here, and the thin gray lines of veterans here braved the rather chilly weather to do honor to their fallen comrades."[45] Although the letter proved nothing about Frank's knowledge of the Phagan murder, Dorsey used it for maximum emotional effect. "Do you tell me, honest men, fair men, courageous men, true Georgians, seeking to do your duty," he asked the jury,

> that that phrase ["too short a time"], penned by that man to his uncle on Saturday afternoon, didn't come from a conscience that was its own accuser? ... And then listen at this—as if that old gentleman, his uncle, cared anything for this proposition, this old millionaire traveling abroad to Germany for his health, this man from

Brooklyn—an eminent authority says that unusual, unnecessary, unexpected and extravagant expressions are always earmarks of fraud; and do you tell me that this old gentleman, expecting to sail for Europe, the man who wanted the price list and financial sheet, cared anything for those old heroes in gray?"

Frank's uncle, Dorsey concluded to the jury, "cared so little about the thin gray line of veterans, but . . . cared all for how much money had been gotten in by the pencil factory."[46] In this way, Dorsey used an irrelevant document to persuade the jury that Frank and his allies were neither Southerners nor particularly sympathetic to the economic hardships of the people they employed. That Moses Frank was actually a Confederate veteran didn't matter: in Dorsey's narrative, the uncle's racial identity trumped his Southern roots and even his loyalty to the Confederacy. Dorsey apparently hoped to make the jury see Leo Frank as his wealthy uncle's lieutenant, a carpetbagger who had come south to exploit already impoverished people who must tolerate his presence in order to survive.

In that scenario Mary Phagan came to represent all that was genteelly pathetic about the New South. A good Christian member of the Bible school, a girl who had looked forward to the annual Confederate Memorial Day, a daughter of destitute but proud former farmers who held tightly to their traditions, she represented everything that Frank did not. The story of Mary Phagan was widely circulated in the South as her tale came to take on the popular appeal of a myth, a novel, a sensational cautionary tale. Tom Watson's didactic and sentimental tone was typical: "Brave Southern girl! Death itself would not rob Mary Phagan of the proofs, that she fought for her innocence to the very last."[47] One of the many ballads to Phagan describes the murder victim as "Bright as the morning light, And modest as the dew"; she "Came to draw her money / And to see the parade that day." Coming to town to collect her small pay and attend the Confederate Memorial Day parade, Mary Phagan— according to this popular rendition of her story—pays for her chastity with her life:

Sweet as the fragrance of a dewey rose,
Pure as the drifted snow,
She died, defending her virtue,
By the cruel cord & blow.[48]

This ballad and others exemplify what Jeffrey Melnick has called the "public obsession with Phagan's 'virtue.'"[49]

Abraham Cahan called the case a "junk novel" because it had all the earmarks of a simplistically sketched story of virtue and vice, drawing on the popular literary conventions that we have seen exploited in other murder cases.[50] The novelistic elements of the case were prominent in both the ephemeral and more lasting documents it inspired—in the many ballads that could be sung repeatedly, published, modified, and passed to future generations. Although these documents were primarily oral and thus subject to eventual extinction, we have seen the immense cultural power of such texts, particularly when they depended on and encouraged collective expressions of rage. Then too, Phagan's champions created more permanent reminders of the case. The text of the gravestone erected at Phagan's Marietta burial site seems anxious to preserve her story for perpetuity; in its reference to "disappearing land marks" it seems to long for a more enduring message than might be found in ballads or even in Civil War monuments. Like the more ephemeral ballads, Phagan's monument celebrates her representative status as an emblem of the Old South even while mourning her tragic death:

> In this day of fading ideals
> And disappearing land marks,
> little Mary Phagan's heroism
> is an heirloom than which
> there is nothing more precious
> among the old red hills of Georgia. . . .
> Many an aching heart in
> Georgia beats for you, and
> many a tear from eyes unused
> to Weep, has paid tribute
> too sacred for Words.[51]

In its anxiety over the loss of historical consciousness, the narrative inscribed on this tombstone does attempt to put the case in historically specific terms, alluding to "fading ideals," "disappearing land marks," and the "old red hills of Georgia." But in the tradition of the "junk novel," those references to larger political and economic changes are finally all but eclipsed by a larger appeal to the timeless conflict between good and evil, innocence and corruption. Even as Phagan's grieving community understood her murder as part of a changing economy that was difficult for them to accept, they represented her murder in terms of a morally simple, timeless drama. We can see the same gesture repeated in Solicitor Dorsey's courtroom presentation, where the prosecutor simplified the murder case as he taunted the defendant: Leo Frank had to murder Phagan, Dorsey argued, because "ah! thank God, she was made of that kind of stuff to which you are a stranger, and she resisted, she wouldn't yield, you couldn't control your passion and you struck her and you ravished her."[52]

By putting the murder case in personal (though racialized) terms, Dorsey stripped the episode of its modern political context and replaced that context with an earlier (though still compelling) narrative of the carpetbagger. Reiterating the moral and cultural differences between Mary Phagan and Leo Frank, Dorsey tried to play on the jury's lingering resentments over Reconstruction, drawing out the political, racial, and economic distinctions between honest Southern workers and ruthless Northern (Jewish) capitalists. Dorsey's case, which neither addressed the particular conditions of factory life nor appealed to the labor reform movement, set the tone for the public discussions that followed. In court and in the public sphere, Frank's case demonstrates how "Jews became the foil for all capitalism's evils, while Georgia's and the nation's most powerful capitalists escaped notice or blame."[53]

In retrospect it might seem that the Phagan murder, the criminal investigation, the trial, and the ongoing press coverage were leading inevitably to Frank's eventual lynching, which one detective accounted for as "a vicarious atonement for the rule of the carpetbagger in the South during the reconstruction period."[54] Like the Haymarket case, the Frank trial in both its official and popular versions clearly touched a nerve regarding capitalism, industrialization, regional tensions, and nativism. When we investigate the specific breed of Southern populism that emerged in the aftermath of Frank's trial, focusing as it did on prejudice against Northerners and Jews, we shall see how these added social conditions further tipped the scales against Frank's chances for exoneration.[55]

IV. A SUCCESSFUL APPEAL

In spite of Frank's eventual fate, his case suggests that in some ways the twenty-six years since the Haymarket executions had a profound effect on judicial processes in the United States. We might even understand Frank's story, despite its tragic conclusion, as an example of a successful national political campaign waged on behalf of a man who had been wronged by the criminal justice system. Unlike the Haymarket anarchists, Leo Frank enjoyed the goodwill of many of America's mainstream daily newspaper editors and publishers. His supporters also had access to considerable funds. By 1914, moreover, many Americans had come to understand that law must not always be allowed to run its course. The Haymarket executions and the public discussions that followed may have had a powerful effect on the willingness of ordinary citizens to take part in discussions about judicial affairs.

Though the trial did not at first garner much attention beyond Georgia—a reporter for the *Atlanta Constitution* complained that "because it is not in New York, the papers of that fickle metropolis have not, in all, carried more than a column of the entire case"—after Frank's conviction the news of an unfair capital murder trial in Georgia began to spread.[56] When in September 1913 Louis Marshall, the president of the American Jewish Committee and a prominent New York lawyer, received an appeal from Atlanta Jews to help Leo Frank mount a campaign for a new trial, he believed that the best way to do so was quietly and without reference to anti-Semitism. He solicited the help of Adolph Ochs, the owner and publisher of the *New York Times*, to editorialize on behalf of Frank. Ochs did so, publishing story after story about the case, and he encouraged other newspapers to follow his lead. Ochs's biographers write that although in the past he had forbidden his newspaper to mount any crusade, during the Frank case he was "emboldened by the perceived security of his position: after eighteen years under his leadership, the *Times*' journalistic preeminence was unassailable, and Ochs, at the age of fifty-six, had become a near-iconic figure in the American press."[57]

To read the editorials and news stories in hundreds of daily newspapers across the nation is to recognize the deep influence of the *New York Times*'s editorial policy, as editors across the nation followed the *Times*'s lead. Burton Rascoe's full-page feature in the *Chicago Tribune*, "Will the State of Georgia Execute an Innocent Man?" reviewed the case with some urgency in December 1914, for Frank was scheduled for execution on January 22. Depending only on newspaper reports and unofficial court transcripts—for there were no court records available—Rascoe compared Frank's case to the sensational Haymarket affair of 1887: "There was the same popular uprising in the Haymarket incident. . . . The demand for a 'victim' to appease popular wrath against public outrages is not peculiar to Atlanta."[58] By 1914 "Haymarket" had become a byword for local prejudice, corrupt trials, and judicial murders, and it could be invoked without ambiguity in an argument like Rascoe's.

The *Atlanta Journal* presented a different case, for it is likely that its striking editorial of March 10, 1914, tending in the same direction as most mainstream newspapers, was less influenced by the *New York Times* than by the *Journal's* own sense of responsibility for the outcome of Frank's trial. Still, the *Journal* did come under attack by the *Times*, which called its earlier editorial policy a "reckless, sensational way that powerfully tended to inflame public passion."[59] Departing from its usual policy, the *Journal* issued an impassioned plea for a new trial:

> We recognize the justice of the rule that precludes the press from discussing, editorially at least, cases while pending in court. We have always respected both the necessity and the propriety of this rule. We do not wish to violate it now, but this case is so extraordinary in every phase and detail, so important in the consequences that may follow and so dangerous to the sanctity of the courts and the safety of the people themselves, that ordinary rules do not apply.[60]

William Curran Rogers argues that unlike the Hearst-owned *Georgian*, which was primarily concerned with sales, the *Journal* editors considered it their "social duty" to temper the public indignation against Frank so that he could have a second, fairer trial.[61] The topic of editorial responsibility looms large in the *Journal's* editorial: "Responsibility for the enforcement of the law and the punishment of crime rests largely but not exclusively upon the courts. The press also has its share of responsibility, and it seems to The Journal that the time has come for the press to speak. The Journal will do so now even though every other newspaper in Georgia remains silent."

Harboring a reasonable doubt as to Frank's guilt, the *Journal* continued, editors must speak out. "In this respect the press is responsible no less than the courts. Its duties are not in conflict but in aid of the courts. It is the amicus curiae, the friend of the court, in such matters." This friend of the court concluded that "Leo Frank has not had a fair trial. He has not been fairly convicted and his death without a fair trial and legal conviction will amount to judicial murder."[62]

Large and small, almost every mainstream daily newspaper in the country agreed. So did a number of prominent national magazines that featured stories on the Phagan murder and Frank trial: *Colliers* in December 1914, the *Outlook* in December 1914 and June 1915, the *Literary Digest* in January 1915, *Everybody's Magazine* in March 1915, and the *New Republic* in July 1915. All of these stories advocated a new trial.

Those who depended for their information upon newspaper reports of the case certainly found much to doubt about the legitimacy of Frank's trial. Although the campaign for a new trial, like the Haymarket efforts, extended beyond the pages of the mainstream dailies, in Frank's case the newspapers were not the enemies of the campaign as they had been in Chicago, so the web of influence spread much more effectively than it had twenty-six years earlier. In California, influential and wealthy Jews made their views known, writing sermons, lectures, and letters, circulating petitions, recruiting non-Jews, and going on lecture tours across the country.[63] The Anti-Capital Punishment Society of America became involved in the case, though that issue was so controversial that many advocates for Frank's life tried to separate his case from their larger distaste for the death penalty.[64]

A number of religious leaders spoke out vehemently in favor of a new trial. At first these were mostly Northern rabbis, but they tried to involve Gentiles as well: Rabbi Joel Blau, arguing that the Frank case was no longer either a sectional or a racial question, urged his congregation to write to Governor Slaton and to "plead with your Gentile friends to write similar letters."[65] Rabbi Stephen Samuel Wise published his sermon in the *Free Synagogue Pulpit* in 1915, lamenting that "it is necessary for a Jew to speak touching the case of Leo Frank. It would have been infinitely better if non-Jews had arisen throughout the land, as they ought to have done, to plead on behalf of this man."[66] Rabbi Alexander Lyons's Brooklyn sermon, "Prejudice in American Life," was "mailed to thousands of people in all the larger towns of Georgia" in late 1914.[67] In that sermon, Lyons argued that Jews and Gentiles alike believed Frank should have a new trial. "There is in many quarters a conviction—which is shared by a number of distinguished Christians, such as, for instance, Justice Holmes of the Supreme Court—that Leo M. Frank was not tried entirely upon pertinent facts," he argued.

In March 1914 a number of Christian clergymen joined the efforts of these Jewish religious leaders. In a letter to the *Atlanta Journal*, Reverend C. B. Wilmer recommended a new trial for Frank.[68] That same month the *Washington Post* reported that a number of Christian ministers in Atlanta were advocating a new trial in their sermons;[69] a week later the *New York Times* ran another story, "More Pastors Urge Retrial for Frank," adding to the list of Georgia ministers who were lending their voices to the commutation effort.[70] And the movement spread beyond the South as well. In April 1915, the Reverend S. Edward Young preached in Brooklyn, calling for a nationwide appeal on Frank's behalf. In May of that year, evangelist Billy Sunday preached in Paterson, New Jersey, claiming that if he "were Governor of Georgia Frank would go free tomorrow."[71] The emphatic if belated response of Christian ministers from Georgia and beyond suggests that many preachers eventually came to see the wisdom of Rabbi Stephen Wise's urgent exhortation:

> If public opinion can be stifled in a democracy, then democracy has passed and we
> dwell under the shadows of a deadening and degrading despotism. But if we are
> quick to demand that there be no muzzling of opinion and stifling of conviction in
> the far away State of Georgia, it behooves us to be equally alert in demanding that

at every forum of opinion in our city and State, whether the press or the university, every side be heard.[72]

In petitions sent to Georgia's governor, every side was heard and opinions tended to break down along regional lines. Whereas most exhortations to uphold Frank's sentence came from the South, particularly Georgia, appeals for a commutation came in from other states. Outside of the South, mass meetings were called in order to protest Frank's death sentence and to circulate petitions for clemency or commutation. Toward the climax of that movement in the fall of 1915, over one hundred thousand letters arrived at the governor's office from every US state as well as Canada and Mexico; a number of these letters came from governors and legislators from across the country. Mass meetings were held in major cities all over the United States. In Chicago alone, over twenty thousand petitions generated over five hundred thousand signatures calling for a new trial. And in May 1915, Frank himself received over fifteen hundred supportive letters a day.[73]

The campaign mounted nationally in defense of Frank was in some ways more organized than that leveled on behalf of the Haymarket anarchists. Because of their superior cultural power, moreover, Frank's many supporters were more successful than those who had defended the working poor on trial in the Cook County Courthouse. Some of the Haymarket advocates, drawing on their earlier experience, responded more quickly this second time around. Samuel Gompers, Eugene Debs, and Clarence Darrow, who had achieved nationwide fame in the years since Haymarket, voiced their opposition to Frank's death sentence almost as soon as it became national news in 1914. Debs, for instance, issued a statement from Terre Haute, Indiana, in late 1914, urging conscientious Americans everywhere to speak out in Frank's defense: "This is not a cause that concerns the State of Georgia alone. The Constitution of the United States has been violated, and its protection denied a citizen charged with crime in a prejudiced community, and this of itself is sufficient to make the case of Leo Frank the case of every American citizen. Let public sentiment be aroused until lynch law is rebuked in Georgia, and Leo Frank given a fair trial and a just verdict."[74] As the governor's days in office waned, these Midwestern labor leaders increased their efforts. Acting as the president of the American Federation of Labor, Samuel Gompers wrote Georgia's governor to "appeal that your great prerogative be exercised in commuting the sentence of Leo M. Frank from death to a life term of imprisonment."[75] Toward the end of Governor Slaton's term, a mass meeting was held on a day designated "Leo M. Frank Day" in Chicago, where Clarence Darrow was one of the scheduled speakers.

Unlike the clemency movement of 1887, the national press response to these many demonstrations was almost unanimous in calling for a new trial. Even in Georgia, with the exception of Mary Phagan's hometown Marietta newspaper and those of a few rural towns, most daily newspapers came to harbor grave doubts about Frank's guilt. Believing that Frank at the very least had not had a fair trial, they supported a commutation of the sentence until such a trial could be arranged. And in one of the most dramatic differences from the Haymarket case, the United States Supreme Court did not rule unanimously on Frank's motion for an appeal on the grounds of a reasonable doubt. Justice Oliver Wendell Holmes's dissent was widely quoted by Frank's defenders. Holmes argued that "mob law does not become due process of law by securing the assent of a terrorized jury. We are not speaking of mere disorder, or mere irregularities in procedure, but of a case where the processes of justice [were] actually subverted."[76] Writing for himself and Charles Evans Hughes, the other dissenting justice, Holmes concluded by declaring "lynch law as little valid when practiced by a regularly drawn jury as when administered by one elected by a mob intent on death."[77] Though Holmes and Hughes were minority voices on the bench, their opinions found a far-reaching and approving audience. As the *San Francisco Chronicle* correctly predicted, "The opinion of the country will be with the dissenting Justices."[78]

The national political campaign launched on behalf of Leo Frank was clearly not without its effect; by the time Governor Slaton commuted Frank's sentence in June 1915, most Americans applauded what the *Atlanta Journal* called his "courageous act."[79] And when in August of that year Frank was lynched, most of the nation agreed that the event constituted "Georgia's Shame."[80]

V. THE PROBLEM OF PUBLIC SENTIMENTS

What then happened in Georgia? Dinnerstein contends that the effort to win a new trial was poorly organized, with too many people working without an organizer.[81] But the campaign to defend Frank was also impaired by a number of philosophical blunders and miscalculations. It would appear, for one thing, that while they recognized the constant efforts required of individuals who wish to intervene in official procedures of justice, and while they rightly calculated how to go about doing so, Frank's advocates meanwhile lost track of Elizabeth Cady Stanton's insight that "law is powerless when at variance with public sentiment."[82] Clearly, Frank's defenders in Georgia disregarded local sentiments in their zeal to change the minds of the nation. Louis Marshall's strong warning that nothing should be done or published to "arouse the sensitiveness of the southern people and engender the feeling that the north is criticizing the courts and the people of Georgia" was not always heeded.[83] Atlantans were often reminded that their initial police investigation had been flawed; after the trial was concluded they were repeatedly asked to consider new evidence. In 1914 the *New York Times* editorialized that "[t]he case [had] been minutely inquired into by Mr. Edward Marshall. . . . His conclusion that Frank is innocent [had] been reached by many other careful students of the case, while it would seem to be practically impossible for any candid man to hold the opinion that the trial was fair, that the best possible defense of the prisoner was made, or that the verdict of the jury was in accordance with the evidence, which did not even establish a remote probability of guilt."[84] Late in 1914 the press reported that Berry Benson, a prominent Augustan, "had made a painstaking investigation and analysis of the Frank case" and believed Frank to be innocent.[85] In early 1915 the *New York Times* ran a story written by "one of the best known criminal investigators in the United States," New York's former Second Deputy Commissioner of Detectives George S. Dougherty. "Certainly none is better qualified," the editors wrote, "to shrewdly draw deductions from the clues and evidence available to students of the famous Frank case." Citing evidence available at trial and subsequently, Dougherty explained why he was "absolutely convinced of the innocence of Leo M. Frank."[86] The constant reminders from the North that Atlanta's law enforcement agencies were corrupt or incompetent could not have helped the Frank team win local support in Georgia.

By far the most inflammatory investigator called to revisit the Frank case was Detective William J. Burns. As MacLean points out, Frank's defenders failed to consider the consequences of involving "the most notorious union-busting private detective in the country" as an advocate for this condemned man.[87] This latest evidence of insensitivity was just part of a pattern of apparent indifference to the working poor of Atlanta. When Frank's lawyers hired Burns with money they had raised through the Frank defense fund, the detective discovered new evidence, collected new affidavits, and persuaded prosecution witnesses to repudiate their earlier testimony, which they claimed had been coerced. Frank's supporters saw that Burns's work found an audience in Northern newspapers, but in the South, Burns was nearly lynched by Atlantans who resented his interference. As Herbert Asbury later recalled, Burns "only succeeded in intensifying public feeling against Frank."[88] Frank's supporters seem to have misunderstood that even in the face of strong international support, they would not convert Georgians to their side unless they actively worked to persuade them not only that Frank was innocent, but also that Georgia would be ill-served by Frank's death.

Given the powerful legacy of postwar resentment in the South, the failure of Frank's advocates to appreciate the significance of Georgia sentiments was a grave miscalculation indeed. Their very success in shaping public opinion elsewhere in the country became a liability when they neglected to work on Southern attitudes. Whether or not Georgians considered all pro-Frank press coverage to be the result of a Jewish conspiracy, as Tom Watson did, they did understand the national press campaign as yet another episode of Northern interference in their own local affairs. Eugene Debs surely only alienated Georgians when he cited the South for its appalling judicial record. The South, he declaimed, "is blinded by race prejudice, one of the inheritances of chattel slavery. There is no law and no justice for the black man in that section. I have traveled over it long enough to know. The bare suspicion of guilt is sufficient warrant to lynch a 'nigger.' It is in this atmosphere and environment that Frank, 'the damned Jew,' has been railroaded."[89]

Debs, who by 1914 had become a hero of the working class for having served time in prison for standing up to the railroad in 1895, might easily have used his influence with Atlanta's factory workers to persuade them that Frank was not an enemy of the working poor. Instead of forging a class-based alliance with these people who were so responsive to Tom Watson's populist appeals, Debs merely highlighted the regional and racial tensions that were making the Frank case so explosive. When we recall that the Ku Klux Klan began as an extralegal institution devoted to protecting the authority of local law over federal intervention, it is hard to escape the conclusion that the lynching of Leo Frank was yet another episode in the long history of regional rebellion that began with the Civil War, endured through Reconstruction, and persisted into the early decades of the twentieth century—and more, that Georgians saw the national press campaign on Frank's behalf as yet another imposition of the federal government's will on an unreconstructed South. All the bitterness of this impoverished region surged up against the idea that Northerners were once again imposing their values on Georgia.

Seeing its work only in narrow legal terms rather than in the larger symbolic and emotional terms that many Georgians brought to the case, the Frank clemency campaign—in spite of its modest accomplishment of a commutation of sentence to life in prison—perhaps felt itself too successful, too confident of the influence it exerted upon Georgia's leading newspapers. Finding themselves eventually capable of changing the verdict against Frank, they grew indifferent to, even contemptuous of, the sentiments of the commoners in Georgia who felt themselves strongly attached to Mary Phagan and the life she represented, and who believed that Frank was guilty of her murder.[90] Leo Frank's allies made no effort to win these people over; while mass demonstrations on Frank's behalf were taking place all over the nation, they were conspicuously absent in Georgia, where most protests were organized by people who wanted to see Frank executed. When Frank's allies disregarded the people of Georgia, whose rural values invested Mary Phagan with powerful iconic meaning, they grew careless and endangered Frank's life. No one will ever know, for instance, what rage might have been provoked by Governor John Slaton's wry comment in his commutation order, that "there is every probability that the virtue of Mary Phagan was not violated on the 26th day of April."[91] We do know that Tom Watson was deeply angered: "Shame upon those white men who desecrate the murdered child's grave," he declaimed, "*and who add to the torture of the mother that lost her,* by saying Mary was an unclean little wanton."[92] To a grieving populace that believed in the symbolic purity of Mary Phagan, such words as Slaton's may well have seemed like a renewed sexual assault, and Watson's outraged rejoinder only chafed their wounds.

Rather than recognizing and trying to heal those wounds, and perhaps spurred on by their success at the national and international levels and encouraged by the many disparaging things being said of Georgians in the national press, the Frank team accepted and even endorsed the very elitism that had enraged the commoners of Atlanta. As MacLean notes, Frank's attorney had "described those who believed his client guilty as 'ignorant people,' referred to the courtroom audience as 'that gang of wolves' and 'a vicious mob,' and characterized one white worker who had testified against Frank as 'the ugliest, dirtiest reptile . . . [whose] habitat was in the filth.'"[93] Throughout the trial, Frank's lawyers pitted themselves against not only the prosecution witnesses but also the entire community from which these witnesses were drawn, the community that also included the much-lamented murder victim herself. As Hasian explains, the defense team "portrayed themselves as progressives who were trying to maintain law and order in a wilderness of hate and prejudice."[94] Satisfied with the voices of the nation's editorial pages, Frank's friends not only made no effort to appeal to the masses, particularly in rural Georgia, and to convince the world that the working poor of Georgia opposed Frank's execution, but they even actively antagonized this population. They displayed a good measure of contempt for these very people, and in doing so they damaged their cause in Georgia even as they built a coalition of influential people across the nation.

VI. LYNCH LAW AND POPULAR JUSTICE

Given how seldom white people were lynched in the deep South, it might not seem surprising that Frank's supporters made no greater effort to change the sentiments of Georgia's rural masses; perhaps they could not imagine Frank's eventual fate at the hands of a lynch mob. And yet, even without the help of hindsight we may say that Frank's lynching was always a strong possibility. To read the contemporaneous press accounts of the case is to see that, to people who disapproved of the judicial outcome, lynching was almost a trope for sloppy justice. Critics of the guilty verdict called Frank's death sentence a legal lynching. The Rabbi Stephen Wise contended that since "the spirit of the law was violated in his trial from beginning to end, if Leo Frank be hanged, he will have been lynched just as truly as if he had been slain by the mob within or without the courtroom."[95] The New York World described the verdict as "more the due process of lynch law than the due process of statute law,"[96] while the Atlanta Journal argued that Frank's "death without a fair trial and legal conviction will amount to judicial murder."[97] After Frank's actual lynching the New Republic described the man's entire treatment, with the exception of Governor Slaton's commutation order, as "one prolonged lynching."[98]

At the same time, those who feared that Frank's wealthy and influential connections would eventually buy his release claimed that Georgians must rise up and defend their laws against Northern interference, and they saw lynch law as a legitimate if desperate legal process. As W. Fitzhugh Brundage notes, Southern whites defended the legitimacy of extralegal violence by appealing to American traditions. "Popular justice, they boasted, reflected the vigor of both democratic and communal values in the South; lynchers defended, rather than endangered, civilization."[99] Threats were construed as political lobbying; as the Chicago Tribune reported, "The telephones of the police and the solicitor general were kept busy during the investigation and trial with the threats of an outraged populace that 'unless you hang the Jew we will get you.'"[100] When the lynching was finally performed, the New York Times reported that "Frank was told from the start that he was to be executed, as the courts had directed that he be, and every effort was made by the 'vigilance committee' to see that the 'legal hanging,' as they termed the lynching, was carried out in an orderly manner."[101] If the campaign for a commutation was successful with the governing elite beyond Georgia, then, it ultimately failed because those who saw themselves as representative Georgians were not convinced that Frank was innocent. Indeed, they only saw in Leo Frank the arrogance of one who had access to national spheres of power that excluded them as rural Southerners.[102] Given that wealthy and internationally recognized people were lobbying on the other side, moreover, they did not believe that they possessed the political power to lobby successfully for the fulfillment of their wishes. And they refused to believe that it was their lot to accept what they saw as injustice in the executive branch.[103] In taking the law irrevocably into their own hands, they proved that, to keep its authority, law must build coalitions among the diverse groups that constitute "public sentiment." Just as Reconstruction had failed because the federal government forced its policies on Southerners without attempting to win their consent, so too in the case of Leo Frank: a technical legal victory ended disastrously because Frank's supporters failed to distinguish law from public sentiments, or to appreciate the power of the latter.

It is hard to escape the conclusion that the Frank defense campaign's miscalculations were the more damaging in comparison to the unapologetically populist propaganda campaigns being launched by those who wanted to see Frank executed. Leo Frank's Southern enemies deliberately drove a wedge between Southerners who saw themselves as ordinary and oppressed people—those who labored long hours to make ends meet—and those who controlled Southern capital. Atlanta's popular folk singer, Fiddlin' John Carson, emerged at the center of the anti-Frank movement and appeared daily throughout Atlanta, singing variations of "The Ballad of Mary Phagan" and even selling sheet music. One of those ballads reminds audiences that Phagan's grieving mother lost not just a daughter but a source of income: "For Mary was her sole support / With her little pay."[104] Another version contains an upbeat call to action:

> Now come all you good people
> Wherever you may be;
> Suppose that little Mary
> Belonged to you or me.[105]

C. P. Connolly reported that the lyrics to this song "sold like hot cakes" on the streets of Atlanta.[106] Tom Watson, who joined the movement to ensure Frank's execution and eventually became its most aggressive and intolerant voice, had begun his political career as a grassroots populist and was well versed in the tactics of a populist campaign. Watson's weekly and monthly newspapers, in which he editorialized about the Frank case, tended to be read aloud and passed from household to household.[107] Since the anti-Frank campaign actively fostered the impression that urban newspapers were an elitist medium where a poor person could find no justice, the propaganda generated by the movement took full advantage of oral forms: folk songs, mass meetings, and speeches. Watson and others waged a relentless propaganda campaign that galvanized many poor white workers in Atlanta, arousing their anger and calling them to action. Meanwhile, hardly any rallies in support of Frank were staged in the South. All the songs and poems about the murder and trial were apparently written by Mary Phagan's advocates and concluded that Frank deserved his death sentence. In the words of one ballad,

> Judge Roan passed the sentence;
> He passed it very well;
> The Christian doers of heaven
> Sent Leo Frank to hell . . .[108]

Frank's party refused to use these weapons, thinking that their salvation would come from the judicial or executive branch of government, not from the Georgia populace.

As we have seen in the Haymarket case, populist oral forms owed much of their success to the collective spirit they helped to generate. Whereas the authors of mainstream newspaper articles and editorials tended to be anonymous and to seem remote, populist messages delivered in songs and other oral forms seemed to come from the people themselves. Tom Watson highlighted his own connection to the people in his unmistakable editorial persona, where he directly appealed to his readers. In going over the evidence of the murder case, for instance, he lamented that Mary Phagan was "DEAD! Dead in her tender youth, in the flower of her maidenhood, in her glory of virginal purity—dead, as *your* little girl may be, some day, if other Leo Franks escape just punishment, *through the machinations of Big Money.*"[109] While appearing to his readers as one of them, Watson also attempted to expose the owners and editors of the major dailies as part of an elite group that had no sympathy for Georgia's working poor.

Although he exaggerated the Jewish conspiracy, Watson was correct in perceiving that Frank's allies wished to remain largely anonymous, hiding behind influential institutions. Unlike Watson, who understood that his effectiveness depended on his ability to identify himself with "the people," the many assimilated Jews who supported Leo Frank worried that mass protest meetings would identify their cause with an immigrant population from which they had worked to disassociate themselves. Frank was himself an assimilated German Jew who impressed Abraham Cahan, the editor of the Yiddish-language *Forward*, as profoundly uninterested in his Judaism. Jeffrey Melnick describes Cahan's assessment of Frank:

> To introduce Frank to readers Cahan called the jailed man an "authentic German Jew," using the word "yehudi" to describe him. In Hebrew "yehudi" simply means "Jew," but in Yiddish it means "Western Jew," and often carries a scornful tone. Addressing his heavily Eastern European audience, Cahan noted that Frank's religious feeling apparently developed only in recent days, and in the manner of "Yehudim," not that "of our Jews."[110]

Though Cahan was himself a secular Jew who paid little attention to the Hebrew faith,[111] he was distressed to find Frank so little interested in the social questions relevant to his people and discouraged to see Frank denying the role of anti-Semitism in his own fate. Like many of Atlanta's German Jews, Frank was well assimilated into bourgeois Atlanta culture. He considered himself a white man in the context of the Southern judicial process and was willing at first to accept the usual course of Southern justice. Considering himself safe in a culture whose racist standards he thought affected only African Americans, Frank did not consider turning his predicament into a case for civil rights.

Whereas Atlanta's Eastern European Jews had conspicuously ghettoized themselves in the center of the city,[112] a number of Atlanta's longer-established German Jews enjoyed the privileges of the upper and middle classes. Many of these more privileged Jews, as David Levering Lewis has shown, "embraced an ideology of extreme cultural assimilation."[113] After the labor turmoil of the 1870s and 1880s, many assimilated Jews and members of other groups whose status as full Americans was not quite secure feared that rampant immigration and labor unrest would further jeopardize their full membership in American society. To fend off the effects of nativism and racism, they remained silent on many political issues and instead tried to pass unobtrusively into the mainstream. As Louis Brandeis advised in 1910, "Habits of living or of thought which tend to keep alive differences of origin or classify men according to their beliefs are inconsistent with the American ideal of brotherhood, and are disloyal."[114] Among "disloyal" thoughts was the notion that a Jew could not get a fair trial; as long as Atlanta's German Jews believed that Leo Frank, as a white man, would receive justice, they preferred to keep silent and assume that he would be treated fairly. Lindemann notes that "the characteristic response of Atlanta's Jewish establishment was to urge respect for the authorities and to express their belief that Frank would get a fair trial."[115] Even after the campaign for a new trial gained national momentum, Atlanta's German Jews "wanted as little publicity and public excitement as possible, a strictly legalistic approach, and were reticent to make an issue of anti-Semitism."[116]

Outside the South, as we have seen, mass meetings were held to protest the Frank verdict. Among the protesters in Northern cities were recent Jewish immigrants from Eastern Europe whose experiences with European socialism (and, no doubt, memories of Haymarket) committed them to outspoken acts of propaganda. These defenders of Frank "looked to mass demonstrations and popular campaigns on Frank's behalf and were lightning-quick to bring up charges of anti-Semitism in this as in other matters."[117] Meanwhile, what was true for wealthy New York Jews was also true for Frank's community of established Atlanta Jews: they were "ashamed of the appearance, the language, and the manners of the Russian Jews," according to Lucy Dawidowicz, "aghast at their political ideologies, and terrified lest the world crumble by a mad act of a Jewish radical."[118] Jacob Schiff, a prominent New York Jew and Leo Frank defender who had pleaded with Jewish leaders of the Lower East side to urge immigrants not to speak Yiddish to their children and complained of the noisy militancy of Eastern European Jews, clearly preferred that the Frank campaign take place quietly and be ostensibly driven by the newspaper industry rather than by individuals and immigrant groups.[119]

Although many socialists, particularly in Northern cities, stood up to defend Leo Frank, the condemned man's clear desire to accept American conditions as they were in 1914 and the efforts of his local Jewish advocates to be unobtrusive in their attempts to save his life may have finally harmed his cause with local Southerners. Unlike the Haymarket anarchists, who deliberately martyred themselves to a purpose that they felt passionately about and that they had clearly spent much of their working lives studying, Leo Frank had little to say about the system of American justice; nor was there anything he could say against the factory system in Georgia. Louis Marshall, confident that Frank's case was "legally and morally impregnable," was convinced that Frank would be acquitted.[120] And so the Frank defense team relied on the jury system, relying as well on the local Southern tradition that a black suspect will always be convicted before a white suspect; they played upon this racism and they put their faith in the benefits of whiteness when they might have tried a little harder to win allies from the working poor who regarded them as enemies. Afraid of propaganda—which, they feared, had come to be associated with foreigners, radicals, and mass protest movements like the one for labor reform and which would call attention to their alien roots—they took a more timid approach, allowing the opposition to Frank to monopolize the oral, ephemeral, and immediate forms of propaganda like mass meetings, songs, speeches, and verse, while they relied on printed arguments in the national press. Even after Frank's lynching, when public outrage across the nation had peaked, the Jewish community refused to use the occasion to raise public awareness about issues that called for reform. When in September 1915 two filmmakers approached Frank's widow about using moving pictures to bring the case more immediately to the public eye, Lucille Frank refused.[121]

While Frank's allies in the South kept a low profile and relied on mainstream daily newspapers and the courts, Tom Watson took full advantage of populist forms and arguments to convince his fellow Georgians that Frank was guilty and deserved execution—and, what was more, that the people of Georgia deserved to see that execution carried out. What resonated most strongly for many poor Georgians was Watson's populist argument that an outraged public has the moral and legal authority to take the law into its own hands when its elected officials become incapable of executing the laws they were entrusted to uphold. Appealing, as we have seen before, to American revolutionary leaders, Watson asserted again and again that democratic power rests in the hands of the people. "When mobs are no longer possible," he declared, "liberty will be dead."[122] It may have been a reactionary argument, as Nancy MacLean has noted, but it was a compelling one for many people.[123] Even the mayor of Atlanta defended Frank's lynching, calling it the enactment of the people's will and a just penalty for an unspeakable crime.[124]

By juxtaposing the Haymarket case with the Leo Frank case, we can begin to consider the relative efficacy of public protest movements. Unlike Frank's Jewish friends and family in Atlanta, the Haymarket anarchists were unwilling to assimilate into a society whose flaws they readily identified. This is not to say they were hostile to American society in its ideal version: they took for granted the ideas of

Thomas Paine, Thomas Jefferson, Henry David Thoreau, and John Brown, and until they learned otherwise they assumed that the American people's veneration of these heroes implied approval of their revolutionary principles. But they also wanted to make American society conform to the revolutionary ideals of the European social- ists they had studied and in some cases known personally. In some ways their lack of access to mainstream publications may have been an advantage, for it forced them to use the more immediate and often more powerful oral forms of propaganda. Twenty-seven years later Mary Phagan's Marietta townspeople, urged on by Tom Watson, demonstrated the power of these same oral forms to maneuver public sen- timents using the arguments that had once powered a revolution. Frank's allies, meanwhile—reluctant to make themselves conspicuous—provide a case study in ineffective propaganda campaigns.

Had they been less afraid of xenophobia, regional and racial prejudice, what might have changed? If they had politicized Leo Frank's murder trial, as the Hay- market anarchists had done, they certainly would have had to answer for the deplorable conditions in the Atlanta Pencil Factory and in other local factories. But in doing so they may have been able to force the public to confront larger questions about the Southern economy and about nativism as a displacement of economic troubles, and they may have been able to begin a genuine and productive discussion about labor reform that could have united Northern and Southern laborers. They might have challenged Tom Watson's xenophobic populism, offering instead an alliance between factory workers of the South and the racially diverse labor move- ment of the North. Instead, they allowed demagogues to pit poor and oppressed Southern workers against Jews and foreigners, thus ensuring that neither group would create an opportunity to better its economic conditions.

Chapter Four

NO OTHER
REMEDY

*Community Awakening and
the Lynching of Emmett Till*

T he tragic outcome of the Leo Frank case taught Americans fighting racial violence the importance of inviting large-scale community involvement in social
questions. When a fourteen-year-old black boy was lynched in 1955, the opponents
of racial violence turned once more to popular literary forms in order to reach people
in ways that mainstream newspapers did not always allow.

Those who had hoped to save Leo Frank's life, as we have seen, were unable to
build enduring alliances that crossed racial, class, and regional lines. After Frank's
lynching, however, disillusioned citizens who deplored the brutal administration of
Southern justice acknowledged the wide-ranging effects of every incident of racial
violence and began building the coalitions that had eluded Frank's allies. Labor
leaders in the North concerned themselves with the economic roots of Southern violence and spoke out against lynchings while trying to unify the working poor of all
races, particularly in the feudal South, still dominated by a sharecropping system
that differed only nominally from slavery. Many American Jews, understanding the
connection between racial violence directed at blacks and their own tenuous hold on
civil rights, joined the NAACP and worked to enact federal legislation to discourage
mob violence and vigorously punish lynchings when they occurred.

Jack Greenberg was one such crusader, a staff attorney with the NAACP Legal
Defense and Educational Fund who argued many civil rights cases before the US

LE DROIT DE VIVRE, PARIS
OCTOBER 1, 1955

NEVER FORGET THAT ONE WHITE NOTE IS WORTH TWO BLACK ONES.

— Et n'oubliez pas qu'une blanche vaut deux noires ! (Dessin de Grambert.)

Editorial cartoon, *Le Droit de Vivre*, October 1, 1955.
Courtesy of *Ligue Internationale Contre le Racisme et
l'Antisemitisme (LICA)*, International League against
Racism and Anti-Semitism

Supreme Court, including the 1954 *Brown v. Board of Education* case that resulted in the desegregation of public education. When Greenberg discussed the lack of a federal law against lynching in 1959, he noted that "often the sole available protection [from racially motivated violence] for minorities is vigorous enforcement of ordinary state laws forbidding violence against the person. It is probably redundant to note that where prosecutors will not prosecute or juries will not convict, there usually is no other remedy than the exercise of political power and general community awakening."[1]

I. THE MURDER AND THE ACQUITTAL

Greenberg was writing just four years after the notorious 1955 murder of Emmett Till, the fourteen-year-old Chicago schoolboy who was brutally beaten, shot, weighted down with a rusty cotton gin, and thrown in the Tallahatchie River while visiting his sharecropping relatives in Money, Mississippi. The story of Emmett Till's murder is still familiar to many Americans, not simply because this kind of brutality against a child was unusual even in the Jim Crow South, but because the case was widely covered in the international press at a time when nearly 65 percent of American households owned televisions.[2] Those who read newspapers saw the Associated Press photograph of the boy's mother, Mamie Bradley, as she met his coffin at the Illinois Central Train Terminal; watching television they saw footage of the three-day public viewing of the boy's bloated and unretouched body in Chicago. They heard, too, about the antics in the segregated courtroom where Roy Bryant and J. W. Milam stood trial for Till's murder, and they saw the men's triumphant poses before newspaper photographers after an all-white jury acquitted them.[3] When Jack Greenberg referred to "juries [that] will not convict," he was perhaps thinking of the Till murder trial above all others. "The fairness of the criminal law," he wrote, "is conditioned by community attitudes," which are in turn related "to political forces."[4] If a jury, "the most unfettered of all judicial bodies in that it may acquit for any or no reason," decides against conviction, then the best response, according to Greenberg and hundreds of other outraged witnesses of the Emmett Till case, was to undertake a systematic community awakening.[5] What David Halberstam has called "the first great media event of the civil rights movement," the Emmett Till murder was just about unprecedented among lynchings in the intensity of the public scrutiny it attracted and, consequently, the degree and scope of the rage it generated.[6] Like many other murder trials we have been considering, the official jury verdict did not end public discussions of the matter. As an *Ebony* reporter assigned to the trial recalled thirty-one years later, the verdict ended only one stage of the Till case. If the official legal battle against Till's murderers ended with an acquittal for murder and a failure to indict for kidnapping, the fight for full civil rights for black Americans in the South was just getting underway.[7] The Till case "was not the end," as Clotye Murdock Larsson later recalled, but "rather a terrible beginning."[8]

Although, as Jacqueline Goldsby has shown, media attention in the case was more intense than for any previous lynching, public opinion followed the familiar pattern that we have observed in the Leo Frank case. Initially, most Southern newspapers strongly condemned the slaying, which they understood as an isolated incident. "The nation was shocked at the fury of a senseless Mississippi crime," wrote Tom Etheridge of the *Jackson Daily News*.[9] Political leaders, too, deplored the slaying; Governor Hugh White warned that Mississippi "will not tolerate" such deeds.[10] But as Northern reporters, labor unions, and the NAACP condemned the crime as a lynching rather than a murder and attributed it to the widespread disregard for black lives in the Jim Crow South, these same individuals came to bristle at the words of meddling outsiders and to resent that Northerners insisted on identifying Mississippi politicians, courts, clergy, and newspapers with the violent criminals responsible for Till's murder. Though NAACP executive secretary Roy Wilkins perhaps put the case more strongly than others, his charge was widely echoed by indignant people all over the world: "it would appear that the State of Mississippi has decided to maintain white supremacy by murdering children."[11] Meanwhile, as shame over the murder turned to resentment of outside interference in what many regarded as a local crime, the majority of Mississippi whites, particularly white sharecroppers in Money, where the two men lived, became more interested in defending the murderers than in seeking justice for a black child from Chicago who had provoked such widespread sympathy, indignation, and publicity. The defendants, at first unable to find a lawyer willing to represent them, were eventually overwhelmed by the assistance of their white neighbors: all five lawyers practicing in Sumner offered to represent the men *pro bono*, and a defense fund garnered an estimated $10,000.[12]

Although the official trial took place during five days in September, the Till case in fact involved three separate trials: the first, the judgment of the two white men (and perhaps other unidentified accomplices)[13] that found Emmett Till guilty of several indiscretions worthy of death; the second, the courtroom trial of these alleged lynchers, covered by the international press; and the third, the court of public opinion, which—to judge by the documentaries, poems, and books still being issued on the Till case—is still deliberating on the meaning of Till's murder and the events it generated. If recent events are any indication, moreover, these trials cannot be kept distinct: with the release of Keith Beauchamp's 2002 documentary about Till's murder, the United States Justice Department reopened the case in 2004.[14]

The first trial was private and subject to dispute: whoever witnessed what happened to Emmett Till in J. W. Milam's tool shed, where the boy was taken after being abducted from his grandfather's cabin, only Milam and Bryant ever told the story, and they did so only after they had been cleared of murder charges. Emmett Till's crime has never been fully established, apart from the allegation that he insulted Carolyn Bryant, owner of the store in Money, where he had gone to buy bubble gum. Did the Chicago boy whistle at Mrs. Bryant, as several of his cousins at different times recalled?[15] Or was the whistle, as Mamie Bradley maintained, just the habit of a boy who had been left with a stutter after a bout of polio—a boy whose mother advised him to whistle when the words wouldn't come? If he was indeed showing off to his Southern friends, proving that he was capable of flirting with a white woman, did he call her "baby," as another cousin remembered?[16] Did he ask her for a date? Did he grab her by the waist and use "unprintable" language, as Carolyn Bryant testified in court?[17] Was he being playful or threatening?

What happened in the store has remained in dispute, but in some ways it hardly matters: according to Till's murderers, they lynched the boy not because of what he said to Mrs. Bryant but because of his conduct in J. W. Milam's barn four days later. In an interview granted after their acquittal, Bryant and Milam claimed that they had only meant to scare Emmett Till. As Milam explained, "I didn't intend to kill the nigger when we went and got him—just whip him and chase him back up yonder." But Till boasted about having white girlfriends. "I counted pictures o' *three* white gals in his pocketbook before I burned it," Milam said. "What else could I do? No use lettin' him get no bigger!"[18]

If lynching is generally understood as a racially motivated form of extralegal punishment—punishment exacted by avengers who do not trust the courts to issue swift and correct vengeance—then it is clear that whatever the specific infringement that called for his death, Emmett Till's crime involved white fears—and, presumably, black aspirations—regarding miscegenation. Perhaps Bryant and Milam believed they were protecting a specific woman's purity, or perhaps they hoped to defend white female sexual purity in general, particularly during an era when, they believed, people outside of the South had lost their regard for racial boundaries. But lynchings often resemble their official counterparts, capital trials, in the sense that the pursuit of "justice" (however inapt that word in the case of racist mob violence) involves more than the specific crime written on the bill of indictment. In Till's case, his conduct toward Carolyn Bryant was only the pretext for his murder; in the deep South both influential leaders and poor whites like Bryant and Milam were already seething over larger social crimes brought on by the federal government. In an era when, as Louis Burnham remarked in 1955, "the forward surge of the Negro people is the most distinctive and progressive feature of Southern politics," Southern blacks trying to exercise their right to vote provoked white racists to resentment and terrorism.[19] Earlier that summer, two separate Mississippi mobs had killed black men for presuming to vote. On May 6, the Reverend George Lee had declared, "If God gives me grace and I'm living on the second day of August, I'm going to march boldly to the courthouse and register" to vote; the next day he was shot to death.[20] On August 13, Lamar Smith, active in the black voter registration effort, was shot in broad daylight in front of the Brookhaven courthouse. Three months after Emmett Till's murder, Gus Courts, head of the Belzoni, Mississippi, NAACP and another leader in the voting rights movement, was shot and nearly killed. None of these crimes was ever prosecuted.[21] The Belzoni sheriff investigating the Lee murder failed even to make an arrest, explaining that the shotgun fragments found in Lee's head "could have been fillings from his teeth."[22] The deep reluctance of local law officials to prosecute these crimes suggests their eagerness to obey the many political leaders who advised whites to resist federal intervention and prevent black citizens from exercising the rights granted them by the federal government.[23]

Emmett Till, of course, was not old enough to vote, but he represented both the federal judiciary's interest in Southern race relations and the defiant belief among many white supremacists, including Mississippi Circuit Court Judge Tom Brady, that the Supreme Court had no means of enforcing its decrees "in the face of a solid adverse public opinion."[24] Till's presence in rural Mississippi aggravated fears of a fully desegregated and miscegenated South. As Whitaker notes, "Nowhere does the fear based on sex show up more clearly than in the disputes surrounding the 1954

Supreme Court decision."[25] Till was murdered, as many have noted, during the summer preceding what was supposed to be the first school year in a newly desegregated South. In May of that year, the US Supreme Court had banned segregation in public schools in the now famous case of *Brown v. the Board of Education*. Mississippi Circuit Court Judge Tom P. Brady not only denounced the decision as the judiciary's usurpation of "the sacred privilege and right of the respective states of this union to educate their youth," "the greatest travesty of the American Constitution and jurisprudence in the history of this nation,"[26] but even encouraged Southern state governments and private citizens alike to "prevent the enforcement of the Supreme Court's edict as quickly as possible."[27] Brady's pamphlet, *Black Monday* (a reference to the *Brown* decision), was widely distributed throughout the South, where resentful whites, forming White Citizens' Councils, sought to prevent implementation of the Brown decision. Though Milam and Bryant were not members of such a group, they seem to have shared the white supremacist ideology being promulgated all over Mississippi. Four years after their trial, one of Bryant and Milam's defense attorneys speculated that his clients "wouldn't have killed [Till] except for Black Monday [the *Brown* decision]. The Supreme Court of the United States is responsible for the murder of Emmett Till."[28] Although Judge Brady later confessed that the Till murder "upset me very much," the violence meted out to the Chicago youth who did not understand the ways of the South was entirely predictable given the climate of hate and hostility that arose in the aftermath of *Brown*. Indeed, just the year before Till's murder Brady himself had anticipated and nearly encouraged something very similar: "If trouble is to come," he wrote,

> we can predict how it will rise. . . . The fulminate which will discharge the blast will be the young negro schoolboy, or veteran, who has no conception of the difference between a mark and a fathom. The supercilious, glib young negro, who has sojourned in Chicago or New York, and who considers the counsel of his elders archaic, will perform an obscene act, or make an obscene remark, or a vile overture or assault upon some white girl. For they will reason, "Has not the Supreme Court abolished segregation in the schools, swimming pools and passenger trains? Is not the Federal Government behind us and will it not protect us? We need but assert ourselves and abolish every vestige of segregation and racial differences." This is the reasoning which produces riots, bloodshed, raping and revolutions.[29]

Laying the blame upon the Supreme Court, Brady all but urged his fellow white Southerners to do what they could to resist the court's order to desegregate the South.

Although we cannot know what Bryant and Milam were thinking as they beat and shot Emmett Till, they later described their violent act in terms of a larger battle between Mississippi and the federal government. As J. W. Milam explained to William Bradford Huie after his acquittal, the Chicago boy represented federal intervention in the South and reminded his murderers of the desperate measures necessary to preserve their Jim Crow way of life. "I just decided," he explained,

Milam

it was time a few people got put on notice. As long as I live and I can do anything about it, niggers are gonna stay in their place. Niggers ain't gonna vote where I live. If they did, they'd control the government. They ain't gonna go to school with my kids. And when a nigger even gets close to mentioning sex with a white woman, he's tired o'livin.' I'm likely to kill him. Me and my folks fought for this country, and we've got some rights. I stood there in that shed and listened to that nigger throw that poison at me, and I just made up my mind. "Chicago boy," I said, "I'm tired of 'em sending your kind down here to stir up trouble. Goddam you, I'm going to make an example of you—just so everybody can know how me and my folks stand."[30]

Whatever their private reasons for murdering Till—and whether they had even intended to kill him at the outset—in this widely circulated interview Bryant and Milam confirmed for the world what had already been suspected. In the words of the *Cleveland Call and Post*, "The lynching of Emmett Louis Till is but one more casualty in Mississippi's defiant, seditious campaign of rebellion against federal authority. Once sly and submerged, this daily sedition has flared white hot since the United States Supreme Court outlawed segregated schools, then issued no specific formula for compliance with the edict."[31]

As we shall see, opponents of this Jim Crow sedition took their fight to an international battlefield, seeking to change the ways of the South by first changing people's hearts, and then rewriting the law. Although they disagreed emphatically with President Eisenhower, who refused to intervene in the Till proceeding, calling it a local matter, and who insisted that "coercive law" was "powerless to bring about complete compliance" where "the great mass of public opinion is in bitter opposition," they did recognize that public opinion would have to be changed in order to win this latter-day Civil War.[32] Warning in 1949 that "the efforts to achieve full citizenship status must not be concentrated on a single front," Julius J. Adams had endorsed an "educational, political, economic, philosophical, psychological and social" operation.[33] In 1956 his wife, Olive Arnold Adams, observed that African Americans had not kept pace with racist whites in "establishing the kind of educational program and propaganda machinery that would equip us psychologically and philosophically for greater mass participation in American life."[34] Holding her own race partly responsible for the outbreak of violence throughout the South after *Brown*, Adams wrote her pamphlet on the Emmett Till lynching in order to redress the imbalance, "to demonstrate how cleverly planned has been the propaganda that has for so long kept us second-class citizens in our own country."[35] Other pamphlets followed as critics of the Emmett Till case began to understand that private citizens would have to undertake the difficult project of changing hearts and minds.

International journalists began the process even before a verdict in the murder trial was rendered, as they reported daily from the Sumner, Mississippi, courthouse where an all-white jury heard testimony in a segregated courtroom. Whatever the outcome of the criminal trial would be, these journalists gave the world an opportunity to witness the ways of Southern courtrooms when white men stood trial for the murder of a black person. Many journalists who had traveled from outside the South were shocked by what they saw. I. F. Stone, for instance, noted that the sight of the sheriff greeting black reporters with a racial epithet was one of a series of scenes that "imprint themselves unforgettably."[36] A United Press correspondent reported Sheriff Strider's explanation for segregating journalists: "We haven't mixed so far down here and we don't intend to."[37] A *Jet* reporter noted that the judge "perhaps unwittingly set the pattern for what would be acceptable courtroom conduct by uncapping a Coca-Cola and sipping it while the jury was being selected. The gesture of informality apparently delighted two spectators present, for they too decided to quench their thirsts, promptly opened and drank some cans of beer without being rebuked by bailiffs or the court."[38] While Bryant and Milam stood trial for murder, the world was judging the larger culture that bore a large responsibility for their deeds; this unofficial world court would soon issue its own verdict on Southern justice.

II. LITERARY PROTESTS

Unlike the defenders of Leo Frank, who hoped that by keeping a low profile and suppressing their accusations of anti-Semitism they might more effectively change the minds of white Southerners, people who sought justice in the Till lynching believed that they must reach the widest possible audience, and they did not shy away from angry and impassioned attempts to awaken the world to the crimes of Mississippi. Christopher Metress argues that among African American writers of imaginative literature, "a new type of jury has convened," one that continues to try the case to this day.[39] Responses to the case were not limited to black writers, nor to the works of famous and established literary figures. As in previous murder cases we have seen, many pamphlets and broadsides were published by individuals and organizations and were distributed widely at public gatherings. The NAACP organized a series of speaking tours featuring among others Mamie Bradley, Roy Wilkins, A. Philip Randolph, Medgar Evers, Representative Charles Diggs (a black Congressman from Michigan who witnessed the Milam and Bryant murder trial), and Ruby Hurley, an NAACP field officer who investigated the Till murder.[40]

Theatrical productions were also staged. Although the texts of many of these plays are no longer extant, we can guess at their ideological bent by noting the performers and organizers. Soon after the verdict was rendered, the Ohio Labor Youth League staged a play based on the case. Performed at the Jewish Cultural Club of Cleveland, the play suggests that Jews and communists felt they had a stake in the search for justice in this case. Wade Dente's play, *A Good Place to Raise a Boy*, was performed in New York, probably in 1956. Although the text of this play, too, has apparently been lost, a promotional flyer suggests its socialist slant:

> The awakening of the Negro in Mississippi, the Poor Whites becoming aware of their plight as equal to the Negro; this is the story the author unfolds, in making a literary epic of the EMMETT TILL STORY. The whole story was never told in the newspapers. Unless this story is told, the valiant efforts of the few Negroes and Poor

whites struggling in the South will be useless. That's why everyone who hates despots, who has ever felt the boot of Racial Suppression and Extinction MUST SEE "A GOOD PLACE TO RAISE A BOY."[41]

We know nothing of two other plays, no longer extant, except what we can infer of the writers and performers. Richard Davidson, author of *Mississippi*, which was performed in New York in 1956, also wrote two poems about the case that he published in *The Daily Worker*. A Jewish poet and playwright and member of the Communist party—which actively protested the lynching of Till and the acquittal of his killers—Davidson was a regular contributor to labor and communist periodicals. Although we know just as little about the 1956 play *What Can You Say to Mississippi?* we do know that its stars, Ossie Davis and Ruby Dee, were deeply concerned about the civil rights of their fellow black Americans, and we can guess that this play, too, was a deliberate propaganda effort. Ossie Davis, after all, had contributed to a $100,000 reward for information leading to the conviction of those responsible for a quadruple lynching in Monroe, Georgia, in 1946.[42]

We can surmise that these plays, like many early literary responses to the Till case, were overtly political, expressing outrage and the contention that the episode was not an isolated event but part of a systematic effort to deny an entire race of people their human and civil rights. Louis Burnham's claim that "[f]rom one end of the South to the other, . . . a public climate has been created in which a Negro's life is worth no more than a white man's whim" was repeated by writers who identified Mississippi as the agent of this terror, even in some cases neglecting to mention the specific individuals involved.[43] Langston Hughes's poem "Mississippi—1955," written on the day the verdict was issued and first published in the *Chicago Defender*, is dedicated "To the Memory of Emmett Till" but focuses on a generalized, almost timeless terror in Mississippi. Two voices speak, the first uttering a lament, "That tears and blood / Should mix like rain / And terror come again / To Mississippi." The second voice immediately chides the first for forgetting that terror has always been a way of life in Mississippi:

> *Come again?*
> *Where has terror been?*
> *On vacation? Up North?*
> *In some other section*
> *Of the nation,*
> *Lying low, unpublicized?*

The first voice, corrected, repeats but revises its earlier pronouncement:

> Oh, what sorrow,
> Pity, pain,
> That tears and blood
> Should mix like rain
> In Mississippi!

And terror, fetid hot,
Yet clammy cold
Remain.

These two voices allow Hughes to express both lamentation for the death of the unnamed Till and rage over the quick and ineffective trial, a trial whose predictable outcome was part of Mississippi's systematic terror against blacks.[44] Apart from the dedication, the poem does not mention Till by name or refer explicitly to the crime or the trial; it depends upon an audience that is familiar with the case and does not need to be reminded of the specific facts that provoked the poem.

Earnest Wakefield Stevens's "Blood on Mississippi," published after the verdict in the *Cleveland Call and Post* (October 15, 1955), focuses on the murderers but refrains from naming them, presenting them instead as a kind of archetype, the "Mississippi savage":

Murder always will be murder
But of all the ways to kill—
It was down right most revolting
How they slaughtered Emmett Till—

While the world looks on with a "shudder" and the speaker wonders how his country can "flood / Other lands with purer air / When its own is drenched in blood," the state of Mississippi bears the burden of guilt for this crime:

Bow your head low, Mississippi,
For the damage you have done
To the efforts of our country
In its fight for everyone.

What a mockery of Justice!
What a stinking, rotten smell!
Only down in Mississippi
Can one really prevue Hell.[45]

The balladlike meter and simple values of this poem present the Till case in the starkest possible terms: the murder was savage, the trial corrupt, and the effect of both events upon the struggle for human rights (at home and abroad) profoundly damaging.

Martha Millet's "Mississippi," which appeared in the October 1955 issue of *Masses and Mainstream*, opens with "The blood cries out / speaking truth to your lies, / Mississippi." As angry as Stevens's poem, "Mississippi" is more complicated in that, rather than seeing Till's murder as an exceptional act of violence, the poem connects his lynching with a history of Southern brutality. In the course of this long poem, which begins with the Indians naming the Mississippi river, the voice of the dead child calls out for understanding:

"What have they done?" cries the child.
"Why have they beaten me, tortured me,
wound me in wire from the cotton gin
that tore our years across,
that made them rich . . .
sunk me deep in the river of no forgetting?"

This innocent voice not only summons the reader's deepest compassion but prompts a pitiless historical examination of Mississippi. The bloated body of Emmett Till rises from a river "heavy with juices of black men / rearing a feudal domain on breaking backs." Till's blood contradicts the falsehoods of the South's official tradition, circulated in its genteel romances: "fathering forcibly young / on the black woman in the nights / your romances do not record." The speaker connects such hypocrisy with the modern-day courtroom scene, where white witnesses "swear on the Good Book still / with the same old southern flourish / that whips a slave to death / between juleps."

Like many other poets protesting the lynching and the jury verdict, Millet reminds her readers of America's ideal, with its "laws that were made *for* men, *by* men, / not in man's despite" and its

Constitution, written in blood
on drumheads on this soil
that was lava with men's
high hopes, brightness, love[.]
What have you done with equal rights
of all Americans
to life, to liberty, to
the pursuit of happiness?

Though the courtroom verdict has nullified these promises to all Americans, rendering Mississippi "a southern Third Reich" for blacks, Millet's speaker warns that "a voice of held-in power," "voice of John Brown, Thoreau, Mamie Bradley," will erupt from Mississippi, demanding retribution. As the poem nears its conclusion, the dead child's voice merges with that of the speaker, who asks, "What have they done to you, / Emmett Till—?" As the voice of the child joins the voices of outraged citizens, living and dead, we are left not exactly where we began, though the poem concludes with the same statement of hopeless anger that introduced its meditations: "The blood cries out." Having been given a larger historical context in which to understand the child's murder, Millet's readers can begin to see this episode of racial violence within the context of a much longer history of white supremacy and the exploitation of cheap labor.[46]

Other literary responses seem to call for a particular reaction to the lynching and acquittal. In both his poetry and his fiction, Langston Hughes echoed the demand of US Representative Adam Clayton Powell Jr. for a "national boycott of anything that comes from Mississippi."[47] In one of Hughes's "Simple" stories published in the

Chicago Defender, Jesse B. Semple announces to his friend, "Anybody can have the South that wants it, not me." In this story—unlike so many other Simple stories in its nearly humorless tone—these two black men discuss the Till slaying as a practical matter. The friend asks Simple, "If you were [in Mississippi], how would you go about protecting yourself?" Simple's answer is uncompromising: "in the first place, I would not be there . . . Neither would I send my child there on a vacation. But if I ever found myself there, Lord help me, I would know it was a nightmare. . . . I would at least get on to Chicago."[48] This story is a nearly unmasked political directive to avoid setting foot in Mississippi. Indeed, as Simple continues to answer his friend, his rage mounts to a pitch that we seldom see in Simple stories, and his fury is untempered by humor:

Me! ME—I can feel them fists in MY own face right now and them white men's kicks here in the middle of ME right now and their big old hairy old hands around MY throat so I cannot cry out loud, and that rope tied unto ME with that heavy old iron wheel from the cotton gin pulling ME down in that muddy old dirty old stinking sluggish old river which the water of is cold and full of mud and there ain't no mud like Mississippi mud—filthy—and there ain't no fist like the hard fist of a man that would hit a child BAM! in the face hard like they hit that boy and there ain't no heart as hard as the heart that would do a thing like that to no mother's son living! There ain't nobody so cruel in all the world as them men in Mississippi and I do not want to talk about it anymore, so do not ask me what I would do if I was there, nor how I would protect myself because I might be forced to show you, so do not ask me.

Arnold Rampersad notes that Simple's life is not "stamped with an uninflected stoicism" or "a total acceptance of the force of racism." Instead, Simple is sustained by "a philosophy and a language to match the repressive world in which [he lives], and . . . a potent weapon as well. That weapon is humor, a native wit" that constitutes "a necessary response to the morally twisted world in which racism forces blacks to live."[49] As the above passage suggests, however, the lynching of Emmett Till found Hughes and his creation without the solace of humor. Hughes's rage unadorned by literary device, he allows Jesse Semple to utter his fury while reminding people of conscience to stay out of Mississippi.

In his unpublished "Money, Mississippi, Blues," Hughes recovers his rage sufficiently to tell the plain story of a hardworking Chicago mother who sent her child to Money, Mississippi, where he was beaten beyond recognition, killed, and returned to her in a wooden box. The poem, set to music by Jobe Huntley, begins with a blunt statement:

I don't want to go to Money, honey,
not Money, Mississippi!
no, I wouldn't go to Money, honey,
down in Mississippi.
There's pity, sorrow, and pain
in Money, Mississippi.

After telling the story of Emmett Till's murder, the speaker ends where he began, drawing out the economic significance of his statement by punning on "Money":

No, I wouldn't want to go—
for no kind o'Money—
to Money, Mississippi,
not Money, Mississippi!

Like Simple, determined to stay out of Mississippi for his own safety, this speaker maintains that no bribe could bring him to Money, Mississippi. In playing on the name of the town he reminds his readers of the economic consequences for Mississippi if Northerners refuse to visit, vacation, or buy in Mississippi, and if Southern blacks migrate north.[50] As the *Cleveland Call and Post* avowed, "the best possible weapon" against Mississippi "is economic pressure. Without its half-paid plantation slaves and masses of ignorant Negroes to exploit, the Mississippi white man would have to produce, with his own sweat, his own economy."[51] Langston Hughes, too, understood the value of political and economic pressure, and he understood as well the role of art in transforming public beliefs and inspiring public actions. Although there is no indication that his song was ever recorded, Hughes did offer the proceeds of such a recording to the NAACP. Inspired by a performance of Billie Holiday's "Strange Fruit," this famous and widely admired writer considered "how many more people are reached when poetry is combined with music." Hughes explained to NAACP public relations director Henry Lee Moon that he had written "The Money, Mississippi, Blues" "in popular style" and that Huntley had supplied it with "a simple singable melody" in the hope that the song would be an effective fund-raiser and political weapon in the fight against racism in Mississippi.[52]

Although, as we have seen with the Haymarket elegies, it is difficult (and perhaps unwise) to draw too fine a distinction between political poetry and elegies, many of the early poems that responded to the Till murder seem dedicated primarily to the business of giving language to a massive public in its earliest stages of mourning. Richard Davidson's "Requiem for a Fourteen-Year-Old," which Metress identifies as the first creative work published about the Till murder, appeared in the *Daily Worker* on September 12, 1955—less than two weeks after Till's body was discovered and a week before the trial began. An effort to imagine Emmett Till as a private individual rather than a symbol of racism, "Requiem," unlike many of the poems to follow, scarcely draws on the public information about the boy that appeared repeatedly in newspaper accounts of the crime and instead focuses on the collective memories of those who knew him, those who lived in his Chicago community. The poem is set in the Chicago church where the funeral service was performed, though it makes no distinction between those inside the church and the thousands who stand on the sidewalks "listening to the words piped over speakers."[53] "The street remembers him," the speaker tells us, as he paints a picture of Till using details that eluded official newspaper reports. The voice of the speaker who narrates the event—"Ten thousand heard the service which gave him / To the cooling earth"—sometimes gives way to the voices of those who knew the boy:

> Man, he could feel the ground real easy under his shoes.
> There was a lot of fun in growing up.
> Except maybe when some damn fool made a crack
> About being colored.

The few details that are familiar to those who read the newspaper are provided not by the speaker, in some effort to write an authentic history, but by the other voices in the poem, as they discuss what they know of the boy, both from direct experience and from the newspapers:

> There is talking among the ten thousand.
> Some are crying, some with eyes closed
> Just thinking.
> A little kid wonders why and doesn't quite understand.
> A Bishop thunders words across the wires.
> People look up and listen.
>   (Nobody will forget how it happened.
>   Finding his body banged up.
>   Finding murder on the long, hot streets.
>   Somebody said he had the absolute nerve
>   Whistling at a white woman that way,
> Somebody said he was a damn young punk.)
> Others remember him.
> A nice kid with his cap slung back on his head . . .

These community voices share memories, debate the significance of Till's death, discuss what they have read in the newspapers, and try to come to some collective understanding of Emmett Till and his murder. The poem is not exactly apolitical: a parenthetical statement notes that "[a]uthorities have promised quick action in the case," while the poem ends with the ironic juxtaposition of Washington politics, where "somebody remarked / about the need for a strong colonial policy." But the poem dwells emphatically on the simple pathos of this death, the death of a lively child, murdered for his very liveliness, and the community's collective effort to remember him before laying him to rest. The poem seems, too, an appropriate first literary response—a reminder that Emmett Till was above all an individual, even if the importance of his death in the incipient civil rights movement would mean perhaps the eclipse of his personality as he became an icon in a political movement.

By the time Davidson published his second poem about the case, "A Cause for Justice" (in the *Daily Worker*, October 11, 1955), the fourteen-year-old boy had become a "cause" rather than a mere boy. By then Bryant and Milam had been acquitted, and Davidson's second poem focuses on the defendants and their families as they sit easily in the courtroom, hear the verdict ("settled in a quick hour"), then walk "casually" home.[54] The speaker dwells on the arrogance of these people, triumphant after the verdict, vain over the media attention they have attracted but irritated that outsiders think the case more significant than it is:

Mrs. XX makes an early appointment at the hairdresser,
Switches on the radio and wonders why all the excitement still goes on,
A trial is a trial and somehow the news of yesterday
Gets lost with hairstyles of tomorrow.

In between these details of the self-absorbed white families, we are reminded of the other point of view. The poem does consider the murder victim, but only in parenthetical stanzas that quietly interrupt the main action, and the child is more emblematic here than in that earlier poem. He is symbolized by a "soft grave and silent trees / And the echo of a boy's voice that is not lost in the headlines of yesterday / But is alive and clear and commands / Our attention." Emmett Till is a life cut short, the life of any boy murdered and unavenged. Like Davidson's earlier "Requiem," this poem closes with a community voicing its feelings, only here we sense that the community is larger, has become an international population that did not know the boy personally but has come to feel that he represents something larger than his own life:

We will not forget Emmett Louis Till
In tomorrow's problems or last week's good news.
We will not forget him in breakfast food
Or in the rush of winter bells.
We promise the voice that commands our attention
The earth that was his earth
Will not wilt and die in a quick hour's decision.

Our anger does not rest in a soft grave near silent trees
But grows as his young voice grows
His death becomes a part of our living flesh.
His killing a waking cry of our conscience.
His murder a country's shame and our fight
To erase that shame and to promise a rising voice
That justice will be done.

In this final promise to the dead boy, and in this exhortation to readers to join the campaign to remember Emmett Till and the larger fight for justice, Davidson's "Cause for Justice" joins a tradition of protest poems that use the death of an innocent as the instigation for a larger battle. Mary Parks's "For Emmett Till," published in the *Daily Worker* (October 13, 1955), closes with a similar gesture:

Remember him, every living thing,
Each birch tree leaf and blue bird wing—
Remember him, stars, remember him sun,
Remember him, People—he was our son.
Avenge him together, O black and white—
That the sun may rise on this monstrous night.[55]

For Mary Parks, too, Emmett Till was a symbol of the deep fissure between American ideals and practices; her poem opens with an innocent meter and content whose grimness lies in what we know is to come:

> Boyhood years are a time to sing
> Of birch tree leaf and a blue bird wing—
> For summer days and a lad exploring,
> For a high blue sky with a baseball soaring.
> Boyhood years are a time for learning,
> School each year when the leaves are turning,
> Dreaming the long bright years ahead—
> But not a time for a boy to be dead.

The simple language and joyful imagery of these opening lines come to an abrupt halt with the final line of this first stanza. The next stanzas continue in a child's vocabulary but they address the irony that Till was killed in a land that prides itself on freedom:

> The teacher spoke about Plymouth Rock,
> The Pilgrims, the Mayflower; was it to mock
> Those others who came on the slavers' ships,
> Braver than lions, tougher than whips?
> Our country threw out the English king,
> But we never threw out that other thing.
> We hold these truths, the teacher said
> To be self-evident—and dead.

By ending this stanza with the same stressed word as the first, the poet links the dead Emmett Till with the dead values of American society. To remember Till is to remember liberty, and to resurrect the dead boy in memory is, perhaps, to restore those "self-evident" truths to their place of proper authority. The emblem of a betrayed promise, Emmett Till also serves in this poem as the inspiration for the fight that will finish the Civil War, that tragic episode in American history when "terrible rivers of blood were shed / To prevent such things as this boy being dead."

Literary Pillars

William Faulkner and Robert Penn Warren

The novelist William Faulkner was so deeply disturbed by the Till lynching that he issued a press dispatch from Rome, predicting that if he and his countrymen "have reached that point in our desperate culture when we must murder children, no matter for what reason or what color, we don't deserve to survive, and probably won't."[56] Just five years earlier in his Nobel Prize acceptance speech, Faulkner had praised the human spirit, "capable of compassion and sacrifice and endurance" and proclaimed that the writer was duty-bound to write about these things. It is his privilege to help man endure by lifting his heart, by reminding him of the courage and honor and hope and pride and compassion and pity and sacrifice which have been the glory of his past. The poet's voice need not merely be the record of man, it can be one of the props, the pillars to help him endure and prevail.[57]

Some of the best literature to be written in the wake of the Emmett Till case shares Faulkner's assumption that the writer can save the human race by appealing to humankind's best virtues rather than its worst faults. While the players in the Till case—an innocent black schoolboy and two grown, armed white men—might tempt a writer to reduce the story to stark representatives of good and evil, the best writers refrained from doing any such thing. Robert Penn Warren's *Segregation: The Inner Conflict in the South* was published in 1956 after the writer returned to his native South in the aftermath of *Brown*. Although it does not explicitly address the Till lynching, it does explore the confrontations between the "angry and ambitious and disoriented and dispossessed" whites, those who, in the words of one, wish to preserve "what you might name the old Southern way, what we was raised up to,"[58] and Southern blacks, who—as one of them maintained—wished primarily to end "the constant assault on his ego."[59] Allowing black and white Southerners to share their own impressions of their cultural crisis, Warren sedulously avoided offending that "instinctive fear, on the part of black or white, that the massiveness of experience, the concreteness of life, will be violated; the fear of abstraction."[60] Instead, a picture emerges of the depth of the Southern crisis in the many statements Warren collected, the many partial portraits he sketched. Some of these seem simplistic—Warren himself acknowledges that the teenaged white boy who can only say "I hate them bastards" represents the "cliché of hate"[61]—while others seem gropingly honest, like the white man, frustrated with a race prejudice he has inherited: "it ain't our hate, it's the hate hung on us by the old folks dead and gone. Not I mean to criticize the old folks, they done the best they knew, but that hate, we don't know how to shuck it. We got that God-damn hate stuck in our craw and can't puke it up."[62] Or the white woman who, admitting that she "can't feel the same way about a Negro as a white person," also "pray[s] I'll change."[63]

One of the black men whom Warren interviewed, a Southern professor, suggested that "the future now would be different, would be hopeful, if there could just be 'one gesture of graciousness' from the white man—even if the white man didn't like the Supreme Court decision, he might try to understand the Negro's view, not heap insult on him."[64] And here, it seems, is Warren's suggestion for resolving the racial crisis in the South: to remind his readers, black and white alike, of the ideals of the human heart that Faulkner had named in his Nobel Prize speech, particularly the "compassion and pity and sacrifice which have been the glory of [the human] past."[65] Warren understood that these ideals would not emerge on their own, but needed the writer to prop them up in the face of countervailing forces—tradition, economic misery, and what one of his interviewees identified as the need for "something to give [one] pride. Just to be better than something."[66] If cultural forces could be built up over so many generations of slavery, Reconstruction, and Jim Crow, they could be undone with effort and goodwill. In the words of a white former-segregationalist who had come to accept the *Brown* decision, "A man can hate an idea but know it's right, and it takes a lot of thinking and praying to bring yourself around. You just have to uncover the unrecognized sympathy in the white man for the Negro humiliation."[67]

Gwendolyn Brooks

Warren's compassionate portrait of a South in crisis perhaps served as a model for other writers who more explicitly reconstructed the Till case in their own creative writings. The title of Gwendolyn Brooks's 1960 poem, "A Bronzeville Mother Loiters in Mississippi. Meanwhile, a Mississippi Mother Burns Bacon," suggests a symmetry between the two mothers, one black, one white; one the mother of the lynched boy, the other the object of his alleged overtures. The poem focuses on the white woman, never named but figured as the "milk-white maid" of some ballad, though her thoughts often invoke the image of the bereaved black mother.[68]

The symmetry and difference between these two women is extended in formal and cultural terms, as well, as the poem considers the differences between a romantic Southern tradition and its horrifying reality. The poem invokes that tradition in its opening lines, as the speaker refers to an unnamed event that "From the very first . . . had been like a / Ballad. It had the beat inevitable. It had the blood." In its content, Brooks's poem considers the ballad, a traditional form devoted to communal events like murders, told in the vernacular and "written so close to a community," according to Mark Strand and Eavan Boland, "that it is almost coauthored by it."[69] Brooks's poem, however, does not draw on the ballad's form, its regular meter, its four-line stanzas, its communal origins. "A Bronzeville Mother . . ." is written in an open form without the regularity of a ballad's meter and without its predictable rhymes. Its form adopts the irregular meter of conversation, or rather of private thought, as we follow the unspoken reflections of the Mississippi mother as she burns bacon.

Why is this mother burning her bacon? Her thoughts are elsewhere, surely not primarily in her kitchen as she prepares breakfast for her family. Indeed, the poem explores the disjunction between this woman's prosaic life as a poor white housewife and the romance of the "milk-white maid" she has come to know in ballads. The poem is not principally about her burning bacon, but that incident is centrally identified in the title, a pivotal moment in the poem. It is a central incident because the woman "hasten[s] to hide" her burnt bacon "in the step-on can." We begin to see in this detail that her life is less than ideal; she must hide her burnt bacon because her family is poor and cannot afford to waste food, because she fears being judged as less than the ideal wife against which she patterns herself, and because her husband is a violent man.

As the poem moves back and forth between the ideal world of the ballad, where one's identity as a "maid mild . . . made the breath go fast," and the actual world of this Mississippi mother's daily existence, we see that even the romantic world of the ballad is not of her making, not of her choosing, beyond even her comprehension. She must fit herself to the "four-line stanzas of the ballads she had never quite / Understood—the ballads they had set her to, in school." Though she has not written this tradition, she accepts it, sees herself "set . . . to" it, and accepts that to be the maid of the ballad, "Pursued / By the Dark Villain. Rescued by the Fine Prince," was "worth anything." The premise of that belief, invented by the romantic Southern tradition of chivalry, informed by fears of sexuality and secured by white supremacist masculine violence, comes under scrutiny as the woman recalls her encounter with a black boy and the bloodshed that ensued.

Just as readers are meant to see the gulf between the open form of Brooks's poem and the ballad whose romantic content supplies the tightly prescribed ideal of Southern womanhood for this Mississippi mother, so does the mother, as she cooks breakfast, begin to discern the gaps between her actual encounter with the youth she identifies as the "Dark Villain" and the romantic narrative of such episodes in ballads. The villain, she recalls, was a mere child, "with eyes still too young to be dirty, / And a mouth too young to have lost every reminder / Of its infant softness." Her husband the "Fine Prince," on the other hand, stood against this child with a "Mature solidness whose lack, in the Dark Villain, was impressing her." The child was too young, too innocent to be an adequate villain, and her hero was less than heroic, taking with him a "heavy companion to hack down (unhorsed) / That little foe." Even the crime fades to insignificance as the mother fails to remember "what that foe had done / Against her, or if anything had been done." If the Dark Villain's youth is marked with "infant softness," the Fine Prince is young in a different way, his "magnificent shell of adulthood" barely concealing "the baby full of tantrums."

As she thinks back over the events that led to the killing, this mother cannot recall the justification for her husband's avenging violence. "The one thing in the world she did know and knew / With terrifying clarity was that her composition / Had disintegrated." Her composition—a memory, perhaps, of her difficult schooldays—is something composed, in prose or with the threads of tradition. Her identity as a milk-white maid has depended upon the truth of the rest of the ballad, in particular upon the malice of the Dark Villain whose malice is now in question; as she interrogates herself about the villain's guilt, this Mississippi mother's identity as a pure Southern woman (an identity composed and artificial, but no less necessary) begins to unravel, and "although the pattern prevailed, / The breaks were everywhere" and "she could think / Of no thread capable of the necessary / Sew-work." As the truth of her ballad falters, the woman's composition disintegrates, like the body of Emmett Till himself, a body that had been so brutally beaten that, according to one report, "a piece of his skull . . . fell loose from his head when [it] was recovered."[70]

Unlike Mamie Bradley, who chose not to repair the damage to her boy's body but to display it for all the world to see, this Mississippi mother recomposes herself with comb and lipstick. If the "necessary / Sew-work" to repair her psychic composition cannot be found, her physical recomposition is possible—and equally "necessary": "It was necessary / To be more beautiful than ever." She must compose her beauty so that her husband does not wonder whether she had been "worth it." In the ideal world of ballads, to be the maid or the hero, granted "Happiness-Ever-After," is "worth anything." But in the actual world, where this "anything" acquires a specific value, demands a concrete memory—"the blood, the cramped cries, the little stuttering bravado, / The gradual dulling of those Negro eyes, / The sudden, overwhelming *little-boyness* in that barn"—it is possible to think that the romance of Southern womanhood is not worth *that*.

When the Fine Prince eats his breakfast, resentful over the "meddling headlines" from Northern papers, and glances "almost secretly" at his hands in a gesture that might recall the guilty Lady MacBeth, we wonder if he hasn't reached the same conclusion. Gwendolyn Brooks does not make her readers privy to this man's thoughts, only reveals the succession of his responses: the stealthy glance at his hands, the violent desires and racist contempt he expresses in front of his children:

> What he'd like to do, he explained, was kill them all.
> The time lost. The unwanted fame.
> Still, it had been fun to show these intruders
> A thing or two. To show that snappy-eyed mother,
> That sassy, Northern, brown-black—
>
> Nothing could stop Mississippi.
> He knew that. Big Fella
> Knew that.
> And, what was so good, Mississippi knew that.

The Fine Prince is a welter of confused emotions: guilt, resentment, rage, jealousy, and Southern pride, as his words take on the cast of the White Citizens Councils that may have informed the violence of his real-life counterparts. He barely launches his political meditation, however, when his children—like their father, babies "full of tantrums"—break out in a fight, the one hurling the molasses jar across the table at his brother. Faced with this new domestic turmoil, the Fine Prince resolves it as he has resolved other crises, with brutality: leaning across the table he "slapped / The small and smiling criminal."

In an instant, without naming Mamie Bradley, the Mississippi mother begins to identify with the mother of the Dark Villain in her fears for her small children:

> She did not speak. When the Hand
> Came down and away, and she could look at her child,
> At her baby-child,
> She could think only of blood.
> Surely her baby's cheek
> Had disappeared, and in its place, surely,
> Hung a heaviness, a lengthening red, a red that had no end.

The images she calls up remind the reader (if not the mother herself) of the mutilated body of Emmett Till. This mother's baby, whose "cheek / Had disappeared," stands in as a morbid reminder of Emmett Till, whose own cheek had been blown away by a shotgun. One of the new conditions this mother must get used to is fear for her children, fear that she "could not protect them," a fear "tying her as with iron." Readers would have to recall—for Brooks does not gloss these images—that Emmett Till's body had been found tied to a rusty cotton gin, "as with iron." But even without recognizing the specific references to the Till lynching, the images of physical brutality, of kidnapping and murder, are unmistakable, and they link this Mississippi mother to the Bronzeville mother of the title.

She thinks consciously of that "Other Woman" only once, as she tries to bear the sexual advances of her husband, which she can only regard in the context of his violence. "Gripped in the claim of his hands," she considers that she cannot protect her children against him, that his hands seep a "red ooze" that spreads over her shoulders "[a]nd over all of Earth and Mars." Heaving with sickness she is tormented by the "decapitated exclamation points in that Other Woman's eyes." The images swirl in this last scene, where the Mississippi mother understands that she belongs to the Fine Prince, that she is his to revere, to protect, to possess, and that her composition as the "maid mild" requires those "decapitated exclamation points," symbol of grief and outrage, in the black mother's eyes.

The poem ends with the image of the magnolia, the emblem of Southern romances and of Mississippi but an emblem, too, of hypocrisy and an almost artificial sweetness. Here, the white woman's hatred for her husband "burst[s] into glorious flower" as the poem asks us to consider "the last bleak news of the ballad." In rewriting the magnolia, this "glorious" symbol of Southern tradition, as an icon of hatred, Brooks asks us to share the Mississippi mother's awakening insight that this tradition she has been raised to embrace is not one of unmitigated loveliness as the ballads would have it, but relies on hypocrisy, cruelty, and deception to keep it intact. Juxtaposing the white woman's "glorious flower" with the "last bleak news of the ballad," the poem asks us to see beyond the myths of tradition, to see the particular episodes of hatred and violence that unite victims of different races.

James Baldwin

Like Gwendolyn Brooks, James Baldwin also used the Till case as an occasion to explore and perhaps begin to understand the heart of the white aggressor in order to help others understand as well. Baldwin's chosen medium, the play, offered him an opportunity to search and portray the minds of an array of characters—white and black, criminal and victim, editor, clergyman, shopkeeper, parent and child, friend and lover. But his primary objective in writing the play, as he claims in his "Notes for Blues," was to "draw a valid portrait of the murderer," to fulfill the "duty to try to understand this wretched man" in order to begin liberating the man's offspring.[71] *Blues for Mister Charlie* opened in New York in April 1964. Even as he was preparing his play for production, Baldwin confessed his misgivings about the American theater, noting that it seemed to him "a series, merely, of commercial speculations, stale, repetitious, and timid."[72]

Baldwin hoped that his production could transcend this stale form. His play tells the story of Richard Henry, a young black man who returns to his native Mississippi after having spent several years in New York. Richard is murdered by Lyle Britten, a white racist, in the opening scene of the play, which concludes with the murderer's trial and acquittal. Rather than make money on the theater, James Baldwin hoped to enlighten his audiences, to "bear witness to the reality and the power of light."[73] We can see him trying to realize that goal in his first set of stage directions, which demand that the "audience should always be aware" of the courthouse, American flag, church steeple, and cross.[74] Though this simple direction serves to emphasize the stage's doubleness—always shadowing the props of the courthouse when the scene is the church, and those of the church when the scene is the courthouse—it also introduces at the very outset the responsibilities of Baldwin's theater audience. Those who view the production are simultaneously theatergoers, courtroom spectators, and churchgoers, witnesses in the many religious and juridical senses of that term, and to observe their roles dutifully they must remain "always . . . aware."

Baldwin deliberately violated the unity of time when he studded his play with a series of flashbacks. Several reviewers found the device distracting, confusing, and unnecessary, while others praised the grace with which the playwright interlaced past and present.[75] The device not only allowed Baldwin to feature Richard Henry prominently in the play while also depicting his murder in the first scene; more significantly, it enables the dead Richard to haunt the play, haunt the people of Plague-town, USA, the way Emmett Till haunted and continues to haunt Mississippi, Chicago, and the United States. In the opening scene, Lyle shoots Richard, who "falls out of sight of the audience, like a stone, into the pit."[76] In this opening action Richard becomes an invisible man, out of sight—and reminds readers of the claim often made of Emmett Till, that had he "been a Mississippi farm boy instead of a Chicago lad on vacation in Mississippi, the world probably would never have known his fate"[77]; he would have been just another murdered black youth to fall, in Baldwin's words, "out of sight." But Richard, like Emmett, defies the tradition of Southern violence that obscures the violence of his death; he returns throughout the play to haunt the living, both characters and audience. In Baldwin's notes to the play, the writer confessed that he had been similarly haunted by Emmett Till and his story. "I do not know why the case pressed on my mind so hard," he writes, "but it would not let me go."[78] If the dead Richard Henry's frequent returns to Plaguetown are surreal, they are also symbolically appropriate, given the way that Emmett Till's bloated body resurfaced three days after his murder and his story continued to haunt those who read about it.

Many of Baldwin's critics complained that his play takes no interest in the political and economic causes and consequences of racial oppression in the South—the very social and economic dynamics that critics of the Till case were eager to publicize.[79] Baldwin was not unaware of these arguments; his white liberal character, Parnell, speaks for "social justice" but is dismissed by the other whites as "Communistic," just as many white defenders of Till's murderers denounced all talk of civil rights as communist propaganda.[80] When Parnell seeks a class-based explanation for Southern racial violence, his friend Meridian, the black father of the slain youth, will hear none of it. The murderer, Parnell explains, is "a poor white man" from a class "just as victimized in this part of the world as the blacks have ever been!" But Meridian insists on being spared "the historical view," since Lyle Britten, whatever his marginal economic status, is "responsible for Richard's death."[81] In these exchanges we see the playwright groping for a psychological rather than a sociological explanation. No doubt aware that the mobs responsible for murders and the juries responsible for acquittals are comprised of individual men, Baldwin wished to understand the psyche of the Southern white heart in order to go about changing it.

Baldwin's portrayal of that heart drew both praise and condemnation. Although some reviewers found the murderer, Lyle Britten, a convincing and even sympathetic portrayal—Nathan Cohen, for instance, saw in Rip Torn's performance "a baffled and earnest man adhering to a code which gives him a position whereby the Negro, any Negro, is his inferior"[82]—many more dismissed Baldwin's white characters, particularly the murderer, as stereotypes and "pasteboard creations."[83] Some conceded that the racist stereotype had once been a fact but was now "an anachronism."[84]

The conviction, just nine years after the Till lynching, that rabid racists like Lyle Britten were an anachronism testifies to the value of Baldwin's play, if only as a means of awakening Northern liberals who refused to believe in the ardent segregationist. Much of Lyle's speech, in fact, is very closely patterned on the words of Emmett Till's killers as they were reported by William Bradford Huie.[85] Lyle's confidence that he will elude conviction—"I ain't worried. I know the people in this town is with me. I got nothing to worry about"—resembles the confidence that had allowed Byrant and Milam to speak openly to Huie about the murders.[86] As Huie explained, the murderers feared neither prosecution nor ostracism:

> They took it for granted before the trial that every white neighbor, including every member of the jury and every defense attorney, had assumed that they had indeed killed the young Negro. And since the community had swarmed in their defense, Milam and Bryant assumed that the "community," including most responsible whites in Mississippi, had approved the killing.[87]

Baldwin makes the attitudes of his white community just a bit more explicit than any recorded statements by the actual whites of Tallahatchie County, Mississippi: as one of Lyle's white townspeople says, Lyle is "a good man, and he's done a lot for us, and I know you all know what I'm talking about."[88] One would be hard-pressed to dismiss this statement as an inauthentic sentiment, since Milam claimed to have received "letters from all over the country congratulating me on my 'fine Americanism.'"[89] Lyle's statements to his victim, too, might have been taken straight from Huie's account of the actual murder. Reminding Richard Henry of his proper place,

Lyle says, "Nigger, you was born down here. Ain't you never said sir to a white man?"[90] His attitude, if not his words, is a near echo of J. W. Milam, who objected to Till's failure to say "sir": "Don't say 'Yeah' to me: I'll blow your head off."[91] Perhaps the most striking reiteration of J. W. Milam, the more imposing of Till's two murderers, is Lyle Britten's assertion that his violent act was a necessary response to the unruliness of his black victim. Recalling Richard's defiance even after being shot, Lyle says in the last speech of the play, "I had to kill him then. I'm a white man! Can't nobody talk that way to *me!*"[92] Though many of Baldwin's critics condemned Britten's character as a stereotype, Britten closely resembles the actual J. W. Milam, who insisted that he, too, had no choice, once Emmett Till proved impossible to intimidate. "What else could we do?" Milam asked Huie.[93]

The nearly undifferentiated characters who make up "whitetown," too, though allegorical and almost surreal, also speak what we might call historically authentic sentiments. One character notes that the old ways, when the South remained segregated—"they had their ways, we had ours"—was a system in line with what "God intended."[94] If Baldwin gives her the words of an ignorant stereotype, they were words widely circulated in the South just eight years earlier, when Robert Penn Warren toured his native South and encountered a handbill that proclaimed, "Segregation is the law of God, not man."[95] No doubt Baldwin witnessed such sentiments when he returned from Europe in 1956, visited the South to see what was happening, and enlisted in the civil rights movement, working with James Meredith and Medgar Evers in Mississippi; certainly these same feelings were much on display in 1964, the year his play was performed on Broadway. If liberal whites in the North did not believe that, their disbelief only confirmed Baldwin's theory that the white liberal is more willfully blind—and perhaps, finally, more dangerous—than the segregationalist.

It is worth taking Baldwin at his word and considering that he intended his depiction of Lyle Britten as an attempt to understand the murderer, to understand the "spiritual darkness" that enables his crimes.[96] Or, as Baldwin explained on another occasion, "what happens to the poor white man's . . . mind" is that "raised to believe . . . that no matter what disaster overtakes [him], there is one consolation like a heavenly revelation—at least [he is] not black."[97] People like this, Baldwin maintained, "cannot be dismissed as . . . total monster[s]." And indeed, at times Baldwin makes Lyle's "spiritual darkness" almost intelligible: capable of loving a black woman, Lyle never permitted himself to do so openly and legally because he refused to see her as his equal. We begin to understand this refusal when we consider that Lyle has exhausted himself working a piece of land that hardly bears fruit, knowing all along that had his parents been born sooner, before the Civil War, he would have been a rich man. Determined to preserve what he can of an old social order for his son, Lyle imposes himself on the most virile black man who crosses his path. His racial antagonism is irrational, but since it does not make him monstrous in his own eyes, Baldwin is determined to examine its sources in order to see how it might be undone. Though it might be an overstatement to assert, as Darwin Turner does, that Baldwin treats Lyle's character "gently," neither is the murderer an unmitigated monster.[98] When he speaks his mind, as Baldwin allows him to do, he is exonerated in his own eyes, and audiences see not the "wild-eyed, nigger-hating, stereotyped redneck villain" that they perhaps wished, but rather "a real man who was backed into a corner."[99]

Neither is Richard Henry, the black victim of Lyle's violence, an entirely winning character. Perhaps because they found Baldwin's white characters so unappealing, many critics of the play claimed that his black characters were exaggeratedly virtuous. Susan Sontag, for example, described Baldwin's characters as masks, "figures, simple and definite, whose identity is easily stated, who arouse quick loves and hates." A "shorthand way of defining virtue and vice," the mask enables simplification, and "'the Negro' is fast becoming the American theater's leading mask of virtue."[100] But Richard Henry, the figure whose situation, if not his character, is loosely based on Emmett Till, is hardly without faults.

Though his father, Meridian, has insisted all his life on nonviolent resistance to racist violence, Richard returns to his Southern home full of anger, announcing his intention to "take one of the bastards with [him]" in a violent struggle[101] and believing he can "make [himself] *well* with hatred."[102] And, as many of Baldwin's critics have pointed out, Richard is obsessed with sex, with pointing out his own virility and the impotence of the white men he encounters. Sexuality is the "motive force" for the play, but especially for Richard's actions.[103] As Philip Roth has observed, Richard Henry is no less despicable, "pathetic in his adolescent masculine pride," than the man who kills him.[104] What are we to make of the centrality of sexual aggression in Baldwin's play? In reducing racial strife to sexual fear and competition between white and black men, does Baldwin trivialize what was happening in the South, does he "denigrate the Negro's search for justice" as several reviewers believe?[105]

Perhaps—but only if the action that prompts Richard's murder was without counterpart in the real world. As we know, Baldwin had a specific counterpart in mind, and in his dramatization he points out that the Emmett Till murder was set in motion by an utterly trivial series of events. It is hard to believe that a theater reviewer assessing the play was ignorant of the Till murder, but there is no other way to read this dismissal of Baldwin's plot: "Surely the Negro tragedy is that people are victimized for lesser but weightier reasons than insulting a white woman and her husband, which is what Richard does in this play."[106] If Baldwin's play displaces racial and economic strife with the emasculation of black men by white men who fear their own emasculation, then that is because emasculation was one of the most dramatic forms that actual racial violence often took. Insofar as the plot of *Blues for Mister Charlie*, like the Emmett Till lynching itself, is part of a larger history of the lynching of black men, then it is entirely appropriate that Baldwin's play explicitly address white fears of black male sexuality, and that civil rights and manhood be conflated. As Meridian Henry observes on the witness stand, "manhood is a dangerous pursuit, here."[107]

John McCarten, reviewing the play for the *New Yorker*, argued that Baldwin's "case" was impaired by his characterization of Richard and Lyle, who were both "objectionable by any sane standards."[108] Given that Baldwin based his play on the lynching of a black child who was widely depicted in the press as entirely innocent, even Christlike,[109] we must consider Baldwin's characterization of Richard a deliberate choice and inquire into the effects of his decision to make his victim older, more aggressive, and more openly sexual than Emmett Till had been. Of course, Baldwin did not go so far as to make Richard the aggressor at the time of his death. Though Richard had earlier determined to drink deeply of the cup of hatred, by the time of his final confrontation with Lyle he seems ready to let it go. He asks his murderer, "Do we need all this shit? Can't we live without it?"[110] On the other hand, he is not prepared to apologize or to stoop to Lyle, only to acknowledge that they are equals: "You a man and I'm a man."[111] His nonviolence is not cowardly, for he declares to his lover that he will never "run no more from white folks" but will "stay and be a man—a *man*!—right here."[112] And yet he deliberately faces his death without the gun that he once vowed he would always take with him. His murder is therefore an unequivocally unjust act, even as Baldwin makes it impossible for audiences to pity the victim. While Baldwin's revision of his victim's character might seem to undermine his point—by making it harder for audiences to sympathize with Richard—in fact he makes a stronger case than one that owes its force to sentimental regard for the victim, the kind of sentimentality that erupted after Emmett Till's slaying. And in the nine years since the Till lynching, as the civil rights movement gained force in the deep South, Baldwin's point was more necessary than ever. Embodying, in the words of one reviewer, "the spirit that moves militant young Negroes to assert their individual rights," Richard Henry demands a response of outraged justice, not of pity.[113] If Baldwin's audiences are to remain "always aware" of the social and moral problems he wants them to acknowledge, their awareness must persist even if they personally dislike Baldwin's protagonist.

Unlike the complaints about Baldwin's inauthentic characters, the widespread objections to his courtroom scenes, which constitute the entire third act of *Blues*, cannot be so easily dismissed. Taubman spoke for many reviewers when he noted that Baldwin "does not worry about the niceties of legal procedure."[114] These scenes, unlike the speeches of Baldwin's characters, do not lend themselves to comparison with the trial of Till's murderers, which was thoroughly reported in the national and international press. Had Baldwin wished to draw on the actual trial, he would have had access to ample material. His play reaches its most stylized and fantastic in this final act, where even the prosecution becomes hostile to the black witnesses, and where church and state become conflated not only in the stage props (flag and cross) but also in the stage directions that identify one attorney as "counsel for the bereaved." Although many of Baldwin's black witnesses invite comparisons to the brave blacks who testified against the defendants in the Till murder trial—Papa D., for instance, sheds his role of the Uncle Tom and shocks blacks and whites alike by calling Lyle an "oppressor"—Baldwin's trial itself is patently unfair, unlike the actual murder trial in Sumner, Mississippi.[115] While witnesses of the Sumner trial praised the fairness of the judge, prosecution, and proceedings, Baldwin's state attorney is hostile to his own witnesses, as if to highlight the impossibility of justice. In this courtroom scene Baldwin disregards all realist conventions, opting instead for an expressionism that may have rung true to those who understood the acquittals in the Till case as a fantastic interpretation of the evidence amassed against the defendants.[116]

In the climax of both the play and the trial, the liberal white editor, Parnell, a friend of both the murder defendant and the victim's father, is called to testify. His testimony has been the subject of speculation throughout the town, as blacks and whites wonder whether he will protect his white friend, whom he knows to be guilty, or betray him in the name of justice and civil rights. He is called to the stand after Lyle's wife has testified that Richard Henry had assaulted her. In a question that surely would not be allowed in any actual trial, Parnell is asked to pass judgment on Mrs. Britten's testimony regarding an encounter that he did not witness. "Mrs. Britten has testified," begins the attorney, "that Richard Henry grabbed her and pulled her to him and tried to kiss her. How can those actions be misconstrued?"[117] Parnell, unable to question the attorney's assumption that Jo Britten's testimony is accurate, can only respond, "Those actions are—quite explicit."[118] Parnell's friends in the black community take his response as a betrayal, though one that is conditioned by longstanding Southern race relations: "You can't never go against the word of a white lady, man, not even if you're white."[119] Critics of Baldwin's play have followed suit unanimously, agreeing with Driver, who notes that when Parnell has to choose, "it is the truth he lets go."[120]

In strict terms, of course, Parnell has not lied at all: he is not asked to verify the "actions" that Jo Britten described, only to interpret them, and neither the prosecuting attorney nor the judge objects to the question. It is true, as critics have charged, that Baldwin's representation of a trial is hardly realistic. But critics have overlooked the larger point of these scenes: that what is strictly true, and what the judicial process allows, is often at odds with what we might properly consider authentic truth and justice. Of course, Baldwin exaggerates the distinction between abstract justice and courtroom justice, between actual guilt and the legal establishment of guilt. But when Meridian Henry laments that "[t]he truth cannot be heard in this dreadful place," he utters a complaint that was made repeatedly by critics of the Till murder trial.[121] Even though most observers conceded that the proceedings were fair, they were troubled by the judicial process's institutional constraints on full disclosure. As Huie's editors at *Look* announced in their introduction to his first article about Till's lynchers, the magazine was presenting to its readers "for the first time, the real story of that killing—the story no jury heard."[122] If Baldwin's courtroom scenes are implausible, they nevertheless capture the sense that many black Americans shared after the outcome of the actual Till murder trial: that in spite of their deluded hopes for a fair trial, the acquittal of two white men charged with murdering a black boy had been from the start a foregone conclusion.

Harper Lee

Harper Lee's 1960 novel, *To Kill a Mockingbird*, also dramatizes the certainty that a trial pitting the word of a black man against that of a white woman will favor the woman whatever the strength of the evidence. Although the facts of Lee's fictional court case, where a black man stands trial for his life, are slightly different from those of the Till case and Baldwin's dramatic rewriting, the rape trial that provides the climax of *To Kill a Mockingbird* pivots on the word of a black man, Tom Robinson, as he tries to defend himself against the accusation of a white woman. Like Baldwin's Plaguetown, USA, Harper Lee's Maycomb, Alabama, is a town where even an honest and respectable black man "can't never go against the word of a white lady." Tom understands this rule well enough to be careful in his testimony. He does not charge that Mayella Ewell, the chief state's witness, has lied on the witness stand; he maintains simply that she's been "mistaken in her mind" about his conduct toward her.[123] Tom, like all the adults in Maycomb, understands the force of the cultural rule that favors a white woman over a black man. In Maycomb only the children are naive enough to think that the evidence presented in the case will clear Tom of the charge. Although Atticus Finch puts up a valiant defense, he knows from the outset that his client has no chance of an acquittal. As he tells his children, he is fighting for Tom's life in spite of the fact that "we were licked a hundred years before we started."[124]

As Patrick Chura has argued, Lee's novel dramatizes the "collective erosion of faith in legalism" to follow the conclusion of the Emmett Till case.[125] A much more realistic form than the one Baldwin had chosen, Harper Lee's novel demonstrates, by means of details more or less accurately borrowed from the Till murder trial, the legitimate reasons for this profound loss of faith. As Chura notes, Tom Robinson's rape trial resembles the murder trial that took place in Sumner, Mississippi, five years before the novel's publication. Atticus Finch, like the attorney who prosecuted Bryant and Milam, earnestly seeks justice and makes an impassioned plea to the jury. Likewise, the judge who hears this case is, as Atticus tells his children, "a good judge": "Judge Taylor might look lazy and operate in his sleep, but he was seldom reversed" and all agree that he, like Judge Swango in Sumner, has solemnly sought a just verdict.[126] As in the Till case, the press emerges in Lee's novel—this time in the form of Mr. Underwood, the owner, publisher, and editor of the *Maycomb Tribune*—as "a determined advocate of civil rights."[127] Like the Till murder trial, Tom Robinson's rape trial is procedurally rational and just; Tom has been represented by a loyal and competent attorney, the judge has allowed fair testimony, and the defense has presented a sound case. As Jem Finch concludes after witnessing nearly the whole trial, "He's just gone over the evidence . . . and we're gonna win, Scout. I don't see how we can't."[128] Unlike Baldwin's surreal Plaguetown courtroom, Lee's Maycomb courtroom, like the ideal courtroom, is procedurally rational, orderly, and just.

Which is not to say that the culture of the courtroom—its traditions, the conduct of its spectators—is in keeping with the ideal of justice. While the rest of the town throngs to the courthouse on opening day, the Finches' neighbor, Miss Maudie, declares that she will stay at home: "'t's morbid, watching a poor devil on trial for his life. Look at all those folks, it's like a Roman carnival."[129] In many ways, the conduct of Judge Taylor's courtroom, its "alarming informality," resembles its real-life counterpart in Sumner.[130] Like Judge Swango, who presided over the Sumner murder trial, Judge Taylor has "one interesting habit. He permitted smoking in his courtroom but did not himself indulge."[131] The smoking, drinking, and picnicking at the "gala occasion" of Tom Robinson's rape trial resemble the irreverent conduct of the spectators who witnessed the Till trial.[132] A critic of this Southern courtroom would not be out of line to conclude (as critics of the Till trial did) that the casual atmosphere trivializes the cause of justice for black people, that white spectators are unable to realize what it means under such circumstances to be a black man on trial for his life.

And, of course, though the novel's young narrator registers no overt protest, Lee's Maycomb courtroom, like the one in Sumner, is racially segregated. Colored spectators must sit in the balcony, and Southern decorum requires them to wait for the whites to enter the courtroom before they ascend the stairs. These segregated conditions are reported, of course, by Scout, who describes this tradition matter-of-factly, without protest. But she does not subscribe to the feelings of white supremacy that undergird segregated public accommodations; indeed, when Atticus's children arrive at the courthouse too late to find seats in the white-only section, they cheerfully agree to be seated above with their friends among the colored spectators.

The children do, however, observe and condemn the more meaningful racial inequalities they observe during the trial, inequalities only symbolized by the segregated seating arrangements in the Maycomb courthouse. They are guided by Atticus's powerful closing statement, where he points out an unalterable law of Southern race relations: the "evil assumption," relied on by Tom Robinson's accuser and her family, "that *all* Negroes lie, that *all* Negroes are basically immoral beings, that *all* Negro men are not to be trusted around our women."[133] Of course, like Milam and Bryant, the Ewells find that their moment as celebrities and heroes is short-lived; they rely on a racial hierarchy that officially ranks them ahead of even the most honorable blacks and confers temporary status for their racial tyranny, but after the trial they discover that middle-class whites have as much contempt for them as ever. As Atticus explains, Mayella Ewell's father "thought he'd be a hero, but all he got for his pain was . . . was, okay, we'll convict this Negro but get back to your dump."[134] Even so, they have destroyed one black life with relative impunity even though the entire town knows how disreputable they are.

Harper Lee relies on her readers to be more perceptive than Scout and Jem and to discern other references to de facto slavery embedded in her narrative. One of these is the detail, reminiscent of Emmett Till's murder, that Tom Robinson's arm is permanently maimed from a childhood accident when he caught his arm in a cotton gin.[135] The detail provides evidence that Tom could not have assaulted Mayella Ewell in the way she had described, but it also reminds attentive readers familiar with the Till lynching that Emmett Till's body had been weighted down with a cotton gin fan before being sunk in the Tallahatchie River. Bryant and Milam may not have been imaginative men, but at least one reporter remarked on the symbolism of using this piece of machinery to help terrorize a black youth on the verge of manhood.[136]

Other references to the deep South during the Eisenhower years could not have been discerned by Lee's main characters, of course—for the novel is set a generation earlier, during the Great Depression—but surely Lee intended for her readers to see the ironies of a world where the Ku Klux Klan can be pronounced a thing of the past. Atticus, the wisest and most pragmatic character in the novel, explains to his children that "[w]ay back about nineteen-twenty there was a Klan, but it was a political organization more than anything. Besides, they couldn't find anybody to scare."[137] For Atticus, the Klan is a historical curiosity, a once-impotent organization, now entirely defunct, that could not effectively have terrorized the lives of blacks and Jews. "The Ku Klux's gone," he assures his children. "It'll never come back."[138] This conversation is more than just the optimistic pledge of a liberal author determined that the evils of a past era will not repeat themselves; on the contrary, given the prevalence of the White Citizens Councils throughout the South in the years following the *Brown* decision, we should take these statements as Lee's ironic warning that the forward march of racial justice is far from inevitable. Indeed, many of the respectable white characters in Lee's novel—the women in the missionary circle who weep for "the squalid lives of the Mrunas," among others—disapprove of Atticus's spirited defense of Tom Robinson.[139] And after Robinson's death in the prison yard, the white community buzzes with racist judgments about the futility of civilizing a Negro. "Just shows you, that Robinson boy was legally married, they say he kept himself clean, went to church and all that, but when it comes down to the line the veneer's mighty thin. Nigger always comes out in 'em."[140] Although such pronouncements have a long history, they were closely associated with the publications of the White Citizens Councils, the organizations that sprang up after *Brown* to replace the discredited Klan.[141] Tom Brady's *Black Monday*, for example, argues that the only race of human being not to evolve is the Negro race, which "remained in a primitive status. . . . His inheritance was wanting. This is neither right nor wrong; it is simply a stubborn biological fact."[142] If Atticus Finch believes that in 1935 such sentiments are on the wane, Harper Lee seems intent on warning her reader that by 1960, only five years after the Till lynching, not only had these beliefs lingered but they had gained more force as the official ideology of a growing number of white supremacist organizations, organizations with an unquestionable influence on ordinary whites in the deep South.

Perhaps the most authentic aspect of Lee's novel, if we are reading it as a response to the Till case, is its critique of jury verdicts. At the conclusion of his closing statement, Atticus reminds the jury that the courtroom is the one place in America that recognizes the equality of all people. "Our courts have their faults, as does any human institution," he tells them, "but in this country our courts are the great levelers, and in our courts all men are created equal." But he also knows, as he reminds the jurors, that "a court is no better than each man of you sitting before me on this jury. A court is only as sound as its jury, and a jury is only as sound as the men who make it up."[143] Although the jury have not yet retired to deliberate, and Atticus speaks with optimism rather than defeatism, his insight ought to be enough to discourage the most sanguine observer. The black Reverend Sykes, who has had a lifetime of experience with the hearts of white men, cautions Jem not to place his confidence in the evidence when the outcome will be determined by white men: "I ain't ever seen any jury decide in favor of a colored man over a white man."[144]

It was a point lamented again and again in the wake of the Sumner acquittal: however fair-minded the judge, however assiduous the attorneys, and however compelling the evidence, a white jury could not be trusted to reach a righteous verdict in a criminal trial that pitted white against black. Tom Robinson is "given due process of law," is "tried openly and convicted by twelve good men and true"; and his defense attorney fights for him "all the way," using "every tool available to free men to save Tom Robinson."[145] In the end, though, as Atticus has predicted all along, and as his disenchanted children learn, "in the secret courts of men's hearts Atticus had no case."[146] Whatever the merits of the particular case, such juries—all-white in both the Sumner murder trial and the fictive Maycomb rape trial—consider it their primary responsibility to uphold the social arrangement of white supremacy. As Atticus explains to his children, "Those are twelve reasonable men in everyday life, Tom's jury, but you saw something come between them and reason. . . . There's something in our world that makes men lose their heads—they couldn't be fair if they tried. In our courts, when it's a white man's word against a black man's, the white man always wins."[147]

The point had been raised before, for years after the Sumner acquittal. We'll recall that in 1959, just the year before Harper Lee published her novel, Jack Greenberg had advised that "where prosecutors will not prosecute or juries will not convict, there usually is no other remedy than the exercise of political power and general community awakening."[148] We might consider Lee's novel as yet another attempt to move readers to compassion and outrage, to change the hearts of individuals so that their sense of reason and justice prevails over their traditional prejudices.

Just as James Baldwin had hoped to change the hearts of the oppressor's children, so did Harper Lee place her hope in the younger generation. Jem, Scout, and their friend Dill model a point of view unclouded by racism; as they observe Tom's trial from the colored balcony, they resemble the many non-Southerners who refused to take their appointed seats in Sumner, Mississippi, as black or white observers, looking instead through racially neutral eyes. Like the many outsiders who observed the Milam and Bryant murder trial, Atticus's children marvel at the distortions in logic required by a tradition of white supremacy. Jem, as we have seen, is sure of an acquittal because he does not understand the power of such a tradition. Dill, watching the contemptuous cross-examination of Tom Robinson, begins to weep and cannot stop. He must leave the courtroom so his sobs do not disturb the proceedings. Though Scout tries to persuade him that Mr. Gilmer is just doing his job, Dill makes an important distinction: "Mr. Finch didn't act that way to Mayella and old man Ewell when he cross-examined them. The way that man called him 'boy' all the time and sneered at him, an' looked around at the jury every time he answered . . . it just makes me sick."[149]

When, in a bitter mood, Atticus responds to Jem's outrage over the guilty verdict, he does not console his son but shares his bitterness. "How could they do it,"
Jem demands. Atticus has no reassuring explanation. "I don't know," he replies, "but
they did it. They've done it before and they did it tonight and they'll do it again and
when they do it—seems that only children weep."[150] The pity, of course, is that most
children grow up to be adults, grow up to learn the ways of Jim Crow and to let their
reason be clouded by the indefinable something that enables the Maycomb jury to
disregard the testimony of an honorable black man in favor of the clear lies of an
ignoble white family.

Harper Lee captures Atticus Finch's children at a pivotal point in their development, when they are beginning to understand how Southern communities function
but before they have lost their ability to share the point of view of their black neighbors. Dill is able to sob at Tom Robinson's treatment in court because, Mr. Raymond
notes, "things haven't caught up with [his] instinct yet. Let him get a little older and
he won't get sick and cry."[151] As if to forestall this hardening, Atticus repeatedly
advises his children of the wisdom of "a simple trick": "You never really understand
a person," he tells them, "until you consider things from his point of view— . . . until
you climb into his skin and walk around in it."[152] He is speaking in particular of
Scout's white schoolteacher, but his metaphor—that of exchanging skin with
another person—provides a central trope for this book about race relations. If juries
are composed of individual men, then they must be won over as individuals, and this
can be done by forcing them to consider the world from another point of view.[153]

Lee's novel is narrated by a child, Scout, a flexible person who is able when she
thinks of it to put herself in another person's place, to walk around in his skin. She
has a good model for such behavior. Atticus cannot bring himself to despise Mayella
Ewell, the woman who has caused his client so much trouble, whose false accusation
has endangered Atticus's life and those of his children, because he is able to walk in
her skin, to see her as "the victim of cruel poverty and ignorance."[154] He cross-
examines her compassionately, not cruelly. He does not go so far in his compassion
as to share her desperation and believe her lie—for, as he says, he's "in favor of
Southern womanhood as much as anybody, but not for preserving polite fiction at the
expense of human life."[155] Conscience, he maintains, is not subject to majority
rule,[156] and the Tom Robinson case "goes to the essence of a man's conscience."[157]
Still, he insists that one can preserve one's principles while considering other points
of view. He demonstrates, moreover, that if, in practicing the "simple trick" he
teaches Scout, those principles seem less persuasive than they once did, then they are
probably matters simply of tradition, not of conscience, and they can safely be abandoned. He demonstrates, that is, how to take hold of what Jack Greenberg regarded
as the only extralegal remedy possible for racial injustice: the "general community
awakening," which is a matter, finally, of separate individual awakenings.

Harper Lee presents these awakenings as a series of lessons simple enough for
a child to understand, though they often elude adults. This novel that opens with
Scout's complaint about a misguided teacher ends in nearly the same place, as Scout

tries to understand the contradiction of her teacher, who hates Hitler but thinks Tom Robinson's conviction is an appropriate lesson for local blacks, who "were gettin' way above themselves, an' the next thing they think they can do is marry us."[158] The teacher seizes on Scout's definition of democracy—"Equal rights for all, special privileges for none"—in order to boast that the United States is such a place. "Over here we don't believe in persecuting anybody," she tells her students. "Persecution comes from people who are prejudiced."[159]

To Kill a Mockingbird does not altogether dismiss the lessons of the schoolroom, nor does it reject the values of the courtroom, where in theory, anyway, a pauper can be "the equal of a Rockefeller."[160] It is important that Scout Finch and readers of the novel continue to believe that in its ideal form, democracy is a political institution worth having, and even in its corrupted form it is worth trying to save. But the courtroom and the schoolroom, places where reason is presumed to rule dispassionately, have much to gain from the lessons of compassion, the "simple trick" of trying to see the world from another point of view. This trick is even more critical when it crosses the color line, that arbitrary boundary installed for the explicit purpose of discouraging true sympathy. Six years after the *Brown* decision, whose result if enforced would have done much to dissolve an important barrier to developing this sympathy in the formative years of children, five years after the Emmett Till lynching, and just a year after Jack Greenberg advocated a "general community awakening," Harper Lee offers the extralegal means of compassion to help resolve the problem of racist institutions.

Cover of *Newsweek*, November 29, 1976.
© 1976 Newsweek, Inc. All rights
reserved. Reprinted by permission.

Chapter Five

WITNESSES
TO AN
EXECUTION

Norman Mailer's
Spectacle of Death

T he civil rights movement brought about a striking decline in the number of state-sponsored executions from the 1950s until the end of the 1960s. When the US Supreme Court imposed a moratorium on executions in 1972, declaring that the nation's application of the death penalty constituted "cruel and unusual punishment," many abolitionists predicted that it was only a matter of time before the court would find capital punishment itself unconstitutional. As Jack Greenberg affirmed, "There will no longer be any more capital punishment in the United States."[1] Greenberg and others were wrong, of course; rather than accepting the demise of this penal practice, state legislators drafted new capital punishment statutes that would address the concerns spelled out in the 1972 *Furman* decision. In 1976 the Supreme Court revisited the issue, finding that the nation's "standards of decency"[2] had not evolved significantly enough to abolish the practice. "It is now evident," the court explained, "that a large proportion of American society continues to regard" capital punishment "as an appropriate and necessary criminal sanction."[3] The question of public sentiments about capital punishment figured prominently in the decision to reestablish this ultimate sanction. Americans would soon have a chance to weigh in on the topic, as the debate over capital punishment turned from an abstraction to an actual case.

And the 1979 publication of Norman Mailer's historical novel, *The Executioner's Song*, followed in the tradition of execution literature I have been examining, turning readers into virtual witnesses and inviting them to take part in a debate about this particular capital case and capital punishment more generally.

I. GARY GILMORE'S CAPITAL OFFENSES

In 1976 Gary Gilmore was sentenced to execution in the state of Utah for the murders of two men. The crimes were not particularly grisly, though they were dispassionate. But because Gilmore had spent nearly eighteen of his thirty-six years incarcerated (almost half of that time in solitary confinement) and had a history of prison violence and escapes, the district attorney sought the death penalty. Because Gilmore forbade his court-appointed lawyers to call to the stand his girlfriend, the only witness who might be able to generate compassion for the defendant, his lawyers declined to call a single witness. Instead, they put their hopes in an appeals hearing and encouraged their client to do the same. The jury deliberated for just eighty minutes before returning a conviction.

Nobody could have predicted that Gilmore would become the first person executed in the United States in ten years, since the 1967 execution of Luis Monge. Because the Supreme Court had annulled all existing death penalty laws in 1972, over four hundred inmates were being held on death row at the time of Gilmore's arrest. Since appeals processes could take years, it seemed unlikely that Gilmore would become the first man executed in a decade.

When it came time to appeal, however, Gilmore, who had already warned his lawyers that he would not petition the court, accepted his death sentence and refused to appear at the hearing. His lawyers appealed on his behalf, winning a brief stay of execution in the Utah Supreme Court. Gilmore immediately fired them and hired Dennis Boaz, a debt-ridden lawyer without a practice who also happened to be an aspiring writer. Seeing a chance to make money on Gilmore's story, Boaz took the case for a fifty percent share of any proceeds and—knowing that the story would be worth more if the man were executed—was in court two days later, pleading for an execution without further delay. In the ensuing weeks, Utah's governor Calvin Rampton ordered a second stay of execution and asked the State Board of Pardons to review the case.

The public interest in Gilmore's life escalated sharply after November 15, 1976, the day originally scheduled for the execution, when Gilmore and his girlfriend, Nicole Barrett, attempted to take their lives by overdosing on Seconol. The story became front-page material for *Newsweek*, while *Time* ran an article titled "Death-Row Dramatics." Soon Gilmore had fired Dennis Boaz and sold exclusive rights to his story to a Hollywood producer, Lawrence Schiller, for $100,000 plus a share in future publications. Schiller's interviews with Gilmore led to a posthumous interview published in *Playboy* and eventually a book and a motion picture.

This fascination with Gilmore's life and execution suggests what he himself discovered in his frustrated attempts to die: that as the first American nearing execution under revised death penalty statutes, he represented political, moral, and social issues much larger than himself. As Richard Giauque of the American Civil Liberties Union argued, "Society has an interest in this wholly apart from Mr. Gilmore's wishes."[4] The case raised several pressing questions for the American public: not only whether Gilmore had the right to insist that his death sentence be executed, but whether the majority of Americans had any appetite to see Gilmore, or indeed any other death-row inmate, put to death by a state government. Capital punishment had been declared unconstitutional in 1972 based on "evolving standards of decency" that held the death penalty cruel and unusual,[5] and when the court reversed itself in 1976, it concluded that state death penalty laws expressed "the community's belief" in the validity of capital punishment.[6] State legislatures could be trusted to assess the moral consensus of their communities without federal intervention, the court decided. But was there a moral consensus over capital punishment, and if so what was it? The flesh-and-blood figure of Gary Gilmore gave the nation a chance to test its convictions regarding the ultimate sanction, and until the debate was at least aired if not resolved, Gilmore's fate was not his alone.

If that were not so then Gilmore might easily have gotten his wish to die, since both he and the state of Utah desired a speedy execution. The condemned man repeatedly insisted that his decision to die was a private one, involving nobody else; it just happened to coincide with the sentence rendered in a Utah courthouse. Instead, the many appeals that were filed against Gilmore's wishes resulted in delay after delay, clearly signaling the far-reaching repercussions of an execution. Both individuals and groups sought reprieves. Members of Gilmore's family wished to save his life; strangers from the ACLU and the NAACP appealed on behalf of other death-row inmates, for whom Gilmore's execution would set a deadly precedent. These appeals continued until the very end, while Gilmore remained equally determined to see his sentence performed. Early in the morning of his last day, the ACLU unsuccessfully solicited a stay of execution from the US Supreme Court. Gilmore was executed before a firing squad on January 17, 1977, just six months after the murders for which he was sentenced.

II. PUBLIC DEBATE AS LITERARY FORM: THE EXECUTIONER'S SONG

Gilmore's case provides a fascinating modern example of the hold that executions take on the public imagination, since the event was well documented in the press and in Norman Mailer's novel *The Executioner's Song*, published in 1979. Described as "new journalism," the novel lacks a narrator and offers instead what Mailer called "photographic realis[m]," material without interpretation.[7]

The novel represents a symphony of voices, both real and invented,[8] of the convicted man, his family, his victims, and the attorneys and journalists involved in the case. Every scene, every detail, is rendered either from the point of view of a partic-ular character or from a printed source. In this heterogeneous form, Mailer replicated the vigorous debate that ensued once Gilmore accepted his death sentence. Much of the novel is composed of newspaper accounts and some of the more than 12,000 pages of interviews conducted first by Schiller and others during Gilmore's final months and later by Mailer himself, supporting the novelist's claim to journalistic realism despite many authorial liberties.

The author's chosen form raises some of the same issues I have been following in this history of capital cases, issues also posed by Jürgen Habermas in *The Struc-tural Transformation of the Public Sphere*. In bourgeois society, we will recall, the state's authority is monitored by informed critical discussions among the people, who follow political events in the press and "compel public authority to legitimate itself before public opinion."[9] Since Mailer's depiction of the prolonged battles over the execution involves religious groups, human rights advocates, lawyers, writers, and others hoping to capitalize on the event, the criminal can be seen as the palpable object upon which battles for social and political authority fastened. The many voices (private and official) replicate the public meeting place we have seen before, both in Nathaniel Hawthorne's famous novel and in the many printed responses to capital cases that I have been considering. The instrument of this meeting place, of course, is the printed page, that of both the newspaper and the self-published literary text. In Mailer's novel, a single text brings together a variety of printed and spoken points of view, enabling characters to voice their opinions and readers to reflect on the many viewpoints presented. Mailer's own explanations of his novel suggest that he intended something similar to Habermas's public debates or the printed debates I have been discussing. As Mailer told William F. Buckley, he had hoped to

> write a book that will really make people think in a way they haven't quite thought before. This material made me begin to look at ten or 20 serious questions in an altogether new fashion, and it made me humble in that I just didn't know the answers. . . . I thought it might be very nice for once just to write a book which doesn't have all the answers, but poses delicate questions with a great deal of evi-dence and a great deal of material and let people argue over it.[10]

Buckley points out the "utility of this new form" that Mailer has invented: "so many people on reading [his] book will be invited to speculate on [Gilmore's] motives and on the motives of the people who are major characters."[11] As Buckley noted, the author intended that the debates figured within the novel continue beyond its pages, as readers elaborate and deliberate upon the "serious questions" raised by Gilmore's life. Given that the *Furman* Supreme Court decision of 1972 insisted that "evolving standards of decency" could justly be measured only by considering the sentiments of a knowledgeable public—"people who were fully informed as to the purposes of the penalty and its liabilities"—Mailer's decision to foster a debate within and beyond the pages of his novel had important consequences beyond those we typi-cally associate with the conversations within novel-reading communities.[12] As we shall see, the debate that Mailer both reflected and helped to shape looked to the figure of the condemned criminal in order to consider the uses of objectivity and compassion when regarding convicts.

Mailer's most important innovation, considering the social and political significance of his theme—and considering, as we have seen, the historically tendentious uses of execution literature—might be his readiness to facilitate debate rather than to insist on a thesis. Early critics of the novel were nearly unanimous in expressing their surprise at this uncharacteristic contribution from a man whose ideas were already so familiar (not to say emphatic) to his readers. Joan Didion wrote that, given what she had heard of "this 'Gary Gilmore book,'" it "seemed one of those lives in which the narrative would yield no further meaning. . . . It might well have been only another test hole in a field [Mailer] had drilled before, a few further reflections on murder as an existential act, an appropriation for himself of the book he invented for *An American Dream*."[13] John Garvey confessed, "When I saw that *Playboy* was excerpting something from a book by Mailer on the execution of Gary Gilmore I imagined a third-person Mailer under another name trying to figure out how he felt about a person getting shot. It promised to be a tasteless thing, brilliant and low."[14] Instead, the finished novel (and indeed, the very process of writing it) surprised even its author, who admitted that his initial plans fell away as he wrote. "When I began the book," Mailer explained,

> I thought I would probably do an essay on the nature of capital punishment, on what to do with our prisons, on why people murder, on karma, on a dozen different things. I was drawn to the book because Gary Gilmore embodied all these questions. And I discovered as I wrote it, as the material came in and as I went out and got more material . . . that I knew less and less. Or let me put it this way, I knew more and more and I understood less and less.[15]

A bewildered author assembling material, Mailer created the ideal conditions for an exchange of opinion. The world he invokes in *The Executioner's Song* is a world of public debate about a number of pressing political and ethical questions relevant to the life of Gary Gilmore and the society he left behind; Mailer's straightforward, unembellished style invites his readers to participate in that debate and to reexamine their culture's standards of decency.

In some ways Mailer's novel is the almost unrecognizable descendent of its colonial precursor, the execution sermon, whose primary purpose was to explain a punishment as the inevitable and just outcome of a willful crime. Nevertheless, Mailer's novel preserves many of the original elements of execution literature. When colonial executions were controlled by both church and state, as we have seen, one stated and highly emphasized purpose was to enable the condemned individual to repent of his sins. Often the execution was delayed until spiritual counselors could be confident that they had done everything possible to bring their charges to full penitence and, they hoped, eventual redemption. In Mailer's novel, Mike Deamer, the deputy attorney general of Utah, tells the prison warden to prepare for Gilmore's execution and then reflects on the event as colonial clergymen had done three hundred years before:

> Deamer felt we were here on earth to be tested on whether we could live right-eously. Repentance was the key. An individual had to make restitution in his life-time for what he'd done wrong, except for those few crimes for which you could not obtain forgiveness in this life. One was murder. . . . To repent, you had to allow your life to be taken. Deamer didn't feel, therefore, that by giving the go-ahead, he was rendering null and void the existence of Gary Gilmore. Rather, he was enabling Gilmore to pass on to the spiritual sphere where at some point down the road of eternity, the man would obtain forgiveness for these murders.[16]

While few other characters in Mailer's novel hold Deamer's peculiar position on the death penalty, its very utterance indicates that even among those who support capital punishment, the reasons for its implementation differ widely. Here, through Deamer, Mailer reminds his readers of a powerful earlier tradition, one whose concern for the condemned man had been all but lost in twentieth-century America, bent on demonstrating the people's vengeance. When, for example, the attorney general and Gilmore are both in court arguing for the same outcome, the spokesman for the state insists "that Gilmore was not going to die because he wanted to, but because it was the lawful proper sentence for what he had done."[17] These two different justifi-cations for Gilmore's execution remind readers that the purpose of capital punish-ment has evolved as America developed from a religious to a secular community, and that further development in the penal code is therefore likely.

Executions, as we have seen, have always been intended to regulate the behavior of subjects by providing examples of those who break the law. The earliest printed accounts of executions furthered that ambition by stating clearly and vigor-ously the relationship between crime and punishment. When Mailer includes the voice of Noall Wootton, the prosecuting attorney, he seems to be briefly recalling that tradition. Wootton

> had made up his mind to go for Death after looking at Gilmore's record. It showed violence in prison, a history of escape, and unsuccessful efforts made at rehabilita-tion. Wootton could only conclude that, one: Gilmore would be looking to escape; two: he would be a hazard to other inmates and guards; and, three: rehabilitation was hopeless. Couple this to a damned cold-blooded set of crimes.[18]

Wootton's horror at the "cold-blooded" crimes seems to explain and justify Utah's position in seeking the death penalty, one that is enforced by Mailer's grim depic-tions of the murders themselves. But Mailer challenges this position even as he pres-ents it, and not least because Wootton's is only one among hundreds of viewpoints we encounter. Wootton is clearly identified with the executioners of the story from his initial appearance at Gilmore's trial until the execution, which he is reluctantly compelled to attend. But the executioner of the book's title, the one whose song we hear, is not simply Wootton; Mailer means us to see in that figure Gilmore himself, as well as the state of Utah.[19] The criminal and his prosecutor are paired ineluctably from the beginning: both are identified with executions and both seek the execution of Gary Gilmore. The paradox of Wootton's distaste for Gilmore and Gilmore's obscene remarks to Wootton in the face of their coinciding interests only emphasizes the profoundly intricate ethical dilemma posed by Gilmore's last months.

That ambivalence is clear when the jury delivers its death sentence and Mailer turns to the prosecutor for his thoughts. "Noall had this bothersome feeling now. It was in the impression he had had all the way that Gilmore was more intelligent than himself. Wootton knew damned well that Gilmore was more educated. Self-educated, but better educated. 'Jesus Almighty,' Wootton said to himself, 'the system has really failed with this man, just miserably failed.'"[20] Here, as if for the first time, the prosecuting attorney identifies with his adversary and sees him not primarily as a cold-blooded killer but as an intelligent man who has been destroyed by the criminal justice system, the very system that Wootton represents. His reflections, too late to save Gilmore and inappropriate, anyway, for the man who represents the state's determination to execute, nevertheless undermine his unambiguous official position. In their desire for an execution, Wootton and Gilmore share a conviction: when Gilmore insists on going ahead with his execution, he explains in terms that would have been familiar to Wootton. "I just believe I ought to be executed, I feel myself responsible," he says, as if he has internalized the arguments of the prosecution. But when he elaborates, he voices the very thought that has come over Wootton: "I've been in eighteen years and I'm not about to do another twenty. Rather than live in this hole, I'd choose to be dead."[21] Here Gilmore implies both that the prison system has failed to train or rehabilitate him and, more alarmingly, that its conditions are not preferable to death by a firing squad. But when the prosecuting attorney says these things, we are forced to take them more seriously, to see Gilmore through a sympathetic consciousness that is all the more compelling for being Wootton's.

In this way, Mailer undercuts the official position of government regarding capital punishment, at times replacing the detached, official voice of the law with a more humane and compassionate voice. Soon after the murders, as if to anticipate the upsurge of sympathy to come, Mailer supplies us with the thoughts of Lieutenant Nielsen, the officer assigned to the Gilmore murder case. "In police work, you had to play a part from time to time. Nielsen liked that. The thing is, for this role, he was supposed to show compassion. From past experience, he knew it wouldn't be altogether a role. Sooner or later, he would really feel compassion. That was all right. That was one of the more interesting sides of police work."[22]

Eschewing a narrative center, Mailer extends whatever sympathy Gilmore merits by means of other characters. For this task, the novelist looks not only to Gilmore's close friends and family, but to people capable of more detachment, even to those who represent the law. When the parole officer, Mont Court, examines Gilmore's artwork, he considers that there must be more to Gilmore than violence. "In these paintings Court was able to see a part of the man simply not reflected in the prison record. Mont Court saw tenderness. He thought, Gilmore can't be all evil, all bad. There's something that's salvageable."[23] As Court's very name suggests, even agents of the laws Gilmore has broken can be inclined to offer their charity rather than hard justice.

A different kind of sympathy emerges when we turn to the voices of those who knew Gilmore before the murders and who can testify to a different side of the condemned man. Gilmore's cousin, Brenda Nicols, remembers Gilmore not as an international celebrity who understands how to manipulate the press but as a newly released convict who struggles with the mundane tasks of earning and spending money. In prison so long that he doesn't know what to do with his freedom, Gilmore finds himself daunted by so ordinary a venture as buying clothes. When he arrives at her door newly paroled and wearing a pair of black plastic shoes, Brenda thinks, "Wow, that's really cheap. They didn't even give him a pair of leather shoes to go home in."[24] Later, in a department store, Gilmore stands around helplessly, never having bought clothes before:

> After a while, he said, "Hey, I don't know how to go about this. Are you supposed to take the pants off the shelf, or does somebody issue them to you?"
>
> Brenda really felt sorry for him. "Find the ones you want," she said, "and tell the clerk. If you want to try them on, you can."
>
> "Without paying for them?"
>
> "Oh, yeah, you can try them on first," she said.[25]

Other characters offer similar depictions of a helpless but earnest man trying to adapt to his unfamiliar freedom. Spencer McGrath, Gilmore's boss, is impressed by Gary's stoicism:

> It was all of a week before Spencer McGrath learned that Gary was walking to work whenever he couldn't hitch a ride, and he only found out because there had been some snow that morning and Gilmore came in late. It had taken him longer to walk all the way.
>
> That got to Spencer. Gilmore had never told a soul. Such pride was the makings of decent stuff. McGrath made sure he had a ride home that night.[26]

Although these passages rarely offer full-fledged arguments, recording instead detached vignettes and apparently apolitical thoughts and feelings, they do lay a foundation for one possible argument against capital punishment in Gilmore's case: that after years of incarceration, Gilmore was unable to survive in the world outside of prison, a world whose rituals might seem natural to those of us trained to observe them, but were altogether bewildering to a man who had spent most of his adult years behind bars. Freedom for Gilmore was a burden that he could not endure.

On the other hand, Mailer takes care not to diminish Gilmore's impulsiveness, immaturity, and hostility during his three months of freedom. We see a man who embarrasses his cousin by talking loudly in the movie theater, tells obscene prison stories to friends and strangers, steals drive-in movie speakers to retaliate against management regulations, pilfers beer and groceries, picks fights that he can't win, violates his parole by leaving Utah, and smashes a woman's car windshield because she will not have sex with him. If at times we see him sympathetically, Gilmore is no hero in the first half of Mailer's novel.

The heroic, tragic language is reserved for his mother, Bessie, once a beautiful woman, "a farm girl who wouldn't work in the sun and wore large sun hats and long gloves," now "poor as a church mouse," faded and arthritic and alone.[27] The widow of a violent drifter and con man, the bereaved mother of a son who died of complications from a stab wound, Bessie is living in a hot trailer in Oregon when she hears the news of the Utah murders. "There was a suction-type feeling inside the trailer. If anybody made the wrong move, it would all disintegrate."[28] Joan Didion notes that "a desolate wind seems to blow through the lives of these women."[29] Bessie is one of the women whose sufferings are intensified by Gary's actions. Unable to stop her son's violence and forbidden by him to appear at his trial and plead for his life, Bessie can do nothing but seek refuge in memories. "That childhood might exist no longer, but she tried to live in it now. It was better than floods of misery that a son of her flesh had killed the sons of other mothers. That burned in her heart like the pain which flared in the arthritis of her knees. Pain was a boring conversationalist who never stopped, just found new topics."[30]

Like Noall Wootton, Bessie Gilmore provides a complicated response to her son's crimes. Heartbroken at the violence he has visited upon innocent victims, she nonetheless understands that his acts might be partly explained by his experiences. Her grief for his victims melts into grief for their murderer. "Yes, Gary was a sad and lonely man, one of the most sad and one of the most lonely. 'Oh, God,' thought Bessie, 'he was in prison so long, he didn't know how to work for a living or pay a bill. All the while he should have been learning, he was locked up.'"[31]

More than sympathy for Gary Gilmore, however, these scenes summon tragic pathos for his mother, bestowing on the housebound widow a magnificent stature that is not matched by any other character in Mailer's novel, not even the convicted man himself. Here, for example, is a private look at the woman as she sits helplessly at home:

> The only thing to be said for these present hours under the heat of the sun and the airless night of the trailer was that heat never made her feel as alone as the winter damp. Winter was the time when she felt so cold she had need of all the life she had lived. But now at the age of 63, Bessie could feel old as 83 in the cold snowbound cemetery of all those feelings that had frozen in the middle of July by the word that Gary had killed two boys. She kept seeing the face of Mr. Bushnell whose face she did not know, but it did not matter, for his head was covered with blood.
>
> "Oh, Gary," whispered the child that never ceased to live in the remains of her operations and twisted joints, "Oh, Gary, how could you?"[32]

The long, mournful cadences of Mailer's sentences in passages like these attest that the pain instigated by Gilmore's crimes is not confined to the friends of the victims;

the difficulties raised by Gilmore's life and death cannot be easily laid out into neat moral and political positions.

III. "AN ACTOR PLAYING A SAINT"

Though he never matches his mother's heart-wrenching dignity, Mailer's Gary Gilmore rises dramatically in stature once he faces the appeals board and declares his intention to die. Father Meersman, one of Gilmore's spiritual counselors, describes what drew him and many others to the condemned man. Speaking at Gilmore's memorial service, Meersman explains:

> I came into his life because of a very unusual statement I heard a man make when he was condemned to death. I told him that when I met him the first time. I said it's quite an unusual statement and if you mean it, why I will offer you all that I can to bring it about. And the statement that he made is one I imagine that you've all heard: I wish to die with dignity.[33]

Though most of his associates initially suspect Gilmore's sincerity, even his opponents in court come to believe and respect him, and they locate their regard in his resolve to die with dignity. In his spoken and written communications to the court, Gary impresses onlookers with his calm eloquence and intelligence. After the first stay of execution, when Gilmore writes a letter to the court, his message is so compelling that the newspapers print it. "Don't the people of Utah have the courage of their convictions?" he challenges them. "You sentence a man to die—me—and when I accept this most extreme punishment with grace and dignity, you, the people of Utah want to back down and argue with me about it."[34] Here and elsewhere, Gilmore's logical explication of cause and effect highlights the illogic and absurdity of the criminal justice system. He later addresses the board of pardons with a similar challenge: "Your Board dispenses privilege, and I have always thought that privileges were sought, desired, earned and deserved, and I seek nothing from you, don't desire anything from you, haven't earned anything and I don't deserve anything either."[35] In his simple interpretation of his sentence, Gilmore implicitly provokes the criminal justice system either to abolish the death penalty or to face up to it by implementing the death sentences that have been passed, to decide once and for all whether it countenances state-sponsored executions. By forcing the state of Utah to execute him without delay, he deprives them of the customary lengthy process, one purpose of which is to give the government time to convince itself that execution is an appropriate punishment. As David Guest proposes, a prompt execution is sometimes "more traumatic for one's executioners."[36]

Speaking plainly and intelligently, Mailer's Gilmore impresses lawyers and judges with his calm acceptance of his death sentence. Over dinner on the night of an appeal, the attorney general describes the convict to his family as "on an intellectual par with the Court. In fact, Hansen could not think of another case in which the accused person seemed to be able to understand and deal with lawyers and Judges as peers. . . . You never had the feeling he was contemptuous of the Judges or of the lawyers' right to argue for him, or against him. That added dignity."[37] The district attorney is also struck by Gilmore's composure. "Earl knew he wouldn't call it admiration, but during the Board of Pardons Hearing, he did get to feel good about the way Gilmore was conducting himself. The man was on a hunger strike, yet his intellect was keen."[38]

Mark Edmundson argues that "the climax of the book . . . comes when Gilmore, having been condemned and imprisoned for the two murders, chooses to force the state of Utah to carry out his sentence and execute him."[39] Gilmore's "triumph of wit," his "most imaginative act," "consists in capitulating and becoming just the kind of well-disciplined subject everyone always wanted him to be, but at the wrong moment. The most imaginative act of Gilmore's life, and the costliest to himself, is to pretend to possess no imagination whatever" when he declares that he didn't know his death sentence "was a joke."[40] Though Gilmore might, as Edmundson argues, wield his apparent compliance in deeply satiric ways, he does not seem ironic to the many witnesses of his day in court. Lawrence Schiller, observing Gilmore in court, is reminded of "a movie [he] saw once about the Middle Ages where a fellow in a white smock trudged in to be burned at the stake. Here, it was loose white pants and a long white shirt, but the effect was similar. Made the prisoner look like an actor playing a saint."[41] In accepting his death sentence calmly, Gilmore does what countless criminals (penitent or not) have done since the beginning of state-sponsored executions: he transforms widespread anger at his crimes into admiration and awe for a man who looks death in the eye without flinching. His act is also highly political. Though the state might maintain that appeals processes ensure that no unjust death sentence is carried out, Gilmore's initially fruitless refusals to appeal underscore a deep contradiction in the logic of death penalty statutes: the state wants to wield its authority over its subjects but cannot abide the risk of seeming bloodthirsty. Hence the seemingly endless rounds of appeals and the de facto mandatory appeals process in a state with no official requirement for appeals. Gilmore forces the public to confront these contradictions, even if it means forfeiting his life to do so. No longer a two-bit thief and killer, Gary Gilmore becomes almost a martyr to his government's sense of public order and to the "standard of decency" embraced by twentieth-century American society.

Because the spectacle of death, as we have seen, often generates sympathy for the condemned criminal rather than unqualified endorsement of a society's laws, state governments began privatizing executions in the 1830s. Still, as I have been arguing, published eyewitness accounts require the reader vicariously to experience the execution. As Guest contends, Mailer's detailed narrative of Gilmore's life and death "rhetorically reinstates the public scaffold."[42] So while governments perform executions in part to regulate the behavior of the citizenry, the spectacle of death, particularly death at the hands of official leaders, often generates sympathy for the condemned criminal, even at the expense of governing authority. Benjamin Rush had warned of this unexpected, sometimes dangerous sympathy in 1787, and we see it vividly in Mailer's novel as in Gary Gilmore's life. The more Gilmore insists on being executed, the more public sympathies encircle him.

We can understand the profound media attention after Gilmore's suicide attempt in part according to this historical tendency to become absorbed with a man who faces his death without struggle, even when his death is a socially sanctioned penalty for two violent crimes. Edmundson argues that the most heroic characters in the novel are those who, "liv[ing] strongly in the knowledge of death receive some share of Mailer's elegiac tones."[43] In Gilmore's failed suicide attempt, the public perhaps saw evidence that the man really wished to die. Although the media response was by no means unanimously sympathetic—indeed, both *Time* and *Newsweek* magazines featured deeply critical stories in the aftermath of Gilmore's overdose—still, his story took a personal turn after the incident, as newspaper coverage began emphasizing the "human interest" elements of his life, including his romance with Nicole Barrett.

Mailer uses Tamera Smith, a rookie newspaper reporter, to demonstrate the public's growing engagement not with the legal issues of Gilmore's case but with the romantic subplot of his story. When she first observes Gilmore at his preliminary hearing, she is captivated by the presence of Gilmore's girlfriend, Nicole. "Tamera felt humiliated for [Gary] in leg manacles, walking in short jerky steps like he was a spavined monster or something, but it was the girl who drew her. . . . The drama of it came right over Tamera. There's another woman in the story besides the widows, she said to herself."[44] What *Newsweek* called "a Bonnie and Clyde Patina" Tamera Smith sees as a moving love story.[45] Knowing about Nicole's suicide pact with Gary, Smith reads Gary's letters to Nicole in preparation for the story she plans to write after Nicole's death. Mailer represents the allure of this romantic subplot within the story, not just in Tamera's exhilaration but also in the haphazard reactions of Dennis Boaz, the lawyer who has signed on to help Gilmore win his legal battle for execution. Boaz changes his mind after Gilmore's suicide attempt and decides that he must fight to save his client's life. Here, Boaz is driven not by any moral or political belief about the cruelty of capital punishment: he has come to believe that "even in an ideal society, we might still need the death penalty. Capital punishment, properly applied, could say a lot about being responsible for one's actions."[46] Rather, Boaz has been persuaded by the media attention to this romantic melodrama and convinces himself that Gilmore's sentence might be commuted and the man transferred to a medium-security prison that allows connubial visits. "Cottage incarceration was what he was talking about."[47] Though ludicrous, Boaz's interest in Gilmore's romantic life was shared by countless others and encouraged by the press. While Gilmore awaited execution, he received over forty thousand personal letters, many of them love letters from strangers. More than ten years after the execution, moreover, Nicole Barrett was interviewed on the television show *A Current Affair*.[48]

The Barrett-Gilmore romance becomes tawdry in Mailer's treatment not because of the elements of their relationship but because of the way that strangers feed greedily on the details while the media indulges their appetite. These intimate details, however, are not of themselves distasteful, for Mailer conveys them not from a judging distance but as if from the minds of the characters themselves. In this way the novel expands our vista by offering private glimpses into the minds of virtually every person involved in Gilmore's life, from the wives of the men he murders to every minor actor engaged in the legal battles that ensue. Arlett notes that Mailer's frequent use of free indirect speech enables him empathetically to fuse his voice and sensibility with those of his characters.[49] The book takes on the proportions of a Russian novel as minor characters come and go, enjoying genuine authenticity as long as they engage our attention.[50]

It is true, of course, that not all characters figure as magnificently as those who are acutely aware of their own mortality, and perhaps even, as Edmundson again argues, that the victims and their wives "don't rate the tragic tones that Gary and Nicole get."[51] But John Hersey is surely mistaken when he argues that Mailer "does not do anything like justice to the vision of the kindly people of the town of Provo, firmly (and perhaps, in the context of this drama, disastrously) fixed and drenched in Mormon ideas of the correctional effects of love and decency."[52] These characters may live simply, unassailed by the recurring dreams of beheadings that have tormented Gary Gilmore since childhood. And their approach to life may be innocent, as we see in this description of the Jensen marriage:

> He never raised his voice and neither did she. If, occasionally, she felt like speaking sharply, she wouldn't. They had decided right from the beginning that they would never leave each other without kissing goodbye. Nor would they go to bed with personal problems unsolved. If they were mad at each other, they would stay up and talk it out. They were not going to sleep even one night being mad at each other.[53]

Though not made, perhaps, of the stuff of Greek heroes, these characters are nevertheless vividly present to readers in their full—albeit ordinary—humanity, and their deaths are no less tragic for their law-abiding integrity. Mailer's sympathetic narrative stance, I believe, triumphs precisely because it forces readers to understand and feel for vastly different characters, characters whose own interests are profoundly at odds with each other. For example, at the end of a chapter devoted to Gilmore's suicide attempt and his cousin Brenda's frustrated attempts to see him in the hospital, Mailer abruptly places a newspaper excerpt regarding the widow of one of the murder victims. "Bushnell's widow, who is expecting another child shortly after the first of the year, has gone to California to live with her mother-in-law. Family members say she goes to pieces at a mention of her husband's name."[54] As Robert Merrill contends, "If we read this book as Mailer conceived it, we must feel compassion for nearly everyone."[55]

By juxtaposing these two scenes—Brenda's tormented worry about Gilmore and Debbie Bushnell's bereavement—Mailer makes it nearly impossible for readers to take a resolute ethical position on the central question of the novel, whether Gilmore should be executed by the state. Our sympathies are directed toward those who love the condemned man, and just as we get involved in their side of the story, we are reminded of the profound suffering that Gilmore has caused, which will endure long after his execution. Mailer claims that he was aiming for this confusion of values and convictions, for such bewilderment is the defining element of fiction. As for nonfiction,

> you read it because you want to know what the author definitively thinks about a subject. . . . Whereas I think in fiction, . . . we want to create life. We want to give the readers the feeling that they are participating in the life of the characters they're reading about. And to the degree that they're participating in it, they shouldn't not nec-essarily understand everything that's going on any more than we do in life.[56]

Mailer's book is so deeply complicated because its author takes seriously the pains and beliefs of nearly all its characters. To do so is to understand that the web of hard-ships, rightly seen from a distance, cannot easily be disentangled. Suffering abounds in this novel, and though individual characters might trace their difficulties to a par-ticular cause, readers with a wider view see those causes entwined with still earlier ones. Bessie Gilmore, for instance, lives in a cheap trailer because the Mormon Church refused to help with her mortgage payments after her husband's death. When a longtime family friend, familiar with Bessie's troubles, learns of the murders, she thinks, "I'll bet a nickel he knew those boys were Mormons before he killed them."[57] Though Mailer does not explicitly link any of these incidents, he offers them to us readers to connect as we can. When Gary inflicts suffering on the families of two young Mormon men, he is returning in rage the hardships that the church had vis-ited upon his mother. But when his mother considers her son's bleak future, she reflects as well on the lost futures of his victims and enables us to understand that aggressors are also the casualties of aggression.

Several readers have charged Mailer with distorting the ethical dimensions of the Gilmore story by identifying too thoroughly with the murderer at the expense of his victims and those who live peaceable lives, by allowing his own admiration to penetrate the story, "causing uneasiness in some readers who consider the prisoner's inexcusably barbaric crime."[58] Whereas Mailer believes that with his decision not to appeal, Gilmore "begins to rise a degree in stature,"[59] some of his readers regret that the novelist allows the murderer to recreate himself, in Edmundson's phrase, as a romantic original. Garvey worries that by making Gilmore "look more interesting than the con he was" Mailer effectively falsifies the real Gary Gilmore.[60] Guest com-plains about the novel's ideological agenda, explaining that "by diminishing the stature of those who conform, and by elevating the stature of those who rebel, the novel . . . finds meaning in Gilmore's crimes by retelling his story as a narrative of incarceration, murder, and redemption."[61] Scheffler argues that Mailer's depiction warps a truth about incarceration that he ought to have addressed more honestly. "An exploration of the real Gary Gilmore," she writes, "should more appropriately focus on the great loss of humanity that occurs when a prison setting proves more con-genial than society to a man who has spent his life incarcerated. Not at all a final tri-umph of the spirit, Gilmore's story dramatically shows how imprisonment can become a habit incapacitating a man to survive decently outside."[62] In this criticism,

Scheffler indicates her desire for a more naturalistic novel, one with a more explicit polemic about the destructiveness of the criminal justice system. We might say she wants a book more in keeping with the one Mailer had expected to write, a book about "what to do with our prisons."[63] We could say the same for Mailer's other critics, who want the novel to take a particular ideological position.

Norman Mailer anticipated such criticisms, acknowledging that

> an awful lot of people are going to resent this book and they're going to say there's something just swinish about glorifying a two-time killer and a bad man . . . There's no doubt in my mind that if you write a book, particularly a long book, about one person you've affected their place in history . . . you've altered the nature of that man's life and that man's record. He is taken more seriously."[64]

While this novel does immortalize Gilmore's life and record, however, it would be a mistake to argue that Mailer's Gilmore is categorically heroic. For one thing, as I have tried to show, during his brief experience of freedom Mailer's Gilmore is selfish, impulsive, and violent. Mailer has confessed his exasperation with the raw materials of Gilmore's personality:

> I found as I was doing the research on him that some of the time I'd come across turns of mind in him that were startling and impressive—And then just about the time I would begin to feel I was really dealing with a man who is possessed of, let's not say superior intelligence, but certainly good intelligence, he would say or do something that I thought was so dumb that he would be disappointing.[65]

Nor does Mailer disguise these elements in his depiction of Gilmore. In his letters to Nicole from prison Gary is at times manipulative and obscene; when he convinces Nicole to take her life, he displays a selfish disregard for her two young children and for her future. While he appears at times "saintly,"[66] he also comes across as smug, arrogant, and childish.

While readers may wish to consider this depiction of Gilmore as part of Mailer's longstanding attraction to violence, there is yet another way of understanding the fictional Gilmore's charismatic allure, one that places Mailer in the much larger historical tradition of execution literature that we have been exploring. If we recall the early American criminal narratives, we will remember that when convicted criminals stand before the public and honestly admit to their crimes and explain their pasts, they command the (sometimes unwilling) respect and sympathy of that public. In his depiction of the condemned Gary Gilmore, Mailer takes part in a literary tradition that extends back to the earliest colonial American execution sermons and dying confessions.

If Mailer has affected Gilmore's place in history, then—and there is no question but that he has—we need to consider the historical dimensions of Gilmore's legacy. What, in other words, are the social and ethical consequences of Mailer's relentless look at Gilmore's last nine months? As I have been arguing, it would be too simple merely to contend that Mailer's work has conferred a heroic rank upon Gilmore. But we are compelled, as Mailer suggests, to take more seriously the man and his role in American cultural history, to ponder more thoughtfully the questions his execution forced the American public to consider. Mailer's choice of subject for such a project is fitting, because the 1972 *Furman* decision seemed to point the way toward permanent abolition of the death penalty. That it did not—that Gilmore's execution in 1977 instead ushered in a new era of capital punishment—is part of the story that continues beyond the pages of Mailer's novel.

When a person is sentenced to death by his government, his or her situation throws into sharp relief the truth that John Locke pointed out about civilized living: that by belonging to a civil society, we abridge our rights in exchange for certain protections and services. We agree to live within the limits of our laws or to serve society's sentence if we violate those laws. Death, of course, is the most extreme sentence, and it reminds us of Rousseau's contention that political subjects are never really free, but always owned and governed by their communities. When subjects are sentenced to death, they eventually give up their lives to the cause of social order, but in the meantime they give their lives over to the purpose of setting an example for all other subjects. They become of necessity public figures, publicly owned. We have seen this from the beginning of American executions—from the subjects who spoke their last words to a receptive audience, to those who addressed their audiences indirectly through the printed word. In all cases the condemned criminal takes part in a staged drama enacted in the name of civilized society.

Mailer's narrative treatment of Gilmore emphasizes this role of the political subject, for at no time are we allowed to enter the central character's thoughts in an unmediated way, as we are with all of the others. Instead, everything we know of Gilmore is first filtered through the perceptions of some other source. Mailer has explained his impression that, after reviewing thousands of pages of interviews, he still "didn't understand [Gilmore] at all."[67] Though the novelist believed that Gilmore was perfectly sane, his conduct remained "off the normal spectrum of human behavior."[68] Mailer's narrative form emphasizes his sense of Gilmore's elusive personality. Without a central narrator to interpret or diagnose the novel's focal point, Gilmore can only be explained by those individuals who, each having access only to his or her own private impressions, attempt to make sense of his place in their own lives.[69] Arlett notes that in this novel whose primary instrument is free indirect discourse ("which affords . . . penetrations of individual personality"), Gilmore alone "seems not to admit entry via free indirect speech, as though he, the center of the mystery of the American temper, is finally an unavailable keystone."[70] We gain access to the man, of course, through his letters to Nicole and excerpted interviews with his lawyers and press agent, but we are never allowed to enter the man's private consciousness.

Mailer explained to Buckley that were he "writing a more conventional novel," he "would have made every effort to get into his mind, and . . . would have attempted to explain him."[71] Instead, he provides his readers with a nearly exhaustive collection of eyewitness accounts of the condemned man, then leaves us, like those who knew Gilmore directly, to "speculate on [Gilmore's] motives."[72] What we discover, perhaps to our dismay, is how inadequate these materials are for any real understanding of the man. As Edmundson rightly maintains, "Gilmore doesn't provide enough fixity" for us to begin to understand him.[73]

John Hersey takes Mailer to task for his chosen literary tool, free indirect speech, which employs "Mailer tag lines" or characteristically Maileresque diction and presents it "as if *within the point of view of a character*. This is not reporting," he contends; "it is projection."[74] Much critical ink has been spilled trying to determine whether Mailer is present or absent as an authorial voice in his novel. While many readers praise him for suppressing his own ego and allowing his materials to speak for themselves,[75] others observe that an authorial voice penetrates the impressions of Mailer's characters. For Hersey, journalism is at fault when it poses as documentary truth and attempts to conceal the author's personality and judgments. I wish to propose, however, not only that what Hersey sees as authorial projection is unavoidable in the context that Mailer has chosen, but even further, that Mailer knew exactly what he was doing when he chose to approach Gilmore only through the subjectivities of his other characters. By refusing to offer us entry into Gilmore's mind, Mailer dramatizes how all of our impressions of others are necessarily limited by our own consciousness. By using his own idioms to convey the thoughts of his characters, he indicates that even the most generous attempts to see from another person's point of view are inescapably limited. Sympathy resembles nothing so well as it resembles projection. As the philosopher and economist Adam Smith declared in 1759, all we can ever know of another's feelings is what we conceive "we should feel in a like situation."[76]

The sympathetic, subjective narrative stance of the novel, in other words—the attitude described as "new journalism"—is the perfect form for approaching a man whose impending execution has riveted both the nation and the international community. As we have seen in our exploration of earlier criminal narratives, the sympathy of the masses is a near certainty when a person condemned to execution accepts his death willingly and graciously, as Gilmore had done. The epistemological limitations of sympathy do not make it any less powerful. If we recall Benjamin Rush's concerns, that widespread sympathy is also a possible threat to the authority of the government agents who issue the death sentence. Here is Rush, writing in 1787 against public executions:

> By an immutable law of our nature, distress of all kinds, when *seen*, produces sympathy, and a disposition to relieve it. This sympathy, in generous minds, is not lessened by the distress being the offspring of crimes: on the contrary, even the crimes themselves are often palliated by the reflection that they were unfortunate consequences of extreme poverty—of seducing company—or of the want of a virtuous education, from the loss or negligence of parents in early life.[77]

We might also add, of course, "of a life spent behind bars." The point here is that when a criminal facing death is exposed to public scrutiny, it is difficult to prevent the public from dwelling on mitigating circumstances and coming to identify with the criminal, often at the expense of the state. Mailer seems to have chosen his form expressly in order to explore this aspect of popular sympathies.

IV. ORCHESTRATING PUBLIC SYMPATHIES

The phenomenon is even more dramatic in an age of mass-media news coverage. In addition to Mont Court, Noall Wootton, and Lieutenant Nielsen—all agents of the law who, as individuals, are able to look briefly beyond the official record into the heart of another human being—Mailer also provides us with an enormous media machine whose role it is to tell Gilmore's story in such a way as to create public interest. What happens when private sympathetic responses like those we have seen are orchestrated and broadened? Somewhere in the middle of the novel, Mailer reports a conversation between Stanley Greenberg and David Susskind, two television writers interested in producing a documentary on Gary Gilmore's life, crimes, and the battle being waged over his impending execution. Greenberg is "aroused" by the possible political effects of such a documentary:

> "What fascinates me about this Gilmore case," he was saying, "is that it's an open commentary on the utter failure of our prison system to rehabilitate anybody. Why, the guy's been in and out his whole damn life and he just keeps getting worse.... Secondly, it could offer a wonderful statement about capital punishment and how godawful it is, eye for an eye. I even think that reaching a large audience can probably save the guy's life."[78]

Greenberg and Susskind imagine a documentary that, like the novel Mailer eventually wrote, will depict Gilmore as a human being whose life has been ruined by repeated incarcerations and a violent, unstable childhood. A successful documentary will see to it that viewers, modulating their rage over Gilmore's violent acts, will reflect upon the social conditions that made such acts inevitable, and will turn instead against the "godawful" solution of capital punishment.

By shifting their focus from an account of crimes and punishments to the circumstances that led to Gilmore's violent behavior, Greenberg and Susskind hope to prompt the kind of public discussion that does not restrict itself to an official version of social affairs. In this respect their imagined documentary will play upon different human sympathies than the regard for law that legitimates state-sponsored executions. Likewise, Mailer himself broadens the range of sympathetic readings of the case; while he never rules out the point of view of Gilmore's victims or prosecutors,[79] he forces his readers to share the perspectives, as we have seen, of an ever expanding collective of interested parties. The view of Phil Hansen, a criminal defense attorney, seems a comment on Mailer's own narrative strategies:

> Even a person who would swear by capital punishment might have to change their mind if it was their own mother on trial. "My mother's not like that," they would

say. "Something went wrong." People were ready for capital punishment only if they were sentencing a stranger. The approach was to get the Jury feeling like they understood the criminal.[80]

Likewise, Mailer extends narrative space to Gilmore, so that readers will feel they have tried to understand him. Just as Habermas suggested that novels allow their readers entrance into alien subjectivities, thereby enabling the practice of empathy that will later operate in the public sphere, Mailer's novel might at first appear to offer sympathy toward Gilmore as a means of championing the convicted criminal and undermining public authority.[81]

Mailer's use of what I consider a sympathetic narrative stance, however, should not be seen as a remedy for governmental excesses. Although we may be tempted to understand his sympathy as a weapon against the legal system, Mailer undercuts the value of that sympathy. For one thing, Gilmore himself is most articulate and noble when, at the board of pardons hearing, he contests those sympathetic friends and strangers who attempt to commute his sentence.[82] Furthermore, while Greenberg and Susskind do not reject an appeal to sympathy in their documentary, what they have in mind is far different from the kind of publicity eventually generated. As lawyers, press agents, and producers battle for the right to tell Gilmore's story, Susskind bows out, calling the drama "a very sensational, malodorous, exploitative mess."[83] "It's no longer a story about the breakdown of the criminal justice system," he complains, "it's a farce." Calling the case "bizarre and sick," Greenberg adds, "I think anybody who does the story now is jumping on a dead and putrefying body."[84]

That man turns out to be Lawrence Schiller. Outbidding the others for the rights to Gilmore's story, Schiller conducts the interviews that Mailer eventually used for his novel. Although Mailer never appears in his own book, then, he is represented by those who scramble over the "dead and putrefying body," particularly Schiller, represented here as a writer hoping to reform his soiled reputation. As Louis Menand argues, while Mailer does not "place his involvement in [the creation of the story] in the foreground," he solves the "problem" by

> elevating the character of Lawrence Schiller to a key role in the second half of the book. . . . He is a continual reminder that Gilmore's death (and the deaths of the two men Gilmore killed) is being turned to commercial use. You think, what a carrion bird is this Larry Schiller. Then you realize that you are holding in your hands the very commodity he has helped to manufacture. You are a shareholder in Gilmore, Inc.[85]

Less openly greedy than Dennis Boaz—he wants, primarily, to write the big story, not necessarily to get rich off it—Schiller still has his own interests clearly in mind; unlike Susskind and Greenberg, who are interested in the political effects of the Gilmore case, Schiller wants to sell a lurid story. Even his girlfriend accuses him of manipulating Gilmore's friends and family to acquire their rights;[86] his future collaborator, Barry Farrell, calls Schiller a "carrion bird."[87] When Norman Mailer confessed to economic reasons for wishing to write the novel, he linked himself rhetorically to Schiller, absorbing the taint of writing about a death for personal gain. "I've had money troubles the last ten years—" Mailer explained; "lately they've become so pressing that I can't really think of taking on any book unless I see some real possibility of earning at least as much money during the time I write as it will cost me to stay afloat. . . . I've become a commercial writer."[88] Lawrence Schiller, then, in both his methods and his personal interests, represents Mailer himself.

More than nearly any other character, Schiller identifies himself with a commitment to sympathy, but his sympathy is a debased, commercialized pretense. When he learns that he has won the battle over the rights to Gilmore's story, he admits, "I have a big problem. Where are the sympathetic characters?"[89] Finally agreeing to let Gilmore speak to other reporters, he says, "Let Gary talk. Maybe it can help our public posture. Our stance is that we are not here to watch a man die, but to come to understand him."[90]

Schiller's sympathetic attitude to his interviewees both provides the celebrated narrative form and implicates itself in voyeurism and greed. Gilmore's most tragic and noble moment, his appearance at the board of pardons hearing, is also the moment that Mailer chooses to expose Schiller as a vulture. While Gilmore addresses the board, insisting that he neither wishes nor deserves their interference, Mailer moves around the audience, taking his readers inward from the group's absorption with Gilmore to Schiller's private thoughts. "What a screen star this fellow would have made, thought Schiller, and was filled with elation at the thought that he had the rights to his life."[91] Mailer's double entendre makes Schiller's elation more disturbing still: in owning the "rights" to Gilmore's "life," the Hollywood producer not only owns the *story* of that life but in a very literal sense he also directs the outcome of that life, holding the power to influence whether Gilmore lives or dies. As everyone knows, Gilmore's story will only be valuable if he is executed, and it is Schiller's job to produce a best-selling story.[92]

Soon after he dramatizes the death of Gary Gilmore, Mailer inserts this newspaper story from the *Salt Lake Tribune*. It is titled, "Utah Execution: We Came Killing":

> We didn't tell you how we crawled around the sandbags in front of the dead man's chair, the sandbags still fresh with his blood. We didn't tell you how we hurried into the firing squad's canvas booth, and how we squinted out of the vertical slits where the rifles had been, squinted out at the chair and made ourselves a gift of the same view the executioners had viewed.
>
> We didn't tell you how we touched everything, touched every possible surface in the death shed. We didn't tell you of the looks on the faces of the prison guards, who watched in amazement as we went about our doings with such eagerness, such lust. We didn't tell you what we did to the death chair itself—the chair with the bullet holes in its leather back. We didn't tell you that, did we? Didn't tell you how we inserted our fingers into the holes, and rubbed our fingers around, feeling for ourselves, how deep and wide those death holes were. Feeling it all.[93]

This remarkable piece, inserted precisely where Mailer himself has been describing Gilmore's execution in exhaustive detail, sheds ironic light on the entire second half of the novel, devoted as it is to the intense and morbid media coverage of the Gilmore case. The author represents himself and his fellow journalists as scavengers for any admissible detail about the execution. His idioms, however, conflate the journalist's search for evidence with the rhetoric of sympathy and Christianity. The journalists, like a horde of doubting Thomases, probe the holes in the execution chair for evidence that Gilmore, this man whose life we have been following for almost a thousand pages, is really dead. And as if prefiguring Mailer's own attempts to see from every possible vantage point, they exchange places with Gilmore's executioners, as if thereby to feel for themselves the sensations of those riflemen. But their "feeling" is only tactile, not emotional, as the horrified faces of the prison guards attest. These attempts to report every detail, to feel it all, may resemble a sympathetic posture (whose idioms suggest exchanging places: we walk a mile in someone's shoes; we see from another person's perspective; we climb, as Atticus Finch advises, into someone else's skin), but they are really just empty, parodic gestures, betokening morbid curiosity but no real sympathy at all.

This newspaper clipping gives readers a rough sense of how Mailer himself came upon the details he uses in these last chapters. Although it is true that Mailer was not present for the execution—he did not get involved in the project until after Gilmore's death—his sources were among those in attendance. And indeed, these final chapters describe Gilmore's last moments with relentless detail. As Guest notes,

> Mailer's obsession with detail seems to increase as the narrative approaches the moment of death. The account of Gilmore's final forty-eight hours and the disposal of his body, at 157 pages, is as long as a good-sized novel. More than ten pages are devoted to the few minutes that Gilmore spends strapped in the execution chair. The narrative lingers over the shooting and the thirty seconds or so required for Gilmore's death and then follows the body into the autopsy room.[94]

Guest contends that Mailer's obsessively detailed description of Gilmore's last moments and later of his lifeless body, which we see being pulled apart over the course of five pages, "is a politically loaded act."[95] Since executions are private affairs, performed behind closed doors (and often in the middle of the night), Mailer's vivid description "is capable of provoking outrage," particularly because "the behavior of the condemned man in the moments before death is restrained and dignified enough to highlight the indignity of subsequent proceedings."[96] In his meticulous use of detail, Mailer makes his readers virtual witnesses to Gilmore's execution and postmortem, imaginatively overturning state laws that restrict public access to information about the death penalty. Death penalty abolitionists have taken issue with such laws, protesting that private executions, in the words of John D. Bessler, "denigrate" democracy by "keep[ing] the public in the dark about the facts surrounding capital punishment," leaving citizens therefore "unable to judge for themselves the morality of the death penalty."[97] Mailer allows us to judge for ourselves and offers an array of responses that suggest the kinds of discussions that might be possible in a more open society.

Many of the witnesses to Gilmore's execution register the profound disgrace of the manner of it and its immediate aftermath. Mailer turns to Ron Stanger, one of Gilmore's attorneys, who is present at the scene:

> Stanger was furious. The moment Gilmore was shot, everybody should have been walked out, and not served for a party to all this. Even as Sam was examining the body, Gary fell over into Meersman's hands. The padre had to hold the head while Sam went fishing all over Gilmore's back to locate the exit wounds. Blood started coming onto Meersman's hands, and dripped through his fingers, and Vern began to weep. Then Father Meersman wept.[98]

In continuing the spectacle long after Gilmore's death, Mailer indicates that the widespread obsession with Gilmore's life cannot be so easily laid aside. Even dead, Gilmore still fascinates those who have been following his life for so many months (or pages). Since Gilmore can no longer speak to his spectators, they must look to his corpse and his surroundings for an ultimate comment on his life. These final scenes grotesquely highlight the public's insatiable curiosity.

But what are we to make of the following scene, where Mailer follows the corpse into the autopsy room, lingering over the unrecognizable, "pulverized" heart, the organs and entrails, watching as pieces of Gilmore's body are sampled and put in solution? Mailer explains that, even though he was essentially sympathetic to Gilmore's wish to be executed, he "wanted the reader to feel . . . what it means when we kill a man. That even this man who wanted to die and succeeded in getting society to execute him, that even when he was killed, we still feel this horrible shock and loss."[99] To be sure, the scene is shocking; the police guard hired to oversee the autopsy, whose eyewitness account Mailer provides, finds the procedure "really gruesome."[100] But when the autopsy is finished, the coroners

> took all the organs they did not need for dissection and put them back into the body and head cavities, and drew his face up, pulled it right back taut over the bones and muscles, like putting on the mask again, fit the sawed-off bone-cap back on the skull, and sewed the scalp, and body cavity. When they were all finished, it looked like Gary Gilmore again.[101]

It looked like Gary Gilmore again: we have seen the innards of this man—whose own subjectivity has been both a focus of intense interest and, finally, a complete mystery. And now, having seen him dismantled and put back together, we are tempted to believe that nothing has changed him, not our intense scrutiny, not scalpels and stitches, not bullet holes. I take this scene both as a metaphor for the (ultimately unsatisfying) attempts to explain Gilmore (the coroner looks for brain tumors but announces that "everything . . . looked to be just fine") and, finally, for the man's recalcitrance in the face of our efforts to understand him on our own terms.[102] Whatever he may "look like," the private Gary Gilmore is radically at odds with our own sense of his communal meaning. If we wish to believe that our desires for him resemble his own, we must do so at our own peril—for sympathy, as John Hersey unwittingly suggests, is really just projection.

The Executioner's Song should be regarded not as a detached chronicle of Gilmore's last months but as part of the events surrounding his execution, a novel that enacts the problem of sympathy and public debate in its own procedures. The novel provokes interest in the ways in which depictions of Gilmore seemed calculated to shape other responses: how did compassion or objectivity operate in discussions about the crimes and execution? When does compassion for the condemned man interfere with his own wishes? Or with the interests of public order and history? When, in other words, does sympathy turn into a sentimental attempt to reshape Gilmore's life in a way that is palatable to readers?

Mailer's afterward grapples with these questions even when the author confines his comments to stylistic issues. For instance, when Mailer admits to having edited Gilmore's letters and interviews, he speaks of his attempt to rehabilitate the prisoner's image:

> Gilmore's interviews were trimmed, and very occasionally a sentence was transposed. The aim was not to improve his diction so much as to *treat him decently*, treat him, let us say, *half as well as one would treat one's own remarks* if going over them in transcript. . . . With Gilmore's letters, however, it seemed fair to show him *at a higher level than his average.* One wanted to demonstrate the impact of his mind on Nicole, and that might best be achieved by allowing his brain to have an impact on us.[103]

Hersey observes that while Mailer is being "wonderfully careful" here, his readers will nevertheless doubt the authenticity of Gilmore's letters.[104] I am more concerned with the effects of our need to view the condemned man sympathetically, "to treat him," as Mailer puts it, "decently." When sympathy is in large measure projection, then we are all implicated in the process of turning our hero into something we would like him to be, and Mailer dramatizes that course even as he calls attention to it.[105]

Although there is no way of judging the authenticity of the Gilmore letters included in The Executioner's Song, I think it's safe to consider them a collaborative effort between Gilmore and Mailer. Here, then, is one of their finest: an early prison letter to Nicole, written just after Gilmore's arrest. Ruminating on the possibility of execution from his prison cell, before his trial even begins, he writes,

> What do I do, rot in prison? growing old and bitter and eventually work this around in my mind to where it reads that I'm the one who's getting fucked around, that I'm just an innocent victim of society's bullshit? What do I do? Spend a life in prison searching for the God I've wanted to know for such a long time? Resume my painting? Write poetry? Play handball? Eat my heart out for the wondrous love you

gave me that I threw away Monday nite because I was so spoiled and couldn't immediately have a white pickup truck I wanted? What do I do? We always have a choice, don't we?[106]

I find this letter a lucid commentary on Mailer's novel because the bitter possibilities that Gilmore proposes ironically are echoed in the novel as legitimate choices by those who wish to offer him sympathy. More than once we hear both the argument that Gilmore is the real victim, and the more remarkable contention that his artistic and poetic nature should be saved and his life spared. Gilmore's letter suggests that these sympathetic positions, dramatized in the very form of the novel, are as violent as the desire to execute him.

Chapter Six

THE SWEETHEART OF DEATH ROW

Karla Faye Tucker and the Problem of Public Sentiments

I n many ways, the 1998 execution of Karla Faye Tucker in Huntsville, Texas, resembled the hangings of colonial criminals publicly executed for murder three hundred years earlier. The political difficulties that Benjamin Rush worried about in the eighteenth century surfaced dramatically in the Tucker case, where a grieving public turned with rage upon the state of Texas.

Karla Faye Tucker's execution was reminiscent of colonial hangings because she so eagerly spoke in public about her hopes for redemption after her death. For early New Englanders, as Daniel E. Williams notes,

> death was not dissolution, the extinction of identity; rather, the destruction of the flesh represented the transition from a lesser to a greater world. . . . Consequently, for those who believed in innate depravity and in the necessity of conversion, death became the most significant event in life. When crowds of people jammed their way into churches to catch a glimpse of [a condemned criminal], and when they pressed about him at the gallows, they watched to see how he would confront that most dreadful moment of divine decree.[1]

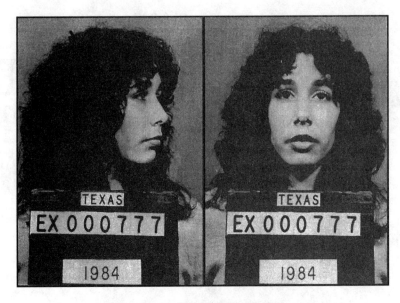

**Mug shots of Karla Faye Tucker,
1984. Courtesy of the Texas
Department of Corrections.**

To be sure, Karla Faye Tucker's execution by lethal injection was a private affair, attended only by prison officials and the fifteen witnesses in the public viewing gallery: five invited by the condemned criminal, five representing her murder victims' families, and five members of the press. But in symbolic terms the execution was intensely public: the *Houston Chronicle* called the weeks leading up to the event "television's longest vigil for a condemned murderer."[2] During the first of her fourteen-plus years on death row, Tucker had refused to grant interviews, not wanting to compound the pain of her victims' families. But once she decided to appeal her sentence and seek clemency, and particularly after December 1997 when the US Supreme Court refused to hear her appeal, Tucker drew international attention to her case. During the last few months of her life, she seemed ubiquitous, granting a "record number of TV interviews" and providing the subject of countless network talk shows.[3] The relentless media campaign waged by Tucker's lawyers and advocates—including former prosecutors, the siblings of her victims, members of Amnesty International, and the Christian evangelist Pat Robertson—made Tucker "a virtual guest in American living rooms" during the last weeks of her life, according to the *New York Times*.[4] Her life and death were fascinating and, for many people, gut-wrenching events that for a time nearly eclipsed all other public matters, as an international audience considered the state of Karla Faye Tucker's soul.

Tucker, who had become a born-again Christian and later married a Christian minister while on death row, serves as an anachronistic reminder of the profoundly spiritual dimension of colonial executions, where the public hanging of a female criminal was nothing unusual. Like those earlier executions, jointly conducted by church and state, Tucker's case forced the public to reflect on her spiritual condition. If we consider those earlier executions, we will recall that condemned criminals were given ample time and clerical attention to get their souls in order before being put to death. Katharine Garret, executed in 1738, was one of many criminals to "acknowledge the Justice of the Court who has Sentenced me to die this Death; and [to] thank them who have Lengthened the Time to me, whereby I have had great Opportunity to prepare for my Death."[5] The execution of an impenitent criminal could reasonably be regarded as only partly successful: effective in that it permanently banished a malefactor from human society, but a dismal failure insofar as the criminal did not come to recognize and assent to a higher law. Criminals were executed only after every attempt had been made to bring about their sincere repentance.

In our own society, officially intent on separating church and state, Karla Faye Tucker's religious awakening was of course an inadvertent effect of the slow judicial process of capital punishment and not, as in colonial days, a deliberate or necessary component of her official sentence. But to many it came to seem the central issue in debates over Tucker's fate. Pat Robertson, founder of the conservative Christian Coalition and usually a strong advocate of the swift and certain implementation of the death penalty, conceded that if Tucker had been executed more quickly, she may not have found religion, may not have saved her own soul, or may not have become such a powerful witness for Christianity.[6] Still, Tucker's religious awakening constituted Robertson's primary argument for sparing her life. While twentieth-century American executions had evolved almost unrecognizably from their colonial origins, Tucker's case reminds us of the same difficulty that had plagued earlier implementations of the death penalty: the paradox that the more submissively the condemned criminal bows to her punishment, the less willingly the public endorses its government's penal decisions.

I. THE IDEAL PENITENT

Like Rebekah Chamblit, who found spiritual salvation in 1733 while awaiting her execution for infanticide and proclaimed to the world that she had found "more comfort and satisfaction within the Walls of this Prison, than ever I had in the ways of Sin among my vain Companions, and think I wou'd not for a World, nay for ten Thousand Worlds have my liberty in Sin again," Karla Faye Tucker also proved herself a model penitent criminal.[7] For one thing, as many commentators have pointed out, Tucker's race and gender distinguished her from the typical death-row inmate, and her good looks surely added to her appeal. Although Tucker and her lawyers insisted that her gender should not be an issue in her clemency appeal, it no doubt had an effect—what William F. Buckley called a "strain on psychological predispositions"—on those who saw her face and heard her story.[8]

But the other, deeper issue was the undeniable change that Tucker had undergone since being incarcerated in 1983. Almost everyone who laid eyes on her found it nearly impossible to reconcile the calm, gentle, and pious woman with the tough-talking prostitute who had been arrested for a brutal double murder. By all accounts, the murders were memorably grim. Tucker and her boyfriend had used a pickaxe to kill their victims—one of whom was discovered with the axe still embedded in her breast—and Tucker had boasted that she had experienced an orgasm with each blow of the weapon. At the time of the murders the twenty-three-year-old Tucker had been on drugs almost continuously since she was ten years old. Worst of all, when arrested she was unrepentant, even boastful about the crimes.

In prison—alone, initially, for the first time in her life and at last able to wean herself off drugs—Tucker underwent a dramatic change, attending Alcoholics Anonymous meetings and Bible study classes and finally confronting the horror of her crime. Many of her eventual allies believed that Tucker's true character had been hidden for years beneath the violent effect of drugs, that her genuine nature emerged only once she had come clean. Tucker herself acknowledged the effect of drugs, of anger and confusion, of a lack of guidance when she was younger and "most impressionable."[9] But she placed more emphasis on her religious conversion, which she described as an actual transformation of her nature: "God reached down inside of me and just literally uprooted all of that stuff and took it out, and poured Himself in."[10] Like her many allies, Tucker maintained that the woman who had helped to kill two people in 1983 and the woman who had found Christ and put her life in order were two different people.

Tucker's biographer sees the transformation as a deliberate and difficult process rather than a magical event. In prison, Beverly Lowry writes, Tucker "was trying to learn to be someone better, more educated, more forthright. . . . In prison she had learned to become a reader."[11] Part of that effort revealed itself when, after her own trial and death sentence when she had nothing to gain, Tucker cooperated with prosecutors and testified against her partner in crime, Danny Garrett. Though she had been criticized for doing so, Tucker "had made new allegiances," Lowry writes; "her pact was with God now."[12] Or, as Tucker explained, she had changed from "being a part of the problem to being a part of the solution."[13] Designated as the "Pickaxe Murderess" when she was arrested in 1983, she later came to be known by the title given to her by an employee of the Texas Department of Criminal Justice, "The Sweetheart of Death Row."

The phrases that denote Tucker's transformation are striking in their confidence and consistency: After spending an hour on the air with her, the talk show host Larry King pronounced the condemned woman "obviously . . . not the same person as she was 14 years ago."[14] The prosecutor who in 1983 thought of Tucker as "the embodiment of evil" later called her a "completely different person who, in my opinion, is not capable of those atrocities."[15] The former police detective who investigated the case said, "I really think she is a different person."[16] Tucker's former acquaintance, a witness to the murders who testified against Tucker and her boyfriend, argued that if Texas followed through on the sentence, the state would not be "executing the same person that did these crimes."[17] Tucker's attorney, who had formed such a strong dislike for his client when he met her that he was reluctant to take her case, came to see her as two separate beings, the criminal self waning as the generous self emerged. "There's another girl inside there," he had told his wife. "She's just now starting to come out."[18] Tucker's biographer, who, like everyone else who had met her, knew that the woman was in fact guilty of two grisly murders—whose job, indeed, was to elicit and report the details of those murders—nevertheless was so attracted to her subject that she often forgot about the crimes. Karla Faye Tucker, she wrote, "is who she is now to me, this warm, loving girl, my friend. The murders seem like some chapter in a worn old book."[19] Although in strictly legal terms, as the *New York Times* pointed out, "this is still the same Karla Faye Tucker who helped to kill two people 14 years ago," most people who came to know her through interviews or in person drew a sharp distinction between the cold, unfeeling, murderous drug addict of 1983 and the gentle, sweet, deeply spiritual woman on death row.[20] To look at this "serene" woman, Lowry wrote, "you want to believe that people change, that confession helps, that there is hope."[21]

Like the many colonial criminals who embraced Christianity when confronting their own deaths and endeared themselves to the public with their piety, Tucker spoke earnestly and consistently for the Christian promise of everlasting life for penitent sinners. Unlike those earlier condemned criminals, Tucker was given nearly fifteen years to prove herself an unwavering convert. She did so partly with the example she set in her death-row community, a community that would have been impossible, she believed, without the women's mutual belief in Christ;[22] their spiritual belief transformed their prison home to what the inmates called "Life Row."[23] She did so also with her apparent submission to God's will. Even in the last days of her life, as she worked to convince the Texas Board of Pardons and Paroles to commute her sentence to life in prison without parole, Tucker insisted that the outcome of her efforts, whatever it was, would be part of God's plan for her life. When Larry King marveled at the startling coalition of allies she had assembled to her cause, people from both the left and the right, civil libertarians as well as conservative Christians, Tucker explained that she had nothing to do with the groundswell of support for her cause. "I didn't get them for me. God did. And . . . what they're really speaking out for is for the cause of Christ."[24] As she mused on the possibility that she would be executed in fewer than three weeks, Tucker maintained that she would walk to her death without fear or resentment, "still speaking out for the love of God [who had] . . . already saved my life."[25] Speaking serenely about the redemptive power of Christ's love, she convinced many people, religious and otherwise, that a human being removed from brutal conditions and forced to reflect on her deeds can indeed earn her own redemption. And in that respect she prompted a debate over the social and legal consequences of rehabilitation.

When Beverly Lowry explains this rehabilitation—she notes that Tucker had been "born again . . . as the person she might have been the whole way through"—

she points to the evangelical earnestness that won Tucker allies from all sides.[26] Christians of course approved of Tucker's enthusiastic testimonials on behalf of Christian love. Tucker's husband, Dana Brown, a prison chaplain, maintained that his wife had "literally reached thousands of people for Jesus Christ and probably will continue through her testimony."[27] Others considered Tucker "a textbook example of redemption" not because she won converts to Christianity but because she had devoted her life to helping people accept the possibility of change for the better.[28] In prison after beginning Bible study and Alcoholics Anonymous classes, Tucker encouraged other inmates to do the same. As she reached out to troubled people beyond her prison walls, writing essays and making videotapes for antidrug outreach campaigns, she tried to provide the kind of ethical guidance she had been denied as a teenager. Partly an attempt to atone for her crimes, partly a response to the call she had heard from other prison evangelists, Tucker's outreach efforts while in prison were the fruits, she said, of her "gut-wrenching need . . . to help people."[29] "I can't take back the lives I took," she explained, "but I can help save lives now."[30] When an evangelical commentator described Tucker as a "miraculously sweet-spirited little soldier in the war against criminal wickedness," he was using highly charged religious language to explain what even secular people had come to recognize: that Tucker, in her own words, had become "part of the solution" rather than part of the problem.[31]

Having rejected her former values and completely refashioned herself, displaying a nature apparently so thoroughly at odds with the one she had left behind, Tucker prompted conversations about the extent to which her neglectful upbringing had determined the course of her early life. Her biography became a part of her story to a degree that is rare in public discussions about death-row inmates, where the crime is usually the focal point, if not the only point, of the story. When James Leibrant, a witness to the murders, asked the world to "give her a chance . . . [because she's] never had a chance before," he alluded to a childhood that had become familiar to those who knew Tucker's case: Tucker's mother, a high-priced prostitute, introduced her daughters to drugs and prostitution when they were children.[32] Desperate to please her mother, Karla Faye took up her mother's interests, getting high at age eight, shooting heroin by age ten, turning tricks at fourteen. When she was thirteen she made the discovery that the man she had known as her father was not her biological father, and, she later acknowledged, "It about devastated my life."[33] But she remained drawn to her mother, with whom, she recalled, she "used to share drugs like lipstick."[34] When Carolyn Moore Tucker died of hepatitis in 1979, Karla Faye went "seriously, uninterruptedly wild."[35] She was twenty years old. Years later, speaking from the death row visiting room, the inmate speculated that her life would have been different if her mother had not died. "It changed me. I turned stone cold to the world."[36]

Although a defendant's upbringing is often introduced at trial as a mitigating factor to be considered at sentencing, after her jailhouse rehabilitation Karla Faye Tucker's grim childhood assumed an importance that is rare in capital cases. Whatever facts her jurors drew on to calculate the possibility of a future menace, Tucker's judges in the court of public opinion often dwelt with pity and indignation on the details of her past. The author of Karla Faye's Original Memorial Homepage, for example, maintained that "The True Story of Karla," much of which was not heard at trial, "will be released in a book by her long-time pastor, David Kirschke."[37] Many of these details were available before Tucker's execution and became part of discussions about the case. As the former Houston detective who cracked the case pointed out, "she never really had a chance as a kid."[38] Of course, the same could be said of many death-row inmates, as Tucker's detractors argued. But unlike many of them, Karla Faye Tucker transformed herself dramatically while in prison, inviting a wide and general application of the term "born-again." As Beverly Lowry explains, "Sometimes imprisoned people experience a childhood they never had. Something like that happened to Karla. . . . Jail has made her a softer person."[39] If the influences of religious faith and a clean environment could have so transformed her character, many wondered how much responsibility Karla Faye Tucker bore for the effects of her negligent upbringing. Her story generated immense sympathy.

And it brought her, as many commentators have pointed out, a surprisingly diverse array of allies. People normally opposed to the death penalty predictably became vocal advocates for her commutation: Bianca Jagger, representing Amnesty International, visited the condemned woman on death row, participated in a protest rally at the state capital, and stood vigil outside the prison on the night of Tucker's execution. Pope John Paul II urged a pardon as "a gesture of mercy which would contribute to a better respect for life."[40] The United Nations Human Rights Commission called for clemency; as did the European Union Parliament; the Italian abolitionist group, "Hands off Cain"; the American Civil Liberties Union; the Texas Coalition to Abolish the Death Penalty; and a group of ministers, priests, nuns, and rabbis who assembled in Houston to plead for Tucker's life. Other less likely allies also emerged out of the political debates as champions of the condemned woman. The usually staunch supporter of capital punishment, Pat Robertson, urged Texas authorities to grant Tucker clemency, asking what good "would be served in Texas to execute her now after 14½ years" and so profound a change?[41] The brother of one of her victims, the sister of another, two prosecutors of Tucker's codefendant, and a juror in her trial all added their voices to those clamoring for clemency.[42] In addition, Tucker made friends of the prison officials at Gatesville, the police detective who arrested her, and countless people who felt they had come to know her through media reports. Governor Bush's office was "flooded with phone calls and faxes" from people lobbying for clemency.[43]

Although not everyone favored clemency—the president of Justice for All, a victims' rights group that opposed commutation, argued that the campaign to save Tucker's life was based on "fraud, lies, ignorance and sexism"—those who did were ideologically divided: some defended Tucker because they disapproved of capital punishment in all its forms, and others were attracted by Tucker's character, biography, religious convictions or charm.[44] Beverly Lowry noticed Tucker's seductiveness at their first meeting when she observed an "obvious if improper affection between guards and prisoner."[45] Tucker charmed an international audience as well, compelling many death penalty supporters to make an exception or, more stunningly, to rethink their ideological positions. The remarkable outcome of Tucker's publicity campaign was a strange coalition of supporters—members of the religious right allied with civil libertarians, families of murder victims defending a murderer—as well as strange divisions: members of one murder victim's family divided between vengeance and forgiveness, the Christian Coalition split over the question of clemency.

This death-row inmate, a former prostitute and drug user, unquestionably guilty of two grisly murders, became the figure of a modern-day parable, like the ancient Mary Magdalene or Saint Augustine, or like the nineteenth-century fictional heroine Hester Prynne. In the many descriptions of the reformed Tucker we can see echoes not only of the pious colonial malefactor who walked unresistingly to her execution but also of the martyred Christian saint. Whether they believed her a saint or were merely drawn to the imagery traditionally used to describe martyrs, both journalists and partisans of Karla Faye Tucker depicted the woman awaiting execution in terms that would not have been out of place in the *Lives of the Saints*. Like Hester Prynne, suggesting for her nineteenth-century narrator the "image of Divine Maternity,"[46] Tucker paradoxically struck many observers as an icon of near saintliness. A Houston reporter imagined the scene of her execution nearly two months before the actual event: "An attractive, 38-year-old woman is strapped to a gurney in Texas's execution chamber, her dark, shoulder-length curls splayed across the antiseptic white sheet that covers the hard, cold deathbed. Her charcoal-colored eyes are transfixed ethereally while she utters her final entreaty to the God who she says miraculously transformed her in jail."[47] That same reporter later called Tucker "a Bible-reading, angelic-looking woman," a description that was reinforced when an image of Tucker looking heavenward was circulated around the world.[48] During her trial, newspaper reporters regularly "mentioned the jail-issue white plastic cross" that hung around the defendant's neck.[49] As the execution neared, Pat Robertson declared that if Governor George W. Bush "lets this sweet woman of God die, he's a man who shows no mercy."[50] The spokesperson for the Texas Coalition to Abolish the Death Penalty called Tucker "the Mother Teresa of the Texas prison system."[51] Tucker's biographer described how Tucker looked as she talked about heaven during their last encounter: "She's as radiant as a heater, turned up high."[52] This writer was not alone in describing Tucker with the same quasi-sexual language that had been traditionally used in portrayals of Christian martyrs; Tucker's spiritual advisor noticed with mixed feelings that her protégé emitted "a bridal radiance" during the last weeks of her life. "A bride walking down the aisle has a single focus: to be with her bridegroom. I saw that same eagerness in Karla, almost as if she wanted to run down the aisle to be with Christ. The joy and anticipation of what her life would be with her beloved Jesus transformed her appearance. In all she said, in all she did, I witnessed an increasing intimacy between the Bridegroom and Karla—and knew I was losing her."[53] Zealous to tell readers about Tucker's last hours, journalists reported that the inmate had been fasting for several days. In these detailed accounts of her demeanor, Tucker appeared as an almost saintly victim of persecution. Though she remained modest in her appeals for clemency, she nevertheless hazarded a comparison with Christ, explaining her fight for clemency by recalling that Jesus, too, had "asked God for the cup to be removed, and if he can ask it, I don't have to feel ashamed to ask that either."[54] It was an association to be echoed on the night of her execution, as opponents of capital punishment displayed signs outside the Huntsville prison proclaiming, "Jesus was a victim of the death penalty." Fasting, praying, talking sweetly of Christian love, Karla Faye Tucker perhaps seemed the closest thing to a saint that American audiences had encountered in many years.[55]

Although her execution was of course not literally a public event, audiences who wanted to be present at the ritual were enabled by live broadcasts and vivid descriptions from inside the execution chamber to be virtual witnesses to an execution that garnered an extraordinary amount of public interest. In spite of her battle against the death sentence, Tucker herself had plainly given much thought to her final moments. Having confessed to feeling "no fear" just three weeks before her execution, Tucker attributed her buoyant spirits to "joy of the Lord": "I know what forgiveness is, even when I did something so horrible. I know that because God forgave me and I accepted what Jesus did on the cross. When I leave here, I am going to be with Him."[56] She told one reporter that if her sentence were carried out, she would walk into the execution chamber thinking about "Jesus coming and escorting me home."[57] In her final moments Tucker lived up to the promise of the Christian fortitude she had demonstrated all along. Like Esther Rogers, executed in 1701 for the murder of her infant child and walking piously to her death "with that Composure of Spirit, Cheerfulness of Countenance, pleasantness of Speech" that "melted the hearts" of those who witnessed her death, Tucker impressed her audiences with her Christian fortitude at the hour of her death.[58] Witnesses to her execution described her as "calm, composed and contrite."[59] Her widely reported dying words, spoken with a smile, were of love and redemption: "I love all of you very much. I am going to be face to face with Jesus now," she said, before beginning a silent prayer.[60]

In her piety and in her compliance with her sentence once she had finally exhausted all avenues to clemency, Tucker performed this secular state ritual as if she were a colonial subject cooperating with both church and state. In so doing she transformed a bureaucratic process—what had become a "quick, sombre, businesslike" procedure whose brutality was masked by a series of pseudo-medical rituals[61]—into a drama that upset the familiar routine in what one overseas journalist denounced as the "murder capital of the world."[62] Church leaders like Pat Robertson were praying for miracles,[63] but so too were ordinary people, like the tearful French reporter who, broadcasting live outside the Huntsville execution chamber, told his television audience, "We're hoping for a miracle here, if Karla Faye Tucker is to live."[64]

Although by the 1990s lethal injections had become, in the words of Andrew Sullivan, "as routine in Texas as a backyard cook-out," Tucker's execution had as much in common with the emotional public hangings of colonial days as it did with the very different, calculatedly dispassionate modern Texas routine.[65] The many television shows devoted to Tucker in the weeks and days before her execution might be regarded as latter-day execution sermons, organized attempts to interpret the impending execution to the American public. Court TV's "A Question of Mercy," for example, revealed in its title, like execution-day sermons, the central question that organized the way its producers wished viewers to understand Tucker's case. Although this program refrained from advancing a specific argument and sought instead a balance of opinions appropriate to a democratic society, the medium of television seems to have replaced the colonial pulpit as a widely popular and accessible site to hear discussion about a notorious crime and its punishment.[66]

In addition, as we have seen, this technically private execution was not, in fact, a private affair. An estimated two hundred reporters from around the world covered the execution from outside the prison gates. They reported not only the behavior of the crowds that had gathered to be on-site for the execution, but also the media updates issued regularly by prison officials. Reporters were given press packs containing information about the last meals of many death-row inmates; they learned that Tucker had requested that her last meal be a peach, a banana, and a tossed salad with Italian dressing.

They also learned that Tucker refused to eat this last meal, electing to continue a fast she had begun several days earlier. An information officer gave reporters a minute-by-minute account of Tucker's last day, so the world could know that at 10:20 AM, the condemned woman read to her family from the *Bible*, at 11:50 her husband said a prayer, at 11:54 Tucker cried for the first time, and at 11:55 she and her family said their last goodbyes through the plastic screen that divided them before Tucker was taken to the Huntsville unit to await execution.[67] In many ways, this modern-day execution offered the public an even more intimate view of the condemned woman's last hours than that shared by actual spectators of earlier public executions. If the audience outside the prison could not witness Tucker's actual death, they could watch a video of the death-row inmate singing a hymn, as they sang along or prayed, or—in the case of those who supported the execution—jeered, applauded, or chanted football cheers. And they were officially informed when Tucker was pronounced dead.

The few journalists allowed inside the viewing chamber, of course, were able to report other details: Tucker's last words, the responses of her family and friends and of the families of her victims who had come to watch her die. Reporters were able to describe Tucker's affect: she smiled and seemed calm throughout the process, several of them noted. But one journalist was saddened that Tucker was denied any physical contact with her family before she died. "I know if I were Karla I would have wanted a last-minute hug or kiss. But that wasn't allowed."[68] In all of these ways, readers and television viewers were able to take part vicariously in Tucker's execution, to share their approbation for the event or to share the sadness of the woman's loved ones who watched her die. Assisted by reporters, they were able to regard their feelings as part of a larger community reaction.

As Governor Bush observed of what for some state executives would have been a difficult decision, "Every death penalty is an emotional moment."[69] If this is so, then executions in Texas are emotional in spite of the best efforts of the Texas Department of Corrections. As many reporters, mostly foreigners, noted in their coverage of Tucker's case, the state is "successful at bureaucratizing executions."[70] "Texas bureaucrats ran back and forth, spoke occasionally with journalists and distributed nice information folders," seethed the Swedish evening *Expressen*.[71] "Prison officials," wrote another reporter, "make it as painless as they can for everyone involved. . . . The names and the crimes and the details begin to blur in my mind."[72] Even the hearse waiting to carry the dead woman away from the prison was tactfully concealed behind a gray shroud.[73] The very point of executions—the pursuit of vengeance—seemed to be cloaked in the professional language of psychotherapy, as David Rose argued in *The Irish Times*; "the death of a murderer, it is claimed, enables the relatives of his victim to achieve 'closure.'"[74]

Karla Faye Tucker was unusual because she overcame the organized anonymity of the execution process and extended that "emotional moment" from herself and her family to an international community of virtual witnesses. The rage of foreign journalists describing the Texas ritual can be seen in their accounts of Texas bureaucracy: "By handing out press packs describing Karla's every sad move on her final day, by strapping her down, then allowing the relatives in to observe the deadly chemicals as they exploded into her pathetic body, America actually thought it was behaving in a civilised manner," raged one journalist.[75] Some of them tried to make Tucker's death seem as violent as possible. Describing the procedure that would happen on the following day, Joanna Coles wrote that Tucker's

> ankles, wrists, elbows and neck will be strapped with pale leather buckles to the only piece of apparatus in the room, a white sheeted, thin mattress bed. At 6 p.m., her right sleeve will be rolled up and her arm rubbed with disinfectant. Twenty seconds later, it will be injected with a lethal dose of pancuronium bromide, potassium chloride and sodium thiopental. Within seconds her heart will suffer a massive shock and her organs swell, the drugs poisoning them too severely to make them useful to anyone else.[76]

Others pointed out that however quick and apparently painless the procedure, however clinically it is described to those who care to know about it, "all execution is degrading and inhumane."[77]

II. A CONVERSATION ABOUT JUSTICE

Karla Faye Tucker compelled audiences to think about capital punishment not simply in terms of abstract justice—the simple calculus of a life for a life—but also in broader ethical terms: by entering the homes of an international audience in the weeks before her death, she forced that audience to consider what it means to be part of a society that deliberately and dispassionately takes human lives in its pursuit of justice. Many journalists who reported her case pointed to her inescapable humanity, a quality that is often masked by the elaborate and highly bureaucratized ritual of execution. The international media, noted a criminal justice scholar, "are putting not only a face but also a personality on the death penalty."[78] A French newspaper argued that Tucker had retained her humanity while on death row, demonstrating that "one should never despair of mankind."[79]

The widespread outrage over Tucker's execution, as well as the sympathy and admiration aroused by her conduct during her many years on death row, can be explained only partly by the changing attitudes toward capital punishment in the three hundred years since executions were first publicly enacted in the New World and capital offenses more broadly defined. When we consider the many ways in which Tucker's public performance resembled that of the ideal penitent criminal of the seventeenth and early eighteenth centuries—her prayerful demeanor, her words of remorse, her evangelical encouragement, her willingness to serve as an example of sin and forgiveness, her courageous but humble last words: in short, her model behavior—we should also recall that the most successfully staged scenes of contrition were precisely those that inadvertently undermined the very authority (religious and secular) that they were meant to endorse. When the criminal was sincerely penitent, the rituals of execution day were formulaic and predictable but no less moving. That they often moved audiences to rage rather than approval was an unwanted but nearly unavoidable effect of public executions. Support for the death penalty, as Julia Reed argues, is easier to muster in a society "encouraged . . . to keep [its] distance" from the death penalty process.[80]

In her pious but no less theatrical performance of her role as the penitent criminal, Tucker not only "smiled her way into hundreds of thousands—if not millions— of homes across the country" but also forced Americans to identify with a death-row inmate.[81] No longer was the condemned criminal a faceless, soulless brute, as he had become under America's increasingly routine, anonymous, and racist system of capital punishment, where executions not only took place in the middle of the night, but were rarely even reported, let alone described and discussed in the news. Instead, with her talk of Jesus and heaven, Karla Faye Tucker, remarkably, compelled the authorities responsible for her execution to acknowledge their human connection to her.[82] As in the early days of colonial executions when church and state leaders had no interest in obscuring the similarities between criminals and the law-abiding witnesses to their executions—but, rather, instructed witnesses to "consider, *who it is that maketh you to differ*, and admire and adore his distinguishing Grace"—Tucker's execution prompted comparisons between herself and those who had never thought about death-row inmates.[83] Dick Weinhold, chairman of the Texas Christian Coalition, echoed many a colonial minister in reminding Americans to "reflect on our own failures and sin. We should reflect on the concept that none of us is better than Karla Faye Tucker, and realize that there, but for the grace of God, go I."[84] Tucker's execution inspired sermon-like pronouncements from civil leaders as well. Refusing to commute her sentence, Governor George W. Bush nevertheless asked God to "bless" the condemned woman. Allan Polunsky, chair of the Texas Board of Criminal Justice, declared that Tucker's "religious awakening could in no way excuse or mitigate her actions in the world she just left, but hopefully will provide her redemption in the world she just entered."[85] While lawmakers were talking of spiritual redemption, some of Tucker's advocates said they "felt joy" after her execution "because they believed Ms. Tucker had gone home to Christ."[86]

There were others, of course, who responded differently, with tears, with anger, with challenges to the judicial system in the United States and especially in Texas. When the execution had been confirmed to the audience outside the Huntsville prison, demonstrators responded with cries of "murder, murder" and "end the killing in Texas."[87] Some responses took the form of general rage, like that manifested by the "outraged citizens calling from around the world [who] rained obscenities and invective on prison secretaries who have nothing to do with it."[88]

Other responses were more specific. Many railed against a penal system motivated solely by vengeance. "Karla Must Die to Sate Bloodlust," shouted the London *Observer*.[89] Bianca Jagger, speaking for Amnesty International, condemned a system of justice that completely neglects "mercy and rehabilitation."[90] European journalists denounced the execution as "barbaric."[91]

Part of the outrage was a response to the behavior, covered heavily in the American and international press, of the crowd outside the Huntsville prison. Although many were lobbying against the execution, others came to Huntsville to support and take part in the event. As the primary defenders of capital punishment, they were poor advertisements for dispassionate justice. Florence King, a self-proclaimed conservative, called them "populist yahoos,"[92] while the *Mirror* condemned them as "blood-lusting fanatics."[93] As many protestors prayed silently or sang gospel songs, other demonstrators behaved like undisciplined soccer fans, chanting macabre slogans and displaying grim signs that announced, "Axe and ye shall receive," "You Pick-ed Your Death," and "Have a nice day Karla Faye." Many of these people arrived in costume, several dressed as witches and one arrayed as the grim reaper, complete with a pickaxe, which was confiscated by the police. Elsewhere in Huntsville, businesses took ghoulish advantage of the execution, advertising "killer prices" and "Killer Karla Karaoke" night, while the city's mayor joked that executions are always "a shot in the arm" for the local economy.[94]

While ideological exchanges among the different crowds at the Huntsville prison might have been expected, the hooligan behavior dismayed many observers, especially foreign journalists, who described the crowd's conduct in detail, denouncing it as "grotesque" and "morbid."[95] The *London Guardian* described a carnivalesque scene, noting that many schoolchildren were present for the revelry. The European press gave extensive coverage to the chaos that erupted as Tucker's supporters tried to give some dignity to the occasion. Their "prayers drowned out by the carnival of death fanatics," Tucker's supporters tried to maintain an atmosphere of solemnity but were faced instead with bedlam.[96] When a loudspeaker announced that "Karla's last wish was to have a song," many in the crowd jeered, some of them yelling, "It's time to die." Tucker's minister then begged the crowd to allow a final hymn, pleading, "Come on guys, the lady is about to die." In response, the crowd shouted even louder.[97] As a musician sang "Amazing Grace," noted the *Mirror*, "the death fiends drowned her voice";[98] the prevailing sound was not the hymn but chants of "Kill the bitch" and "Have a nice day Karla Faye."[99] When Tucker's allies sang "We Shall Overcome," her enemies responded with a more raucous song, the sports stadium classic, "Hey, Hey, Goodbye," sung "so loudly," one reporter lamented, "that Tucker must have heard them."[100] Although religious leaders and their followers tried to observe some of the traditional execution-day rituals—prayer, hymns, and solemnity—they had clearly lost control in this volatile setting, where freedom of speech prevailed over a single interpretation of the execution. The result was a cacophonous, "baying mob" that invited comparisons to a lynch mob.[101] Meanwhile, reporters and television producers fought for position. "In the glare of the spotlight," one reporter confessed, "we behaved poorly."[102]

John D. Bessler observes that states began privatizing executions after 1830 in part to prevent the shameful mob behavior that took place at the gallows, behavior that fell far short of "the occasion's solemnity."[103] No doubt lawmakers worried that if their primary argument for state-sponsored executions was the need to uphold law and order, the boisterous and, at times, savage crowds that gathered to celebrate executions hardly helped them to make their case. The same may be said of the carnivalesque atmosphere that prevailed outside the Huntsville prison on the night of Tucker's execution: if the state of Texas were putting Tucker to death solemnly and reluctantly, the enthusiastic crowds who assembled to taunt the woman and her supporters seemed to represent the state's vengeful unconscious. Critics of the execution took revolted note of their conduct.

With near unanimity, foreign critics of the execution pointed to the contradiction between America's regular use of the death penalty and its posture as "the self-appointed arbiter of world human rights."[104] While the United Nations Human Rights Commission led a world condemnation of Tucker's execution, Pope John Paul II acknowledged feelings of bitterness over "the contradiction of certain western societies embracing maximum human rights while also putting a strong sense of revenge into practice."[105] The *Irish Times* editorialized that the death penalty "does not sit comfortable with the annual survey of human rights provisions around the world published by the U.S. State Department."[106] Many commentators agreed with Brian Reade's assessment that "the most obnoxious aspect of [the] execution was the blind arrogance of it all."[107]

In the United States, many critics believed that this execution would further warrant an evidently declining trust in government. American opponents of Tucker's execution pointed to domestic problems that could already be discerned in the context of capital punishment. Amnesty International, for example, detailed "mounting evidence that the behaviour of the [Texas] Board of Pardons is undermining public confidence in the administration of justice. Although general support for the death penalty remains high, nearly half of Texans would oppose an execution where there is evidence that the inmate has 'shown signs of turning his or her life around.'"[108] When support for the death penalty plunged to a thirty-year low in the days following Tucker's execution, many concluded that faith in the government's oversight of the process was indeed waning. The American Civil Liberties Union, always critical of state-sponsored executions, reminded the world that Tucker's execution was exceptional only because of her race and gender, not in its shocking evidence of a corrupt process. In a statement issued on the day of the execution, the ACLU said, "The fact that a white woman has now drawn a ticket in this deadly lottery does not make the system any less racist or unfair."[109]

And, of course, countless Web sites emerged after the execution, devoted to memorializing Karla Faye Tucker, expressing pious sentiments and feelings of grief and rage. In some ways these sites served as virtual funeral rites, enabling visitors to post the kinds of memorial sentiments they might say at a funeral or leave at a tomb. Unlike the thousands of sentimental visitors who had paid homage to the slain Sarah Cornell at her graveside in nineteenth-century New England, twentieth-century sympathizers could memorialize Tucker from their homes, offices, and public libraries. Messages addressed to the dead woman were typical. "Thank you Karla," read one, "for you [sic] beautiful witness to our Lord and Savior Jesus Christ. His love in you was so apparent and I am deeply grieved by you [sic] death. I feel as though a dear friend died."[110] Another site published the lyrics to "The End," a song written for Tucker by Melody Kirschke and sung outside the Huntsville prison on the night of Tucker's death. Although the occasional unsentimental visitor posted a note of resistance, like the one who marveled "to see so many people feeling sorry for a killer!!!!!!!!" these remarks were unusual and often met with opposition. As one respondent wrote, "If you don't like this site the way they have it, *don't come here!*"[111] Although technically open to all opinions, these Web sites indicate a near consensus that Tucker had made a convincing case for institutional mercy, at least among the ordinary people who were moved to comment on her situation.

If, as I have been arguing, television and newspapers replaced the seventeenth-century pulpit as a source of interpretive authority on the case, the Internet assumed the function once belonging to broadside publications: it represented, that is, the marketplace of public opinion with its unofficial, mass responses to the execution. If an earlier age of citizens discussed topical issues in a bourgeois public sphere, those who logged on to the Internet in order to take part in discussions about the Tucker case could not so easily be identified as "bourgeois." To be sure, they all had access to Internet connections, but the anonymity of their chosen form gives us very little information about them. What we do know is that their virtual conversations about the Tucker affair show them to be a reading (and television-watching) public who were, for a time at least, deeply concerned with this legal matter and in many cases scarcely able to separate their private feelings from their political thoughts. While many offered political opinions—hoping, for instance, that Tucker's execution "might bring us closer as a Nation by seeking appropriate alternatives to the death penalty"— others posted more visceral sentiments: "I never met her, but I miss her," read one.[112]

Whether their comments were primarily of a public or a private nature, the individuals who formed these congregated virtual communities fit Habermas's description of a "forum" where "private people" congregate in public and "read[y] themselves to compel public authority to legitimate itself before public opinion."[113] While some registered mere outrage—"The justice system is broken! Who will fix it?"—others proposed specific means of redress: "I ask/beg others of Spirit to contact Gov. Bush and ask him to stop such killing. Remember Karla by remembering that 400 people are on Texas' death row. Karla killed two and asked and got God's forgiveness. Texas killed 37 last year alone."[114] The verdict on Karla Faye Tucker seems to have been decided in her favor at these Web sites, and now public opinion was turning its judgment on George W. Bush, the state of Texas, and the system of capital punishment.

These expressions might be seen as a kind of abortive sympathy, which in the eighteenth century Benjamin Rush described as a feeling that, having no effective outlet (since in this case the law insisted upon Tucker's execution), does damage by turning "secretly" against the state. Those who sympathized with Tucker but in general supported capital punishment found themselves in a most difficult position, since in their identification with the condemned woman they were forced to confront a contradiction in their own values. We cannot know how many such people grappled with these feelings, but surely there were many who found themselves sharing the anguish of one death penalty supporter who, without surrendering his conviction that capital punishment should remain in place, acknowledged, in the weeks before the execution, "I can't stand it if they kill Karla Faye."[115] Or the distress of the woman who encountered Tucker's story on television some four years after the execution and posted her comment to a Web site: "i watched the tv show also," she wrote, "and i think what she did was wrong but she desurved a second chance that she did not get. i also think that she desurved what she got. im very confussed" [sic].[116] Those who sympathized fully with Tucker, however, were able to turn their sympathies to good use and avoid some of this writer's confusion. Like other penitent criminals we have been considering, Tucker fully accepted divine justice and thoroughly repented of her crimes, thereby garnering widespread admiration. But unlike ideal penitents, she contested human justice, took issue with her sentence and with the state's position, and appealed for her sentence to be commuted to life imprisonment. While the eighteenth-century Patience Boston "receive[d her] Sentence with Silence in [her] Heart as well as Lips," and thanked her judges "for their Tenderness as well as Faithfulness," Tucker questioned the wisdom and necessity of her death sentence.[117] Contrite but determined to take full advantage of Texas's alleged provision for clemency, she differed from colonial criminals in giving her audience a legitimate cause to champion: that of forcing the Texas Board of Pardons and Paroles to articulate its guidelines for clemency.

III. THE PURPOSE OF CLEMENCY

Tucker waged her appeal on two fronts: with a video and letter to Governor Bush asking for clemency, and with what the *Houston Chronicle* called an "all-out legal blitz to spare her life."[118] Her argument centered on the fact of her rehabilitation. Prison officials and law enforcement officers all acknowledged that Tucker had undergone a remarkable change in the years since her arrest. Since her death sentence had followed inexorably from the jury's prediction that she would pose a future threat (one of the two Texas requirements for imposing the death penalty), Tucker cited her evidence to the contrary as an argument for clemency. Though juries do the best they can with the evidence they have, Tucker's lawyers argued, they sometimes fail to predict accurately. The clemency process ought to provide a means of review in cases like Tucker's where the inmate has surprised everyone.

The problem Tucker confronted in making her case was that the Texas Board of Pardons and Paroles does not consider rehabilitation as a mitigating factor. Governor Bush consistently argued that his own review process should consider just two questions: whether there is any doubt about guilt, and whether the courts have had adequate opportunity to review all legal issues.[119] The Board of Pardons and Paroles gave no guidelines for making an appeal; indeed, as Tucker's advocates pointed out, the board had a dismal record of considering appeals for clemency, never having met as a group and having recommended a commutation only once in seventeen years, "despite compelling grounds for mercy."[120] When Peggy Griffey, head of the Capital Litigation Division for the Texas attorney general's office, was pressed to explain the rules of commutation, she could only say they were "within the discretion of the governor's office."[121] Larry King and others gave Tucker a platform from which to explain her dilemma and publicly request a chance to speak to all members of the board.[122] She wished them particularly to consider the fact of her transformation. If prison is supposed to rehabilitate people, she argued, then the system should acknowledge a genuine rehabilitation when it happens.[123] In remaining silent on the topic, the Texas Board of Pardons and Paroles seemed tacitly to acknowledge that the Texas penal system was motivated solely by vengeance, which the Supreme Court had explicitly dismissed as a legitimate motive for punishment.[124]

The talk show host Larry King, in particular, embraced Tucker's cause and elaborated on her argument that the Board of Pardons and Paroles operated in unnecessarily and unfairly obscure ways. On live television the day after his hour-long interview with Tucker herself, King quizzed two of the state's representatives in the case, Victor Rodriguez, chair of the Texas Board of Pardons and Paroles, and Peggy Griffey. The answers he elicited demonstrated not only that Texas had no clear guidelines for clemency review, but also that the people in charge of the process could not even imagine a successful appeal. Griffey could not explain the rules governing commutation, for example, and neither she nor Rodriguez could describe a hypothetically successful case for commutation. Griffey explained that she had no "example ready for you. I think that it's very hazardous to second guess the jury," while Rodriguez evaded King's request for an example by musing over "what . . . we [are] talking about when we say 'commute.'" King noted that the Texas BPP does not give guidelines to those seeking clemency. What argument, he asked Rodriguez, "would be something that would open you to commutation?" Again Rodriguez failed to respond, saying instead "I don't want to lay out today what I may or may not do with the case," and that, in any event, Tucker's appeal "is for her to make." "But you give them no guideline as to what you need to hear," King persisted. Rodriguez replied that the board's "fundamental rule . . . is to do what's right." While Larry King's interview demonstrated vividly that any inmate appealing for clemency was fighting against an elaborate, illogical, and taciturn system dedicated to the illusion rather than the reality of meaningful clemency review, his television audience learned that, in Griffey's words, inmates don't have "some sort of right to any kind of clemency process. . . . Clemency has always been something that's entirely discretionary."[125] Although the US Supreme Court had stated that capital punishment without a meaningful system of executive clemency "would be totally alien to our notions of justice,"[126] Griffey's comments on the Larry King show suggested that Texas considers clemency review unnecessary. By the end of the hour, King had his guests conceding that "it's going to take a miracle" to save Karla Faye Tucker. When he and other journalists publicized Tucker's efforts to win over the institutionally unreceptive Board of Pardons and Paroles, they helped to make the case that Amnesty International would later argue in more detail: that executive clemency, intended to acknowledge and redress legal errors or excessive sentences, is so poorly organized in Texas that it "violates minimum human rights safeguards."[127]

Unlike Gary Gilmore, who had insisted that his fate was a personal matter without ramifications for other death-row inmates, Karla Faye Tucker saw her appeal as possibly affecting many inmates who had genuinely rehabilitated themselves. Rather than fretting as her execution date approached, Tucker appeared "exuberant" and "irrepressible" as she spoke of her legal battles.[128] When Larry King asked her if her life was getting "worse every day," she surprised him by replying, "No. It gets a little more exciting every day. . . . Every day something new comes up and it's exciting to be a part of it because . . . it's going to affect a lot of people."[129] Tucker hoped that her battle would enable other death-row inmates who had "sincerely changed" to "get a serious hearing" from the board of pardons.[130] She was excited, as well, by the visibility of her case as she tried to reach people with the Christian message of redemption. As her husband noted, "the fight is bigger than her. The fight is bigger than the seven women on death row. The fight is bigger than the 400-plus men on death row. It goes on all over this world. . . . She's a classic example that someone can change."[131]

In her letter to Governor Bush, Tucker argued the point that had been raised by her lawyers and other allies: if Texas law allows for the commutation of death sentences, what better case for commutation than someone who had reformed and was able to help society from her prison cell?

In closing her eleven-page letter, Tucker drew on a scriptural precedent for choosing mercy over justice: King David, guilty of murdering a man in battle in order to take his wife, was not put to death as Mosaic law required. Tucker concluded with one of David's psalms, in which he cries out to the Lord for mercy. But, like a minister, she commented on the psalm before ending her letter:

> David cried out, not just for pardon, but for purity; not just for acquittal, but for acceptance; not just for comfort, but for complete cleansing—whatever the cost. Although his heart was crushed by his shame and sorrow over sin, he knew the great breadth of God's mercy. See how, once his sins are confessed, forgiven, and purged, David dares to ask for God's choicest gift: Joy, restoration, God's presence, His Holy Spirit. Then he humbly offers himself to be used as an instrument to show forth God's praise and to teach other transgressors. This psalm evidences that God accepted that offer, just by the mere fact that it is in our Holy Bible.[132]

Tucker probably did not write this passage herself. Its tone and diction are much different from the rest of her letter to Bush. In its parallelism, its cadences, and its alliteration ("not just for pardon, but for purity; not just for acquittal, but for acceptance; not just for comfort, but for complete cleansing") the passage reads more like a sermon than a letter from death row. And in its charge to "See how . . . David dares" to ask for mercy, it resembles a preacher's exhortation to his congregation. Tucker was, of course, not the first condemned criminal to channel the words of her minister; from colonial days to the present, religious leaders have understood that lessons of redemption are best taught by redeemed sinners. The difference was that in Tucker's case, the clergy were not allied with the state; when this penitent criminal spoke in the voice of her spiritual guides, she was pitting herself against the state authorities who had determined her sentence and those charged with upholding it.

Governor Bush, as we know, did not see fit to dispense with the rigor of the law; concluding that "judgments about the heart and soul of an individual on death row are best left to a higher authority," he refused to intervene in the execution.[133] In the weeks leading up to Tucker's lethal injection, many journalists and politicians tried to predict the governor's decision, all agreeing that, in William F. Buckley's words, "George W. Bush has a helluva problem."[134] "Will Mr. Bush have the 2000 presidential elections in mind when the paperwork falls on his desk?" asked Ivo Dawnay. "No one doubts it."[135]

When he announced his decision, Bush spoke with the solemnity and reverence appropriate to a governor launching his subject's soul into eternity. "Like many touched by this case," he declared, "I have sought guidance through prayer."[136] If he did not exactly resemble the nineteenth-century Massachusetts justice who wept openly as he imposed the death penalty on a high-profile, sympathetic criminal, Governor Bush nevertheless played his part well, understanding that if he chose not to appease his conservative Christian allies, he must at least pretend to be tormented by his grave responsibility.[137] Though he was every bit as theatrical as the other players in this drama, however, Bush differed from the others in the evident insincerity of his dramatic role. I have been arguing that the histrionic nature of emotionally charged public executions does not diminish their earnestness; as we have seen, the execution of Karla Faye Tucker, for all its ritualistic predictability, was affecting, and the utterances it inspired were for the most part heartfelt. Bush's performance stands out in its cynicism; though he spoke with piety and, we might say, with compassionate conservatism on the eve of Tucker's execution, when he was on the presidential campaign trail only sixteen months later he revealed the brevity of his role when he mocked the executed criminal. Interviewed by Tucker Carlson of *Talk* magazine about Karla Faye Tucker's clemency appeal, the presidential candidate shocked the reporter with his contemptuous imitation: "'Please,' Bush whimpers, his lips pursed in mock desperation, 'don't kill me.'"[138]

Clearly, George W. Bush could not sustain the aura of solemnity surrounding Tucker's death. But for others—for those who continue to read Linda Strom's *Karla Faye Tucker Set Free: Life and Faith on Death Row* or Beverly Lowry's *Crossed Over*, for those who tuned in to the television movie of Lowry's book, broadcast in 2000, and for the many visitors who continue to read and post messages at the eight or so Web sites devoted to her memory, the fact that Tucker's crime, rehabilitation, and execution were repetitions of a once-familiar colonial ritual did not in the least diminish the emotional power of her case. If the sarcastic governor who refused to pardon a penitent criminal could so easily turn her into a joke, the masses who read her story and vicariously watched her execution would remember her with admiration. In the words of one visitor to the Karla Faye Tucker Brown memorial Web site, "The vision of Karla walking straight and tall in the prison yard will stay with me the rest of my life"[139] (http://books.dreambook.com/ladydaria/faye.html).

Conclusion

ARTFUL UPRISINGS

The Campaign against Capital Punishment

W e have been looking at extraordinary capital cases—crimes and executions that garnered unusual attention in the press and stirred individuals to reflect on them in the public domain, using printed and oral media and a variety of imaginative forms to encourage public consideration of state-sponsored and extralegal executions. Although the public discussions generated by these capital cases often took on larger social issues, as we have seen, they were in every case prompted by particular individuals whose deaths awakened sympathy, indignation, and admiration. In the years following Karla Faye Tucker's death by lethal injection, however, extraordinary executions have become rare as the pace of state-sponsored deaths has accelerated. In Texas alone a record nineteen inmates were put to death in 1995, more than any other state since the death penalty was reinstated in 1976. Texas broke its record in 1997 and continued to exceed the nineteen executions every subsequent year but 2001. (By 2000, the new record, still held by Texas, was forty). A *New York Times* headline noted that "As Texas Executions Mount, They Grow Routine."[1] Whereas in the early days of the modern era of capital punishment, executions were anticipated by days of news activity and always warranted a report on the morning

**Editorial cartoon, Kevin Kallaugher, *Baltimore Sun*,
June 6, 2000. Reprinted with permission of the artist.**

after the event, their commonness two decades later left little time for news coverage between executions, and in any case an indifferent public failed to demand such coverage. Even Betty Lou Beets, Karla Faye Tucker's death-row companion, attracted only slight media attention in 2000 when she became the fourth woman executed in the United States since capital punishment was reinstated in 1976.

Which is not to say that the American public has ceased to pay attention to state-sponsored executions. What attracted most notice by the end of the twentieth century was the very fact that capital punishment had become so unremarkable. Texas, where executions had once taken place in the dead of night to discourage unruly gatherings, quietly changed its policy in 1995, moving executions to the early evening without drawing larger crowds.[2] By the turn of the century everyone knew that state killings were happening in record numbers across the country—particularly in Texas, which had come to represent the horribly routine nature of capital punishment—but by then few people knew or remembered the names of those being put to death. As *New York Times* columnist Bob Herbert complained, "The conveyor-belt of death [in Texas] maintains its steady, mindless pace."[3]

Herbert's bitter objection continues to be precisely the point for a mounting number of Americans who, at the end of the twentieth century and beginning of the twenty-first, are increasingly uneasy about the unemotional, mechanized, sanitized, and anonymous routine of capital punishment and the rising number of inmates being put to death. In the public sphere, newspapers, film, and television companies; nonprofit organizations; and concerned individuals are taking it upon themselves to make the public confront and understand a process that has slipped out of view. John D. Bessler's 1997 book, *Death in the Dark: Midnight Executions in America*, argues that executions should be televised in order to restore the publicity of eighteenth- and early nineteenth-century executions. Americans in that case would not be subject, as they now are, to the many misconceptions about "the facts surrounding capital punishment."[4] Knowing "when and how the state takes a human life," Bessler argues, citizens would be better able to engage in rational debates about their criminal justice system.[5] Other writers, filmmakers, and artists are doing what they can to make the public understand who these death-row inmates are, how the government decides that they deserve death, and in some cases how they in fact die at the hands of the state. Sometimes these writers attempt to generate sympathy for individual death-row inmates, while other times they offer dispassionate but meticulous and critical scrutiny of the death penalty system itself. The musician and longtime opponent of capital punishment, Steve Earle, is moving away from individual capital cases as the subjects for his music. Having written several songs about executions, one based on his friendship with a death-row inmate who was executed in 1998, Earle has since decided that attachment to particular death row inmates often interferes with "political solutions."[6] Home Box Office's 2002 documentary, *The Execution of Wanda Jean*, focuses less on the individual who was executed than on the effort to have her sentence commuted, the arguments about judicial unfairness, and the controversy over executing mentally retarded inmates. While the filmmaker intended "to show [this] death row inmate as a human being,"[7] her film emphasizes "the inequities in the death penalty, not just the inherent immorality but also the haphazard administration of it and public misperception of how the whole thing works."[8] The "unusual" opportunity to observe the death penalty up close, this reviewer found, "offers no eloquent speeches, just blunt and often inarticulate realism," and questions the legal system "by exposing its dreary and loaded mechanisms."[9] Katya Lezin's 1999 book, *Finding Life on Death Row*, offers the stories of six death-row inmates, presenting their crimes "in the context of their entire lives" in an attempt to "humanize individuals who are traditionally reduced to stark numbers and sensationalized facts."[10] The foreword to Levin's book is written by Stephen B. Bright, an appeals attorney and the director of the Southern Center for Human Rights, which handled the appeals of the six subjects of Levin's study. As Bright argues in his preface,

> A society that employs such an enormous, severe, irreversible, and violent penalty, which has been discarded by much of the rest of the world, should at least know whom it is killing. It should understand the process that determines who lives and who dies. The death penalty is authorized for thousands of people who commit crimes each year, but only about 275 are sentenced to death. Even fewer are actu-

ally put to death. Who are those people? How were they selected to die when so many others—some with worse histories of criminal behavior and guilty of far more heinous crimes—were punished with life imprisonment? Are those condemned to death really the worst of the worst criminals in our society? These are questions of fundamental importance.... But the condemned have received too little attention. And as the number of executions continues to increase, less and less attention is being paid to who is being killed and how they were condemned to die.[11]

The artists behind these cultural works clearly wish to change not only the political scene but ultimately the law itself; most hope to bring about at least substantial reform if not complete abolition of the death penalty.

Before considering the effects of art on legislation, we should first attend to shifting public attitudes regarding capital punishment. If we recall that the Supreme Court revisits capital cases periodically in order to assess whether "standards of decency" have evolved to the point where capital punishment itself (or particular applications of it) is no longer constitutional, we will see the importance of cultural works in shaping as well as reflecting a cultural consensus. Insofar as capital punishment is the product of public opinion and is therefore cultural in nature, changing American attitudes to the death penalty are often most powerfully expressed—and can perhaps be most accurately measured—in artistic productions. To look at the cultural, political, and legal debates over capital punishment at the end of the twentieth century is to understand the overlapping and reciprocal nature of these debates. Katya Lezin's book and similar efforts to make the public consider the details of state-sponsored executions, the way the process works and the individuals involved, reached a number of political leaders who, reconsidering the system, agreed that it needed reform. The crisis generated by these leaders—particularly as the 2000 presidential election loomed—in turn inspired a new generation of artists, musicians, and writers to challenge not individual executions but the very system of state-sponsored killings. Although the entire nation was involved in this debate, the national controversy centered once again on Texas and Illinois. To consider the effect of art on public sentiment and of public sentiment on law, we must bear in mind what happened in Illinois and Texas during the last decade or so.

I. THE ILLINOIS MORATORIUM

The newspaper that had beaten the drums for the execution of the Haymarket anarchists in 1887 had become by the late twentieth century a champion of convicted criminals. In 1999 the *Chicago Tribune* ran a series of investigative articles scrutinizing the Illinois capital punishment system and uncovering a pattern of widespread error, incompetence, misconduct, and unfairness.[12] The series called attention to a nearly fifty percent reversal rate of death penalty sentences since Illinois had reinstated capital punishment in 1977; more recipients of death sentences had been exonerated than executed. The *Tribune* investigation concluded that "[c]apital punishment in Illinois is a system so riddled with faulty evidence, unscrupulous trial tactics and legal incompetence that justice has been forsaken."[13] The governor had just started his first term earlier that year and would soon find himself at the center of the national debate over capital punishment. Governor George Ryan was a law-and-order Republican, a longtime supporter of capital punishment who had been a member of the Illinois legislature in 1977 when that body voted to reinstate the death penalty. As Ryan later recalled, "There was great optimism in the air" in 1977, when states were given a chance to reform their death penalty laws. Ryan recalled voting for capital punishment "with the belief that whatever problems had plagued the capital punishment system in the past were now being cured."[14] But in early 1999, he "watched in surprise" when death row inmate Anthony Porter was released from prison after coming within 48 hours of being executed.[15] A month later, another death row inmate was exonerated. When Governor Ryan was confronted with his first scheduled execution in March, he consulted with prosecutors, detectives, and defense attorneys in the case and spent nights reviewing the documents. There was no doubt that the condemned man, Andrew Kokoralies, was guilty of not only the murder he had been sentenced for but also a number of other gruesome murders and mutilations. Still, Ryan was clearly uneasy presiding over an actual state killing, and though he signed the death warrant, by the time the next execution was ready to go on the calendar the governor declared a moratorium, announcing that until he could "be sure with moral certainty that no innocent man or woman is facing a lethal injection, no one will meet that fate."[16] In March, Ryan appointed a fourteen-person commission charged with determining "what reforms, if any, would ensure that the Illinois capital punishment system is fair, just and accurate."[17]

II. THE TEXAS CONVEYOR OF DEATH

In Texas, meanwhile, the nation was watching another governor, George W. Bush, who had campaigned successfully against incumbent Governor Ann Richards in 1994 by calling her "soft on crime" and who during his first term had presided over a record number of executions, including the famous Karla Faye Tucker case.[18] Unlike his counterpart in Illinois, Bush was untroubled by the startling number of death sentences in his state, explaining that "of all the death penalties we have had in our state, I am confident that those that have been put to death have been guilty."[19] Nor was Bush reluctant to execute mentally retarded inmates or juvenile offenders. At a time when a number of states were passing legislation to bar the execution of the mentally retarded, a similar Texas bill died in the State House after Governor Bush announced his opposition: "I like the law the way it is right now," he declared.[20] And after the Texas Senate and House, joining a national effort by state legislatures to reform their death-penalty statutes, unanimously passed a bill to create a state public defender system that would guarantee timely assignment of lawyers to indigent defendants, Governor Bush vetoed the bill.[21] State senator

Rodney Ellis, sponsoring the bill, explained that "if we are going to lead the world in executions, . . . then we should at least make sure that defendants are getting effective representation."[22] The governor's veto meant another defeat for judicial fairness in Texas.

George W. Bush stood out among his fellow political leaders, particularly Governor Ryan, who were losing confidence in a capital system that they had always thought fair and free of errors. What appeared to many Americans as a crisis in Texas was becoming a national issue, not simply because legislators, judges, and governors in other states were beginning to ask the same questions that were plaguing Ryan,[23] but also because Bush became the Republican party's nominee for president in August 2000. Whatever death penalty reforms seemed necessary or imminent to many would surely depend on the person occupying the White House and appointing justices. Capital punishment never became an election issue in the 2000 presidential race because both Bush and his Democratic opponent favored the death penalty, and capital punishment seemed as popular as ever among most candidates for elected office.[24] But to the many people who were feeling apprehensive about the actual implementation of the death penalty, especially in light of revelations by news media and nonprofit organizations devoted to saving death-row prisoners, Bush's confidence in the system and his persistent refusal to consider reforms were troubling features to contemplate in a future president. Many Americans worried that their concerns over capital punishment were not shared by either presidential candidate and would not even be discussed in the election process. But while the two-party electoral system failed to offer a forum for Americans to debate this troubling issue, a number of artists provided other venues in which to do so.

III. THE POLITICAL USES OF ART

Musicians were among the artists who put their medium to work on abolition. Bruce Springsteen and Steve Earle had written songs for the 1995 movie *Dead Man Walking*, and Earle often spoke and performed at various rallies for the abolition of the death penalty. In 2001 the hip-hop band Spearhead released *Stay Human*, an album about a community activist wrongly convicted and sentenced to death. A meditation in music on many of the issues that troubled death penalty opponents, *Stay Human* weaves thirteen songs together with broadcasts from a community radio station that, in following the impending execution and the upcoming gubernatorial election, takes the time to address many of the peripheral issues—police misconduct, racism, poverty, political expediency—that became central issues in the capital trials resulting in so many wrongful death sentences. A compilation released in 2002, *The Executioner's Last Songs*, is devoted entirely to the abolition of the death penalty, and the producers are donating all proceeds to the Illinois Death Penalty Moratorium Project. The album features both new and old songs about prison, crime, and cruelty, about Karla Faye Tucker and George W. Bush, and about Tom

Dooley, the subject of a nineteenth-century Appalachian murder ballad. What the reviewer Tom Wheeler called "a genuinely oppositional undertaking," this album offers a variety of musical traditions—punk rock, country, traditional, rock and roll, rhythm and blues—to lend pathos and rage to the political issue of capital punishment and to demonstrate that political protest is a strong part of the American musical tradition. "Music isn't going to lead the way to radical change," Wheeler wrote. "But it sure as hell can provide the marching tunes."[25]

While musicians provided the soundtrack to a movement, other artists endowed their audiences with an opportunity to reflect on the problems inherent in the death penalty. The playwrights Jessica Blank and Erik Jensen used the theater to engage their audiences in the debate about capital punishment. *The Exonerated*, their theatrical documentary based on the stories of men and women who had been wrongly convicted and sentenced to death, opened in fall 2000 and has subsequently been performed in different formats and with different casts around the country. Drawing on the appeal of famous actors like Steve Buscemi, Jill Clayburgh, Ossie Davis, Brian Dennehy, Richard Dreyfuss, Mia Farrow, Jeff Goldblum, Tim Robbins, Susan Sarandon, Marlo Thomas, Montel Williams, Robin Williams, Debra Winger, and others, Blank and Jensen have employed a rotating cast to continue attracting audiences to their enormously popular play. Unabashed about mixing art and politics, they seek not only to distress and educate their audiences, but also to solicit donations from theater patrons for exonerated ex-prisoners and organizations working to abolish the death penalty.[26] The printed text of the play, published in 2004, acknowledges their debt not only to the artistic community but also to the world of political activism: the writers dole out thanks to creative agencies like the Actors' Gang, the Artists Network, the Culture Project, and the New York State Council for the Arts, as well as to organizations working for the abolition of the death penalty—the Justice Project, the Innocence Project, the Center on Wrongful Convictions—and to individuals like Tim Robbins, Susan Sarandon, and George Soros, known for their left-leaning politics.

The story behind the play's inception further blurs the distinction between art and politics. The idea occurred to the playwrights after an emotional experience at a workshop on wrongful convictions hosted by the Columbia Law School in early 2000, where Blank and Jensen heard from an Illinois inmate who claimed that his false confession had been coerced with torture. Moved to tears by the prisoner's account, the writers found themselves "frustrate[ed] . . . that stories like these are rarely known outside of activist communities."[27] At the time, more and more stories about wrongful convictions were emerging—eighty-seven men and women had been released from death row since 1973—and Governor Ryan had just declared his moratorium on the death penalty in Illinois. Determined to try to locate some of these people and hear their stories, Blank and Jensen traveled the country during that summer, eventually interviewing sixty people who had been freed from death row who described "what it was like to be innocent and on death row."[28] They returned with 150 manuscript pages, which they edited down to a play that featured twelve characters who were freed from death row after lengthy appeals.[29]

The playwrights were probably untroubled by reviews that placed their work "in the tradition of agitprop theater or what journalists refer to as muckraking."[30] The character Delbert, an exonerated man who doubles as a chorus for the entire action, openly identifies with African American poets and novelists who saw their writings as part of a larger effort toward social transformation:

> How do we, the people, get outta this hole, what's the way to fight,
> might I do what Richard and Ralph and Langston'n them did?
> It is not easy to be a poet here. Yet I sing.
> I sing.[31]

To "sing" for Delbert as for Langston Hughes is to compose but also to expose a world in which singing and fighting are synonymous. For Blank and Jensen, too, the fight to bring these stories to life on a stage does not preclude the possibility of making art at the same time. In their directions to actors, the authors insist that actors "be careful not to be didactic. . . . The drama of these stories does not need enhancement."[32] And while the content is serious, "There's a great deal of humor here, too— don't overlook it," they caution.[33] Though they did not add to their interview material, only edited it, the writers carefully structured and staged their play in order to provide what one reviewer called "an artful and moving evening of documentary theatre."[34] The set is sparse, with actors reading their scripts rather than acting a fully staged story. As one reviewer described it, "Nothing stands between the actors and the audience except ten chairs and music stands, facing front. The lack of artifice helps the audience absorb the play's full weight."[35] The dialogue, taken directly from interviews and interspersed with words from the official transcripts of the legal proceedings, adumbrates those proceedings while also breaking free of them. As one reviewer noted, "Seated on stools on a bare stage, the actors take turns in the solo spotlight, probably similar to the one at the tiny table where the initial inquiry took place. This isn't a court briefing where everything is sterile and unaffected. By the end of the uninterrupted, tense and at times unnerving session, folks in the audience are wiping away tears, both men and women."[36] The stories unfold in an organized, coherent way, moving from speaker to speaker and following a general trajectory from the crime and interrogation to the trial, imprisonment, exoneration, and then the after-effects as these characters struggle to reclaim their lives after so many years on death row. Though some theatergoers were probably as troubled as the reviewer who resented the political use of theater (particularly when a donation envelope fell out of her program), most reviewers agreed that the sold-out performances were aesthetically and emotionally satisfying as well as politically provocative.[37] Blank and Jensen, wrote one reviewer, "are theater people as much as American citizens with a cause"; anyone coming to the theater "expecting a play and not a lecture won't feel short changed."[38]

But of course the play follows in the tradition of other political literature we have been considering, and as such its first performances were timed for maximum political effect. Governor Ryan's recent moratorium had put capital punishment in the news if not in the presidential debates. George W. Bush was running for president on a record that was shocking to people who were troubled by state-sponsored executions: As governor, Bush had presided over 145 executions in Texas. When Allan Buchman learned about the play, he offered to donate his New York theater space for three nights. The director of New York's Culture Project, an enterprise that encourages the influence of theater on social values, attached one condition: Blank and Jensen must have a play ready to be performed before the elections in November. They did, and when the production opened in October, the playwrights offered free tickets to George W. Bush and his wife because, they said, they suspected he had no idea what his record number of executions had done to "individuals who were, in fact, innocent."[39]

Bush did not attend the performance, but those who did were confronted with an unsettling question: How had these clearly innocent people all arrived on death row? In their broad outlines, the stories conveyed on stage were familiar to those who had been following the news about exonerations, but the individual stories of overzealous police officers, coerced confessions, prosecutorial misconduct, and substandard legal defense "still beggar belief at second sight."[40] Kerry Cook, on death row for twenty-two of his forty-five years, explains that because of a joyride he took as a ninth grader, "that was pretty much it—after that, any robbery, any broken window, any cat up a tree, everything was just *[his] fault*, as far as the sheriff was concerned."[41] Delbert Tibbs, a black man, notes that an eyewitness description did not match him at all, "except racially," but two weeks after the crime "they gotta find *somebody*, 'cause the small town is in hysterics, you know? There's a nigger running around killing white men and raping white women, and you can't have that."[42] Sunny Jacobs, whose husband and codefendant died in the electric chair based on evidence as shoddy as the facts used against her, describes how the prosecution had withheld exculpatory evidence while the judge kept the jury from hearing that her accuser was getting a reduced sentence in return for his testimony.[43]

Several characters talk about how they came to confess to the crimes that they insist they never committed. Perhaps the most difficult stumbling block for those who cannot fathom how innocent people are sentenced to death, the coerced confession appears in these stories as one of the most damning features of our criminal justice system. The eighteen-year-old David Keaton, brought in for questioning without his parents or a lawyer, was afraid of being beaten by the police. "I didn't know the rules. And they kept on talking', and they were threatenin' me, and all that. And I was afraid. I mean, they would go in there and beat you up, mess you up, hang you up, nobody'd ever hear nothing' else about you. And so I say, Okay, to prevent that, I'm gonna go ahead and confess to the crime. I know I'm tellin' the truth, and the witnesses are gonna know too, 'cause I just wasn't there and they would have seen that."[44] At the time of Keaton's trial, the prosecutor scoffs at the idea of a coerced confession: "There was nobody making those defendants say anything, and this jury knows anyway that of course that would be impossible, impractical. You just can't *make* somebody say something; nobody can!"[45] The point of the play, of course, is that whether juries and ordinary citizens know it or not (and most do not), false confessions can indeed be compelled. The stories of coerced confessions are among the most sickening moments in *The Exonerated.*

The critic who complained that the secondary characters ("various bullies and clichéd characters") were "unconvincing, almost cartoonish" perhaps didn't realize that the lines spoken by these characters were drawn entirely from official documents of courtroom and police proceedings.[46] The stage directions do encourage the feeling of unreality—one cop, for instance, is directed to speak in an "unnaturally fast robotic monotone."[47] And yet, unnatural performances highlight the point of all these stories: that the truth did not matter in these courtrooms, where an array of powerful interests turned a rational and just process into a bizarre theatrical spectacle. Perhaps the most shocking example of this can be found in Gary Gauger's story. Although he did not think he was confessing to the murder of his parents, the police kept Gauger up all night, persuaded him to speculate about the crime, and then used those guesses against him in court. "I was in such a vulnerable and suggestible state from finding my parents and not knowing what happened," Gary recalls. "I was emotionally distraught, I was physically exhausted. I was confused. I had fifteen cups of coffee. I was spaced-out. And the police used that. They said they had all the evidence, that they didn't even *need* my confession."[48] Suggesting that Gary may have blacked out, the police encourage him to speculate on how he might have killed his parents. Gary agrees "to give what they call a 'vision statement'—a hypothetical account of what [he] would have done if [he] had killed [his] parents." The scene shifts abruptly from Gary's guesses—"I guess I would've gotten up that morning. . . . I would've had to have reached out toward my mom"—to the policeman's courtroom testimony, which turns Gary's conditional statements into declarative sentences: "The defendant stated that he got up that morning. . . . He reached up and he grabbed his mother with his left hand and cut her throat with his right." As the audience watches Gary's bewildered but helpful words turned against him, Gary shares his disbelief: "They used that vision statement for a *confession.*"[49] The use of his words is more shocking when we learn that "the autopsies showed that everything I said in those statements was wrong."[50] Scenes like this one are stylized and nightmarish, but they do not distort the actual interrogation and trial as they were recorded in official transcripts.

Although audiences come to know something of the personalities, the histories, and the traumas of the real people depicted in *The Exonerated*, the real achievement of the play is to illustrate the outrageous strangeness and injustice of the capital system itself. We learn that David had wanted to be a minister before his arrest, that the good-natured Gary belonged in the peacenik 1960s, that the upbeat Sunny "didn't want to waste my time being mad,"[51] and that Delbert, whose "whole personality is like an old soul song,"[52] is determined not to give in to fear or malice or racism. But these characters represent others as well—the growing number of people exonerated of capital crimes (the number had reached 102 by 2004, when the play was published) and those who are still wrongly incarcerated on death row—and in suggesting those other, untold stories, the play focuses most of its scrutiny on the criminal justice system, its errors and abuses.[53] The rotating cast and the new parts that Blank and Jensen added periodically—the characters in the 2000 premiere are not identical with those in the published version—suggest that these stories, while individual, also represent a larger crisis.

One of the common threads in nearly every story is the theme of poor legal representation. Sunny, who was never in trouble with the law before her arrest for murder, explains why she didn't hire her own defense attorney. "My parents said, 'Well, you know, we were told we could try and get you a better lawyer, but you *have* a lawyer—they've *appointed* you one—so it's okay.' We didn't know."[54] What there is to know emerges in the other stories, which depict indifferent lawyers who fail to object to the bullying of prosecutors. During Kerry's trial, a witness who had earlier testified that a different man was present at the scene of the crime now points to Kerry as the suspect, and Kerry's lawyer does not argue. "My court-appointed attorney was the former DA who jailed me twice before," Kerry tells us. "He was paid five hundred dollars by the state, and in Texas you get what you pay for."[55]

Nor is the appeals process the reliable safety net that many capital punishment supporters claim. If the former death-row inmates depicted in *The Exonerated* are typical in their experiences of bad legal representation and police and prosecutorial misconduct, they are unusual in the ways their convictions were reversed: these people were freed not by means of the regular appeals process, Jessica Blank explains, but rather through the efforts of volunteers: "a crusading lawyer working pro bono or a group of journalism students, with the funding of a university, who dug back into a closed case or an investigative reporter who didn't let someone's story die in the public eye for ten years."[56] In fact, Blank and Jensen expose the astonishing truth that even after some of their subjects had been cleared of all wrongdoing, they cannot enjoy the rights of free people. Robert Earl Hayes, a former horse groomer, is denied a horse-racing license after his exoneration because he was convicted of a crime. "I can legally get a gun," he marvels, "but I can't get a license to drive a horse. . . . Because of their mistake."[57] More troubling still, a number of these characters tell how they remained on death row for several years after exculpatory evidence emerged. Although Norman Rhodes, the prosecution's star witness against Sunny Jacobs and her husband, confessed in 1979 to the two murders, his testimony did not prevent the execution of Sunny's husband, Jesse Tafero, in 1990. Sunny was not released from prison until 1992. When Gary Gauger's case caught the attention of a Northwestern law professor who enlisted his students in the appeal, the group discovered that a motorcycle gang long under federal surveillance was responsible for the murder of Gary's parents; indeed, the Bureau of Alcohol, Tobacco, and Firearms videotaped one gang member's confession to the murder. But it took another year for Gauger's release, during which time "they fought [my appeal] all the way to the Illinois Supreme Court."[58]

The Exonerated uses an old rhetorical device from public execution sermons in order to bring about identification between the audience and the subject of its gaze, though of course the political effect in this case is very different. Like colonial ministers, urging their congregations to look upon the criminal and "consider, *who it is that maketh you to differ*, and admire and adore his distinguishing Grace," Blank and Jensen's play reminds audiences that the gulf between law-abiding citizens and death-row inmates is not an unfathomable, impassable one.[59] Kerry Cook observes that "at a capital trial, the prosecutors always say, 'He's dangerous, he's a maniac, the sick, twisted murderer.' But I'm no different from you—I mean, I wasn't a street thug, I wasn't trash, I came from a good family—if it happened to me, man, it can happen to anyone."[60] In one of the play's many climactic moments, Sunny turns to the audience and asks them to take "a moment to reflect: From 1976 to 1992, just remove that entire chunk from your life, and that's what happened."[61] In addressing their audiences directly, asking rhetorical questions and insisting on the resemblance between them, these theatrical characters force their audiences to consider how easy it is to find oneself in the wrong place at the wrong time, at the mercy of unscrupulous prosecutors and police investigators, dependent on overworked or indifferent defense attorneys and politicians who find it expedient to secure a conviction at all costs. The religious language is gone but the message from colonial executions remains: *There but for the grace of God go I.*

Whereas colonial execution sermons emphasized the righteousness of the punishment and invited spectators to identify with condemned criminals in order to live blameless lives and avoid their mistakes, these ex-prisoners present themselves as everymen and everywomen victimized by a criminal justice system they now expose, telling the stories they were not permitted to tell in court and asking their audiences to judge a legal system they may have trusted without understanding. The original production consisted of twelve exonerated characters, which, as Jessica Blank points out, is "just like a jury."[62] The direct addresses from these characters to the audience challenge the idea that theatergoers are simply watching theater, and when the actual exonerated people step onto the stage at the end of the production, as they did during many performances, audiences are reminded that they are being asked to judge and, if they side with the exonerated people telling their stories, to act. One reviewer, describing the entrance of "these people you have come to know [who] take their places with the actors," called the finale "one of those transcendent moments."[63] On another occasion, when the actor playing Kerry Cook became sick, the real Cook, traveling with the production, stepped into the role, bringing the other actors to tears as he spoke his lines.[64] Subsequent performances deliberately cast some of the exonerated in their own roles, as if to emphasize that these stories were no fictions, and that the audience was part of a political dialogue, not mere pleasure-seekers. Indeed, the producers seemed to imply, the moral rage of audiences could be harnessed to effect political change.

A 2001 performance of *The Exonerated* emphasized the larger goals of the production by beginning with a series of condemnations of the death penalty written by Albert Camus, Arthur Koestler, and the Dalai Lama. In the hope of "drawing more attention to public debate around the death penalty in America," the Open Society Institute organized a series of "Talk Back" discussions to coincide with the 2002 New

York production of the play; each night the performance was followed by a discussion led by different organizations working for improved justice and an end to capital punishment.[65] Producers planned to take the show on the road, particularly to Texas and Florida, where "executions are a less abstract concern than in New York."[66] The authors of the play clearly hoped that they could convince people to reflect on the political and moral predicament of the death penalty at a time when the topic was becoming more vexed than it had been at any time since its reinstatement in 1976. Jessica Blank described her hope for the play: "If people's hearts are open and they hear these stories, it's our belief with this issue that they cannot, will not be able to, leave the theater being adamantly and unquestioningly pro-death penalty. They will be moved to question things very deeply, and if that happens, we've done our job."[67]

There is ample evidence to suggest that the play has had its intended effect, serving as the catalyst for an earnest discussion among ordinary citizens of a topic that has not been taken seriously in the official political arena. The talk show host Montel Williams, who performed in the San Francisco production of *The Exonerated*, perhaps best embodies the committed but uninformed death-penalty supporter who is forced to reconsider his views after taking into account the detailed stories told in this play. In an interview with the *San Francisco Bay View*, Williams unintentionally performs a political transformation that no doubt would have delighted Blank and Jensen. "I have always been a relatively staunch supporter of the death penalty for certain crimes," he explains, ". . . and I will remain that for the rest of my life." But musing on the finality of death, he begins to voice some of the reservations that have troubled the death penalty since the beginning and that feature prominently in *The Exonerated*:

> Any society that feels that it has the right to employ it should do so judicially and fairly, and until it can do so, it shouldn't be employed. I think there are people sitting on death row right now who are innocent. I think the first thing we need to do is place a moratorium on death row, go through and check every single case and every nuance of these cases and from this day forward try to ensure that we have a guilty person. You know what, it's really funny: the more I keep working with this issue I'm in support of, I keep arguing myself out of it, because a system that is operated by people is not infallible. People make mistakes.[68]

Williams had been playing the role of Delbert Tibbs, and in doing so was forced to imagine himself literally in the position of an innocent man wrongly convicted of a capital crime.

Like Montel Williams, Mary Jo White was a "thoughtful death penalty advocate" when she saw *The Exonerated* in 2003.[69] Unlike Williams, White was not a performer but a member of the judicial branch of government; she had been the top federal prosecutor in Manhattan for nearly ten years and had sought the death penalty on seven occasions, though none of those cases resulted in a death sentence. Though White agreed with the play's depictions of the criminal justice system—that court-appointed lawyers are "paid laughable sums" of money even in capital cases, and that "you have racism all throughout our justice system"—she was most unsettled by "the zealousness of cops" conducting investigations. "The degree to which that permeates the American justice system, I fear, is not insignificant," she said.[70]

IV. WHAT EFFECT ON THE LAW?

"We can always change any law in this country. I'm hoping that this will start a debate and that this debate will make us either fix the system or abolish it until it can be fixed." Montel Williams[71]

"The legislature couldn't reform it. Lawmakers won't repeal it. But I will not stand for it." Governor George Ryan[72]

Given the profound impact of art on individual consciences, we might wonder whether it can have as important an effect on the law itself. It is not unreasonable to think that it might. Though Mary Jo White is no longer a United States attorney, she explained in a *New York Times* interview that her thinking about the death penalty "has evolved several times in my life," and that at times she consulted all kinds of sources for insight into the human effects of capital punishment. She saw the movie *Dead Man Walking* in 1995, and discovered—as she was reminded when watching *The Exonerated*—that abstract justice is far different from actual justice meted out on real people. An execution is enacted on "another human being. If you're going to be abstract about it, you may have one result in your thinking. If you have to face another human being, you may have another."[73]

The example of Governor George Ryan might also seem to argue for the powerful effect of art on law. After all, the governor attended a production of *The Exonerated* at least twice before making his momentous decision to empty Illinois death row, and surely the play helped to make him see the extraordinary human costs of wrongful convictions.[74] Ryan, moreover, did his best to change Illinois law regarding capital punishment. Two years after he announced a moratorium on state executions, the bipartisan commission Ryan established to assess the death penalty issued its report, calling for a far-reaching overhaul of the Illinois system of capital punishment and recommending eighty-five specific reforms that would help to prevent unjustifiable executions. While a narrow majority of the commission supported the abolition of capital punishment, "a strong consensus emerged" among the group "that if capital punishment is retained in Illinois, reforms in the nature of those we have outlined are indispensable to answering the governor's call to better ensure a fair, just and accurate death penalty scheme."[75] The report, widely seen as "the most thorough independent analysis of the modern death penalty," acknowledged that it would be costly to implement its recommendations.[76] In spite of these costs, Thomas P. Sullivan, the former federal prosecutor who helped chair the commission, offered only two alternatives: "Fix the capital punishment system or abolish it," he insisted. "There is no other principled recourse."[77]

But the story of Ryan's attempts to reform the Illinois capital system is finally a bleak one. The Ryan report was issued in April 2002, and in the following nine months the governor worked diligently to persuade the state legislature to pass some of the suggested reforms. That year was an election year, however, and as many had predicted, lawmakers were reluctant to pass expensive legislation that might brand them as "soft on crime." Dismayed by the General Assembly's failure to pass "even one substantive death penalty reform," on January 11, 2003, just three days before the end of his term, Governor Ryan announced a blanket commutation for all Illinois death-row inmates.[78] Speaking before an audience at Northwestern University, where law professors and students had "first shed light on the sorrowful condition of Illinois's death penalty system," Ryan told the crowd that "no matter how efficient and fair the death penalty may seem in theory, in actual practice it is primarily inflicted upon the weak, the poor, the ignorant and against racial minorities." Complaining bitterly about unqualified, overworked, and lazy lawyers who "often didn't put much effort into fighting a death sentence," prosecutors whose standards for determining who gets the death penalty are hidden from public scrutiny, courts that rely on executive clemency in order to "avoid making the kind of major change that I believe our system needs," politicians who win votes by declaring themselves "tough on crime" but who are unwilling to "address the tough questions that arise when the system fails," Ryan declared the state "in a rudderless ship" where the death penalty was concerned. "There is more than enough blame to go around."[79]

Ryan explained that he had not intended to issue a blanket commutation, especially as he consulted the families of crime victims, but as he read through the files of the 167 death-row inmates (a process that took him and his staff three years) he realized that the same errors that haunt the capital system—"error in determining guilt, and error in determining who among the guilty deserves to die"—haunt individual judgments about life and death.[80] "I can't play God," he told his staff as he was sorting through the files of death-row inmates.[81]

When Ryan declared the moratorium in 2000, he urged the political leaders of Illinois to begin a rational discussion of the death penalty. When he emptied death row in 2003, he expressed discouragement over the outcome of his earlier appeal. "While our experience in Illinois has indeed sparked a debate, we have fallen short of a rational discussion," he maintained.[82] Speaking as the executive leader of his state, about to resume the life of an ordinary citizen, Ryan might well have been speaking for many of his fellow citizens, troubled over the death penalty and the failure of their political leaders to address the problem. He was announcing one of the most powerful unilateral actions available to a governor, but he expressed himself in the words of a citizen frustrated by the political imperatives that made real change impossible.

By virtue of his position as governor and the extraordinary step he was taking, Ryan drew the gaze of the entire world. But like any ordinary citizen in a democracy, Ryan used the public arena in order to foster a debate that was not taking place in the legislative and judicial halls. When he stepped down from his podium at Northwestern University and from his position as governor, the debate continued, fueled by other citizens taking advantage of the press and other technologies for communicating in the public sphere that Jürgen Habermas described. The effect of this conversation on death penalty legislation remains to be seen.

Where, as we move into the twenty-first century, is the nation marching with respect to the death penalty? During Governor Ryan's term of office many people saw Illinois as "a national bellwether for efforts to overhaul capital punishment."[83] After Ryan's blanket commutation, many abolitionists at home and abroad believed that what happened in Illinois would signal the end of capital punishment in the United States. The secretary general of the Council of Europe "sincerely hope[d] that this is a step forward to the abolition of the death penalty in the whole of the United States." In Washington, the director of the National Coalition to Abolish the Death Penalty called the announcement "a watershed moment, a turning point in the debate over capital punishment in the United States." Amnesty International pointed to Ryan's example that "change is possible . . . there is an alternative to the empty 'tough on crime' politics of the death penalty."[84] But in his public declaration, the governor seemed deeply pessimistic about the possibility of political change. Was his forward-looking and shocking act a sign of things to come, or had the governor cleaned out death row only that it might be filled again in the same way? What could be expected from a political system where both major party candidates supported capital punishment, where the topic never emerged in debates over an elected office, where even governors found themselves stymied by the legislative process, where one man's conscientious deliberation was seen by many as an affront to government, where even as powerful an institution as the *Chicago Tribune* could provoke outrage among the masses but could not in the end change the nature of the capital justice system?

Governor Ryan, for all his earnest effort to be humane and just, seemed when he left office to be a man living in the wrong century. Many attributed his courageous act to the fact that his political career was finished; no longer an elected official, he could once again be a man. But he also harked back to an earlier age, when political leaders did not demonize criminals but urged the law-abiding public to consider the ways they resembled these unfortunates and to offer them sympathy along with condemnation. It was a dangerous gesture, as we have seen: in identifying with the criminal, spectators might turn against the state. But in urging lawmakers and citizens to see death-row inmates as human beings, Ryan remembered that the purpose of the criminal justice system is twofold: to punish but also to try to reform. He pondered the possibility of rehabilitation for even the most hardened violent criminals and seemed reluctant to deprive such people of an opportunity for redemption. For a brief time he resembled the fictional governor and magistrates of *The Scarlet Letter*, who, in commuting Hester Prynne's capital sentence, incur the wrath of the townswomen, who declare that these men are "merciful overmuch" in this case, where the statute calls for death. In using their discretionary powers to commute Hester's sentence, the magistrates meet the rage of the townspeople with their wiser judgment and offer Hester the chance for rehabilitation—a chance that she uses well by the end of her seven-year struggle.

Governor Ryan, too, encountered much rage, particularly from the prosecutors who had secured death sentences and from the families of those who had been murdered by death-row inmates. "How can one person have all this authority and power?" asked the brother of one murder victim, adding that he hoped Ryan would "spend the rest of his life in prison." The sister of another murder victim declared that "[w]hat they've done to all these victims' families, it's like we were murdered again, our family members, that's how bad it is."[85] Everyone wanted a clearer line between capital offenders and the rest of humanity. Even the governor's wife was angry with his decision.

For a brief time, as he explained his unprecedented act in his final days of office, Governor Ryan resembled Hawthorne's magistrates, lawmakers, and interpreters of the law. But finally he most resembled the disgruntled townspeople in Hawthorne's marketplace. He spoke for ordinary citizens who were beginning to understand the profound capacity for error inherent in the capital justice system. As a political leader about to reenter civilian life, he seemed to voice the frustrations of many—Hawthorne's fictitious townspeople among them—who complain that their political leaders are unresponsive to the desires of citizens.

Governor Ryan's extraordinary act may not after all herald the end of capital punishment. The political process has a much easier time accommodating itself to the smooth-running but error-ridden capital system in states like Texas, where nobody pays much attention, than it does responding to the ethical and legal challenges issued by Governor Ryan's commission. Texas employs a much more modern version of the capital justice system, where inmates are put to death according to an assembly-line model, and where the governor receives "only the most cursory briefings" when reviewing each case.[86] In spite of the wide public support for Ryan's moratorium, the strong if not universal approval of his blanket clemency, and the echoes of his questions among private citizens and political leaders alike, the capital system in the United States may go the way of Texas rather than Illinois. President Bush's first US attorney general, John Ashcroft, persistently overrode local US attorneys who opted not to seek the death penalty, particularly in states where the use of capital punishment was rare. Now that Alberto Gonzales, Governor Bush's state legal counsel, is President Bush's second attorney general, the United States is beginning to look more uniformly like Texas, where Gonzales "repeatedly failed to apprise [Governor Bush] of crucial issues in the cases at hand: ineffective counsel, conflict of interest, mitigating evidence, even actual evidence of innocence."[87] All of these developments mean that Governor Ryan looks more like an angry and impotent ordinary citizen than like a man who once held immense political power.

In his rage, frustration, and sympathy for death-row inmates and their families, George Ryan reminds us of Benjamin Rush's warning to the young nation first testing its new institutions. Be careful of state-sponsored public punishments, Rush cautioned, not because they will desensitize people to the suffering of others, but for exactly the opposite reason. To "generous minds," the spectacle of suffering that they are powerless to relieve provokes a dangerous sentiment. Because the suffering of criminals "is the effect of a law of the state, which cannot be resisted, the sympathy of the spectator is rendered abortive. . . . While we pity, we secretly condemn the law which inflicts the punishment; hence, arises a want of respect for laws in general, and a more feeble union of the great ties of government."[88] The persistence of capital punishment has weakened our credibility with other nations, whose respect for the United States diminishes with every publicized execution, and the more American citizens learn about the process, the more they tend to deplore those who refuse to address their concerns. The public outcry against unjust executions, grown shriller here at home in the new century but still unheeded, might well weaken the government's credibility with its own citizens. In the meantime, generous minds will continue to give artistic shape to their sentiments, though they may have little effect on law itself.

NOTES

ACKNOWLEDGMENTS

1. Ralph Waldo Emerson, "Self-Reliance," in *Ralph Waldo Emerson: Essays and Lectures,* ed. Joel Porte (New York: Library of America, 1983), p. 265.

PREFACE

1. Plato *Republic* 607b5–6.
2. Nathaniel Hawthorne, *The Scarlet Letter* (1850), vol. 1 of *The Centenary Edition of the Works of Nathaniel Hawthorne*, ed. Thomas Woodson, L. Neal Smith, and Norman Holmes Pearson, 16 vols. (Columbus: Ohio State University Press, 1962–85), pp. 62–63.
3. Ibid., p. 63.
4. Ibid.
5. Ibid., p. 66.
6. Ibid., p. 68.
7. Ibid., p. 62.
8. Ibid., p. 51.
9. Ibid.
10. Ibid.
11. Ibid., p. 54.
12. Ibid., pp. 51–52.
13. Ibid., p. 57.
14. Ibid., p. 68.
15. Ibid., p. 63.
16. Jürgen Habermas, *The Structural Transformation of the Public Sphere: An Inquiry*

Into a Category of Bourgeois Society, trans. Thomas Burger (Cambridge, MA: MIT Press, 1989), p. 95.

17. Ibid., p. 96.

18. Benedict Anderson, *Imagined Communities: Reflections on the Origin and Spread of Nationalism* (London: Verso, 1983).

19. See chapter 1 in Kristin Boudreau, *Sympathy in American Literature: American Sentiments from Jefferson to the Jameses* (Gainesville: University Press of Florida, 2002).

20. The phrase is Tompkins's. The novelists she studies all "have designs upon their audiences," wishing to sway readers by "articulating and proposing solutions for the problems that shape a particular historical moment." Jane Tompkins, *Sensational Designs: The Cultural Work of American Fiction, 1790–1860* (New York: Oxford University Press, 1985), p. xi. For Tompkins, these novels had an "enormous impact" on their readers (p. xiii). Crane goes further, investigating not merely the attempt to sway readers or the impact on ordinary citizens, but the specific ways in which literary texts have in fact interacted with and influenced legal and judicial decisions. The "ethical assumptions guiding courts and legislatures" are often expressed in a culture's literary texts, and such texts can and often do bring about reevaluations of the law. Gregg D. Crane, *Race, Citizenship and Law in American Literature* (Cambridge, UK: Cambridge University Press, 2002), p. 2.

THEORETICAL INTRODUCTION TO EXECUTION LITERATURE: EARLY AMERICAN CRIMINAL NARRATIVES, THE POWER OF READING, AND THE PROBLEM OF PUBLIC SENTIMENTS

1. Benjamin Rush, *Essays Literary, Moral and Philosophical*, ed. Michael Meranze (Schenectady, NY: Union College Press, 1988), p. 82.

2. For treatments of sentiment in nineteenth-century culture, see Jane Tompkins, *Sensational Designs: The Cultural Work of American Fiction, 1790–1860* (New York: Oxford University Press, 1985); Ann Douglas, *The Feminization of American Culture* (New York: Knopf, 1977); Gordon Hutner, *Secrets and Sympathy: Forms of Disclosure in Hawthorne's Novels* (Athens: University Press of Georgia, 1988); Roy R. Male, "Hawthorne and the Concept of Sympathy," *PMLA* 68 (1953): 138–49; and Glenn Hendler, "The Limits of Sympathy: Louisa May Alcott and the Sentimental Novel," *American Literary History* 3 (1991): 685–706. For discussions of the role of sympathy in eighteenth-century culture and society, see William Frankena, "Hutcheson's Moral Sense Theory," *Journal of the History of Ideas* 16 (1955): 356–75; John Mullan, *Sentiment and Sociability: The Language of Feeling in the Eighteenth Century* (Oxford: Clarendon Press, 1988); Norman Fiering, "Irresistible Compassion: An Aspect of Eighteenth-Century Sympathy and Humanitarianism," *Journal of the History of Ideas* 37 (1976): 195–218; David Marshall, "Adam Smith and the Theatricality of Moral Sentiments," *Critical Inquiry* 10 (1984): 592–613; Gary Wills, *Inventing America: Jefferson's Declaration of Independence* (New York: Doubleday, 1978); Jay Fliegelman, *Declaring Independence: Jefferson, Natural Language, and the Culture of Performance* (Stanford, CA: Stanford University Press, 1993); and Cathy Davidson, *Revolution and the Word: The Rise of the Novel in America* (New York: Oxford University Press, 1986).

3. For more detailed analysis of this theme, see Marshall. As Louis Masur notes, Benjamin Rush encountered the ideas of Scottish Enlightenment philosophy when he was a medical student in Edinburgh between 1766 and 1768. See Louis P. Masur's excellent book, *Rites*

of Execution: Capital Punishment and the Transformation of American Culture, 1776–1865 (New York: Oxford University Press, 1989), p. 63. Jefferson, too, read widely in moral philosophy, as Fliegelman and Wills point out. See Adam Smith, *A Theory of Moral Sentiments* (London, 1759) and Francis Hutcheson, *An Inquiry into the Origin of our Ideas of Beauty and Virtue; in Two Treatises*, 3rd ed. (London, 1729). For further development of these ideas, see Fiering and Fliegelman.

4. Elizabeth Cady Stanton, "Speech to the Anniversary of the American Anti-Slavery Society," *Liberator*, May 18, 1860. Reprinted in *Elizabeth Cady Stanton, Susan B. Anthony: Correspondence, Writings, Speeches*, ed. Ellen Carol DuBois (New York: Schocken Books, 1981), and Ida B. Wells, *Southern Horrors: Lynch Law in all its Phases* (New York, 1893).

5. Jürgen Habermas demonstrates how widespread this idea was among philosophers and social theorists. Rousseau, Mill, Kant, and Toqueville all ascribed the power of governments in part to the sentiments of the people. See Habermas, *The Structural Transformation of the Public Sphere: An Inquiry into a Category of Bourgeois Society*, trans. Thomas Burger (Cambridge, MA: MIT Press, 1989), pp. 97–98, 103, 134.

6. See chapter 3 of Davidson for a lucid discussion of the debate over novel reading.

7. August 3, 1771. *The Papers of Thomas Jefferson*, vol. 1: 1760–1776, ed. Julian P. Boyd (Princeton, NJ: Princeton University Press, 1950), pp. 76–77.

8. Ibid.

9. Thomas Jefferson, "Female Education," March 14, 1818. *The Complete Jefferson*, ed. Saul Kussiel Padover (Freeport, NY: Books for Libraries, 1943), p. 1085.

10. Benjamin Rush, "Thoughts upon Female Education," in *Essays Literary, Moral and Philosophical*, ed. Michael Meranze (Schenectady, NY: Union College Press, 1988), p. 48.

11. See, for example, Nathaniel Clap, *The Lord's Voice, Crying to His People* (Boston, 1715), p. 76; William Shurtleff, *The Faith and Prayer of a Dying Malefactor* (Boston, 1740); Peres Forbes, *The Paradise of God Opened to a Penitent Thief* (Providence, 1784); Timothy Hilliard, *Paradise Promised to a Penitent Thief* (Boston, 1785); and James Dana, *The Intent of Capital Punishment* (New Haven, CT, 1790), pp. 17–18.

12. For details about execution day, see Masur; Daniel M. Cohen, *Pillars of Salt, Monuments of Grace: New England Crime Literature and the Origins of American Popular Culture, 1674–1860* (New York: Oxford University Press, 1994); and Daniel E. Williams's splendid introduction to his *Pillars of Salt: An Anthology of Early American Criminal Narratives* (Madison, WI: Madison House, 1993).

13. John Tebbel, *A History of Book Publishing in the United States*, vol. 1 (New York: R. R. Bowker, 1972), pp. 4–5.

14. William Shurtleff, *The Faith and Prayer of a Dying Malefactor* (Boston, 1740).

15. Eliphalet Adams, *A Sermon Preached on the Occasion of the Execution of Katherine Garret* (New London, 1738), p. 2.

16. Ibid., p. 4.

17. Shurtleff, preface.

18. Ibid., p. 31.

19. Ibid., p. 19.

20. Ibid., p. 20.

21. Adams, p. 12.

22. Ibid., p. 23.

23. Introduction to *Pillars of Salt*, p. 3.

24. Rebekah Chamblit, *The Declaration, Dying Warning and Advice of Rebekah Chamblit* (Boston, 1733), p. 1.

25. Of the twenty-five known execution materials published in the colonies between 1674 and 1726, fourteen were written by the Mathers. This family dominated the early years of execution materials, publishing eight of the first twelve sermons and histories of convicted criminals. For a list of execution literature, see Ronald A. Bosco, "Early American Gallows Literature: An Annotated Checklist," *Resources for American Literary Study* 8 (1978): pp. 81–107.

26. In Cotton Mather, *Warnings from the Dead* (Boston, 1693), p. 70.

27. Dying statement of Hugh Henderson, in John Campbell, *After Souls by Death Are Separated from Their Bodies* (Boston, 1738), p. 36.

28. John Ury, *The Dying Speech of John Ury* (Philadelphia, 1741), p. 4.

29. John Rogers (Boston, 1701). Reprinted in Daniel E. Williams, pp. 94–109. References here are to the Williams version.

30. Ibid., p. 108.

31. Rush was an impassioned opponent of public punishments of all kinds. Both his "Enquiry Into the Effects of Public Punishments Upon Criminals" and "An Enquiry into the Consistency of the Punishment of Murder by Death, with Reason and Revelation" are reprinted in *Essays Literary, Moral and Philosophical*, pp. 79–94 and 95–105, respectively.

32. Ian Watt describes the private world of the novel, which constituted a "short-cut, as it were, to the heart." Readers find in novels "the same complete engrossment of their inner feelings, and the same welcome withdrawal into an imaginary world vibrant with more intimately satisfying relationships than ordinary life provided." Ian Watt, *The Rise of the Novel: Studies in Defoe, Richardson and Fielding* (Berkeley and Los Angeles: University of California Press, 1957), pp. 195–96. See also Mullan.

33. John Young, *Narrative of the Life, Last Dying Speech and Confession of John Young*. Printed in Christopher Flanagan, *Conversation and Conduct of the Late Unfortunate John Young* (New York, 1797).

34. Ibid., p. 6.

35. Ibid., p. 8.

36. Ibid., p. 4.

37. Ibid., p. 1.

38. Ibid., p. 6.

39. Ibid., p. 4.

40. Henry David Thoreau, "Resistance to Civil Government" (Boston: Elizabeth P. Peabody, 1849).

41. Young, *Narrative of the Life*, p. 5.

42. A more recent disruption may have troubled government officials even more deeply. The Shay's rebellion of 1786 and 1787 resulted from the feelings among many poor farmers and laborers that their new government resembled the old in its apparent indifference to the plight of poor Americans, many of whom had fought valiantly against the British army. Although the rebels were sentenced to death, they were later pardoned, perhaps because of just such fears as those expressed by Benjamin Rush in 1787.

43. See especially chapter 3 in *Rites of Execution*.

44. Williams's anthology, *Pillars of Salt*, contains a number of execution narratives spanning from 1699 to 1796. A review of these accounts reveals that public concerns often focused on the criminal rather than the legal establishment. Levi Ames, executed for burglary

in 1773, became "the most widely publicized criminal in early America," inspiring nine broadside ballads, some of whose titles suggest sympathetic treatment by the authors: *The Dying Groans of Levi Ames, A Solemn Farewell to Levi Ames, The dying Penitent; or, the Affecting Speech of Levi Ames* (all in Williams, p. 186). In 1756, the counterfeiter Owen Syllavan received a stay of execution when, the night before the scheduled event, the gallows were cut down by "Persons unknown" (Williams, p. 149). These and other episodes suggest the profound disruption to public order that was to be feared by private sentiments.

45. *The Columbian Centinel*, August 23, 1797, p. 2.

46. When Thomas Mount was executed for burglary in 1791, his confession revealed an intricately structured underworld of thieves that amazed the public. Calling themselves the American Flash Company, this gang was held together by its own language, songs, and laws. See Mount's *Confession*, reprinted in Williams, pp. 308–35.

47. Margaretta V. Bleecker Faugeres, *The Ghost of John Young* (New York, 1797).

48. A number of poems in *The Lyrical Ballads* focus on the private suffering of law-breakers, without using those criminals to preach the wisdom of law-abiding conduct. See, for instance, "The Convict," whose speaker resembles the one in Faugeres's poem: "I pause; and at length, through the glimmering grate, / That outcast of pity behold." See also "Poor Susan," "The Two Thieves," "The Dungeon," and "The Thorn."

49. 1802 Preface to *The Lyrical Ballads*, William Wordsworth and Samuel Taylor Coleridge. Reprint edited by R. L. Brett and A. R. Jones (London: Methuen, 1963), p. 256.

50. *Discipline and Punish: The Birth of the Prison*, trans. Alan Sheridan (New York: Random House, 1977), p. 16.

CHAPTER ONE: REWRITING THE FALL RIVER MURDER: A FACTORY TOWN TURNS TO SENTIMENTAL NARRATIVES

1. Cited in Ephraim K. Avery, *A Vindication of the Results of the Trial of Rev. Ephraim K. Avery* (Boston, 1834), pp. 23–24.

2. Richard Hildreth, *Report of the Trial of the Rev. Ephraim K. Avery* (Boston, 1833), pp. 23–24.

3. Ibid., p. 25.

4. Ibid., p. 31.

5. Ibid., p. 49.

6. A Member of the Massachusetts Bar, *Celebrated Murders as Shown in Remarkable Capital Trials* (Chicago, 1878), p. 200.

7. Harvey Herndon, *Narrative of the Apprehension in Rindge, N.H. of the Rev. E.K. Avery, Charged with the Murder of Sarah M. Cornell* (Providence, 1833), p. 35.

8. Avery's return to Rhode Island provoked so much excitement both along the way and in the newspapers that Herndon was approached by several editors for a written account of his efforts to locate and arrest the suspect. According to Avery's defense attorneys, thirteen thousand copies of Herndon's thirty-four-page *Narrative of the Apprehension in Rindge, N.H. of the Reverend E.K. Avery* were published before the trial had even begun. See Benjamin Hallett, *The Arguments of Counsel in the Close of the Trial of Rev. Ephraim K. Avery, for the Murder of Sarah M. Cornell* (Boston, 1833), p. 9.

9. Hildreth, *Report of the Trial*, p. 7.

10. Ibid., p. 6.

11. Benjamin Hallett, *Trial of Rev. Mr. Avery: A Full Report of the Trial of Ephraim K. Avery* (Boston, 1833), p. 5.

12. Lincoln Sumner Fairfield, "Table Talk," *North American Quarterly Magazine* 2, no. 10 (1833): 256.

13. Hildreth, "Advertisement" and "Note by the Reporter," in *Report of the Trial*.

14. Anonymous, *Correct, Full and Impartial Report of the Trial of Rev. Ephraim K. Avery, Before the Supreme Judicial Court of the State of Rhode Island* (Providence, 1833), p. 3.

15. David Richard Kasserman, *Fall River Outrage: Life, Murder, and Justice in Early Industrial New England* (Philadelphia: University of Pennsylvania Press, 1986), p. 235.

16. "Mr. Avery," *New England Galaxy*, June 8, 1833.

17. Ibid.

18. Fairfield, "Table Talk," p. 256.

19. Aristides, *Strictures on the Case of Ephraim K. Avery* (Providence, 1833), p. 6.

20. Catharine Williams, *Fall River: An Authentic Narrative* (Providence, 1834), p. 59.

21. Anonymous, *Explanation of the Circumstances Connected with the Death of Sarah Maria Cornell* (Providence, 1834), p. 10.

22. Proteus, *Rhode Island Republican*, September 18, 1833.

23. Reviewed in *Literary Subaltern*, September 7, 1833.

24. *Rhode Island Republican*, September 4, 1833, p. 2.

25. This play, titled *Sarah Maria Cornell; or, the Fall River Murder*, was apparently not the one of the same title, performed in New York, that I discuss below. According to George C. Odell's *Annals of the New York Stage* (New York: Columbia University Press, 1928), the characters' names are different from the one performed at Richmond Hill. Still, it is possible that Clarke's play, which was published and sold in New York, was revised by another party and performed at the Richmond Hill Theater. In either case, I consider them separate documents.

26. Odell, *Annals of the New York Stage*, 3:688.

27. "The Drama Called Sarah Maria Cornell," *New York Mirror*, September 21, 1833.

28. "Richmond-Hill," *New York Mirror*, October 5, 1833.

29. Williams, *Fall River: An Authentic Narrative*, p. 62.

30. Kasserman is an excellent source for the demonstrations that followed Avery's acquittal. See his chapter 9, "Public Justice."

31. The Prescott case is discussed in Karen Halttunen, *Murder Most Foul: The Killer and the American Gothic Imagination* (Cambridge, MA: Harvard University Press, 1998), p. 89.

32. Kasserman (*Fall River Outrage*) describes several occasions when Avery was pursued by angry mobs. In Boston on July 13, for example, Avery sought protection in a nearby shop. Between four hundred and five hundred people surrounded the building to await his reemergence, and only a police escort secured his safety (p. 218).

33. William C. McLoughlin, "Untangling the Tiverton Tragedy: The Social Meaning of the Terrible Haystack Murder of 1833," *Journal of American Culture* 7, no. 4 (1984): 75–84.

34. Ibid., p. 76.

35. Ibid., p. 76.

36. *The Fall River Sourcebook: A Documentary History of Fall River, Massachusetts*, vol. 1 (New York: American History Workshop, 1981), p. 1.

37. Ibid., p. 62.

38. Ibid., p. 6.

39. Ibid., p. 8.

40. "Factory Establishment for Sale," *Fall River Monitor,* June 30, 1827.

41. Thomas Dublin notes that at the Hamilton Company in Lowell, Massachusetts, a typical New England textile factory, 97 percent of the female mill workers were unmarried when they began factory work, and 93 percent remained single until the end of their employment. *Women at Work: The Transformation of Work and Community in Lowell, Massachusetts, 1826–1860* (New York: Columbia University Press, 1979), p. 31.

42. John Coolidge, *Mill and Mansion: A Study of Architecture and Society in Lowell, Massachusetts, 1820–1865*, 2nd ed. (Amherst: University of Massachusetts Press, 1993), pp. 130, 133.

43. Ibid., p. 133.

44. George F. Kengott's study of Lowell, *The Record of a City: A Social Survey of Lowell, Massachusetts* (New York: Macmillan, 1912), pp. 46–48, chronicles the decline of paternalism in one typical factory town.

45. An article in the *Boston Quarterly Review*, for instance, argues that "the great mass" of factory workers "wear out their health, spirits, and morals, without becoming one whit better off than when they commenced labor. . . . Few of them ever marry; fewer still ever return to their native places with reputations unimpaired. 'She has worked in a Factory,' is almost enough to damn to infamy the most worthy and virtuous girl." *Boston Quarterly Review* 3 (1840): 369–70.

46. Thomas Dublin, *Women at Work*, pp. 32–33.

47. William Scoresby, *American Factories and Their Female Operatives* (Boston, 1845), p. 86.

48. Ibid., p. 84.

49. Ibid., p. 92, emphasis in original.

50. Ibid.

51. Ibid., p. 93.

52. American History Workshop, *The Fall River Sourcebook*, pp. 3–4 and 22.

53. Dublin writes that "mill employment represented a stage in a woman's life cycle before marriage; this was demonstrated by the fact that the vast majority of operatives did marry after their sojourn in Lowell" (*Women at Work*, p. 32).

54. Williams, *Fall River*, p. 10.

55. Mary Carr Clarke, *Sarah Maria Cornell, or the Fall River Murder: A Domestic Drama in Three Acts* (New York, 1833), p. 12.

56. Ibid.

57. Ibid., pp. 12–13.

58. Ibid., p. 13.

59. Hallett, *The Arguments of Counsel*, p. 26.

60. Williams, *Fall River*, p. 75.

61. Hallett, *The Arguments of Counsel*, p. 25.

62. Williams, *Fall River*, p. 53.

63. Hallett, *The Arguments of Counsel*, p. 63.

64. Aristides, *Strictures*, p. 13.

65. Ibid., p. 15.

66. Williams, *Fall River*, p. 82.

67. Ibid., p. 85.

68. Ibid., p. 25.

69. Ibid., p. 62.

70. Anonymous, *Brief and Impartial Narrative of the Life of Sarah Maria Cornell; Written By One, Who, Early Knew Her* (New York, 1933), p. 18.

71. Clarke, *Sarah Maria Cornell*, pp. 3–4.

72. Hallett, *The Arguments of Counsel*, pp. 17–18.

73. McLoughlin, "Untangling the Tiverton Tragedy," p. 82.

74. Hallett, *The Arguments of Counsel*, p. 67.

75. Williams, *Fall River*, pp. 65 and 67.

76. Ibid., p. 67. The anonymous author of the *Brief and Impartial Narrative* tells a different story: Cornell's father, he explains, "either consented to, or advised his wife to return with her young and helpless family, to her father in Connecticut, whom he believed better able to support them than himself" (p. 5).

77. Williams, *Fall River*, pp. 67–68.

78. May 20, 1822, cited in Williams, *Fall River*, p. 108.

79. Ibid., p. 112.

80. Ibid., p. 113.

81. Ibid., p. 110.

82. Ibid., p. 116.

83. Ibid., pp. 118–19.

84. Ibid., pp. 121–22.

85. Ibid., p. 75.

86. Ibid., p. 120.

87. Ibid., p. 108.

88. Ibid., p. 112.

89. Ibid., p. 111.

90. Ibid., p. 111. The fire is described in "Report of Factory Fire," *Independent Chronicle and Boston Patriot*, February 4, 1826. Kasserman explains that after the fire, Cornell moved to the nearby Branch Factory rather than leave Slatersville, where she remained only until materials became too scarce. Then she had to move again, this time to Millville, Massachusetts (*Fall River Outrage*, p. 42).

91. Williams, *Fall River*, p. 124.

92. Ibid., p. 4.

93. Ibid., p. 41. The author of the *Brief and Impartial Narrative* suggests that Cornell was promiscuous in her choice of jobs. During her lifetime she "was thus employed in no less number than eleven different factories, situated in various parts of four of the New-England states" (p. 8).

94. Williams, *Fall River*, p. 14.

95. Ibid., p. 9.

96. Clarke, *Sarah Maria Cornell*, p. 13.

97. Ibid., p. 16.

98. Ibid., p. 30.

99. Anonymous, *Brief and Impartial Narrative*, p. 6.

100. Williams, *Fall River*, p. 68.

101. Anonymous, *Brief and Impartial Narrative*, pp. 7–8.

102. Clarke, *Sarah Maria Cornell*, p. 9.

103. Ibid.

104. Williams, *Fall River*, p. 144.

105. Hildreth, *Report of the Trial*, p. 31.
106. Ibid.
107. Williams, *Fall River*, p. 145.
108. Ibid., p. 112.
109. Ibid., p. 115.
110. Ibid., p. 118.
111. Clarke, *Sarah Maria Cornell*, p. 15.
112. Ibid., p. 23.
113. Williams, *Fall River*, pp. 3–4.
114. Avery, *A Vindication of the Results of the Trial*, p. 4.
115. Clarke, *Sarah Maria Cornell*, pp. 8–9.
116. Ibid., p. 9.
117. Ibid., p. 10.
118. Aristides, *Strictures*, p. 92. Although I have been unable to corroborate this claim, the immense popularity of Aristides's series suggests that the public probably seized on and repeated his statement whether it was true or false. The statement was sufficiently incendiary to prompt Avery's colleagues to respond to it in print. Objecting to the claim that even the judges thought Avery guilty, they wrote, "we leave it to a candid and intelligent public to say whether it be likely, even if they had an opinion of his guilt, they would descend so far below the dignity of their office as to lend their influence to a faction which has for its object the nullification of the decision in the case, and the subversion of law and order by means of popular excitement." Avery, *Vindication*, p. 29.
119. Clarke, *Sarah Maria Cornell*, p. 40.
120. Anonymous, "The Death of Sarah M. Cornell" (n.p., 1832).
121. Anonymous, "The Factory Maid" (n.p., n.d.).
122. Anonymous, "Lines Written on the Death of Sarah M. Cornell" (n.p., n.d.).
123. Anonymous, *Brief and Impartial Narrative*, pp. 16–17.
124. Williams, *Fall River*, p. 64.
125. Ibid., p. 131.
126. Hallett, *The Arguments of Counsel*, p. 32.
127. Ibid., p. 43.
128. Aristides, *Strictures*, p. 6.
129. Ibid.
130. Williams, *Fall River*, p. 60.
131. Ibid., pp. 130–35.
132. Anonymous, *The Terrible Hay-Stack Murder: Life & Trial of the Rev. Ephraim K. Avery, for the Murder of the Young & Beautiful Miss Sarah M. Cornell, a Factory Girl of Fall River, Mass.* (Philadelphia, 1877), p. 43.
133. Aristides, *Strictures*, p. 18.
134. Hallett, *The Arguments of Counsel*, p. 74.
135. Aristides, *Strictures*, p. 84.
136. Williams, *Fall River*, p. 3.
137. Williams describes, for instance, certain findings that the sheriff "proposed laying . . . before the court upon [Avery's] trial, but was told they were inadmissible, since it was not any particular act of impropriety in the prisoner's life, previous to the commission of the crime for which he stood indicted, but his general character which they wished to know, and which could alone in this case be considered as evidence" (ibid., p. 77). Determined to recon-

sider the case, Williams describes this evidence of Avery's past conduct, which had not been admitted at the trial.

138. Ibid., p. 101, emphasis in original.

139. Aristides, *Strictures*, p. 18.

140. Ibid., p. 32.

141. Clarke, *Sarah Maria Cornell*, p. 5.

142. Williams, *Fall River*, p. 15.

143. Ibid., p. 3.

144. Clarke, *Sarah Maria Cornell*, p. 44.

145. Ibid., p. 48.

146. Williams, *Fall River*, p. 63.

147. Ibid., p. 17.

148. Ibid., p. 18.

149. Ibid., p. 24.

150. I have found no evidence to support Williams's claim that when the medical details of Cornell's death were presented in court, "No person could hear them unmoved: the very judges, though used to the delineation of crime, and pictures of violence, wept upon the bench; yea wept like children, at the description of her mangled person" (44). This description seems of a piece with the Dr. Wilbur episode, included in order to give readers an example of the sensibility required of them.

151. Clarke, *Sarah Maria Cornell*, p. 33.

152. Ibid.

153. Williams, *Fall River*, p. 22.

154. Anonymous, *Brief and Impartial Narrative*, pp. 22–23.

155. Ibid., p. 24.

156. Perhaps Avery and his friends understood the value of casting Cornell as a sentimental heroine, for Avery's own account of the case emphasizes his own emotional life. Describing his feelings after learning of the suspicion against him, for example, he writes: "Such a day I had never experienced. My feelings were such as to beggar description, and, although supported by conscious innocence, to think of my wife, my infant children, and to inquire in my own mind what will become of them, produced the most thrilling emotions in my heart. But O, thought I, the church! The cause of my Redeemer! Must this suffer reproach by having one of its ministers suspected of crimes that have been, and are, justly ranked as the most hateful among men? And shall this precious cause suffer through me? I do most solemnly declare that I felt more for the church than for myself." Avery, *Vindication*, p. 11.

157. Anonymous, "Lines Written on the Death of Sarah M. Cornell."

158. Anonymous, "The Clove-Hitch Knot," (n.p., n.d.). Readers of this poem are instructed to sing it to the tune of "Auld Lang Syne."

159. Avery, *Vindication*, pp. 26 and 27.

160. Aristides, *Strictures*, p. 7.

161. Ibid., p. 42.

162. Williams, *Fall River*, p. 44.

163. Aristides, *Strictures*, p. 91.

164. Avery, *Vindication*, p. 5.

165. Ibid., p. 73.

166. Hildreth, *Report of the Trial*, p. 143.

167. Clarke, *Sarah Maria Cornell*, p. 46.

168. Herndon, *Narrative of the Apprehension*, p. 33.

169. Aristides, *Strictures*, p. 6.

170. Ibid., p. 4.

171. In his passionate call to revolution, Paine warns his readers that anyone who has witnessed the violations of British soldiers, whose house has been burnt, or whose family has been deprived of bed and bread, who "can still shake hands with the murderers," is "unworthy the name of husband, father, friend, or lover, and whatever may be your rank or title in life, you have the heart of a coward, and the spirit of a sycophant." Thomas Paine, *The American Crisis* (Philadelphia, 1776).

CHAPTER TWO: THE HAYMARKET ANARCHIST TRIAL OF 1886

1. Frederick A. Noble, *Christianity and the Red Flag: A Sermon Preached for the Union Park Congregational Church, of Chicago, Illinois* (Chicago, 1886), pp. 2–3.

2. That chapter was reopened briefly and spectacularly in 1893. The day after a monument to the anarchists was dedicated at Waldheim Cemetery, Illinois Governor John P. Altgeld pardoned the three surviving anarchists and issued his written indictment of the police investigation and trial, *Reasons for Pardoning the Haymarket Anarchists*.

3. Timothy L. Parrish, "Haymarket and *Hazard*: The Lonely Politics of William Dean Howells," *Journal of American Culture* 17, no. 4 (1994): 24.

4. These quotes, from the *New York Sun*, the *Washington Sunday Herald*, and the *Washington Post*, can be found in "The Red Flag in America," *Public Opinion* (May 15, 1886).

5. William M. Salter, *A Cure for Anarchy* (Chicago, 1887), p. 4.

6. John P. Altgeld, *Reasons for Pardoning the Haymarket Anarchists* (Chicago, 1893; reprint, Chicago: Charles H. Kerr, 1986), pp. 45–46.

7. George N. McLean, *The Rise and Fall of Anarchy in America: From its Incipient Stage to the First Bomb Thrown in Chicago* (Chicago, 1888), p. 20.

8. Smith notes that from its first appearance in the May 15, 1886 issue, Thure de Thulstrup's illustration "has been the authoritative visual representation of the event," even though the image is an impossibility, representing simultaneously "the speech that ended before the bomb was thrown, the bomb itself, and the riot that followed." Carl Smith, *Urban Disorder and the Shape of Belief: The Great Chicago Fire, the Haymarket Bomb, and the Model Town of Pullman* (Chicago: University of Chicago Press, 1995), p. 125.

9. John P. Altgeld's pardon statement, issued after a thorough review of the case, insists that "the evidence shows that there were only 800 to 1,000 people present, and that it was a peaceable and orderly meeting; that the mayor of the city was present and saw nothing out of the way, and that he remained until the crowd began to disperse, . . . but as soon as [Police Captain] Bonfield had learned that the mayor had left, he could not resist the temptation to have some more people clubbed, and went up with a detachment of police to disperse the meeting; and that on the appearance of the police the bomb was thrown by some unknown person, and several innocent and faithful officers, who were simply obeying an uncalled-for order of their superior, were killed"—Altgeld, *Reasons for Pardoning the Haymarket Anarchists*, p. 47.

10. In a letter to his brother-in-law, William M. Salter, president of Chicago's Society for Ethical Culture, James argued that "this trying of every case over again by public opinion

after it has been tried by the responsible powers, is a bad thing in itself." November 7, 1887. William James, *The Correspondence of William James,* ed. Ignas K. Skrupskelis and Elizabeth M. Berkeley (Charlottesville: University Press of Virginia, 1992–1997), 6: 285.

11. *Chicago Tribune,* November 14, 1887.

12. Editorial, *Chicago Daily News,* August 20, 1886.

13. *Public Opinion,* May 15, 1886, p. 84; August 28, 1886, p. 384.

14. "Brand the Curs," *Chicago Mail,* May 1, 1886.

15. John D. Lawson, ed., *The Trial of the Chicago Anarchists: August Spies, Michael Schwab, Samuel Fielden, Albert R. Parsons, Adolph Fischer, George Engel, Louis Lingg and Oscar W. Neebe for Conspiracy and Murder; Chicago, Illinois, 1886,* vol. 12 (Wilmington, DE: Scholarly Resources, 1972), p. 174.

16. Smith, *Urban Disorder,* p. 106.

17. *Public Opinion,* May 15, 1886.

18. Parsons traced his paternal ancestry to the Narragansett Bay Puritans of 1632. Oscar Neebe was born in New York but "to give us children a good education" his family returned to Germany when he was a child. He returned to the United States when he was fourteen. (See Philip S. Foner, ed., *Autobiographies of the Haymarket Anarchists* [New York: Humanities Press, 1969], p. 161). Fielden was born in England and the others—Lingg, Spies, Fischer, Engel, and Schwab—were native Germans.

19. *Illustrated Graphic News* 1, vol. 11, May 15, 1886.

20. Paul C. Hull, *The Chicago Riot: A Record of the Terrible Scenes of May 4, 1886* (Chicago, 1886), p. 8.

21. John Higham, *Strangers in the Land* (New Brunswick, NJ: Rutgers University Press, 1955), p. 53.

22. Henry Clews, "Shall Labor or Capital Rule?" *North American Review* (June 1886): 601.

23. Charles Carroll Bonney, *The Present Conflict of Capital and Labor: A Discourse* (Chicago, 1886), p. 32.

24. McLean, *The Rise and Fall of Anarchy,* pp. 10–11.

25. Quoted in Dyer D. Lum, *A Concise History of the Great Trial of the Chicago Anarchists in 1886: Condensed from the Official Record* (n.d.; reprint, New York: Arno Press, 1969), p. 23.

26. Bonney, *The Present Conflict of Capital and Labor,* p. 10.

27. *Illustrated Graphic News* 1, no. 11, May 15, 1886.

28. Noble, *Christianity and the Red Flag,* p. 1.

29. Editorial, *Chicago Tribune,* November 4, 1887.

30. "Current Topics," *Albany Law Journal* 33, no. 20 (1886): 381.

31. Fremont O. Bennett, ed., *The Chicago Anarchists and the Haymarket Massacre* (Chicago, 1887), p. 94.

32. Joseph R. Buchanan, *The Story of a Labor Agitator* (New York: Outlook, 1903), p. 373.

33. I have been unable to determine who took these photographs, now owned by the Chicago Historical Society. Michael Schwab refers to them in an 1891 article in the *Monist,* where he notes that Paul Carus (editor of the *Monist*) had sent them to criminal anthropologist Cesare Lombroso for an article about criminal types. Michael Schwab, "A Convicted Anarchist's Reply to Professor Lombroso," *Monist* 1, no. 4 (1891): 520–24.

34. Carl S. Smith, "Cataclysm and Cultural Consciousness: Chicago and the Haymarket Trial," *Chicago History* 15 (Summer 1986): 42.

35. *Chicago Times,* August 10, 1886.

36. Anonymous, *The Chicago Martyrs* (London: Freedom Press, 1912), p. 6.

37. Lum, *A Concise History,* p. 7.

38. Buchanan, *The Story of a Labor Agitator,* p. 376. Recalling that the *Chicago News* editor, Melville Stone, had "been nearly as bad as the worst in hounding 'the boys,'" Buchanan and the anarchists decided against this interview.

39. Cited in Foner, *Autobiographies of the Haymarket Anarchists,* p. 12. At least one reader joined the clemency movement after encountering these documents. William Dean Howells changed his mind about the Haymarket case after reading Spies's autobiography and Dyer Lum's account of the trial. Paul Avrich, *The Haymarket Tragedy* (Princeton, NJ: Princeton University Press, 1984), p. 302.

40. Joseph E. Gary, "The Chicago Anarchists of 1886: The Crime, the Trial, and the Punishment," *Century Magazine* 45, no. 6 (1893): 833.

41. Ibid. Mrs. Black's letter first appeared in the *Chicago Daily News* (September 22, 1886).

42. Emma Goldman, *Living My Life,* 2 vols. (New York: Knopf, 1931), 1: 10.

43. As a young man Parsons fought for the Confederacy but later regretted his defense of slavery. His wife, Lucy Parsons, was the daughter of former slaves.

44. Foner, *Autobiographies of the Haymarket Anarchists,* p. 55.

45. Lucy E. Parsons, ed., *Famous Speeches of the Eight Chicago Anarchists* (1910; reprint, New York: Arno, 1969), p. 29.

46. Ibid., pp. 37–38.

47. Foner, *Autobiographies of the Haymarket Anarchists,* p. 50.

48. Lum, *A Concise History of the Great Trial of the Chicago Anarchists in 1886,* p. 162.

49. Albert Parsons, *An Appeal to the People of America* (Chicago, 1887). Joseph Buchanan tells of reading a letter from August Spies to Governor Oglesby. Spies had been persuaded by friends and family to sign the appeal for executive clemency. When radical Germans in Chicago learned of the appeal they felt Spies had disgraced himself as a coward, particularly since Parsons, the only American among the condemned men, had refused to sign. Spies corrected his mistake with a letter to the governor, asking that "if a sacrifice of life must be, will not my life suffice?" The letter was published in the *Chicago Tribune* (November 10, 1887).

50. John Turner, "The Tragedy of Chicago," *Freedom* (December 1887): 59.

51. Foner, *Autobiographies of the Haymarket Anarchists,* p. 91.

52. Parsons, *Famous Speeches of the Eight Chicago Anarchists,* p. 33.

53. Ibid., pp. 34, 36.

54. Lum, *A Concise History of the Great Trial,* p. 107.

55. Smith, *Urban Disorder,* p. 162.

56. John C. Kimball, "Rev. John C. Kimball on Anarchy," *Liberty,* December 17, 1887, p. 7.

57. Cesare Lombroso, "Illustrative Studies in Criminal Anthropology: The Physiognomy of the Anarchists," *Monist* 1, no. 3 (1891): 341–42.

58. "The Red Flag in America," p. 85.

59. Foner, *Autobiographies of the Haymarket Anarchists,* pp. 41–42.

60. Ibid., p. 17.

61. Parsons, *Famous Speeches of the Eight Chicago Anarchists,* p. 14.

62. Ibid., p. 15.

63. Paine, *The American Crisis,* p. 121.

64. August Spies, "Revenge Circular" (Chicago, 1886).

65. Albert Parsons, editorial, *Alarm*, March 7, 1885.

66. Bruce C. Nelson, "Anarchism: The Movement Behind the Martyrs," *Chicago History* 15 (1986): 13.

67. Parsons, *Famous Speeches of the Eight Chicago Anarchists*, p. 30.

68. Ibid., p. 35.

69. Ralph Waldo Emerson, *Nature* (1836; reprint, *Ralph Waldo Emerson, Selected Essays*, ed. Larzer Ziff (New York: Penguin Books, 1982), p. 35.

70. Parsons, *Famous Speeches of the Eight Chicago Anarchists*, pp. 102, 104.

71. William M. Salter, *What Shall Be Done with the Anarchists?* (Chicago, 1887), p. 17.

72. Parsons, *Famous Speeches of the Eight Chicago Anarchists*, p. 103.

73. Ibid., p. 12. In *Walden* Thoreau describes the remote sounds of the Concord militia: "It seemed by the distant hum as if somebody's bees had swarmed, and that the neighbors . . . were endeavoring to call them down into the hive again." Henry David Thoreau, *Walden* (1854; reprint, *Portable Thoreau*, ed. Carl Bode [NY: Viking Penguin, 1982]), p. 409.

74. Foner, *Autobiographies of the Haymarket Anarchists*, p. 24.

75. Henry David Thoreau, "Resistance to Civil Government" (Boston, 1849; reprint, *Portable Thoreau*, ed. Bode) p. 120.

76. Foner, *Autobiographies of the Haymarket Anarchists*, p. 125.

77. Parsons, *Famous Speeches of the Eight Chicago Anarchists*, p. 38.

78. Thoreau, "Resistance to Civil Government," p. 122.

79. Ibid.

80. Parsons, *Famous Speeches of the Eight Chicago Anarchists*, p. 39.

81. Kimball, "Rev. John C. Kimball on Anarchy," p. 7.

82. Lawson, *The Trial of the Chicago Anarchists*, p. 29.

83. Ibid., p. 238. John Brown Jr. sent each man a box of grapes and a message containing a statement his own father had issued before his death: "It is a great comfort to feel assured that I am permitted to die for a cause." Louis Ruchames, "John Brown, Jr., and the Haymarket Martyrs," *Massachusetts Review* 5 (Summer 1964): 765–68.

84. Foner, *Autobiographies of the Haymarket Anarchists*, p. 142.

85. Parsons, *Famous Speeches of the Eight Chicago Anarchists*, pp. 42–43.

86. Ibid., p. 38.

87. Kimball, "Rev. John C. Kimball on Anarchy," p. 7.

88. Parsons, *Famous Speeches of the Eight Chicago Anarchists*, p. 64.

89. Hartmut Keil and John B. Jentz, eds., *German Workers in Chicago: A Documentary History of Working-Class Culture from 1850 to World War I* (Urbana: University of Illinois Press, 1988), p. 277.

90. Ibid., p. 264.

91. Ibid., p. 277.

92. Avrich, *The Haymarket Tragedy*, p. 306.

93. Smith, "Cataclysm and Cultural Consciousness," p. 42.

94. Lawson, *The Trial of the Chicago Anarchists*, p. 252.

95. Smith, *Urban Disorder*, pp. 142–43.

96. Foner, *Autobiographies of the Haymarket Anarchists*, p. 100.

97. Parsons, *Famous Speeches of the Eight Chicago Anarchists*, p. 63.

98. Foner, *Autobiographies of the Haymarket Anarchists*, p. 114.

99. Ibid., p. 97.

100. Ibid., p. 71.

101. Parsons, *Famous Speeches of the Eight Chicago Anarchists*, p. 27.

102. Ibid., p. 17.

103. Foner, *Autobiographies of the Haymarket Anarchists*, p. 160.

104. Parsons, *Famous Speeches of the Eight Chicago Anarchists*, preface.

105. Lum, *Concise History*, p. 5.

106. Bennett, *The Chicago Anarchists and the Haymarket Massacre*, p. 145.

107. Avrich, *The Haymarket Tragedy*, p. 330.

108. Henry Adams, "Shall We Muzzle the Anarchists?" *Forum*, July 1, 1886, p. 454.

109. Matthew Mark Trumbull, *The Trial of the Judgment; A Review of the Anarchist Case* (Chicago, 1888), p. 3.

110. Salter, *What Shall Be Done With the Anarchists?* pp. 3–4.

111. Foner, *Autobiographies of the Haymarket Anarchists*, p. 24.

112. Salter, *A Cure for Anarchy*, p. 8.

113. Noble, *Christianity and the Red Flag*, p. 11.

114. J. L. Spalding, "Are We in Danger of Revolution?" *Forum*, July 1, 1886, pp. 405–15, esp. p. 409.

115. Samuel P. McConnell, "The Chicago Bomb Case," *Harper's* 168 (May 1934): 737. There is evidence to suggest that Lingg, who wanted to be martyred for the cause of anarchy and labor reform, understood that public sentiments were turning in favor of his comrades and that he arranged to have bombs smuggled into his cell in order to be caught and stem the tide of sympathy. Such was August Spies's opinion, as he wrote to William Salter: "Lingg, as far as I can judge him, seeks to be martyred. And to be candid, would like the rest of us to go with him. . . . Did he put those instruments into his cell, so that they might *be found?*—This is the question I have been asking myself. If he had them there for any *purpose*, this is the only one that looks plausible to me. He wants to die, thinking thereby to help the cause of labor. . . . Perhaps, he thought that the best and surest way to bring this about, was to place a few bombs in his cell." August Spies, letter to William Salter, November 7, 1887. Manuscript at Harvard University Houghton Library, quoted with permission.

116. Eugene Debs, "The Chicago Anarchists," *Locomotive Firemen's Magazine*, January 11, 1887, p. 13.

117. Adams, "Shall We Muzzle the Anarchists?" p. 450.

118. Matthew Mark Trumbull, "The Trial of the Judgment: Free Speech and Consequential Murder," *Alarm*, November 17, 1888, p. 2.

119. "Of Course!" *Workmen's Advocate*, November 15, 1887, p. 1.

120. Cited in Lewis Wheelock, "Urban Protestant Reactions to the Chicago Haymarket Affair 1886–1893" (Ph.D. diss., State University of Iowa, 1956), p. 145.

121. Bonney, *The Present Conflict of Capital and Labor*, p. 3.

122. Cited in Wheelock, "Urban Protestant Reactions," p. 143.

123. Ibid., pp. 237–38.

124. Bonney, *The Present Conflict of Capital and Labor*, p. 14.

125. Parsons, *Famous Speeches of the Eight Chicago Anarchists*, p. 19.

126. Cited in Wheelock, "Urban Protestant Reactions," p. 133.

127. "A Word to Social Philosophers," *Nation*, November 17, 1887, p. 388.

128. Smith, *Urban Disorder*, p. 128.

129. Salter, *A Cure for Anarchy*, p. 3.

130. Kimball, "The Rev. John C. Kimball on Anarchy," p. 7.

131. Trumbull, *The Trial of the Judgment*, p. 3.

132. Parsons, *Famous Speeches of the Eight Chicago Anarchists,* p. 112.

133. Ibid., p. 52.

134. Eleanor Marx-Aveling, "A Woman's Plea for Mercy," *Pall-Mall Gazette,* November 8, 1887, p. 1.

135. Letter to John G. Whittier, November 1, 1887. William Dean Howells, *Selected Letters of W. D. Howells,* ed. Robert C. Leitz III, et al., vol. 3, 1882–1891 (Boston: Twayne Publishers, 1980), p. 198.

136. Ernst Schmidt, "To All Friends of an Impartial Administration of Justice!" (Chicago, 1887).

137. Ernst Schmidt, "The Defense and Amnesty Campaigns," in *The Haymarket Scrapbook,* ed. Dave Roediger and Franklin Rosemont (Chicago: Charles H. Kerr, 1986), pp. 112–13.

138. Foner, *Autobiographies of the Haymarket Anarchists,* p. 10.

139. Sigmund Zeisler, *Reminiscences of the Anarchist Case* (Chicago: University of Chicago Press, 1927), p. 15.

140. Altgeld, *Reasons for Pardoning the Haymarket Anarchists,* pp. 6–7.

141. Leon Lewis, *The Facts Concerning the Eight Condemned Leaders* (Greenport, NY, 1887), p. 3.

142. Eleanor Marx-Aveling and Edward Aveling, *The Chicago Anarchists: A Statement of Facts* (London, 1887), p. 1.

143. Schmidt, "To All Friends of an Impartial Administration of Justice!"

144. Howells, letter to William C. Howells, November 13, 1887. In *William Dean Howells: Selected Letters,* ed. Robert C. Leitz III, et. al, vol. 3 (Boston: Twayne, 1980), p. 206.

145. Anonymous, *In Memoriam of the Martyrs of the Working People Murdered at Chicago on November 11, '87* (n.p., n.d.), p. 5.

146. Anonymous, *The Chicago Martyrs,* p. 15.

147. This quote comes from an unidentified clipping, probably from the *Boston Transcript,* from Mildred Howells's Haymarket scrapbook in the Houghton Library (quoted with permission). Although not dated, the article was written after the discovery of bombs in Lingg's cell, but before the executions. Samuel Gompers was among many who warned the governor that executions would make dangerous martyrs of the men.

148. Noble, *Christianity and the Red Flag,* p. 4.

149. Parsons, *Famous Speeches of the Eight Chicago Anarchists,* p. 33.

150. Ibid., p. 73.

151. Ibid., p. 24.

152. *New York Tribune,* November 12, 1887, p. 1.

153. Turner, "The Tragedy of Chicago."

154. Avrich, *The Haymarket Tragedy,* p. 385.

155. Kimball, "Rev. John C. Kimball on Anarchy," p. 7.

156. See especially "Can Poetry Matter?" and "The Poet in an Age of Prose" in Dana Gioia, *Can Poetry Matter? Essays on Poetry and American Culture* (St. Paul, MN: Graywolf Press, 1992).

157. Jeffrey A. Hammond notes that the English pastoral elegy "came to play a special role in witnessing the poet's coming of age." *The American Puritan Elegy: A Literary and Cultural Study* (New York: Cambridge University Press, 2000), p. 21. If we turn our attention, however, to the myriad poems written for the newspapers of grass-roots political movements, we will see that anonymous publication was widespread in these venues during the 1880s.

158. Clark D. Halker, *For Democracy, Workers, and God: Labor Song-Poems and Labor Protest, 1865–95* (Urbana: University of Illinois Press, 1991).

159. Daniel Aaron, *Writers on the Left* (New York: Oxford University Press, 1961), p. 205. The phrase "craft consciousness" comes from Alan M. Wald, *Exiles from a Future Time: The Forging of the Mid-Twentieth-Century Literary Left* (Chapel Hill: University of North Carolina Press, 2002), p. 15. Wald's account of America's leftist writers in the 1930s offers a notable contrast to the less self-consciously literary (but no less politically committed) poets of the Haymarket era.

160. Wald, *Exiles from a Future Time*, p. 103.

161. Halker, *For Democracy, Workers, and God*, p. 97.

162. Ibid., p. 2.

163. Ibid., p. 28.

164. Ibid., p. 17.

165. Anonymous, "Paddy Miles's Sentiments," *Chicago Labor Enquirer*, June 16, 1888.

166. Many workers who mourned the Haymarket anarchists were already furious with the Knights, whose motto, "an injury to one is the concern of all," seemed deeply ironic in light of the Knights' refusal to join the clemency movement. While the Knights were officially opposed to the anarchists' militancy and to any suggestion that they defend the convicted men, the organization's leaders found that rank-and-file members were increasingly sympathetic to the anarchists and wished to see the Knights defend them. See Richard Schneirov, "'An Injury to One is the Concern of All': The Knights of Labor in the Haymarket Era," in *Haymarket Scrapbook*, ed. Dave Roediger and Franklin Rosemont (Chicago: Charles H. Kerr, 1986), p. 82.

167. Emma Goldman, "The Crime of the 11th of November," *Mother Earth* 6 (November 1911): 265.

168. Edgar Lee Masters, *The Tale of Chicago* (New York: G. P. Putnam's Sons, 1933), p. 219.

169. Eugene Debs, "The Martyred Apostles of Labor," *Eugene Debs: His Life, Writings and Speeches* (Girard, KS: Appeal to Reason, 1908), p. 263.

170. In the days before Brown's execution, Emerson had called the abolitionist a "new saint awaiting his martyrdom, and who, if he should suffer, will make the gallows like the cross." ("Courage," address delivered November 8, 1859. Cited in James Elliot Cabot, *A Memoir of Ralph Waldo Emerson*, vol. 2 [Boston, 1887], p. 597). The anonymous poem to the Haymarket anarchists was part of Captain Black's funeral elegy, reprinted in a Chicago labor newspaper ("At the Tomb: Speeches Made By Messrs. Black, Reitzel, Morgan, and Currlin at Sunday's Funeral," *Chicago Labor-Enquirer*, November 19, 1887).

171. Georg Biedenkapp, "To the Manes of the 11th of November," *Fackel*, November 12, 1899, and Charles Diether, "The Eleventh of November, 1887," *Der Anarchist*, November 14, 1891.

172. Lydia Platt Richards, "Albert R. Parsons," *Alarm*, December 3, 1887.

173. L. B. G., "To Lucy E. Parsons," *Alarm*, November 19, 1887.

174. Arthur Cheesewright, "Hymn," *Chicago Labor Enquirer*, November 19, 1887.

175. L. S. Oliver, "To My Martyred Comrades, 1897" *Free Society*, December 5, 1897, p. 178.

176. Melissa F. Zeiger, *Beyond Consolation: Death, Sexuality, and the Changing Shapes of Elegy* (Ithaca, NY: Cornell University Press, 1997), p. 21. Jahan Ramazani argues that the modern elegy constitutes not a transcendence of loss but an "immersion in it." See his *Poetry of*

Mourning: The Modern Elegy from Hardy to Heany (Chicago: University of Chicago Press, 1994), p. 4. W. David Shaw explains that modern poets understand that "the pastoral elegy's power to heal and console may be deeply insulting" ("Elegy and Theory: Is Historical and Critical Knowledge Possible?" *Modern Language Quarterly* 55, no. 1 [1994]: 1–16).

177. Ramazani, *Poetry of Mourning*, p. xi.

178. An important exception is Esther Schor, who notes that many elegists "evoked, organized, and directed" sentiment "to serve a variety of political goals" (*Bearing the Dead: The British Culture of Mourning from the Enlightenment to Victoria* [Princeton, NJ: Princeton University Press, 1994], p. 75).

179. George E. Haggerty, "Desire and Mourning: The Ideology of the Elegy," in *Ideology and Form in Eighteenth-Century Literature*, ed. David H. Richter (Lubbock: Texas Tech University Press, 1999), p. 190.

180. Ibid., p. 189.

181. Ramazani, *Poetry of Mourning*, p. 4.

182. As Ramazani notes, "most canonical English elegists had depicted mourning as compensatory" (Ibid., p. 3).

183. Anonymous, "Victoria," *Chicago Labor Enquirer*, November 14, 1887.

184. Anonymous, "The Road to Freedom," *Chicago Labor Enquirer*, June 9, 1888.

185. Halker, *For Democracy, Workers, and God*, p. 136.

186. Fayette Munson, "The Beacon is Burning," *Chicago Labor Enquirer*, December 17, 1887.

187. L. S. Oliver, "To My Martyred Comrades," 1897.

188. L. B. G., "To Lucy E. Parsons."

189. Anonymous, "The Price of Freedom," *Chicago Labor Enquirer*, December 17, 1887. Perhaps this poet hoped his work would be sung at labor rallies, since its model enjoyed a life beyond the printed page. The news that Parsons sang "Annie Laurie" in his last hours traveled extensively and the story became almost legendary. One journalist, reporting that mourners sang "Annie Laurie" during the funeral procession, remarked that "that sad and melodious air . . . must also hereafter find a warm place in the breast of the American anarchist and will have a fresh meaning. Many times along the way the beautiful music of this dreamy lyric brought tears to the eyes of the spectators . . . because of memories which its notes revived in the mind of almost every one who heard it" (*New York Tribune*, November 14, 1887).

190. Fayette Munson, "The Beacon Is Burning," *Chicago Labor Enquirer*, December 17, 1887.

191. Dyer D. Lum, *In Memoriam: Chicago, November 11, 1887* (Berkeley Heights, NJ: Oriole, 1937), p. 20.

192. Albert Richard Parsons, "Last Words," in *An Anthology of Revolutionary Poetry*, ed. Marcus Graham (New York: Active Press, 1929), pp. 108–109.

193. Here again these poets anticipate modern elegists, as Ramazani has described them: "Modern poets direct their melancholic ambivalence not only at themselves and the dead, not only at elegiac and social convention, but also at their own elegies. . . . These and other modern elegists are wracked by . . . the guilty thought that they reap aesthetic profit from loss, that death is the fuel of poetic mourning" (*Poetry of Mourning*, p. 6).

194. Robert Reitzel, "New Year's, 1888," *Fackel*, January 1, 1888.

195. Voltairine De Cleyre, *Selected Works*, ed. Alexander Berkman (New York: Mother Earth, 1914), p. 35.

196. Lathrop Withington, "The Blood-Stained Banner of the West," *Firebrand,* October 13, 1895; S. Robert Wilson, "Murder Most Foul," *Alarm,* December 17, 1887; Voltairine De Cleyre, "The Hurricane," in *Selected Works of Voltairine De Cleyre,* p. 34; Thomas Moore, "Columbia's Shame," *Chicago Labor Enquirer,* November 14, 1887.

197. Edward O'Donnell, "In Memoriam," *Rebel,* November 20, 1895.

198. L. S. Oliver, "The State," in *An Anthology of Revolutionary Poetry,* ed. Marcus Graham (New York: Active Press, 1929), p. 105.

199. David Edelshtadt, "Who Were They?" in *American Labor Songs of the Nineteenth Century,* ed. Philip S. Foner (Urbana: University of Illinois Press, 1975), p. 230.

200. Frances A. Bingham, "The Price of Blood," *Workman's Advocate,* November 5, 1887.

201. C. W. Beckett, "Remember Chicago," *Commonweal,* November 10, 1888.

202. S. Robert Wilson, "Murder Most Foul," *Alarm,* December 17, 1887.

203. Walter Crane, "Freedom in America," *Commonweal,* October 15, 1887.

204. Thomas Moore, "Columbia's Shame," *Labor Enquirer,* November 14, 1887.

205. L. S. Oliver, "The State," *An Anthology of Revolutionary Poetry,* ed. Marcus Graham (New York: Active Press, 1929), p. 105.

206. Anonymous, "The Road to Freedom," *Chicago Labor Enquirer,* June 9, 1888.

207. *Chicago Labor Enquirer,* "At the Tomb."

208. Lum, *In Memoriam,* pp. 15–16.

209. Anonymous, "Where the Gallows Darkly Rose," *Freedom,* December 1887.

210. Voltairine De Cleyre, *Selected Works,* ed. Alexander Berkman (New York: Revisionist Press, 1972), p. 54.

211. L. S. Oliver, "To My Martyred Comrades," *Free Society,* December 5, 1897.

212. Anonymous, "The Road to Freedom."

213. Goldman, "The Crime," p. 265.

214. A. D. Cridge, "The Battle-Hymn of Freedom," *Social Science,* October 29, 1887.

215. Lum, *In Memoriam,* p. 9.

216. De Cleyre, *Selected Works,* p. 54.

217. Walter Crane, "On the Suppression of Free Speech at Chicago," *Commonweal,* July 17, 1886: 123.

218. Munson, "The Beacon is Burning."

219. Anonymous, "The Road to Freedom."

220. Anonymous, "Victoria," *Chicago Labor Enquirer,* November 14, 1887. These poets all had access to this information about the trial and the jurors. Many printed sources provided details about jury selection, including the jurors' ties to the business community and their prejudices against socialists, anarchists, and labor agitators, revealed in the jury selection interviews.

221. Anonymous, "The Road to Freedom."

222. Ibid.

223. J. William Lloyd, "Seven," *Liberty* 19 (1887).

224. Anonymous, "Victoria."

225. Anonymous, "The Road to Freedom."

226. Richards, "Albert R. Parsons."

227. Wilson, "Murder Most Foul."

228. Anonymous, "Our Martyrs," *Alarm,* November 19, 1887.

229. Anonymous, "August Spies," *Alarm,* November 19, 1887.

230. An exception is Cary Nelson, who considers popular and frankly political poetry in his study. But even he overlooks the Haymarket elegists when finding precedents for the modern poets he examines. Cary Nelson, *Repression and Recovery: Modern American Poetry and the Politics of Cultural Memory, 1910–1945* (Madison: University of Wisconsin Press, 1989), p. 235.

231. Beckett, "Remember Chicago."

232. Martin Drescher, "The Day Will Come!" in *American Labor Songs of the Nineteenth Century*, ed. Philip S. Foner (Urbana: University of Illinois Press, 1975), p. 229.

233. Nelson, *Repression and Recovery*, p. 51.

234. Michael Denning, *Mechanic Accents: Dime Novels and Working-Class Culture in America* (New York: Verso, 1998), p. 263.

235. See Michael Denning, pp. 38–55, on the publication of working-class fiction in prominent labor newspapers. As Martin Foran, the author of *The Other Side* (a socialist novel published serially in *The Workingmen's Advocate*) notes in his introduction, "If the laboring class could be made a *reading* class, their social and political advancement and amelioration would be rapid and certain" (quoted in Denning, p. 43).

236. Denning, *Mechanic Accents*, pp. 38–55.

237. As Nelson demonstrates, the literary history that emerges when one considers popular poetry often looks very different from that driven by a consideration of canonical poets. This difference no doubt explains why Ramazani overlooks the much earlier body of anti-elegiac elegies: he admits that his "author-centered" study rests "on the assumption that strong poets have remade the elegy for modernity" (p. x). But Ramazani's assumption commits him to a tautology; the study of poets not generally considered "strong," as I have tried to show, reveals how they, too, may have shaped the tradition of elegies.

238. Nelson, *Repression and Recovery*, p. 127.

239. Goldman, "The Crime," p. 265.

240. Jürgen Habermas, *The Structural Transformation of the Public Sphere: An Inquiry into a Category of Bourgeois Society*, trans. Thomas Burger (Cambridge, MA: MIT Press, 1989), pp. 25–26.

241. Schor, *Bearing the Dead*, p. 97.

242. Gioia, *Can Poetry Matter?* p. 24; and Robert Pinsky, *Favorite Poem Project* http://www.bu.edu/favoritepoem/forteachers/index.html (accessed October 2004).

243. Anonymous, "Where the Gallows Darkly Rose," *Freedom* (December 1887).

244. William Dean Howells, *Selected Letters of W. D. Howells*, ed. Robert C. Leitz III, et al., 6 vols. (Boston: Twayne, 1980), 3: 201.

CHAPTER THREE: WISDOM, JUSTICE, AND MODERATION ABANDONED: THE LYNCHING OF LEO FRANK

1. Burton Rascoe, *The Case of Leo Frank: A Factual Review of One of the Most Sensational Murder Cases in Court Annals* (Girard, KS: Haldeman-Julius, 1947), p. 8.

2. Nancy MacLean, "Gender, Sexuality, and the Politics of Lynching: The Leo Frank Case Revisited," *Under Sentence of Death: Lynching in the South*, ed. W. Fitzhugh Brundage (Chapel Hill: University of North Carolina Press, 1997), p. 165.

3. Rascoe, *The Case of Leo Frank*, p. 8.

4. MacLean notes that "the number of female workers aged sixteen and over in the

city's manufacturing industries doubled between 1900 and 1919 to more than four thousand," while "the earnings of daughters made up from one-quarter to two-fifths of total household income" for the working poor. "Gender, Sexuality, and the Politics of Lynching," pp. 161–62.

5. Mary Phagan's stepfather, understanding the threat to the family that factory employment posed, had asked Mary to quit her job at the pencil factory. Jeffrey Melnick, *Black–Jewish Relations on Trial: Leo Frank and Jim Conley in the New South* (Jackson: University Press of Mississippi, 2000), p. 63.

6. "Attack Is Made on Child Labor," *Atlanta Constitution.*

7. Steve Oney, *And the Dead Shall Rise: The Murder of Mary Phagan and the Lynching of Leo Frank* (New York: Pantheon Books, 2003), p. 6.

8. April 28, 1913.

9. "Business Men Protest Sensational 'Extras,'" *Atlanta Journal,* April 30, 1913.

10. W. E. Thompson, *A Short Review of the Frank Case* (Atlanta, 1914), p. 1.

11. John D. Lawson, *The Trial of Leo M. Frank for the Murder of Mary Phagan, Atlanta, Georgia, 1913.* In *American State Trials,* ed. John D. Lawson, vol. 10 (Wilmington, DE: Scholarly Resources, 1972), p. 297.

12. March 15, 1914.

13. Lawson, *The Trial of Leo M. Frank,* p. 409. Rosser and Arnold's statement was published in the Atlanta newspapers on August 26, 1913, the day of Frank's sentencing.

14. While conceding that Frank "would not have been condemned for [his Jewishness] alone," Dinnerstein nevertheless claims that "The Southern heritage . . . had nurtured strong in-group loyalty which at times manifested itself in a paranoid suspicion of outsiders. Leo Frank as a Northerner, an industrialist, and a Jew represented everything alien to the culture." Leonard Dinnerstein, *The Leo Frank Case* (New York: Columbia University Press, 1968), p. 32. Frey and Frey note that while the majority of Americans supported Governor Slaton's commutation order, a "hard-line anti-Semitic community" was "kept in continual agitation" by propagandists in the South. Robert Seitz Frey and Nancy Thompson-Frey, *The Silent and the Damned: The Murder of Mary Phagan and the Lynching of Leo Frank* (New York: Madison Books, 1988), p. 90.

15. Burton Rascoe, who had covered the case for the *Chicago Tribune,* later wrote that at the time of the Phagan murder trial, "there was a circulation war in Atlanta between the conservative and long-established *Atlanta Constitution* and Hearst's *Atlanta Journal,* and these papers were vying in demands for action on the part of the police. Since the first of the year there had been an even dozen of unsolved rape-and-murder crimes in the city and fourteen such crimes within less than a year. The papers were saying that if the murderers were not speedily found and brought to justice the people would rise up and demand an entire new police force. A political crisis was at hand; and it was plainly up to the city administration to find a scapegoat, innocent or guilty, to save their own hides" (Rascoe, *The Case of Leo Frank,* p. 15).

16. Jim Auchmutey, "A Murder, a Lynching, a Mystery," *Atlanta Journal-Constitution,* June 11, 2000.

17. Lawson, *The Trial of Leo M. Frank,* p. 254.

18. L. O. Bricker, "A Great American Tragedy," *Shane Quarterly* 4 (April 1943): 90. The Reverend Bricker, pastor of Mary Phagan's First Christian Church, spoke out in favor of a new trial in 1914 and assumed partial responsibility for the first, prejudicial trial. "I assume my full share of the responsibility for this condition," he said. "I admit freely that I was wrought up to a pitch that prevented the proper exercise of judgment and decision. . . . I am prompted now to do my best to square my part of this grave responsibility by opening the

problem to discussion in my pulpit, and I invite the attention of all people who feel as I do that they were hasty and not in the proper mood for judgment during the first trial" (*New York Times*, March 14, 1914).

19. Harold Ross, "The Leo Frank Case," in *A Little Girl is Dead*, ed. Harry Golden (Cleveland: World Publishing, 1965), p. 356.

20. This ballad, one of the many "Ballad[s] of Mary Phagan," is printed in Frey and Frey, *The Silent and the Damned*, pp. 140–41.

21. Larry J. Griffin, Paula Clark, and Joanne C. Sandberg, "Narrative and Event: Lynching and Historical Sociology," in *Under Sentence of Death: Lynching in the South*, ed. W. F. Brundage (Chapel Hill: University of North Carolina Press, 1997), p. 26.

22. Gene Wiggins, *Fiddlin' Georgia Crazy: Fiddlin' John Carson, His Real World, and the World of His Songs* (Urbana: University of Illinois Press, 1987), p. 27.

23. Thomas E. Watson, "The Celebrated Case of the State of Georgia vs. Leo Frank," *Watson's Magazine* 21 (1915): 208.

24. The defense deliberately ascribed the hiring of a lawyer not to Frank but to Sig Montag, the factory owner. "Frank didn't call for friends or lawyer," Luther Rosser argued in his summation. "He didn't call for anything. If he had known what he was up against, though, in this police department of ours, he'd probably have called for two lawyers—or even more. But old man Sig Montag, who has been here a long time, knew this old police crowd and he knew their tactics. He was well on to their curves. He knew what danger there was to Frank" (Lawson, *The Trial of Leo M. Frank*, p. 293).

25. Rascoe, *The Case of Leo Frank*, p. 37.

26. *New York Times*, December 13, 1914.

27. Herbert Asbury, "Hearst Comes to Atlanta," *American Mercury* 7 (January 1926): 91.

28. Lawson, *The Trial of Leo M. Frank*, p. 237.

29. Ibid., pp. 329–30.

30. Albert S. Lindemann, *The Jew Accused: Three Anti-Semitic Affairs (Dreyfuss, Beilis, Frank) 1894–1915* (Cambridge: Cambridge University Press, 1991), p. 239.

31. MacLean, "Gender, Sexuality, and the Politics of Lynching," p. 163.

32. Ibid.

33. Lindemann, *The Jew Accused*, p. 239.

34. Melnick, *Black–Jewish Relations on Trial*, p. 13.

35. Burton Rascoe, "Will the State of Georgia Execute an Innocent Man?" *Chicago Tribune*, December 14, 1914.

36. John M. Slaton, "Governor John M. Slaton's Commutation Order," *Atlanta Journal*, June 21, 1915.

37. Lawson, *The Trial of Leo M. Frank*, p. 302.

38. Rascoe, *The Case of Leo Frank*, p. 7.

39. Melnick, *Black–Jewish Relations on Trial*, p. 32.

40. Ibid., p. 16.

41. Rascoe, *The Case of Leo Frank*, p. 3.

42. Marouf Hasian Jr., "Judicial Rhetoric in a Fragmentary World: 'Character' and Storytelling in the Leo Frank Case," *Communication Monographs* 64 (1997): 259.

43. Asbury, "Hearst Comes to Atlanta," pp. 89–90.

44. "Frank Asserts Innocence," *Atlanta Constitution*, August 26, 1913.

45. Lawson, *The Trial of Leo M. Frank*, pp. 321–22.

46. Ibid.

47. Watson, "The Celebrated Case," p. 266.

48. Special Collections Department, Woodruff Library, Emory University. "Atlanta Miscellany Box," 572, no. 2.

49. Melnick, *Black–Jewish Relations on Trial*, p. 64. MacLean, too, notes that Frank's enemies fetishized female virginity ("Gender, Sexuality, and the Politics of Lynching," p. 174).

50. Cahan's phrase is cited in Melnick, *Black–Jewish Relations on Trial*, p. 15.

51. The text of this monument is reproduced in Mary Phagan, *The Murder of Little Mary Phagan* (Far Hills, NJ: New Horizon Press, 1987), p. xi.

52. Lawson, *The Trial of Leo M. Frank*, p. 349.

53. MacLean, "Gender, Sexuality, and the Politics of Lynching," p. 176.

54. *The Denver Post*, August 17, 1915. In the Georgia Department of Archives and History, John M. Slaton Collection, box 48A.

55. Nancy MacLean convincingly argues that the Frank case constitutes an important exception to the rule that populism is generally hostile to sexual and racial conservatism. "Gender, Sexuality, and the Politics of Lynching."

56. *Atlanta Constitution*, August 4, 1913.

57. Susan E. Tifft and Alex S. Jones, "The Family," *New Yorker*, April 19, 1999, p. 47.

58. Rascoe, "Will the State of Georgia Execute an Innocent Man?" p. 1.

59. "Atlanta and the Frank Case," *New York Times*, March 15, 1914.

60. "Frank Should Have a New Trial," *Atlanta Journal*, March 10, 1914.

61. William Curran Rogers, "A Comparison of the Coverage of the Leo Frank Case by the Hearst-Controlled *Atlanta Georgian* and the Home-Owned *Atlanta Journal*, April 28, 1913–August 30, 1915" (master's thesis, University of Georgia, 1950), p. 88.

62. "Frank Should Have a New Trial."

63. Gerald S. Henig, "He Did Not Have a Fair Trial: California Progressives React to the Leo Frank Case," *California History* 58 (1979): 173–74.

64. Frey and Frey, *The Silent and the Damned*, p. 85.

65. "All Urged to Write Appeals for Frank," *New York Times*, December 13, 1914.

66. Samuel Stephen Wise, "The Case of Leo Frank: A Last Appeal," *Free Synagogue Pulpit* 3 (1915): 80.

67. "Retry Leo Frank, Says Rabbi Lyons," *New York Times*, November 29, 1914, p. 13.

68. Wilmer spoke again on behalf of a committee of ministers at Governor Slaton's commutation hearing a year later, where he argued that their appeal was not based on mercy. "We appeal," he said, "on moral grounds and for justice. We appeal against the provincial prejudice which has been evident against outside interference and against the prejudice of Gentiles against Jews." "Both Sides Heard on Frank Appeal," *New York Times*, June 15, 1915.

69. "Pulpit for Frank," *Washington Post*, March 16, 1914.

70. March 23, 1914.

71. "Billy Sunday for Frank," *New York Times*, May 12, 1915.

72. Wise, "The Case of Leo Frank," p. 94.

73. Dinnerstein, *The Leo Frank Case*, pp. 118–19.

74. "Frank Railroaded, E. V. Debs Asserts," *New York Times*, December 28, 1914.

75. Frey and Frey, *The Silent and the Damned*, p. 76.

76. Oliver Wendell Holmes, "Mr. Justice Holmes, Dissenting," in Harry Golden, *A Little Girl is Dead* (Cleveland: World Publishing, 1965), p. 317.

77. Ibid., p. 319.

78. April 21, 1915.

79. "Governor Slaton's Courageous Act," *Atlanta Journal*, June 21, 1915.

80. The *Atlanta Constitution*, August 18, 1915. Atlanta's William Bremen Jewish Heritage Museum contains the newspaper clipping file that Rabbi David Marx collected during the Frank case. In reading the hundreds of clippings from this file, one cannot escape the conclusion that the vast majority of daily newspapers in the United States supported a new trial or executive clemency for Frank.

81. Dinnerstein, *The Leo Frank Case*, p. 105.

82. Elizabeth Cady Stanton, "Letter to the Editor," *New York Tribune*, May 30, 1860.

83. Louis Marshall to Adolph Ochs, January 8, 1914. Quoted in Dinnerstein, *The Leo Frank Case*, p. 91.

84. "Atlanta and the Frank Case," March 15, 1914.

85. "Says His Analysis Vindicates Frank," *New York Times*, December 27, 1914.

86. George S. Dougherty, "Frank Is Innocent, Says Dougherty," *New York Times*, January 10, 1915.

87. MacLean, "Gender, Sexuality, and the Politics of Lynching," p. 164.

88. Asbury, "Hearst Comes to Atlanta," p. 91.

89. "Frank Railroaded, E. V. Debs Asserts."

90. Rascoe concluded that with the exception of Frank's friends, residents of Atlanta generally believed Frank was guilty, whereas "[o]utside of Georgia those who have depended upon newspaper reports of the case are almost invariably of the opinion that Frank [was] innocent of the crime of which he has been convicted." Rascoe, "Will the State of Georgia Execute an Innocent Man?"

91. Slaton, "Governor John M. Slaton's Commutation Order," p. 4.

92. Watson, "The Celebrated Case of the State of Georgia vs. Leo Frank," p. 266.

93. MacLean, "Gender, Sexuality, and the Politics of Lynching," p. 164.

94. Hasian, "Judicial Rhetoric in a Fragmentary World," p. 263.

95. Wise, "The Case of Leo Frank," p. 92.

96. "Anti-Semitism and the Frank Case," *Literary Digest* 50 (January 1915): 85.

97. "Frank Should Have a New Trial."

98. "Leo Frank," *New Republic* 3 (July 1915): 300.

99. W. F. Brundage, *Under Sentence of Death: Lynching in the South* (Chapel Hill: University of North Carolina Press, 1997), p. 3.

100. Rascoe, "Will the State of Georgia Execute an Innocent Man?"

101. "New Inside Story of Frank Lynching," *New York Times*, August 23, 1915.

102. As Steve Oney demonstrates, the people behind the lynching were not poor and without influence, as was typical of lynch mobs. The planners were among Marietta's elite, while the "field commanders," those who carried out the lynching, "were all members of Marietta's petit bourgeois." Oney, *And the Dead Shall Rise*, p. 525.

103. As Valdosta's Reverend Alex Bealer lamented in his first Sunday sermon following the lynching, many people "have lost confidence in the legislative, the judicial and the executive branches of government and have felt justified in taking the administration of the laws into their own hands." "Local Ministers Preach Very Strong Sermons," *Valdosta Times*, August 24, 1915.

104. Olive Woolley Burt, *American Murder Ballads and their Stories* (New York: Oxford University Press, 1958), p. 63.

105. Ibid., p. 62.

106. C. P. Connolly, "The Frank Case," *Colliers*, December 19, 1914, p. 23.

107. Dinnerstein suggests that Watson's newspapers were popular among illiterates who listened while they were read to them. Dinnerstein, *The Leo Frank Case*, p. 96.

108. Cited in Golden, *A Little Girl is Dead*, p. 360.

109. Watson, "The Celebrated Case of the State of Georgia vs. Leo Frank," p. 196.

110. Melnick, *Black–Jewish Relations on Trial*, pp. 35–36.

111. Sanford E. Marovitz, *Abraham Cahan* (New York: Twayne, 1996), p. 30.

112. Frey and Frey, *The Silent and the Damned*, p. 23.

113. David Levering Lewis, "Parallels and Divergences: Assimilationist Strategies of Afro-American and Jewish Elites from 1910 to the Early 1930s," *Journal of American History* 71, no. 3 (1984): 543.

114. Yonathan Shapiro, *Leadership of the American Zionist Organization, 1897–1930* (Urbana: University of Illinois Press, 1971), pp. 61–62.

115. Lindemann, *The Jew Accused*, p. 248.

116. Ibid., p. 265.

117. Ibid.

118. Lucy S. Dawidowicz, *The Jewish Presence: Essays on Identity and History* (New York: Holt, Rinehart, and Winston, 1977), p. 127.

119. Lewis, "Parallels and Divergences," pp. 551, 554.

120. Marshall, letter to Leonard or Herbert Haas, December 24, 1914; quoted in Dinnerstein, *The Leo Frank Case*, p. 111.

121. "Ask to Show Frank Films," *New York Times*, September 14, 1915. On October 16, 1915, Eleanor Rivenburgh also wrote to Lucille Frank, asking permission to write a photoplay that might clear Frank's name. Letter in Brandeis University Leo Frank collection 1, cited in Melnick, *Black–Jewish Relations on Trial*, p. 5.

122. Quoted in "Why Was Frank Lynched? Was it Race Hatred, Dirty Politics, Yellow Journalism?" *Forum* 56 (December 1916): 688.

123. MacLean argues that "Frank's opponents . . . sought solutions in a political ideology developed under conditions that no longer existed. . . . Frank's opponents viewed vigilante activity as a legitimate exercise of popular sovereignty when state policy no longer reflected the citizenry's will. They equated the killing of Frank with a tradition of popular mobilization against the powerful in the service of 'justice.'" MacLean, "Gender, Sexuality, and the Politics of Lynching," p. 177. For another defense of the lynching see Thomas E. Watson, "The Official Record in the Case of Leo Frank, a Jew Pervert," *Watson's Magazine* 21, no. 5 (September 1915): 290–91.

124. Frey and Frey, *The Silent and the Damned*, p. 102.

CHAPTER FOUR: NO OTHER REMEDY: COMMUNITY AWAKENING AND THE LYNCHING OF EMMETT TILL

1. Jack Greenberg, *Race Relations and American Law* (New York: Columbia University Press, 1959), p. 322.

2. Jacqueline Goldsby, "The High and Low Tech of It: The Meaning of Lynching and the Death of Emmett Till," *Yale Journal of Criticism* 9, no. 2 (1996): 256.

3. Murray Kempton, writing for the *New York Post*, noted with disgust that J. W. Milam was "beyond embarrassment, clutching the soft parts of his wife, Juanita's, flesh for

the benefit of photographers and tipping his chair back, totally expansive." September 25, 1955, reprinted in Christopher Metress, *The Lynching of Emmett Till: A Documentary Narrative* (Charlottesville: University Press of Virginia, 2002), p. 107. For a more recent, scholarly assessment of these photographs, see Goldsby, "The High and Low Tech of It."

4. Greenberg, *Race Relations and American Law*, p. 342.

5. Ibid., p. 341.

6. David Halberstam, *The Fifties* (New York: Villard Books, 1993), pp. 436–37.

7. The case was officially closed in 1957 and reopened in 2004.

8. Cloyte Murdock Larsson, "Land of the Till Murder Revisited," *Ebony* (March 1986): 55.

9. September 11, 1955. Reprinted in Metress, *The Lynching of Emmett Till*, p. 41.

10. *Jackson Daily News*, September 2, 1955, reprinted in Metress, *The Lynching of Emmett Till*, p. 21.

11. Quoted in *Memphis Commercial Appeal*, September 1, 1955, reprinted in Metress, *The Lynching of Emmett Till*, p. 18.

12. Stephen J. Whitfield, *A Death in the Delta: The Story of Emmett Till* (New York: Free Press, 1988), pp. 27–34.

13. Keith Beauchamp's 2002 documentary, *The Untold Story of Emmett Louis Till* (Till Freedom Come Productions), argues that in addition to the two men (now dead) tried for the murder, several other men were present at the murder, some of them still alive.

14. Eric Lichtblau and Andrew Jacobs, "U.S. Revives Emmett Till Case Based on New Details in Films," *New York Times*, May 11, 2004.

15. Whitfield, looking at contemporary newspaper reports, maintains that at least two of Till's cousins claimed that Till "was definitely whistling" at Caroline Bryant (*A Death in the Delta*, p. 19). When William Bradford Huie later interviewed the cousins, however, he said that neither of them had mentioned the whistle until he asked them about it; then they only agreed that Emmett "may have whistled, at the store. But it had not struck them as important" (cited in Metress, *The Lynching of Emmett Till*, p. 243).

16. Till's cousin Curtis Jones was interviewed in *Eyes on the Prize: America's Civil Rights Years* (Boston: Blackside Corporation for Public Broadcasting, 1987), episode 1.

17. Metress, *The Lynching of Emmett Till*, pp. 90–91.

18. William Bradford Huie, "What's Happened to the Emmett Till Killers?" *Look*, January 22, 1957; reprinted in Metress, *The Lynching of Emmett Till*, p. 210.

19. Louis Burnham, *Behind the Lynching of Emmett Louis Till* (New York: Freedom Associates, 1955), p. 11.

20. Ibid., p. 3.

21. See Philip Dray, *At the Hands of Persons Unknown: The Lynching of Black America* (New York: Random House, 2002), p. 430; and Michal R. Belknap, *Federal Law and Southern Order: Racial Violence and Constitutional Conflict in the Post-Brown South* (Athens: University of Georgia Press, 1987), p. 32.

22. *St. Louis Post-Dispatch*, February 9, 1956, cited in Belknap, *Federal Law and Southern Order*, p. 32.

23. William Faulkner noted in 1956 that Mississippi was full of "many voices"—the voices of political leaders who, while claiming to uphold the laws of the nation, advocated the strategies of white supremacists explicitly at odds with their oaths of office. William Faulkner, "On Fear: Deep South in Labor: Mississippi," in *Faulkner: Essays, Speeches and Public Letters*, ed. James B. Meriwether (New York: Random House, 1965), pp. 98–99.

24. Tom P. Brady, *Black Monday* (Winona, MS: Association of Citizens' Councils, 1954), p. 18.

25. Hugh Stephen Whitaker, "A Case Study in Southern Justice: The Emmett Till Case" (master's thesis, Florida State University, 1963), p. 12.

26. Brady, *Black Monday,* foreword.

27. Ibid., p. 81.

28. Metress, *The Lynching of Emmett Till*, p. 241.

29. Brady, *Black Monday*, pp. 63–64.

30. Metress, *The Lynching of Emmett Till*, p. 207.

31. "Mississippi Insurrection," *Cleveland Call and Post*, October 8, 1955.

32. Letter to Ralph E. McGill, February 26, 1959, cited in Belknap, *Federal Law and Southern Order*, p. 265.

33. Cited in Olive Arnold Adams, *Time Bomb: Mississippi Exposed and the Full Story of Emmett Till* (Mound Bayou: Mississippi Regional Council of Negro Leadership, 1956), p. 8.

34. Ibid., p. 9.

35. Ibid., p. 10.

36. I. F. Stone, "The Sickness of the South: The Murder of Emmett Till," *The Haunted Fifties*, ed. I. F. Stone (New York: Vintage Books, 1963), p. 107.

37. John Herbers, "Jury Selection Reveals Death Demand Unlikely," *Jackson State Times*, September 19, 1955.

38. "The Strange Trial of the Till Kidnappers," *Jet*, October 6, 1955, pp. 7–8.

39. Christopher Metress, "No Justice, No Peace: The Figure of Emmett Till in African American Literature," *MELUS* 28, no. 1 (2003): 90.

40. "Protest Mounts on Emmett Till Case," *Cleveland Call and Post,* October 8, 1955.

41. Cited in Metress, *The Lynching of Emmett Till*, p. 312.

42. Dray, *At the Hands of Persons Unknown*, p. 382. The information given here about these now-missing plays is based on the research of Christopher Metress, *The Lynching of Emmett Till*, pp. 289–91.

43. Burnham, *Behind the Lynching of Emmett Louis Till*, p. 4.

44. Langston Hughes, "Mississippi—1955," in Metress, *The Lynching of Emmett Till*, p. 294.

45. Ernest Wakefield Stevens, "Blood on Mississippi," in Metress, *The Lynching of Emmett Till*, pp. 302–303.

46. Martha Millet, "Mississippi," in Metress, *The Lynching of Emmett Till*, pp. 302–309.

47. Adam Clayton Powell Jr., "Press Release, Office of Honorable Adam Clayton Powell, Jr., 11 October, 1955," in Metress, *The Lynching of Emmett Till*, pp. 133–36.

48. Langston Hughes, "I Feel Mississippi's Fist in My Own Face, Says Simple," *Chicago Defender*, October 15, 1955, p. 9.

49. Arnold Rampersad, introduction, *Langston Hughes: The Return of Simple*, ed. Akiba Sullivan Harper (New York: Hill and Wang, 1994), p. xviii.

50. Langston Hughes, "The Money, Mississippi, Blues," in Metress, *The Lynching of Emmett Till*, pp. 296–98.

51. "Mississippi Insurrection."

52. Letter to Moon, October 4, 1955, reprinted in Metress, *The Lynching of Emmett Till*, p. 295.

53. Richard Davidson, "Requiem for a Fourteen-Year-Old," in Metress, *The Lynching of Emmett Till*, pp. 291–93.

54. Richard Davidson, "A Cause for Justice," in Metress, *The Lynching of Emmett Till*, pp. 298–300.

55. Mary Parks, "For Emmett Till," in Metress, *The Lynching of Emmett Till*, pp. 301–302.

56. William Faulkner, "Press Dispatch Written in Rome, Italy, For the United Press, on the Emmett Till Case," *New York Herald Tribune*, September 9, 1955.

57. William Faulkner, "Address Upon Receiving the Nobel Prize for Literature, Stockholm, 10 December 1950," in *William Faulkner: Essays, Speeches and Public Letters*, ed. James B. Meriwether (New York: Random House, 1965), p. 120.

58. Robert Penn Warren, *Segregation: The Inner Conflict in the South* (New York: Random House, 1956), p. 13.

59. Ibid., p. 41.

60. Ibid., p. 15.

61. Ibid., p. 11.

62. Ibid., p. 62.

63. Ibid., p. 59.

64. Ibid., p. 56.

65. Faulkner, "Address Upon Receiving the Nobel Prize for Literature," p. 120.

66. Warren, *Segregation*, p. 25.

67. Ibid., p. 58.

68. Gwendolyn Brooks, *The Bean Eaters* (New York: Harper, 1960).

69. Mark Strand and Eavan Boland, *The Making of a Poem: A Norton Anthology of Poetic Forms* (New York: Norton, 2000), p. 77.

70. "The Strange Trial of the Till Kidnappers," p. 8.

71. James Baldwin, *Blues for Mister Charlie* (1964; reprint, New York: Vintage International, 1995), p. xiv.

72. Ibid., p. xiii.

73. Ibid., p. xv.

74. Ibid., p. 1.

75. Howard Taubman ("Theater: 'Blues for Mister Charlie,'" *New York Times*, April 24, 1964) remarked that the shifting scenes "have the smoothness of a dance"; Waters E. Turpin ("A Note on *Blues for Mister Charlie*," in *James Baldwin: A Critical Evaluation*, ed. Therman B. O'Daniel [Washington: Howard University Press, 1977], pp. 195–96) admired the flashbacks, which, he thought, "flow like the turgid, repetitive rhythms of a syncopated blues that has no end" (p. 195). Others found the play's structural complexity its "major flaw" (Carlton W. Molette, "James Baldwin as Playwright," in *James Baldwin: A Critical Evaluation*, ed. Therman B. O'Daniel [Washington: Howard University Press, 1977], pp. 183–88), and the constant flashbacks "mechanistic" (John Simon, "Theatre Chronicle," *Hudson Review* 17 [Autumn 1964]: 421–30).

76. Baldwin, *Blues for Mister Charlie*, p. 2.

77. Burnham, *Behind the Lynching of Emmett Louis Till*, p. 5.

78. Baldwin, *Blues for Mister Charlie*, p. xiv.

79. As Tom Driver observed in his 1964 review for *Negro Digest*, Baldwin "alienated a large part of the liberal intelligentsia by paying scant attention to the political and economic roots of segregation. Marxist and socialist theory have not detained him. Absent also is any concern with the structure of American law and the elective process." Tom F. Driver, "The Review That Was Too True to Be Published," *Critical Essays on James Baldwin*, ed. Fred L. Standley and Nancy V. Burt (Boston: G. K. Hall, 1988), p. 292.

80. Baldwin, *Blues for Mister Charlie*, p. 54.

81. Ibid., p. 41.

82. Nathan Cohen, "A Flawed Talent," *National Review* 16 (September 1964): 780.

83. John McCarten, "Grim Stuff," *New Yorker* (May 1964): 143. Philip Roth called the play "a soap opera designed to illustrate the superiority of blacks over whites." Philip Roth, "Channel X: Two Plays on the Race Conflict," *New York Review of Books* (May 1964): 11. Joseph Featherstone noted that in spite of Baldwin's announced intent to enter the racist's mind, the "trivial" indictment of the South that he manages is the insight that "all this racial fuss stems from the white man's inability to get it up." Joseph Featherstone, "Blues for Mister Baldwin," *Critical Essays on James Baldwin*, ed. Standley and Burt, p. 154. The charge that Baldwin's "inflexible, Negro-hating Southerners are stereotypes" (Taubman, "Theater: 'Blues for Mister Charlie,'") was echoed by many critics.

84. Gregor Roy, "Play of the Month: Blues for Mister Charlie," *Catholic World* 199 (July 1964): 264.

85. Baldwin mentions Huie's interviews in his "Notes for Blues," where he explains that the Till case provided the impetus for his play.

86. Baldwin, *Blues for Mister Charlie*, p. 56.

87. Huie, "What's Happened to the Emmett Till Killers?"

88. Baldwin, *Blues for Mister Charlie*, p. 48.

89. Huie, "What's Happened to the Emmett Till Killers?"

90. Baldwin, *Blues for Mister Charlie*, p. 119.

91. Huie, "What's Happened to the Emmett Till Killers?"

92. Baldwin, *Blues for Mister Charlie*, p. 120.

93. William Bradford Huie, "The Shocking Story of Approved Killing in Mississippi," *Look*, January 24, 1956.

94. Baldwin, *Blues for Mister Charlie*, p. 48.

95. Warren, *Segregation*, p. 25.

96. Baldwin, *Blues for Mister Charlie*, p. xiv.

97. James Baldwin, "The American Dream and the American Negro," *New York Times*, March 7, 1965.

98. Darwin T. Turner, "James Baldwin in the Dilemma of the Black Dramatist," in *James Baldwin: A Critical Evaluation*, ed. Therman B. O'Daniel (Washington: Howard University Press, 1977), p. 191.

99. Molette, "James Baldwin as Playwright," p. 187.

100. Susan Sontag, "Going to Theater, Etc.," *Partisan Review* 31 (Summer 1964): 389.

101. Baldwin, *Blues for Mister Charlie*, p. 22.

102. Ibid., p. 21.

103. Gordon Rogoff, "Muddy Blues," *Commonweal* 80 (May 1964): 299.

104. Roth, "Channel X," p. 11.

105. Cohen, "A Flawed Talent," p. 781.

106. Ibid.

107. Baldwin, *Blues for Mister Charlie*, p. 103.

108. McCartin, "Grim Stuff."

109. Mamie Bradley, for instance, insisted on comparing her son to Christ, an only son sacrificed to "remedy a condition." In an interview with the *Chicago Defender*, Bradley told of a vision in which a "presence" told her, "Mamie, it was ordained from the beginning of time that Emmett Louis Till would die a violent death. You should be grateful to be the mother

of a boy who died blameless like Christ." Ethel Payne, "Mamie Bradley's Untold Story," in Metress, *The Lynching of Emmett Till,* p. 232. See also Mattie Smith Colin, "Mother's Tears Greet Son Who Died a Martyr," *Chicago Defender,* September 10, 1955.

110. Baldwin, *Blues for Mister Charlie,* p. 118.

111. Ibid., p. 119.

112. Ibid., p. 99.

113. Henry Hewes, "A Change of Tune," *Saturday Review* 47 (May 1964): 36.

114. Taubman, "Theater: Blues for Mister Charlie."

115. Baldwin, *Blues for Mister Charlie,* p. 87.

116. Turpin notes that the expressionism of the final scenes must have seemed authentic to blacks, since "for the Negro, life in America has to assume the fantastic" (Turpin, "A Note on *Blues for Mister Charlie,*" p. 196).

117. Baldwin, *Blues for Mister Charlie,* p. 113.

118. Ibid., p. 114.

119. Ibid.

120. Driver, "The Review That Was Too True to Be Published," p. 292.

121. Baldwin, *Blues for Mister Charlie,* p. 105.

122. Metress, *The Lynching of Emmett Till,* p. 201.

123. Harper Lee, *To Kill a Mockingbird* (Philadelphia: Lippincott, 1960), p. 210.

124. Ibid., p. 84.

125. Patrick Chura, "Prolepsis and Anachronism: Emmett Till and the Historicity of *To Kill a Mockingbird,*" *Southern Literary Journal* 32, no. 2 (2000): 17.

126. Lee, *To Kill a Mockingbird,* p. 201. William Bradford Huie maintained that Judge Swango, "with his aristocratic fairness, his assured informality, his respect for the Anglo-Saxon legal heritage, . . . captured the admiration of everyone." Huie, *Wolf Whistle and Other Stories* (New York: New American Library, 1959), p. 29.

127. Chura, "Prolepsis and Anachronism," p. 12.

128. Lee, *To Kill a Mockingbird,* p. 214.

129. Ibid., p. 170.

130. Ibid., p. 176.

131. Ibid.

132. Ibid., p. 171.

133. Lee, *To Kill a Mockingbird,* p. 217.

134. Lee, *To Kill a Mockingbird,* p. 263. Chura ("Prolepsis and Anachronism," p. 10) notes the resemblance, again, to Bryant and Milam, poor whites (or "peckerwoods") who thought they'd be heroes in the white community after their acquittal but in fact were ostracized by both whites and blacks, could find no work, could not rent land, and "suffered disillusionment, ingratitude, resentment, misfortune" (Huie, "What's Happened to the Emmett Till Killers?").

135. Lee, *To Kill a Mockingbird,* p. 197.

136. *Commonweal,* for instance, described Till's body as "weighted down—symbolically enough—with a cotton gin pulley"—"Death in Mississippi," p. 603.

137. Lee, *To Kill a Mockingbird,* p. 157.

138. Ibid.

139. Ibid., p. 241.

140. Ibid., pp. 253–54.

141. A press release from the Jewish Labor Committee, dated November 28, 1955,

claims that these councils were direct successors to the Ku Klux Klan. "These councils," according to the JLC, "pose a threat to the internal security of the United States and [are] no different from Communist or Nazi agencies operating in our midst." Jewish Labor Committee, "JLC Calls for Federal Action in New Mississippi Shooting. Calls for Internal Security Committee Action on White Citizens' Councils" (New York: Jewish Labor Committee, 1955), pp. 1–2.

142. Brady, *Black Monday,* p. 2.

143. Lee, *To Kill a Mockingbird,* p. 218.

144. Ibid., p. 221.

145. Atticus resembles the attorneys who prosecuted Emmett Till's murderers, whom Huie described as "skilled, determined, and eloquent." Huie, *Wolf Whistle,* p. 29.

146. Lee, *To Kill a Mockingbird,* p. 254.

147. Ibid., p. 233.

148. Greenberg, *Race Relations and American Law,* p. 322.

149. Lee, *To Kill a Mockingbird,* p. 211.

150. Ibid., p. 225.

151. Ibid., p. 213.

152. Ibid., p. 36.

153. This is a lesson that Jem and Scout learn on the night that they dissuade a lynch mob determined to drag Tom Robinson from the jail and willing to kill Atticus in the process. "A mob's always made up of people, no matter what," Atticus tells them. "You children last night made [the mob leader] stand in my shoes for a minute," and it was enough to remind him of his humanity. "A gang of wild animals *can* be stopped, simply because they're still human" (p. 157).

154. Lee, *To Kill a Mockingbird,* p. 216.

155. Ibid., p. 158.

156. Ibid., p. 114.

157. Ibid., p. 113.

158. Ibid., p. 260. Writing before the civil rights movement, the American philosopher and educational reformer John Dewey made a similar point in 1939: "To denounce Nazism for intolerance, cruelty and stimulation of hatred amounts to fostering insincerity if, in our personal relations to other persons, if, in our daily walk and conversation, we are moved by racial, color or other class prejudice; indeed, by anything save a generous belief in their possibilities as human beings, a belief which brings with it the need for providing conditions which will enable these capacities to reach fulfillment." John Dewey, "Creative Democracy— The Task Before Us," *John Dewey and the Promise of America* (Columbus, OH: American Education Press, 1939).

159. Ibid., pp. 258–59.

160. Ibid., p. 218.

CHAPTER FIVE: WITNESSES TO AN EXECUTION: NORMAN MAILER'S SPECTACLE OF DEATH

1. Quoted in Michael Meltsner, *Cruel and Unusual: The Supreme Court and Capital Punishment* (New York: Random House, 1973), p. 291. Robert Sherrill laments that the court squandered this chance, "the best chance it had ever had, and probably the best chance it

would ever have in the next hundred years (considering how seldom liberal judges are appointed), to escape from the death-penalty dilemma." Robert Sherrill, "Death Trip: The American Way of Execution" *Nation*, January 8–15, 2001, p. 24.

2. *Furman v. Georgia*, 408 US 238 (1972).

3. *Gregg v. Georgia*, 428 US 153 (1976).

4. Norman Mailer, *The Executioner's Song* (1979; reprint, New York: Modern Library, 1993), p. 642.

5. *Furman v. Georgia*.

6. *Gregg v. Georgia*.

7. John W. Aldridge, "An Interview with Norman Mailer," *Partisan Review* 47 (July 1980); reprinted in J. Michael Lennon, *Conversations With Norman Mailer* (Jackson: University Press of Mississippi, 1988), p. 269.

8. I say "invented" because although Mailer insists on the authenticity of his journalism (he declared that he lived up to his intention to "stay out of the book entirely," to avoid using "anything that doesn't come from interviews or documents," and to be "absolutely scrupulous about what people told [him] to the best of [his] ability"), many of the idioms are his own. The quotes from Mailer come from Aldridge, "An Interview with Norman Mailer," p. 265; and William F. Buckley Jr., "Crime and Punishment: Gary Gilmore," interview with Norman Mailer, *Firing Line*, October 11, 1979. Reprinted in Lennon, *Conversations with Norman Mailer*, p. 231. For a discussion of Mailer's use of free indirect speech, see Robert M. Arlett, "The Veiled Fist of a Master Executioner," *Criticism* 29 (Spring 1987): 215–32.

9. Jürgen Habermas, *The Structural Transformation of the Public Sphere: An Inquiry into a Category of Bourgeois Society*, trans. Thomas Burger (Cambridge, MA: MIT Press, 1989), pp. 25–26.

10. Buckley, "Crime and Punishment: Gary Gilmore," p. 243.

11. Ibid.

12. *Furman v. Georgia*.

13. Joan Didion, "I Want to Go Ahead and Do It," *New York Times Book Review*, October 7, 1979; reprinted in J. Michael Lennon, *Critical Essays on Norman Mailer* (Boston: G. K. Hall, 1986), p. 79.

14. John Garvey, "The Executioner's Song," *Commonweal* 5, no. 107 (1980): 139–40.

15. Buckley, "Crime and Punishment: Gary Gilmore," p. 229.

16. Mailer, *The Executioner's Song*, p. 920.

17. Ibid., p. 505.

18. Ibid., p. 286.

19. Mailer "realized . . . only after [he'd] finished [the book] and the title had been there a long time" that "Gilmore is also the executioner, in the sense that this is the story of an executioner who, in his turn, is executed." Buckley, "Crime and Punishment: Gary Gilmore," p. 236.

20. Mailer, *The Executioner's Song*, p. 426.

21. Ibid., p. 459.

22. Ibid., p. 269.

23. Ibid., p. 51.

24. Ibid., p. 12.

25. Ibid., p. 24.

26. Ibid., p. 59.

27. Ibid., p. 300.

28. Ibid., p. 296.

29. Didion, "I Want to Go Ahead and Do It," p. 81.

30. Mailer, *The Executioner's Song,* p. 299.

31. Ibid., p. 296.

32. Ibid., pp. 301–302.

33. Ibid., p. 964.

34. Ibid., p. 494.

35. Ibid., p. 640.

36. David Guest, *Sentenced to Death: The American Novel and Capital Punishment* (Jackson: University Press of Mississippi, 1997), p. 141.

37. Mailer, *The Executioner's Song,* p. 509.

38. Ibid., p. 644.

39. Mark Edmundson, "Romantic Self-Creations: Mailer and Gilmore in *The Executioner's Song,*" *Contemporary Literature* 31, no. 4 (1990): 438.

40. Ibid., p. 438–39.

41. Mailer, *The Executioner's Song,* p. 638.

42. Guest, *Sentenced to Death,* p. 134.

43. Edmundson, "Romantic Self-Creations," p. 442.

44. Mailer, *The Executioner's Song,* pp. 512–13.

45. "Death Wish," *Newsweek,* November 29, 1976, p. 26.

46. Mailer, *The Executioner's Song,* p. 486.

47. Ibid., p. 576.

48. The episode is described by Mikal Gilmore, *Shot in the Heart* (New York: Doubleday, 1994), pp. 376–78.

49. Arlett, "The Veiled Fist of a Master Executioner," p. 224.

50. Mailer explains that the character of Gary Gilmore was "quintessentially American and yet worthy of Dostoevsky"—Aldridge, "An Interview with Norman Mailer," p. 270. In another interview Mailer compared his chosen form to the nineteenth-century novel, in which "you get a study of people in society with their character impinging on society"—Melvyn Bragg, "A Murderer's Tale: Norman Mailer Talking to Melvyn Bragg," in Lennon, ed., *Conversations with Norman Mailer,* p. 259.

51. Edmundson, "Romantic Self-Creations," p. 442.

52. John Hersey, "The Legend on the License," *Yale Review* 70 (1979): 310.

53. Mailer, *The Executioner's Song,* p. 200.

54. Ibid., p. 563.

55. Robert Merrill, *Norman Mailer Revisited* (New York: Twayne, 1992), p. 178. John Garvey perceptively argues that Mailer writes compassionately and "without condescension" about the Mormon families in his novel. "What I mean by that," he explains, "is the tendency of some writers who deal with criminality to see in the victims a naiveté or smugness of stuffy respectability which draws violence, almost justifiably. What Mailer shows us is the horror which occurs when decent people happen on a man like Gilmore at the wrong moment" ("The Executioner's Song," p. 140).

56. Buckley, "Crime and Punishment," p. 244.

57. Mailer, *The Executioner's Song,* p. 440.

58. Judith A. Scheffler, "The Prison as Creator in 'The Executioner's Song,'" *Modern Critical Views: Norman Mailer,* ed. Harold Bloom (New York: Chelsea House Publishers, 1986), p. 190.

59. Bragg, "A Murderer's Tale," p. 256.

60. Garvey, "The Executioner's Song," p. 142.

61. Guest, *Sentenced to Death*, p. 159.

62. Scheffler, "The Prison as Creator," pp. 190–91.

63. Buckley, "Crime and Punishment," p. 229.

64. Bragg, "A Murderer's Tale," pp. 253–54.

65. Buckley, "Crime and Punishment," p. 233.

66. This is Mailer's word: "So by the end of the book," Mailer says, "we know him well, even intimately, but his moral personality is considerably more saintly or malevolent than I can pretend to tell you" (Aldridge, "An Interview with Norman Mailer," p. 264).

67. Aldridge, "An Interview with Norman Mailer," p. 263.

68. Bragg, "A Murderer's Tale," p. 257.

69. These efforts all fail. "What's striking throughout the text," Edmundson notes, "is the inability of all the institutional agencies and their functionaries, prison psychiatrists, social workers, wardens, and the rest, to come up with a description of Gilmore that isn't jargon-ridden and flat-minded. No one can describe to anyone else's satisfaction why Gilmore committed the murders." Edmundson, "Romantic Self-Creations," p. 445. The same can be said of the ordinary people who share their memories of Gary.

70. Arlett, "The Veiled Fist of a Master Executioner," p. 224.

71. Buckley, "Crime and Punishment," p. 233.

72. Ibid., p. 242.

73. Edmundson, "Romantic Self-Creations," p. 445.

74. Hersey, "The Legend on the License," p. 306.

75. See, for examples, Garvey, "The Executioner's Song"; Steven G. Kellman, "Mailer's Strains of Fact," *Southwest Review* (Spring 1983): 126–33; and Aldridge, "An Interview with Norman Mailer."

76. Adam Smith, *A Theory of Moral Sentiments* (London, 1759), p. 9. Smith's book begins with a chapter devoted to sympathy.

77. Benjamin Rush, *Essays Literary, Moral and Philosophical*, ed. Michael Meranze (Schenectady, NY: Union College Press, 1988), p. 82.

78. Mailer, *The Executioner's Song*, p. 572.

79. He had wanted, he said, to include the perspectives of the executioners, but the actual gunmen remained anonymous and the prison warden refused to be interviewed (Buckley, "Crime and Punishment," pp. 230–31).

80. Mailer, *The Executioner's Song*, p. 382. Hansen's strategy does not work. During the trial and mitigation hearings, Gilmore notices that the jury never look at him. Given a final chance to say something to the jury before they retire to deliberate on a sentence, Gilmore announces, "Well, I am finally glad to see that the Jury is looking at me" (Mailer, p. 425).

81. Habermas, *The Structural Transformation of the Public Sphere*, pp. 50–51.

82. He is less noble, but no less emphatic, in his "open letter from Gary Gilmore to all and any who still seek to oppose by whatever means my death by legal execution. Particularly: ACLU, NAACP. I invite you to finally butt out of my life. Butt out of my death" (Mailer, *The Executioner's Song*, p. 743).

83. Mailer, *The Executioner's Song*, p. 597.

84. Ibid., p. 598.

85. Louis Menand, "Beat the Devil," *New York Review of Books*, October 22, 1998, p. 30.

86. Mailer, *The Executioner's Song,* p. 604.

87. Ibid., p. 680.

88. Aldridge, "An Interview with Norman Mailer," pp. 262–63.

89. Mailer, *The Executioner's Song,* p. 613.

90. Ibid.

91. Ibid., p. 640.

92. Robert Merrill believes that Schiller redeems himself in the course of the novel. "He deals more honestly with everyone involved than most of us would have done; he suffers acute physical and emotional stress in deciding how far to go in exploiting his material; and he ends up committing himself to doing the best he can for the story rather than his bank account, even rejecting an offer of $250,000 from the *New York Post.*" Robert Merrill, *Norman Mailer Revisited,* p. 170. Even if we share Merrill's assessment, Schiller comes to represent all that is inescapably self-serving in sympathy: it finally tells us more about the spectator who wields it than about the spectacle who receives it.

93. Mailer, *The Executioner's Song,* pp. 972–73.

94. Guest, *Sentenced to Death,* p. 132.

95. Ibid.

96. Ibid., p. 134.

97. John D. Bessler, *Death in the Dark: Midnight Executions in America* (Boston: Northeastern University Press, 1997), p. 208.

98. Mailer, *The Executioner's Song,* p. 936.

99. Buckley, "Crime and Punishment," p. 247.

100. Mailer, *The Executioner's Song,* p. 957.

101. Ibid., p. 958.

102. Ibid.

103. Ibid., p. 998, emphasis mine.

104. Hersey, "The Legend on the License," p. 304.

105. Edmundson suggests that Gilmore's "energy" is "inimical to cultural forms, including literary forms," and including even the form of Romantic self-creation that Mailer thought he saw in Gilmore. Edmundson, "Romantic Self-Creations," p. 446.

106. Mailer, *The Executioner's Song,* pp. 288–89.

CHAPTER SIX: THE SWEETHEART OF DEATH ROW: KARLA FAYE TUCKER AND THE PROBLEM OF PUBLIC SENTIMENTS

1. Daniel E. Williams, ed., *Pillars of Salt: An Anthology of Early American Criminal Narratives* (New York: Madison House, 1993), p. 2.

2. Ann Hodges, "The Execution of Karla Faye Tucker: TV Turns Last Day on Death Row into Media Marathon," *Houston Chronicle,* February 4, 1998.

3. Ibid.

4. Sam Howe Verhovek, "Karla Tucker Is Now Gone, But Several Debates Linger," *New York Times,* February 5, 1998.

5. "The Confession and Dying Warning of Katharine Garrett," in *A Sermon Preached on the Occasion of the Execution of Katharine Garret,* ed. Eliphalet Adams (New London, 1738), p. 43.

6. "Obviously," Robertson acknowledged to Larry King, "God gave her some mercy

and grace to do just that. And if she were executed, she would go to be with the Lord forever in heaven, so she would be a winner in that one." Larry King, "Karla Faye Tucker: Does She Deserve to Die?" *Larry King Live,* January 15, 1998.

7. Rebekah Chamblit, *The Declaration, Dying Warning and Advice of Rebekah Chamblit* (Boston, 1733), p. 3.

8. William F. Buckley, "Dark Night for George W.," *National Review*, January 26, 1998, p. 59.

9. Larry King, "Karla Faye Tucker, Live From Death Row," *Larry King Live,* January 14, 1998.

10. Ibid.

11. Beverly Lowry, "The Good Bad Girl," *New Yorker*, February 9, 1998, p. 71.

12. Beverly Lowry, *Crossed Over: A Murder, a Memoir* (New York: Knopf, 1992), p. 188.

13. *Larry King Live,* January 14, 1998.

14. *Larry King Live,* January 15, 1998.

15. Kathy Walt, "Karla Faye's Last Chance," *Houston Chronicle*, February 1, 1998.

16. Ibid.

17. Ibid.

18. Lowry, *Crossed Over,* p. 159.

19. Ibid., p. 173.

20. Sam Howe Verhovek, "As Woman's Execution Nears, Texas Squirms," *New York Times,* January 1, 1998.

21. Lowry, *Crossed Over,* p. 13.

22. Ibid., p. 197.

23. Linda Strom, *Karla Faye Tucker Set Free: Life and Faith on Death Row* (Colorado Springs: Waterbrook Press, 2000).

24. King, *Larry King Live,* January 14, 1998.

25. Ibid.

26. Lowry, *Crossed Over,* p. 198.

27. Kathy Walt, "Tucker Dies After Apologizing," *Houston Chronicle*, February 3, 1998.

28. Joanna Coles, "A Few Hours to Live."

29. Lowry, *Crossed Over,* p. 188.

30. Coles, "A Few Hours to Live."

31. Ellen Goodman, "Karla Faye Tucker Gave Death Row a Human Face," *Houston Chronicle*, February 15, 1998.

32. Walt, "Karla Faye's Last Chance."

33. Karla Faye Tucker, "Letter to Governor Bush," www.agitator.com/dp/98/karlaletter.html, 1998.

34. Lowry, *Crossed Over,* p. 129.

35. Ibid., p. 139.

36. Ibid., p. 99.

37. Straightway, *Karla Faye's Original Memorial Homepage*, http:www.straightway.org/karla/karla.htm, 2001.

38. Daniel Pedersen, "Praying for Time," *Newsweek*, February 2, 1998, p. 66.

39. Lowry, "The Good Bad Girl," p. 75.

40. *Agence France Presse,* February 2, 1998.

41. *Larry King Live,* January 15, 1998.

42. According to the prosecuting attorney, several jurors had not wanted to assign the death penalty but had no choice under Texas law. Lowry, *Crossed Over,* p. 180.

43. Sam Howe Verhovek, "Divisive Case of a Killer of Two Ends as Texas Executes Tucker," *New York Times,* February 4, 1998.

44. Ibid.

45. Lowry, "The Good Bad Girl," p. 70.

46. Nathaniel Hawthorne, *The Scarlet Letter* (1850), *The Centenary Edition of the Works of Nathaniel Hawthorne,* ed. Thomas Woodson, L. Neal Smith, and Norman Holmes Pearson, vol. 1 (Columbus: Ohio State University Press, 1962–1985), p. 56.

47. Walt, "Execution May Haunt Texas: Tucker Case Likely to Bring Unprecedented Scrutiny," *Houston Chronicle,* December 15, 1997.

48. Walt, "Should Tucker Be Executed?" *Houston Chronicle,* February 1, 1998. This photograph appeared in European newspapers.

49. Lowry, *Crossed Over,* p. 155.

50. Walt, "Execution May Haunt Texas: Tucker Case Likely to Bring Unprecedented Scrutiny," *Houston Chronicle,* December 15, 1997.

51. Polly Ross Hughes and Stephen Johnson, "Many Still Fighting to Stop Tucker's Execution," *Houston Chronicle,* February 3, 1998.

52. Lowry, "The Good Bad Girl," p. 77.

53. Strom, *Karla Faye Tucker Set Free,* pp. 183–84.

54. *Larry King Live,* January 14, 1998.

55. Karen Beckman observes that the images of Tucker that were circulated in the press presented this death-row inmate as the "idealized white woman" whose image could be traced back to the Renaissance. The production of such images, Beckman argues, underscored Tucker's distinction from the typical death-row inmate who was barely noticed by the mainstream media. Karen Beckman, "Dead Woman Glowing: Karla Faye Tucker and the Aesthetics of Death Row Photography," *Camera Obscura,* 19, no. 1, p. 6.

56. *Larry King Live,* January 14, 1998.

57. Pedersen, "Praying for Time," p. 67.

58. John Rogers, *Death the Certain Wages of Sin to the Impenitent: Life the Future Reward of Grace to the Penitent* (Boston, 1701), p. 108.

59. Michael Graczyk, "Tucker Dies With Her Eyes Wide Open," *USA Today,* February 4, 1998.

60. Ibid.

61. Tracey Duncan, "I Cannot Face Execution Number 9 in Texas," *Daily Telegraph,* February 5, 1998.

62. Walt, "Karla Faye's Last Chance," *Houston Chronicle,* February 1, 1998.

63. *Larry King Live,* January 15, 1998.

64. Christopher Burns, "World Watches as Minutes Tick Down for Texas Woman's Execution," Associated Press, February 3, 1998.

65. Andrew Sullivan, "Muddled Minds United by the Feminist Martyr of Death Row," *London Sunday Times,* January 18, 1998.

66. Rob Feldman, "A Question of Mercy," Court TV, 1998.

67. Joanna Coles, "Ghoulish and Good Gather For Last Hours," *Guardian,* February 4, 1998.

68. Walt, "I Watched Killer Smile as She Died," *London Daily Mail,* February 4, 1998.

69. Walt, "Karla Faye's Last Chance."

70. Walt, "Should Tucker Be Executed?" The statement is from Tim Flanagan, dean of the College of Criminal Justice at Sam Houston State University in Huntsville, TX.

71. Cited in *Agence France Presse,* February 4, 1998.

72. Duncan, "I Cannot Face Execution Number 9."

73. Ibid.

74. David Rose, "No Mercy," *Irish Times,* February 7, 1998.

75. Brian Reade, "Yanks Are the Real Savages," *Mirror,* February 6, 1998, p. 11.

76. Joanna Coles, "A Few Hours to Live," *Guardian,* February 3, 1998.

77. "Lethal Lapse in Ethical Standards; There is No Such Thing Anywhere as a Civilized Execution," *Guardian,* February 4, 1998.

78. Walt, "Should Tucker Be Executed?"

79. "World Reacts to Karla Faye Tucker's Execution in Texas," *Agence France Presse,* February 4, 1998.

80. Julia Reed, "Capital Crime," *Vogue,* March 1998, p. 340.

81. Walt, "Should Tucker Be Executed?"

82. John D. Bessler points out that the transition to private executions (along with gag laws that prohibited the press from covering executions or interviewing condemned criminals prior to their executions) was motivated by the fear that publicity would garner support for the abolition of capital punishment. John D. Bessler, *Death in the Dark: Midnight Executions in America* (Boston: Northeastern University Press, 1997), p. 71. Tucker's example amply illustrates the grounds for this fear, as publicity of her case provoked sympathy for the condemned woman and opposition to her execution.

83. William Shurtleff, *The Faith and Prayer of a Dying Malefactor* (Boston, 1740), p. 20.

84. Hughes and Johnson, "Many Still Fighting to Stop Tucker's Execution."

85. *Houston Chronicle,* February 4, 1998.

86. Verhovek, "Divisive Case of a Killer of Two Ends as Texas Executes Tucker."

87. Joerg-Michael Dettmer, "Media Furore and Prayer: Karla Faye Tucker Executed in Texas," *Deutsche Presse-Agentur,* February 4, 1998.

88. Duncan, "I Cannot Face Execution Number 9."

89. January 4, 1998.

90. "The Execution of Karla Faye Tucker: Tucker's Final Words, Thoughts From Others," *Houston Chronicle,* February 4, 1998.

91. "Europeans Call Penalty Barbaric," *New York Times,* February 4, 1998.

92. Florence King, "The Misanthrope's Corner," *National Review,* March 9, 1998.

93. Reade, "Yanks Are the Real Savages."

94. Alex Renton, "'I Love You All' . . . Then She Was Dead," *Evening Standard,* February 4, 1998.

95. Andy Lines, "Sickened By Sight of the Execution 'Party': Baying Mob Cheer as Karla Faye Tucker is Executed," *Mirror,* February 5, 1998; "World Reacts to Karla Faye Tucker's Execution in Texas."

96. Lines, "Sickened By Sight of the Execution 'Party.'"

97. Joanna Coles, "Ghoulish and Good Gather For Last Hours."

98. Lines, "Sickened By Sight of the Execution 'Party.'"

99. Renton, "'I Love You All'"; Coles, "Ghoulish and Good Gather for Last Hours."

100. Lines, "Sickened By Sight of the Execution 'Party.'"

101. Ibid.
102. Duncan, "I Cannot Face Execution Number 9."
103. Bessler, *Death in the Dark,* p. 207.
104. Rose, "No Mercy."
105. "World Reacts."
106. "Europeans Call Penalty Barbaric."
107. Reade, "Yanks Are the Real Savages."
108. Amnesty International, "Killing Without Mercy: Clemency Procedures in Texas" (1999).
109. Sam Howe Verhovek, "Karla Tucker is Now Gone, But Several Debates Linger," *New York Times,* February 5, 1998.
110. http://books.dreambook.com/ladydaria/tucker98.html (1998).
111. Ibid.
112. Ibid.
113. Jürgen Habermas, *The Structural Transformation of the Public Sphere: An Inquiry Into a Category of Bourgeois Society,* trans. Thomas Burger (Cambridge, MA: MIT Press, 1989), pp. 25–26.
114. http://books.dreambook.com/ladydaria/tucker98.html (1998).
115. Lowry, "The Good Bad Girl," p. 62.
116. Anonymous, "Karla Faye Tucker Murdered By Gov. George Bush on Behalf of the Government of the United States of America?" http://www.greenspun.com/bboard/q-and-a-fetch-msg.tcl?msg_id=0002L8 (2002).
117. Williams, *Pillars of Salt,* p. 135.
118. Walt, "Tucker Dies After Apologizing."
119. *Larry King Live,* January 15, 1998.
120. Amnesty International, "Killing Without Mercy."
121. *Larry King Live,* January 15, 1998.
122. She was granted only one meeting, but it was a highly unusual one: Victor Rodriguez, the chair of the BPP, drove to the Gatesville prison to speak with Tucker in person.
123. *Larry King Live,* January 14, 1998.
124. "Punishment as retribution has been condemned by scholars for centuries," the court observed in 1972, "and the Eighth Amendment itself was adopted to prevent punishment from becoming synonymous with vengeance." *Furman v. Georgia,* 408 U.S. 238 (1972).
125. *Larry King Live,* January 15, 1998.
126. *Gregg v. Georgia,* 428. U.S. 153 (1976).
127. Amnesty International, "Killing Without Mercy," p. 1.
128. Lowry, "Good Bad Girl," p. 62.
129. *Larry King Live,* January 14, 1998.
130. Pedersen, "Praying for Time," p. 67.
131. Walt, "Karla Faye's Last Chance."
132. Tucker, "Letter to Governor Bush."
133. Verhovek, "Divisive Case of a Killer of Two Ends as Texas Executes Tucker."
134. Buckley, "Dark Night for George W."
135. Ivo Dawnay, "Texans Shrink from Taking a Woman's Life," *Sunday Telegraph,* January 11, 1998.
136. R. G. Ratcliffe, "The Execution of Karla Faye Tucker: Bush Prayed for Guidance Before Denying Tucker's Appeal," *Houston Chronicle,* February 4, 1998.

137. The story of the judge is told by Daniel M. Cohen, *Pillars of Salt, Monuments of Grace: New England Crime Literature and the Origins of American Popular Culture, 1674–1960* (New York: Oxford University Press, 1994), p. 194.

138. Tucker Carlson, *Talk Magazine* (September 1999).

139. http://books.dreambook.com/ladydaria/tucker98.html (1998).

CONCLUSION: ARTFUL UPRISINGS: THE CAMPAIGN AGAINST CAPITAL PUNISHMENT

1. Sam Howe Verhovek, "As Texas Executions Mount, They Grow Routine," *New York Times*, May 25, 1997.

2. Ibid.

3. Bob Herbert, "In America: Tainted Justice," *New York Times*, August 6, 2001.

4. John D. Bessler, *Death in the Dark: Midnight Executions in America* (Boston: Northeastern University Press, 1997), p. 208.

5. Ibid., p. 210.

6. Ann Powers, "Death Penalty Ignites a Coalition of Musicians," *New York Times*, June 27, 2001.

7. Dimitra Kessenides, "The Execution of Wanda Jean," Salon.com (accessed March 15, 2002).

8. Julie Salamon, "Human Face of Execution in Oklahoma," New York Times, September 6, 2002.

9. Ibid.

10. Katya Lezin, *Finding Life on Death Row: Profiles of Six Inmates* (Boston: Northeastern University Press, 1999), p. xviii.

11. Ibid., pp. ix–x.

12. The series began on November 14, 1999 with "Death Row Justice Derailed"; an additional four articles appeared over the next four days.

13. Ken Armstrong and Steve Mills, "Part One: Death Row Justice Derailed," *Chicago Tribune*, November 14, 1999.

14. "In Ryan's Words, 'I Must Act,'" *New York Times*, January 11, 2003.

15. Ibid.

16. Ken Armstrong and Steve Mills, "Ryan: 'Until I Can Be Sure': Illinois is First State to Suspend Death Penalty," *Chicago Tribune*, February 1, 2000.

17. Scott Turow et al., "Preamble to the Report of the Illinois Governor's Commission on Capital Punishment, April 2002," in Scott Turow, *Ultimate Punishment: A Lawyer's Reflections on Dealing with the Death Penalty* (New York: Farrar, Straus, and Giroux, 2003), p. 119.

18. Fox Butterfield, "On the Record. Governor Bush on Crime: Bush's Law and Order Adds Up to Tough and Popular," *New York Times*, August 18, 1999.

19. Ibid.

20. As president, Bush later indicated that he did not understand his own state's capital punishment laws. "We should never execute the mentally retarded," he announced. "And our court system protects people who don't understand the nature of the crime they've committed nor the punishment they are about to receive." Raymond Bonner, "Drawing a Line on Death," *New York Times*, June 24, 2001, Week in Review. Bush's mistake was to confuse

"people who don't understand" the nature of the crime or punishment with "the mentally retarded," who were not protected from execution until the Supreme Court ruled in 2002 that such executions were unconstitutional. But even after this ruling, the Supreme Court failed to offer guidelines for determining who qualified as mentally retarded, leaving such inmates again at the mercy of sometimes unmerciful state governments.

21. Butterfield, "On the Record."

22. Rodney Ellis, "Senate Criminal Justice Committee Passes Ellis Bill to Strengthen Texas' Indigent Criminal Defense Network," press release, Austin, TX, April 21, 1999.

23. Nine other states had established similar commissions to reexamine their states' death penalty statutes. Jodi Wilgoren, "Few Death Sentences or None Under Overhaul Proposed By Illinois Panel," *New York Times*, April 16, 2002. Even Supreme Court Justice Sandra Day O'Connor expressed deep reservations about the capital system, suggesting that postconviction DNA testing should be used in capital cases, and that "perhaps it's time to look at minimum standards for appointed counsel in death cases and adequate compensation for appointed counsel when they are used." "Justice O'Connor Expresses Concern on Death Penalty," *New York Times*, July 4, 2001.

24. The exception, of course, was Green Party candidate Ralph Nader, who insisted that capital punishment was an ineffective deterrent and that it had been unfairly applied. See Jennifer Bleyer, "Race Matters, But Class Matters More, Says Nader," *NewsforChange*, September 21, 2001. Working Assets, www.workingforchange.com (2000). See also Matt Welch, "Nader Lets Loose," *NewsforChange* (accessed October 20, 2000). Working Assets, www.workingforchange.com (2000). But because Nader was so marginalized by the two-party system, his passionate opposition to capital punishment never affected the discussions between the two major party candidates.

25. Tom Wheeler, "Musicians Against the Death Penalty," *Counterpunch* 8 (June 2002).

26. C. J., "*The Exonerated:* The Theater of Life and Death," *Revolutionary Worker* 1078 (November 13, 2000), online at rwor.org/a/v22/1070-79/1078/exoner.htm (2000). As of February 2004, the play had raised over $500,000 for the exonerated people it depicts.

27. Playbill notes, quoted in C. J.

28. Jessica Blank and Erik Jensen, *The Exonerated* (New York: Faber and Faber, 2004), p. xi.

29. Eventually they pared these characters down to six and added dialogue from court transcripts, affidavits, and the transcripts of police interrogations. Hugh Hart, "Life after Death Row: Two Actors Traveled the Country to Meet People Wrongly Convicted. The Result: A Drama and a New Perspective," *Actors' Gang*, April 7, 2002 www.theactorsgang.com/news5.htm (2002).

30. Elyse Sommer, "*The Exonerated.*" *Curtain Up: The Internet Theater Magazine of Reviews, Features, Annotated Listings*, www.curtainup.com/exonerated.html.

31. Blank and Jensen, *The Exonerated*, p. 8.

32. Ibid., p. xv.

33. Ibid., p. xvi.

34. Richard Connema, "Robin Williams and Amanda Plummer Extraordinary in West Coast Premiere of *The Exonerated*," *Talkin' Broadway Regional News and Reviews: San Francisco*, December 1, 2003, www.talkinbroadway.com/regional/sanfran/s413.html (2003).

35. Michael Criscuolo, "Show Listings: *The Exonerated*," Nytheatre.com, October 5, 2002, www.nytheatre.com/nytheatre/exonerated.htm (2002).

36. Wanda Sabir, "Montel Williams in *The Exonerated*," *San Francisco Bay View*, December 3, 2003, www.sfbayview.com/120303/montel120303.shtml (2003).

37. Lucia Mauro writes, "I couldn't help but be disturbed over the propaganda-esque nature of the experience." "*The Exonerated* at the Shubert Theatre," *Chicago Theater*, February 2003, www.chicagotheater.com/revExoner.html.

38. Sommer, "*The Exonerated*."

39. Amy Goldwasser, "*The Exonerated*," Salon.com, October 20, 2000.

40. Philip Fisher, "*The Exonerated* (Revisited)," *British Theatre Guide*, 2004, www.britishtheatreguide.info/reviews/exonerated2-rev.htm (2004). Fisher's comment came after seeing the play for the second time.

41. Blank and Jensen, *The Exonerated*, p. 13.

42. Ibid., p. 23.

43. Ibid., p. 43.

44. Ibid., p. 20.

45. Ibid., p. 44.

46. Mauro, "*The Exonerated* at the Shubert Theatre."

47. Blank and Jensen, p. 23.

48. Ibid., p. 30.

49. Ibid., pp. 31–33.

50. Ibid., pp. 32–33.

51. Ibid., p. 66.

52. Ibid., p. 4.

53. Blank and Jensen refer to the 102 death-row inmates exonerated between 1973 and 2004: "We consider every one of their stories to be part of this play." Ibid., p. xiii.

54. Ibid., p. 43.

55. Ibid., p. 16.

56. Goldwasser, "*The Exonerated*."

57. Blank and Jensen, *The Exonerated*, p. 71.

58. Ibid., p. 64.

59. William Shurtleff, *The Faith and Prayer of a Dying Malefactor* (Boston, 1740), p. 20.

60. Blank and Jensen, *The Exonerated*, pp. 47–48.

61. Ibid., p. 66.

62. Quoted in Goldwasser, "*The Exonerated*."

63. C. J., "*The Exonerated*: The Theater of Life and Death."

64. Sabir, "Montel Williams in *The Exonerated*."

65. Open Society Institute, "New Death Penalty Play, *The Exonerated*, Features Post-Performance Q & A With Experts and Audience," press release, New York, October 17, 2002.

66. Michael Ellison, "Escape from the Electric Chair," *Guardian*, January 3, 2001.

67. Goldwasser, "*The Exonerated*."

68. Sabir, "Montel Williams in *The Exonerated*."

69. Adam Liptak, "The Death Penalty: A Witness for the Prosecution," *New York Times*, February 15, 2003.

70. Ibid.

71. Sabir, "Montel Williams in *The Exonerated*."

72. "In Ryan's Words: 'I Must Act,'" *New York Times*, January 11, 2003.

73. Liptak, "The Death Penalty: A Witness for the Prosecution."

74. Ibid.

75. Jodi Wilgoren, "Illinois Panel: Death Sentence Needs Overhaul," *New York Times*, April 15, 2002.

76. Ibid.

77. Wilgoren, "Few Death Sentences or None."

78. "In Ryan's Words: 'I Must Act.'"

79. Ibid.

80. Ibid.

81. "Ryan Changes Stand on Death Penalty," Associated Press, January 13, 2003.

82. "In Ryan's Words: 'I Must Act.'"

83. Wilgoren, "Illinois Panel."

84. Barry James, "Clearing of Illinois Death Row is Greeted By Cheers Overseas," *New York Times*, January 14, 2003.

85. Jodi Wilgoren, "Citing Issue of Fairness, Governor Clears Out Death Row in Illinois," *New York Times*, April 12, 2003.

86. Alan Berlow, "The Texas Clemency Memos," *Atlantic Monthly* 292 (July/August 2003): 91.

87. Ibid., p. 91. See also "After John Ashcroft," *New York Times*, November 11, 2004.

88. Benjamin Rush, *Essays Literary, Moral and Philosophical*, ed. Michael Meranze (Schenectady, NY: Union College Press, 1988), pp. 82–83.

BIBLIOGRAPHY

Aaron, Daniel. *Writers on the Left*. New York: Oxford University Press, 1961.

Adams, Eliphalet. *A Sermon Preached on the Occasion of the Execution of Katharine Garret*. New London, 1738.

Adams, Henry. "Shall We Muzzle the Anarchists?" *Forum* 1 (July 1886): 445–54.

Aldridge, John W. "An Interview with Norman Mailer." In *Conversations with Norman Mailer*, edited by Michael Lennon. Jackson: University Press of Mississippi, 1988. Originally published in *Partisan Review* 47 (July 1980): 262–70.

Altgeld, John P. *Reasons for Pardoning the Haymarket Anarchists*. Chicago: Charles H. Kerr, 1986.

American History Workshop. *The Fall River Sourcebook: A Documentary History of Fall River, Massachusetts*. Vol. 1. New York: American History Workshop, 1981.

Amnesty International. "Killing Without Mercy: Clemency Procedures in Texas." London: Amnesty International, 1999.

Anderson, Benedict. *Imagined Communities: Reflections on the Origin and Spread of Nationalism*. London: Verso, 1983.

Anonymous. "August Spies." *Alarm*, November 19, 1887, p. 1.

Anonymous. *Brief and Impartial Narrative of the Life of Sarah Maria Cornell; Written by One, Who, Early Knew Her*. New York, 1833.

Anonymous. *The Chicago Martyrs*. London: Freedom Press, 1912.

Anonymous. "The Clove-Hitch Knot." N.p., n.d.

Anonymous. *Correct, Full and Impartial Report of the Trial of Rev. Ephraim K. Avery, Before the Supreme Judicial Court of the State of Rhode Island*. Providence, 1833.

Anonymous. "The Death of Sarah M. Cornell." N.p., 1832.

Anonymous. *Explanation of the Circumstances Connected with the Death of Sarah Maria Cornell*. Providence, 1834.

Anonymous. "The Factory Maid." N.p., n.d.

Anonymous. *In Memoriam of the Martyrs of the Working People Murdered at Chicago on November 11, '87*. N.p., n.d.

Anonymous. "Lines Written on the Death of Sarah M. Cornell." N.p., n.d.

Anonymous. "November 11, 1887." *Alarm*, December 3, 1887, p. 3.

Anonymous. "Our Martyrs." *Alarm*, November 19, 1887, p. 3.

Anonymous. "Paddy Miles's Sentiments." *Chicago Labor Enquirer*, June 16, 1888, p. 2.

Anonymous. "The Price of Freedom." *Chicago Labor Enquirer*, December 17, 1887.

Anonymous. "The Road to Freedom." *Chicago Labor Enquirer*, June 9, 1888, p. 2.

Anonymous. *The Terrible Hay-Stack Murder: Life & Trial of the Rev. Ephraim K. Avery, for the Murder of the Young & Beautiful Miss Sarah M. Cornell, a Factory Girl of Fall River, Mass.* Philadelphia, 1877.

Anonymous. *Trial At Large*. New York, 1833.

Anonymous. "Victoria." *Chicago Labor Enquirer*, November 14, 1887, p. 4.

Anonymous. "Where the Gallows Darkly Rose." *Freedom*, December 1887, p. 59.

Aristides. *Strictures on the Case of Ephraim K. Avery*. Providence, 1833.

Arlett, Robert M. "The Veiled Fist of a Master Executioner." *Criticism* 29 (Spring 1987): 215–32.

Asbury, H. "Hearst Comes to Atlanta." *The American Mercury* 7 (January 1926): 87–95.

Avery, Rev. Ephraim K. *A Vindication of the Results of the Trial of Rev. Ephraim K. Avery*. Boston, 1834.

Avrich, Paul. *The Haymarket Tragedy*. Princeton, NJ: Princeton University Press, 1984.

Baldwin, James. *Blues for Mister Charlie*. 1964. Reprint, New York: Vintage International, 1995.

Beauchamp, Keith. *The Untold Story of Emmett Louis Till*. Till Freedom Come Productions, 2002.

Beckett, C. W. "Remember Chicago." *Commonweal* 4, no. 10 (November 1888): 357.

Beckman, Karen. "Dead Woman Glowing: Karla Faye Tucker and the Aesthetics of Death Row Photography." *Camera Obscura* 19, no. 1: 1–41.

Belknap, Michal R. *Federal Law and Southern Order: Racial Violence and Constitutional Conflict in the Post-Brown South*. Athens: University of Georgia Press, 1987.

Bennett, Fremont O., ed. *The Chicago Anarchists and the Haymarket Massacre*. Chicago, 1887.

Berlow, Alan. "The Texas Clemency Memos." *Atlantic Monthly* 292 (July/August 2003): 91–96.

Bessler, John D. *Death in the Dark: Midnight Executions in America*. Boston: Northeastern University Press, 1997.

Biedenkapp, Georg. "To the Manes of the 11th of November." *Fackel*, November 12, 1899.

Bingham, Frances A. "The Price of Blood." *Workmen's Advocate* 5 (November 1887): 3.

Black, William P. "Funeral Elegy." *Chicago Labor Enquirer*, November 19, 1887, p. 1.

Blank, Jessica, and Erik Jensen. *The Exonerated*. New York: Faber and Faber, 2004.

Bleyer, Jennifer. "Race Matters, But Class Matters More, Says Nader." *NewsforChange*, September 21, 2000, http://www.workingforchange.com (accessed 2003).

Bloom, Harold, ed. *Modern Critical Views: Norman Mailer*. New York: Chelsea House, 1986.

Bonney, Charles Carroll. *The Present Conflict of Capital and Labor: A Discourse*. Chicago, 1886.

Bosco, Ronald A. "Early American Gallows Literature: An Annotated Checklist." *Resources for American Literary Study* 8 (1978): 81–107.

Boudreau, Kristin. *Sympathy in American Literature: American Sentiments from Jefferson to the Jameses*. Gainesville: University Press of Florida, 2002.

Brady, Tom P. *Black Monday*. Winona, MS: Association of Citizens' Councils, 1954.

Bricker, L. O. "A Great American Tragedy." *Shane Quarterly* 4 (April 1943): 89–95.

Brooks, Gwendolyn. *The Bean Eaters*. New York: Harper, 1960.

Brundage, W. F. *Under Sentence of Death: Lynching in the South*. Chapel Hill: University of North Carolina Press, 1997.

Buchanan, Joseph R. *The Story of a Labor Agitator*. New York: Outlook, 1903.

Buckley, William F., Jr. "Crime and Punishment: Gary Gilmore." Interview with Norman Mailer. Transcript of *Firing Line*, October 11, 1979. Reprinted in *Conversations with Norman Mailer*, edited by Michael Lennon, 228–51.

———. "Dark Night for George W." *National Review*, January 26, 1998, p. 59.

Burnham, Louis. *Behind the Lynching of Emmett Louis Till*. New York: Freedom Associates, 1955.

Burt, Olive Woolley. *American Murder Ballads and their Stories*. New York: Oxford University Press, 1958.

Cabot, James Elliot. *A Memoir of Ralph Waldo Emerson*. Boston, 1887.

Campbell, John. *After Souls by Death Are Separated from Their Bodies*. Boston, 1738.

Carlson, Tucker. *Talk Magazine*, September 1999.

Chamblit, Rebekah. *The Declaration, Dying Warning and Advice of Rebekah Chamblit*. Boston, 1733.

Cheesewright, Arthur. "Hymn." *Labor Enquirer*, November 19, 1887.

Chura, Patrick. "Prolepsis and Anachronism: Emmett Till and the Historicity of *To Kill a Mockingbird*." *Southern Literary Journal* 32, no. 2 (2000): 1–26.

C. J. "*The Exonerated*: The Theater of Life and Death." *Revolutionary Worker* 1078 (November 13, 2000). http://www.rwor.org/a/v22/1070-79/1078/exoner.htm (accessed December 2003).

Clap, Nathaniel. *The Lord's Voice, Crying to His People*. Boston, 1715.

Clarke, Mary Carr. *Sarah Maria Cornell, or the Fall River Murder: A Domestic Drama in Three Acts*. New York, 1833.

Clews, Henry. "Shall Labor or Capital Rule?" *North American Review* 142 (June 1886).

Cohen, Daniel M. *Pillars of Salt, Monuments of Grace: New England Crime Literature and the Origins of American Popular Culture, 1674–1860*. New York: Oxford University Press, 1994.

Cohen, Nathan. "A Flawed Talent." *National Review* 16 (September 1964): 780–81.

Connema, Richard. "Robin Williams and Amanda Plummer Extraordinary in West Coast Premiere of *The Exonerated*." *Talkin' Broadway Regional News and Reviews: San Francisco*. December 1, 2003, http://www.talkinbroadway.com/regional/sanfran/s413.html (accessed December 2003).

Connolly, C. P. "The Frank Case." *Colliers*, December 19, 1914, pp. 6–24, and December 16, 1914, pp. 18–25.

Coolidge, John. *Mill and Mansion: A Study of Architecture and Society in Lowell, Massachusetts, 1820–1865.* 2nd ed. Amherst: University of Massachusetts Press, 1993.

Cooper, Amanda. "A *Curtain Up* Review: *The Exonerated.*" *Curtain Up: The Internet Theater Magazine of Reviews, Features, Annotated Listings,* November 23, 2003, http:www.curtainup.com/exonerated.html (accessed December 2003).

Crane, Gregg D. *Race, Citizenship and Law in American Literature.* Cambridge: Cambridge University Press, 2002.

Crane, Walter. "Freedom in America." *Commonweal* 3 (October 15, 1887): 333.

———. "On the Suppression of Free Speech at Chicago." *Commonweal* 2 (July 17, 1886): 123.

Cridge, A. D. "The Battle-Hymn of Freemen." *Social Science* 1 (October 29, 1887): 14.

Criscuolo, Michael. "Show Listings: *The Exonerated.*" Nytheatre.com, October 5, 2002, www.nytheatre.com/nytheatre/exonerated.htm (accessed December 2003).

"Current Topics." *Albany Law Journal* 33, no. 20 (1886): 381.

Dana, James. *The Intent of Capital Punishment.* New Haven, 1790.

Davidson, Cathy. *Revolution and the Word: The Rise of the Novel in America.* New York: Oxford University Press, 1986.

Davidson, Richard. "A Cause for Justice." In *The Lynching of Emmett Till: A Documentary Narrative,* edited by Christopher Metress. Charlottesville: University of Virginia Press, 2002.

———. "Requiem for a Fourteen-Year-Old." In *The Lynching of Emmett Till: A Documentary Narrative,* edited by Christopher Metress. Charlottesville: University of Virginia Press, 2002.

"Death In Mississippi." *Commonweal* (September 23, 1955): 603–604.

Debs, Eugene. "The Chicago Anarchists." *Locomotive Firemen's Magazine,* January 11, 1887, pp. 11–13.

———. "The Martyred Apostles of Labor." *Eugene Debs: His Life, Writings and Speeches.* Girard, KS: Appeal to Reason Press, 1908.

De Cleyre, Voltairine. *Selected Works,* edited by Alexander Berkman. New York: Revisionist Press, 1972.

Denning, Michael. *Mechanic Accents: Dime Novels and Working-Class Culture in America.* New York: Verso, 1998.

Diether, Charles. "The Eleventh of November, 1887." *Der Anarchist,* November 14, 1891.

Dinnerstein, L. *The Leo Frank Case.* New York: Columbia University Press, 1968.

Douglas, Ann. *The Feminization of American Culture.* New York: Alfred A. Knopf, 1977.

Dray, Philip. *At the Hands of Persons Unknown: The Lynching of Black America.* New York: Random House, 2002.

Drescher, Martin. "The Day Will Come!" In *American Labor Songs of the Nineteenth Century,* edited by Philip S. Foner. Urbana: University of Illinois Press, 1975.

Driver, Tom F. "The Review That Was too True to Be Published." In *Critical Essays on James Baldwin,* edited by Fred L. and Nancy V. Burt Standley. Boston: G. K. Hall, 1988.

Dublin, Thomas. *Women at Work: The Transformation of Work and Community in Lowell, Massachusetts, 1826–1860.* New York: Columbia University Press, 1979.

Edelshtadt, David. "Who Were They?" In *American Labor Songs of the Nineteenth Century,* edited by Philip S. Foner. Urbana: University of Illinois Press, 1975.

Edmundson, Mark. "Romantic Self-Creations: Mailer and Gilmore in *The Executioner's Song.*" *Contemporary Literature* 31, no. 4 (1990): 434–47.

Ellis, Rodney. "Press Release: Senate Criminal Justice Committee Passes Ellis Bill to Strengthen Texas' Indigent Criminal Defense Network." Austin, TX, April 21, 1999.

Emerson, Ralph Waldo. *Nature, Addresses and Lectures*. Boston: J. Munroe, 1849.

"The Execution of the Anarchists." *Nation* 45, no. 1167, November 10, 1887, pp. 366–67.

Fairfield, Lincoln Sumner. "Table Talk." *North American Quarterly Magazine* 2, no. 10 (August 1833): 256.

Faugeres, Margaretta V. Bleecker. *The Ghost of John Young*. New York, 1797.

Faulkner, William. "Address Upon Receiving the Nobel Prize for Literature, Stockholm, 10 December 1950." In *William Faulkner: Essays, Speeches and Public Letters*, edited by James B. Meriwether. New York: Random House, 1965.

———. "On Fear: Deep South in Labor: Mississippi." In *Faulkner: Essays, Speeches and Public Letters*, edited by James B. Meriwether. New York: Random House, 1965.

———. "Press Dispatch Written in Rome, Italy, For the United Press, on the Emmett Till Case." *New York Herald Tribune,* September 9, 1955.

Featherstone, Joseph. "Blues for Mister Baldwin." In *Critical Essays on James Baldwin,* edited by Fred L. Standley and Nancy V. Burt Standley. Boston: G. K. Hall, 1988.

Fiering, Norman. "Irresistible Compassion: An Aspect of Eighteenth-Century Sympathy and Humanitarianism." *Journal of the History of Ideas* 37 (1976): 195–218.

Flanagan, Christopher. *Conversation and Conduct of the Late Unfortunate John Young*. New York, 1797.

Fliegelman, Jay. *Declaring Independence: Jefferson, Natural Language, and the Culture of Performance*. Stanford, CA: Stanford University Press, 1993.

Foner, Philip S., ed. *Autobiographies of the Haymarket Anarchists*. New York: Humanities Press, 1969.

Forbes, Peres. *The Paradise of God Opened to a Penitent Thief*. Providence, 1784.

Foucault, Michel. *Discipline and Punish: The Birth of the Prison*, translated by Alan Sheridan. New York: Random House, 1977.

Frankena, William. "Hutcheson's Moral Sense Theory." *Journal of the History of Ideas* 16 (1955): 356–75.

Frey, Robert Seitz, and Nancy Thompson-Frey. *The Silent and the Damned: The Murder of Mary Phagan and the Lynching of Leo Frank*. New York: Madison Books, 1988.

Furman v. Georgia, 408 U.S. 238 (1972).

Garvey, John. "The Executioner's Song." In *Modern Critical Views: Norman Mailer,* edited by Harold Bloom. New York: Chelsea House, 1986.

Gary, Joseph E. "The Chicago Anarchists of 1886: The Crime, the Trial, and the Punishment." *Century Magazine* 45, no. 6 (1893): 803–37.

Gioia, Dana. *Can Poetry Matter? Essays on Poetry and American Culture*. St. Paul: Graywolf, 1992.

Golden, Harry. *A Little Girl is Dead*. Cleveland: World Publishing, 1965.

Goldman, Emma. "The Crime of the 11th of November." *Mother Earth*, November 1911.

———. *Living My Life*. 2 vols. New York, 1931.

Goldsby, Jacqueline. "The High and Low Tech of It: The Meaning of Lynching and the Death of Emmett Till." *Yale Journal of Criticism* 9, no. 2 (1996): 245–82.

Greenberg, Jack. *Race Relations and American Law*. New York: Columbia University Press, 1959.

Gregg v. Georgia, 428 U.S. 153 (1976).

Griffin, L. J., Paula Clark, and Joanne C. Sandberg. "Narrative and Event: Lynching and Historical Sociology." In *Under Sentence of Death: Lynching in the South*, edited by W. F. Brundage. Chapel Hill: University of North Carolina Press, 1997.

Guest, David. *Sentenced to Death: The American Novel and Capital Punishment.* Jackson: University Press of Mississippi, 1997.

Habermas, Jürgen. *The Structural Transformation of the Public Sphere: An Inquiry into a Category of Bourgeois Society*, translated by Thomas Burger. Cambridge, MA: MIT Press, 1989.

Haggerty, George E. "Desire and Mourning: The Ideology of the Elegy." In *Ideology and Form in Eighteenth-Century Culture*, edited by David H. Richter. Lubbock: Texas Tech University Press.

Halberstam, David. *The Fifties.* New York: Villard Books, 1993.

Halker, Clark D. *For Democracy, Workers, and God: Labor Song-poems and Labor Protest, 1865–95.* Urbana: University of Illinois Press, 1991.

Hallett, Benjamin. *The Arguments of Counsel in the Close of the Trial of Rev. Ephraim K. Avery, for the Murder of Sarah M. Cornell.* Boston, 1833.

———. *Trial of Rev. Mr. Avery: A Full Report of the Trial of Ephraim K. Avery.* Boston, 1833.

Hammond, Jeffrey A. *The American Puritan Elegy: A Literary and Cultural Study.* New York: Cambridge University Press, 2000.

Hart, Hugh. "Life After Death Row: Two Actors Traveled the Country to Meet People Wrongly Convicted. The Result: A Drama and a New Perspective." *Actors' Gang*, April 7, 2002, www.theactorsgang.com/news5.htm (accessed December 2003).

Hasian, M. J. "Judicial Rhetoric in a Fragmentary World: 'Character' and Storytelling in the Leo Frank Case." *Communication Monographs* 64 (1997): 250–69.

Hendler, Glenn. "The Limits of Sympathy: Louisa May Alcott and the Sentimental Novel." *American Literary History* 3 (1991): 685–706.

Herndon, Harvey. *Narrative of the Apprehension in Rindge, N.H. of the Rev. E.K. Avery, Charged with the Murder of Sarah M. Cornell.* Providence, 1833.

Hersey, John. "The Legend on the License." *Yale Review* 70 (1979): 289–314.

Hewes, Henry. "A Change of Tune." *Saturday Review* 47, no. 9 (May 1964): 36.

Higham, John. *Strangers in the Land.* New Brunswick, NJ: Rutgers University Press, 1955.

Hildreth, Richard. *Report of the Trial of the Rev. Ephraim K. Avery.* Boston, 1833.

Hilliard, Timothy. *Paradise Promised to a Penitent Thief.* Boston, 1785.

Holmes, Oliver Wendell. "Mr. Justice Holmes, Dissenting." In Harry Golden, *A Little Girl is Dead.* Cleveland: World Publishing, 1965.

Howells, William Dean. *Selected Letters of W. D. Howells*, edited by Robert C. Leitz III, et al. Vol. 3: 1882–1891. Boston: Twayne, 1980.

Hughes, Langston. "I Feel Mississippi's Fist in My Own Face, Says Simple." *Chicago Defender*, October 15, 1955, p. 9.

———. "Mississippi—1955." In *The Lynching of Emmett Till: A Documentary Narrative*, edited by Christopher Metress. Charlottesville: University of Virginia Press, 2002.

Huie, William Bradford. "The Shocking Story of Approved Killing in Mississippi." *Look*, January 24, 1956.

———. "What's Happened to the Emmett Till Killers?" *Look*, January 22, 1957.

———. *Wolf Whistle and Other Stories.* New York: New American Library, 1959.

Hull, Paul C. *The Chicago Riot: A Record of the Terrible Scenes of May 4, 1886.* Chicago, 1886.

Hutcheson, Francis. *An Inquiry into the Original of Our Ideas of Beauty and Virtue: In Two Treatises.* 3rd ed. London, 1729.

Hutner, Gordon. *Secrets and Sympathy: Forms of Disclosure in Hawthorne's Novels*. Athens: University of Georgia Press, 1988.

James, William. *The Correspondence of William James*, edited by Ignas K. Skrupskelis and Elizabeth M. Berkeley. Charlottesville: University Press of Virginia, 1992–1997.

Jefferson, Thomas. *The Papers of Thomas Jefferson*, edited by Julian P. Boyd. Vol. 1: 1760–1776. Princeton, NJ: Princeton University Press, 1950.

Jewish Labor Committee. "JLC Calls for Federal Action in New Mississippi Shooting. Calls for Internal Security Committee Action on White Citizens Councils." Press Release, New York: Jewish Labor Committee, 1955.

Kasserman, David Richard. *Fall River Outrage: Life, Murder, and Justice in Early Industrial New England*. Philadelphia: University of Pennsylvania Press, 1986.

Keil, Hartmut, and John B. Jentz, eds. *German Workers in Chicago: A Documentary History of Working-Class Culture from 1850 to World War I*. Urbana: University of Illinois Press, 1988.

Kengott, George F. *The Record of a City: A Social Survey of Lowell, Massachusetts*. New York: Macmillan, 1912.

Kessenides, Dimitra. "The Execution of Wanda Jean." Salon.com, March 15, 2002, www .salon.com/people/feature/2002/03/18/garbus/ (accessed December 2003).

Kimball, John C. "Rev. John C. Kimball on Anarchy." *Liberty*, December 17, 1887, pp. 1, 6–7.

King, Florence. "The Misanthrope's Corner." *National Review*, March 9, 1998, p. 72.

King, Larry. "Karla Faye Tucker: Does She Deserve to Die?" *Larry King Live*, January 15, 1998, CNN.

———."Karla Faye Tucker: Live from Death Row." *Larry King Live*, January 14, 1998, CNN.

Larsson, Clotye Murdock. "Land of the Till Murder Revisited." *Ebony*, March 1986, pp. 53–58.

Lawson, John D., ed. *The Trial of the Chicago Anarchists: August Spies, Michael Schwab, Samuel Fielden, Albert R. Parsons, Aldoph Fischer, George Engel, Louis Lingg and Oscar W. Neebe for Conspiracy and Murder. Chicago, Illinois, 1886*. Vol. 12 of *American State Trials*. Wilmington, DE: Scholarly Resources, 1972.

———, ed. *The Trial of Leo M. Frank for the Murder of Mary Phagan, Atlanta, Georgia, 1913*. Vol. 10 of *American State Trials*. Wilmington, DE: Scholarly Resources, 1972.

L. B. G. "To Lucy E. Parsons." *Alarm*, November 19, 1887, p. 1.

Lee, Harper. *To Kill a Mockingbird*. Philadelphia: J. B. Lippincott, 1960.

Lennon, Michael, ed. *Critical Essays on Norman Mailer*. Boston: G. K. Hall, 1986.

Lewis, Leon. *The Facts Concerning the Eight Condemned Leaders*. Greenport, NY, 1887.

Lezin, Katya. *Finding Life on Death Row: Profiles of Six Inmates*. Boston: Northeastern University Press, 1999.

Lindemann, A. S. *The Jew Accused: Three Anti-Semitic Affairs (Dreyfuss, Beilis, Frank) 1894–1915*. Cambridge: Cambridge University Press, 1991.

Lloyd, J. William. "Seven." *Liberty* 19 (1887): 7.

Lombroso, Cesare. "Illustrative Studies in Criminal Anthropology: The Physiognomy of the Anarchists." *Monist* 1, no. 3 (1891): 336–43.

Lowry, Beverly. *Crossed Over: A Murder, a Memoir*. New York: Alfred A. Knopf, 1992.

———. "The Good Bad Girl." *New Yorker*, February 9, 1998, pp. 60–77.

Lum, Dyer D. *A Concise History of the Great Trial of the Chicago Anarchists in 1886: Condensed from the Official Record*. New York: Arno, 1969.

————. *In Memoriam: Chicago, November 11, 1887*. Berkeley Heights, NJ: Oriole, 1937.

MacLean, Nancy. "Gender, Sexuality, and the Politics of Lynching: The Leo Frank Case Revisited." In *Under Sentence of Death: Lynching in the South*, edited by W. Fitzhugh Brundage. Chapel Hill: University of North Carolina Press, 1997.

McCarten, John. "Grim Stuff." *New Yorker*, May 1964, p. 143.

McConnell, Samuel P. "The Chicago Bomb Case." *Harper's* 168 (May 1934): 730–39.

McLean, George N. *The Rise and Fall of Anarchy in America: From its Incipient Stage to the First Bomb Thrown in Chicago*. Chicago, 1888.

McLoughlin, William C. "Untangling the Tiverton Tragedy: The Social Meaning of the Terrible Haystack Murder of 1833." *Journal of American Culture* 7, no. 4 (1984): 75–84.

Mailer, Norman. *Conversations With Norman Mailer*, edited by Michael Lennon. Jackson: University Press of Mississippi, 1988.

————. *The Executioner's Song*. 1979. New York: Modern Library, 1993.

Male, Roy R. "Hawthorne and the Concept of Sympathy." *PMLA* 68 (1953): 138–49.

Marshall, David. "Adam Smith and the Theatricality of Moral Sentiments." *Critical Inquiry* 10 (1984): 592–613.

Marx-Aveling, Eleanor. "A Woman's Plea for Mercy." *Pall-Mall Gazette*, November 8, 1887, p. 1.

Marx-Aveling, Eleanor, and Edward Aveling. *The Chicago Anarchists: A Statement of Facts*. London, 1887.

Masur, Louis P. *Rites of Execution: Capital Punishment and the Transformation of American Culture, 1776–1865*. New York: Oxford University Press, 1989.

Mather, Cotton. *Warnings From the Dead*. Boston, 1693.

Mauro, Lucia. "*The Exonerated* at the Shubert Theatre." *Chicago Theater*, February 2003, http://www.chicagotheater.com/revExoner.html (accessed December 2003).

Melnick, J. *Black-Jewish Relations on Trial: Leo Frank and Jim Conley in the New South*. Jackson: University Press of Mississippi, 2000.

Meltsner, Michael. *Cruel and Unusual: The Supreme Court and Capital Punishment*. New York: Random House, 1973.

Member of the Massachusetts Bar. *Celebrated Murders as Shown in Remarkable Capital Trials*. Chicago, 1878.

Menand, Louis. "Beat the Devil." Review of Mailer's *The Time of Our Time*. *New York Review of Books*, October, 22, 1998, pp. 27–30.

Merrill, Robert. *Norman Mailer Revisited*. New York: Twayne, 1992.

Metress, Christopher. *The Lynching of Emmett Till: A Documentary Narrative*. Charlottesville: University of Virginia Press, 2002.

————. "'No Justice, No Peace': The Figure of Emmett Till in African American Literature." *MELUS* 28, no. 1 (Spring 2003): 87–103.

Millet, Martha. "Mississippi." In *The Lynching of Emmett Till: A Documentary Narrative*, edited by Christopher Metress. Charlottesville: University of Virginia Press, 2002.

Molette, Carlton W. "James Baldwin as Playwright." In *James Baldwin: A Critical Evaluation*, edited by Therman B. O'Daniel. Washington: Howard University Press, 1977.

Moore, Thomas. "Columbia's Shame." *Chicago Labor Enquirer*, November 14, 1887, p. 4.

Mullan, John. *Sentiment and Sociability: The Language of Feeling in the Eighteenth Century*. Oxford: Clarendon Press, 1988.

Munson, Fayette. "The Beacon is Burning." *Chicago Labor Enquirer*, December 17, 1887, p. 2.

Nelson, Bruce C. "Anarchism: The Movement Behind the Martyrs." *Chicago History* 15 (1986): 4–19.

Nelson, Cary. *Repression and Recovery: Modern American Poetry and the Politics of Cultural Memory, 1910–1945.* Madison: University of Wisconsin Press, 1989.

Noble, Frederick A. *Christianity and the Red Flag: A Sermon Preached for the Union Park Congregational Church of Chicago, Illinois, 1886.* N.p., n.d.

Odell, George C. *Annals of the New York Stage.* Vol. 3, 1821–1834. New York: Columbia University Press, 1928.

O'Donnell, Edward. "In Memoriam." *Rebel,* November 20, 1895, p. 21.

"Of Course!" *Workmen's Advocate,* November 15, 1887, p. 1.

Oliver, L. S. "The State." In *An Anthology of Revolutionary Poetry,* edited by Marcus Graham. New York: Active Press, 1929.

———. "To My Martyred Comrades." *Free Society,* December 5, 1897, p. 178.

Oney, Steve. *And the Dead Shall Rise: The Murder of Mary Phagan and the Lynching of Leo Frank.* New York: Pantheon Books, 2003.

Open Society Institute. "New Death Penalty Play, *The Exonerated,* Features Post-Performance Q & A with Experts and Audience." Press Release, New York, October 17, 2002.

Paine, Thomas. *The American Crisis.* Vol. 1, 1776.

Parks, Mary. "For Emmett Till." In *The Lynching of Emmett Till: A Documentary Narrative,* edited by Christopher Metress. Charlottesville: University of Virginia Press, 2002.

Parrish, Timothy L. "Haymarket and *Hazard*: The Lonely Politics of William Dean Howells." *Journal of American Culture* 17, no. 4 (1994): 23–32.

Parsons, Albert. *An Appeal to the People of America.* Chicago, 1887.

Parsons, Albert Richard. "Last Words." In *An Anthology of Revolutionary Poetry,* edited by Marcus Graham. New York: Active Press, 1929.

Parsons, Lucy E., ed. *Famous Speeches of the Eight Chicago Anarchists.* New York: Arno Press and the *New York Times,* 1969.

Payne, Ethel. "Mamie Bradley's Untold Story." In *The Lynching of Emmett Till: A Documentary Narrative,* edited by Christopher Metress. Charlottesville: University of Virginia Press, 2002.

Pinsky, Robert. *Favorite Poem Project,* http://www.bu.edu/favoritepoem/forteachers/index .html (accessed December 2003).

Plato. *The Republic.* Perseus Digital Library, Tufts University.

Powell, Adam Clayton, Jr. "Press Release: Office of Honorable Adam Clayton Powell, Jr., 11 October, 1955." In *The Lynching of Emmett Till: A Documentary Narrative,* edited by Christopher Metress. Charlottesville: University of Virginia Press, 2002.

Public Broadcasting Service. *Eyes on the Prize: America's Civil Rights Years; Awakenings 1954–1956.* PBS, 1986.

Ramazani, Jahan. *Poetry of Mourning: The Modern Elegy from Hardy to Heany.* Chicago: University of Chicago Press, 1994.

Rampersad, Arnold. Introduction to *Langston Hughes: The Return of Simple,* edited by Akiba Sullivan Harper. New York: Hill and Wang, 1994.

Rascoe, B. *The Case of Leo Frank: A Factual Review of One of the Most Sensational Murder Cases in Court Annals.* Girard, KS: Haldeman-Julius, 1947.

"The Red Flag in America." *Public Opinion,* May 15, 1886, pp. 81–87.

Reed, Julia. "Capital Crime." *Vogue,* March 1998, pp. 338–42.

Reitzel, Robert. "New Year's, 1888." *Fackel,* January 1, 1888.

Richards, Lydia Platt. "Albert R. Parsons." *Alarm,* December 3, 1887, p. 3.

Ritz, Wilfred J. *American Judicial Proceedings First Printed Before 1801: An Analytical Bibliography.* Westport, CT: Greenwood Press, 1984.

Rogers, John. *Death the Certain Wages of Sin to the Impenitent: Life the Future Reward of Grace to the Penitent.* Boston, 1701.

Rogoff, Gordon. "Muddy Blues." *Commonweal* 80 (May 1964): 299–300.

Ross, Harold W. "The Leo M. Frank Case." In *A Little Girl is Dead,* edited by Harry Golden. Cleveland: World Publishing, 1965.

Roth, Philip. "Channel X: Two Plays on the Race Conflict." *New York Review of Books*, May 1964, pp. 10–13.

Roy, Gregor. "Play of the Month: Blues for Mister Charlie." *Catholic World* 199 (July 1964): 263–64.

Ruchames, Louis. "John Brown, Jr., and the Haymarket Martyrs." *Massachusetts Review* 5 (Summer 1964): 765–68.

Rush, Benjamin. *Essays Literary, Moral and Philosophical*, edited by Michael Meranze. Schenectady, NY: Union College Press, 1988.

Sabir, Wanda. "Montel Williams in *The Exonerated*." *San Francisco Bay View*, December 3, 2003, www.sfbayview.com/120303/montel120303.shtml (accessed December 2003).

Salter, William M. *A Cure for Anarchy.* Chicago, 1887.

————. *What Shall Be Done With the Anarchists?* Chicago: Open Court, 1887.

Schaack, Michael J. *Anarchy and Anarchists: A History of the Red Terror and the Social Revolution in America and Europe.* New York: Arno Press, 1977.

Scheffler, Judith A. "The Prison as Creator in 'The Executioner's Song.'" In *Modern Critical Views: Norman Mailer,* edited by Harold Bloom. New York: Chelsea House, 1986.

Schmidt, Ernst. "The Defense and Amnesty Campaigns." In *The Haymarket Scrapbook,* edited by Dave Roediger and Franklin Rosemont. Chicago: Charles H. Kerr, 1986.

————. "To All Friends of an Impartial Administration of Justice!" Chicago, 1887.

Schor, Esther. *Bearing the Dead: The British Culture of Mourning from the Enlightenment to Victoria.* Princeton, NJ: Princeton University Press, 1994.

Schwab, Michael. "A Convicted Anarchist's Reply to Professor Lombroso." *Monist* 1, no. 4 (1891): 520–24.

Scoresby, William. *American Factories and their Female Operatives.* Boston, 1845.

Shaw, W. David. "Elegy and Theory: Is Historical and Critical Knowledge Possible?" *Modern Language Quarterly* 55, no. 1 (1994): 1–16.

Sherrill, Robert. "Death Trip: The American Way of Execution." *Nation* 8, January 15, 2001: 13–34.

Shurtleff, William. *The Faith and Prayer of a Dying Malefactor.* Boston, 1740.

Simon, John. "Theatre Chronicle." *Hudson Review* 17 (Autumn 1964): 421–30.

Smith, Adam. *A Theory of Moral Sentiments.* London, 1759.

Smith, Carl S. "Cataclysm and Cultural Consciousness: Chicago and the Haymarket Trial." *Chicago History* 15 (Summer 1986): 36–53.

————. *Urban Disorder and the Shape of Belief: The Great Chicago Fire, the Haymarket Bomb, and the Model Town of Pullman.* Chicago: University of Chicago Press, 1995.

Sommer, Elyse. "*The Exonerated*." *Curtain Up: The Internet Theater Magazine of Reviews, Features, Annotated Listings*, www.curtainup.com/exonerated.html (accessed December 2003).

Sontag, Susan. "Going to Theater, Etc." *Partisan Review* 31 (Summer 1964): 389–99.

Spalding, Rev. J. L. "Are We in Danger of Revolution?" *Forum* 1 (July 1886): 405–15.

Spies, August. Letter to William M. Salter, November 7, 1887. Manuscript collection, Houghton Library at Harvard University.

———. *Revenge Circular*. Chicago, 1886.

Stanton, Elizabeth Cady. Letter to the editor. *New York Tribune*, May 30, 1860.

Stanton, Elizabeth Cady, and Susan B. Anthony. *Elizabeth Cady Stanton, Susan B. Anthony: Correspondence, Writings, Speeches*, edited by Ellen Carol DuBois. New York: Schocken Books, 1981.

Stevens, Ernest Wakefield. "Blood on Mississippi." In *The Lynching of Emmett Till: A Documentary Narrative*, edited by Christopher Metress. Charlottesville: University of Virginia Press, 2002.

Stone, I. F., ed. *The Haunted Fifties*. New York: Vintage Books, 1963.

Strand, Mark, and Eavan Boland. *The Making of a Poem: A Norton Anthology of Poetic Forms*. New York: Norton, 2000.

"The Strange Trial of the Till Kidnappers." *Jet*, October 6, 1955, pp. 6–11.

Strom, Linda. *Karla Faye Tucker Set Free: Life and Faith on Death Row*. Colorado Springs: Waterbrook Press, 2000.

Tebbel, John. *A History of Book Publishing in the United States*. Vol. 1. New York: R. R. Bowker, 1972.

Thompson, W. E. *A Short Review of the Frank Case*. Atlanta, 1914.

Thoreau, Henry David. "Resistance to Civil Government." Boston: Elizabeth Peabody, 1849.

———. *Walden*. 1854. Reprinted in *The Portable Thoreau*, ed. Carl Bode. New York: Viking Penguin, 1982.

Tompkins, Jane. *Sensational Designs: The Cultural Work of American Fiction, 1790–1860*. New York: Oxford University Press, 1985.

Train, Arthur. "Did Leo Frank Get 'Justice'?" *Everybody's Magazine* 32 (March 1915): 314–17.

Trumbull, Matthew Mark. "The Trial of the Judgment: Free Speech and Consequential Murder." *Alarm*, November 17, 1888, p. 2.

———. *The Trial of the Judgment: A Review of the Anarchist Case*. Chicago, 1888.

Tucker, Karla Faye. "Letter to Governor Bush." www.agitator.com/dp/98/karlaletter.html (accessed December 2003).

Turner, Darwin T. "James Baldwin in the Dilemma of the Black Dramatist." *James Baldwin: A Critical Evaluation*, edited by Therman B. O'Daniel. Washington: Howard University Press, 1977.

Turner, John. "The Tragedy of Chicago." *Freedom* (December 1887): 59.

Turow, Scott, et al. "Preamble to the Report of the Illinois Governor's Commission on Capital Punishment, April 2002." *Ultimate Punishment: A Lawyer's Reflections on Dealing With the Death Penalty*, edited by Scott Turow. New York: Farrar, Straus, and Giroux, 2003.

Turpin, Waters E. "A Note on *Blues for Mister Charlie*." In *James Baldwin: A Critical Evaluation*, edited by Therman B. O'Daniel. Washington: Howard University Press, 1977.

Ury, John. *The Dying Speech of John Ury*. Philadelphia, 1741.

Wald, Alan M. *Exiles from a Future Time: The Forging of the Mid-Twentieth-Century Literary Left*. Chapel Hill: University of North Carolina Press, 2002.

Warren, Robert Penn. *Segregation: The Inner Conflict in the South*. New York: Random House, 1956.

Watson, Thomas E. "The Celebrated Case of the State of Georgia vs. Leo Frank." *Watson's Magazine* 21 (1915): 182–232.

Watt, Ian. *The Rise of the Novel: Studies in Defoe, Richardson and Fielding.* Berkeley and Los Angeles: University of California Press, 1957.

Wells, Ida B. *Southern Horrors: Lynch Law in All Its Phases.* New York, 1893.

Wheeler, Tom. "Musicians Against the Death Penalty." *Counterpunch*, June 8, 2002, www.counterpunch.org (accessed December 2003).

Wheelock, Lewis. "Urban Protestant Reactions to the Chicago Haymarket Affair 1886–1893." Ph.D. diss., State University of Iowa, 1956.

Whitaker, Hugh Stephen. "A Case Study in Southern Justice: The Emmett Till Case." Master's thesis, Florida State University, 1963.

Whitfield, Stephen J. *A Death in the Delta: The Story of Emmett Till.* New York: Free Press, 1988.

"Why Was Frank Lynched: Was it Race Hatred, Dirty Politics, Yellow Journalism?" *Forum* 56 (December 1916): 677–92.

Wiggins, G. *Fiddlin' Georgia Crazy: Fiddlin' John Carson, His Real World, and the World of His Songs.* Urbana: University of Illinois Press, 1987.

Williams, Catharine. *Fall River: An Authentic Narrative.* Providence, 1834.

Williams, Daniel E., ed. *Pillars of Salt: An Anthology of Early American Criminal Narratives.* New York: Madison House, 1993.

Wills, Gary. *Inventing America: Jefferson's Declaration of Independence.* New York: Doubleday, 1978.

Wilson, S. Robert. "Murder Most Foul." *Alarm,* December 17, 1887, p. 2.

Wise, Stephen Samuel. "The Case of Leo Frank: A Last Appeal." *Free Synagogue Pulpit* 3 (1915): 79–96.

Wolfe, Tom, and E. W. Johnson, eds. *The New Journalism.* New York: Harper, 1973.

Wordsworth, William, and Samuel Taylor Coleridge. *The Lyrical Ballads.* 1802. Reprint, edited by R. L. Brett and A. R. Jones. London: Methuen, 1963.

Zeiger, Melissa F. *Beyond Consolation: Death, Sexuality, and the Changing Shapes of Elegy.* Ithaca, NY: Cornell University Press, 1997.

Zeisler, Sigmund. *Reminiscences of the Anarchist Case.* Chicago: University of Chicago Press, 1927.

INDEX

Aaron, Daniel, 88, 241n159

abolition of death penalty. *See* death penalty opposition

Actors' Gang, The, 213

Adams, Eliphalet, 24–26, 227nn15–16, 227nn21–22, 259n5

Adams, Henry, 81, 82, 239n108, 239n117

Adams, Julius J., 135

Adams, Olive Arnold, 135, 251nn33–34

admiration. *See* sympathy

Aldridge, John W., 256n7, 258nn66–67, 258n75, 259n88

Altgeld, John, 69, 85, 235n2, 235n6, 235n9, 240n140

American Civil Liberties Union (ACLU), 165, 193, 201, 258n82

American Civil War, 15, 69, 70, 74, 77, 78, 79, 88, 110, 112–15, 122, 144, 152, 237n43

American Revolution, 30, 75–76, 127, 128

Ames, Levi, 228–29n44

Amnesty International, 188, 193, 199, 200, 204, 222, 263n108, 263n120, 263n127

anarchism, 68, 73, 75, 77, 79, 80, 81, 82, 84, 87, 103, 104, 239n115

Anderson, Benedict, 14, 226n18

anti-Semitism, 108, 110–11, 115–16, 118, 119, 126, 136, 245n14, 247n68

Aristides, 41, 48–49, 57, 58, 59, 60, 64, 65, 230n19, 231nn64–65, 233n118, 233nn128–29, 233n134, 234n139, 234nn160–61, 234n163, 235nn169–79

Arlett, Robert M., 178, 256n8, 257n49, 258n70

Armour, Philip, 70

Armstrong, Ken, 264n13, 264n16

Arnold, Reuben, 110

art,

artistic reputation, 14, 16, 88, 89, 102, 241n159

imaginative literature, 11, 14, 60, 61, 87–

104, 132, 136, 141, 144–46, 207, 209, 210, 220, 224
literary status, literary merit 14, 42, 87–91, 100, 102–104, 241n159
political art, 212, 213, 214, 218, 220, 224, 241n159, 242n178, 244n230, 264n6, 265n25
Artists Network, 213
Asbury, Herbert, 113, 121, 246n27, 246n43, 248n88
Ashcroft, John, 223, 267n87
Auchmutey, Jim, 245n16
Aveling, Edward, 86, 240n142
Avery, Rev. Ephraim K., 15, 17, 38–65 passim, 69, 229n1, 229n8, 230n32, 233n114, 233n118, 234n156, 234n159, 234nn164–65
Avrich, Paul, 237n39, 238n92, 239n107, 240n154

Baldwin, James, 149–56, 159, 252nn71–74, 252n76, 252n78, 253nn80–81, 253nn85–86, 253n88, 253n90, 253n92, 253n94, 253nn96–99, 253nn101–102, 253n107, 254nn110–12, 254n115, 254nn117–19, 254n121
ballads. *See* ephemeral literature
Baptist Church, 83
Barrett, Nicole, 164
Bealer, Rev. Alex, 248n103
Beauchamp, Keith, 132, 250n13
Beckett, C. W., 243n201, 244n231
Beckman, Karen, 261n55
Beets, Betty Lou, 208
Belknap, Michal R., 250n21, 250n22, 251n32
Bennett, Fremont O., 236n31, 239n106
Benson, Barry, 120
Berlow, Alan, 267nn86–87
Besant, Annie, 85
Bessler, John D., 183, 200, 209, 259n97, 262n82, 263n103, 264nn4–5
Biedenkapp, Georg, 241n171
Bingham, Frances, 95, 243n200
Black, Hortensia, 73–74, 237n41
Black, William P., 76, 77, 82, 91, 241n170
Blank, Jessica. *See The Exonerated*

Blau, Joseph, 118
Bleyer, Jennifer, 265n24
Boaz, Dennis, 164
Boland, Eavan, 146, 252n69
Bonner, Raymond, 264n20
Bonney, Charles Carroll, 72, 83, 236n23, 236n26, 239n121, 239n124
Bosco, Ronald A., 228n25
Boston, Patience, 202
Boudreau, Kristin, 226n19
Bradley, Mamie, 131, 132, 136, 139, 147–48, 253n109
Brady, Tom, 133–34, 158, 251n24, 251nn26–27, 251n29, 255n142
Bragg, Melvyn, 257n50, 258n59, 258n64, 258n68
Brandeis, Louis, 126
Bricker, Rev. L. O., 109, 245–46n18
Bright, Stephen B., 209–10
broadsides. *See* ephemeral literature
Brooks, Gwendolyn, 146–49, 252n68
Brown, Dana, 192
Brown, John, 78–79, 91, 128, 139, 238n83, 241n170
Brundage, W. Fitzhugh, 123, 246n21, 248n99
Bruno, Giordano, 87
Bryant, Caroline, 132, 133, 250n15
Bryant, Roy, 131–36, 142, 151, 156–59, 254n134
Buchanan, Joseph, 73, 236n32, 237n38, 237n49
Buchman, Allan, 215
Buckley, William F., 166, 178, 189, 205, 256n8, 256nn10–11, 256n15, 257n56, 258n63, 258n65, 258nn71–72, 79, 259n99, 260n8, 263n134
Burnham, Louis, 133, 137, 250nn19–20, 251n43, 252n77
Burns, Christopher, 261n64
Burns, William J., 121
Burt, Olive Wooley, 248nn104–105
Buscemi, Steve, 213
Bush, George W., 193, 194, 197, 199, 202–206, 211–12, 215, 223, 260n8, 260n33, 263n116, 263n132, 263n134, 263n136, 264nn18–20
Butterfield, Fox, 264n18, 265n21

Cabot, James Elliot, 241n170
Cahan, Abraham, 114, 125–26, 247n50
Campbell, John, 228n27
Camus, Albert, 218
capital punishment. *See* death penalty
capital trials, 11
capitalism, 17, 68–70, 76, 78, 80, 83, 84,
    89, 95, 96, 99, 101, 102, 108, 111–12,
    115–16, 124–25
Carlson, Tucker, 206, 264n138
Carmen, Walt, 89
Carson, Fiddlin' John, 124
Carus, Paul, 236n33
Center on Wrongful Convictions, 213
Chamblit, Rebekah, 189, 228n24, 260n7
charity. *See* clemency
Cheesewright, Arthur, 79, 241n174
Chicago. *See* Illinois
child labor, 105–107, 111–12, 245n6
Christian Coalition, 189, 194
Chura, Patrick, 156, 254n125, 254n127,
    254n134
Civil Rights Movement, 16, 129, 131, 135,
    137, 142, 151, 163, 255n158
Clap, Nathaniel, 227n11
Clarke, Mary Carr, 42, 46–47, 49–50, 53–57,
    60, 61, 62, 65, 231nn55–58, 232n71,
    232n96, 232nn102–103, 233nn111–12,
    233nn115–17, 233n119, 234n141,
    234nn144–45, 234nn151–52, 234n167
Clayburgh, Jill, 213
clemency, 12, 15, 17, 28, 29, 69, 81, 82, 85,
    86, 105, 108, 116, 119, 122, 124, 170,
    188, 189, 193–96, 199, 201–205, 209,
    221, 222, 223, 228n42, 237n39,
    237n49, 247n68, 248n80, 259n6,
    262n74, 263n104, 263n108, 263n120,
    263n127, 267nn86–87
Clews, Henry, 71, 236n22
Cohen, Daniel M., 227n12, 264n137
Cohen, Nathan, 151, 253n82, 253nn105–106
Coleridge, Samuel Taylor, 229n49
Coles, Joanna, 197, 260n28, 260n30,
    261n67, 262n76, 262n97
Colin, Mattie Smith, 254n109
Columbia Law School, 213
communism, 70, 92, 136–37, 151, 255n141

commutation. *See* clemency
compassion. *See* sympathy
Congregational Church, 44, 46, 55
Conley, Jim, 107–109, 111
Connema, Richard, 265n34
Connolly, C. P., 249n106
Cook, Kerry, 215, 217, 218
Coolidge, John, 45, 231nn42–43
Cornell, Sarah Maria, 37–65 passim, 107,
    201, 234n156
corporations. *See* capitalism
Council of Europe, 222
Courts, Gus, 133
courts, courtroom. *See* judicial system
Crane, Gregg, 18, 226n20
Crane, Walter, 243n203, 243n217
Cridge, A. D., 243n214
criminal justice system. *See* judicial system
criminal narratives, 28, 29, 30, 31, 32, 33,
    34, 35, 177, 179, 228n44
Criscuolo, Michael, 266n35
cultural belief. *See* public opinion
Culture Project, 213, 215

Dalai Lama, 218
Dana, James, 227n11
Danforth, Samuel, 27
Darrow, Clarence, 119
Davidson, Cathy, 226n2, 227n6
Davidson, Richard, 137, 141–43, 251n53
Davis, Ossie, 137, 213
Dawidowicz, Lucy, 126, 249n118
Dawnay, Ivo, 205, 263n135
Dead Man Walking, 212, 220
death penalty,
    evolving standards of decency. *See* US
        Supreme Court
    juvenile capital offenders, 211
    mentally retarded capital offenders, 209,
        211, 264–65n20
    moratorium on executions, 211, 212, 213,
        214, 219, 220, 223
    opposition, 17, 31–34, 118, 163, 172, 178,
        180, 183, 193, 195, 198, 201–202, 209,
        210, 211–13, 219–21, 222, 262n82
Debs, Eugene, 82, 91, 119, 121–22,
    239n116, 241n169, 247n74, 248n89

De Cleyre, Voltairine, 94–95, 99, 242n195, 243n196, 243n210, 243n216
Dee, Ruby, 137
Dennehy, Brian, 213
Denning, Michael, 102, 244nn234–36
Dente, Wade, 136–37
desegregation, 16, 17, 130, 133–35
Dettmer, Joerg-Michael, 262n87
Dewey, John, 255n158
Didion, Joan, 167, 171, 256n13, 257n29
Diether, Charles, 241n171
Diggs, Charles, 136
Dinnerstein, Leonard, 108, 120, 245n14, 247n73, 248n81, 248n83, 249n107, 249n120
Dooley, Tom, 212–13
Dorsey, Hugh, 112–15
Dougherty, George S., 121, 248n86
Douglas Ann, 226n2
Dray, Philip, 250n21, 251n42
Drescher, Martin, 244n232
Dreyfuss, Richard, 213
Driver, Tom F., 155, 252n79, 254n120
Dublin, Thomas, 231n41, 231n46, 231n53
Duncan, Tracy, 261n61, 262nn72–73, 262n88, 263n102
Durfee, John, 37–38, 43, 46, 49

Earle, Steve, 209, 212
Eddy, Samuel, 57, 64
Edelshtadt, David, 243n199
Edmundson, Mark, 173–76, 179, 257nn39–40, 257n43, 257n51, 258n69, 258n73, 259n105
Eisenhower, Dwight D., 135, 158
Ellis, Rodney, 212, 265n22
Ellison, Michael, 266n66
Emerson, Ralph Waldo, 10, 69, 76, 77, 78, 225n1, 238n69, 241n170
Engel, George, 67, 68, 74, 77, 78, 236n18
ephemeral literature, 12, 14, 15, 23, 40, 43, 61, 63, 67, 72, 73, 80, 81, 85, 86, 88, 90, 99, 100, 102, 103, 104, 109, 114–15, 118, 124–25, 127–28, 135, 136, 146, 201, 209, 212–13, 229n44
Etheridge, Tom, 131
European Union, 193

European revolutions, 75–77, 97, 128
Evers, Medgar, 136, 152
execution-day sermons, 23, 24, 25, 32, 33, 167, 196, 205, 217, 218, 228n25
Execution of Wanda Jean, The, 209
Executioner's Last Songs, The, 212
executions, extralegal. *See* lynching
executions, private, 173, 183, 187, 196, 198, 200, 262n82
executions, public, 12, 15, 16, 19, 23, 28, 29, 33, 34, 97–98, 173, 178, 179, 183–84, 187–89, 195–96, 198, 206, 227n12, 228n31, 262n82
Exonerated, The, 213–20, 265nn26–29, 265n31, 265n33, 266nn35–58, 266nn60–65, 266nn67–68, 266n71
exonerations. *See* wrongful convictions

factories, factory workers, 15, 37, 38, 39, 44–48, 50–55, 70, 80, 105–107, 110–13, 115, 121, 127–28, 231n41, 231n45
Factory Girl, The, 42
Fairfield, Lincoln Sumner, 230n12, 230n18
Farrow, Mia, 213
Faugeres, Margaretta, 32–34, 229n47
Faulkner, William, 144–45, 250n23, 252nn56–57, 252n65
Featherstone, Joseph, 253n83
Feldman, Rob, 261n66
fellow-feeling. *See* sympathy
fiction. *See* novels
Field, Marshall, 70, 85
Fielden, Samuel, 68, 78, 79, 80, 85, 236n18
Fiering, Norman, 226n2, 227n3
First Amendment, 75, 82, 84, 97–98, 118, 200
Fischer, Adolph, 67, 68, 75, 81, 87, 94, 236n18
Fisher, Philip, 266n40
Fisk, Wilbur, 65
Flanagan, Christopher, 29, 34
Flanagan, Tim, 262n70
Fliegelman, Jay, 226n2, 227n3
Foner, Philip S., 236n18, 237n39, 237n44, 237nn47–51, 237nn59–60, 238n74, 238n76, 238n84, 238n96, 238nn98–100, 239n103, 239n111, 240n138, 243n199, 244n232

Foran, Martin, 244n235
Forbes, Peres, 227n11
forgiveness. *See* clemency
Foucault, Michel, 34, 229n50
Frank, Leo, 15–16, 17, 105–28, 129, 131, 136
Frank, Lucille, 127, 249n121
Frank, Moses, 114
Frankena, William, 226n2
Franklin, Benjamin, 21
free speech. *See* First Amendment
Frey, Robert Seitz and Nancy Thompson-Frey, 245n14, 246n20, 247n64, 247n75, 249n112, 249n124

Galilei, Galileo, 87
Garret, Katherine, 24, 189, 259n5
Garrett, Danny, 190
Garvey, John, 167, 176, 256n14, 257n55, 258n60, 258n75
Gary, Joseph, 73, 85, 237nn40–41
Gauger, Gary, 216, 217
Georgia, 105–106, 108–10, 113, 115–25
Giauque, Richard, 165
Gilmore, Gary, 16, 17, 162–86, 204
Gilmore, Mikal, 257n
Gioia, Dana, 88, 104, 240n156, 244n242
Goldblum, Jeff, 213
Golden, Harry, 247nn76–77, 249n108
Goldman, Emma, 74, 98, 103, 237n42, 241n167, 243n213, 244n239
Goldsby, Jacqueline, 131, 249n2, 250n3
Goldwasser, Amy, 266n39, 266n56, 266n62, 266n67
Gompers, Samuel, 69, 119, 240n147
Gonzales, Alberto, 223
Goodman, Ellen, 260n31
Gortatowsky, Joseph Dewey, 110
Gould, Jay, 80
government, 15, 16, 18, 19, 21, 22, 25, 26, 28, 29, 30, 32, 34, 54, 78, 79–80, 92, 95–103, 108, 120, 125, 131, 133, 169, 172–73, 178, 180, 181, 199, 200, 202, 203, 205, 209, 215, 218, 222, 224, 226n5
Graczyk, Michael, 261nn59–60
Greece, ancient, 11
Greenberg, Jack, 129–31, 159–61, 163, 249n1, 250nn4–5, 255n148

Greene, Albert, 48, 59
Griffey, Peggy, 203
Griffin, Larry J., Paula Clark, and Joanne C. Sandberg, 110, 246n21
Grinnell, Julius, 78, 85
Guest, David, 172, 173, 176, 257n36, 257n42, 258n61, 259nn94–96

Haas, Herbert and Leonard, 249n120
Habermas, Jürgen, 14, 18, 103, 166, 181, 202, 222, 225–26nn16–17, 227n5, 244n240, 256n9, 258n81, 263n113
Haggerty, George E., 242nn179–89
Halberstam, David, 16, 131, 250n6
Halker, Clark D., 88, 89, 93, 102, 241n158, 241nn161–64, 242n185
Hallett, Benjamin F., 40, 229n8, 230n11, 231n59, 231n61, 63, 232n72, 232n74, 223nn126–27,134
Halttunen, Karen, 230n31
Hammond, Jeffrey A., 240n157
Hands Off Cain, 193
Hasian, Marouf, Jr., 113, 123, 246n42, 248n94
Hathaway, Lucy, 55
Hawthorne, Nathaniel, *The Scarlet Letter*, 12–13, 16, 166, 194, 222–23, 225nn2–15, 261n46
Hayes, Robert Earl, 217
Haymarket anarchists, 15, 17, 67–104, 105–106, 108, 110, 116–20, 125–28, 141, 210
Hearst, William Randolph, 107–108, 117, 245n15
Henderson, Hugh, 228n27
Hendler, Glenn, 226n2
Henig, Gerald S., 247n63
Herbers, John, 251n37
Herbert, Bob, 208, 264n3
Herndon, Harvey, 65, 229nn7–8, 235n168
Hersey, John, 175, 179, 185, 257n52, 258n74, 259n104
Hewes, Henry, 254n113
Higham, John, 71, 236n21
Hildreth, Richard, 40, 229nn2–5, 229nn9–10, 230n13, 233nn105–106, 234n16
Hilliard, Timothy, 227n11
Hitler, Adolf, 161
Hodges, Ann, 259nn2–3

Holliday, Billie, 141
Holmes, Lizzie, 81
Holmes, Oliver Wendell, 118, 120,
    247nn76–77
Howells, Mildred, 240n147
Howells, William Dean, 85, 86, 104,
    237n39, 240n135, 240n144, 244n244
Hughes, Charles Evans, 120
Hughes, Langston, 137–38, 139–41, 214,
    251n44, 251n48, 251n50
Hughes, Polly Ross, 261n51, 262n84
Huie, William Bradford, 134, 151–52, 155,
    250n15, 250n18, 253n85, 253n87,
    253n89, 253n91, 253n93, 254n126,
    254n134, 255n145
Hull, Paul C., 71, 236n20
Hume, David, 21
Huntley, Jobe, 140–41
Hurley, Ruby, 136
Huss, John, 87
Hutcheson, Francis, 21, 227n3
Hutner, Gordon, 226n2

identification. *See* sympathy
Illinois, 16, 67–72, 81, 84, 85, 118–19, 131,
    141, 150, 210–11, 212, 213, 220–23,
    264n16, 246n17, 265n23, 267nn75–77,
    267nn83–85
Illinois Supreme Court, 81, 85, 217
immigrants, 70–72, 79, 88, 108, 125–28
industrialization, 50, 53, 70, 80, 81, 89, 104,
    107–109, 111–12, 115–16
infanticide, 24, 28, 189, 195
Innocence Project, 213
insurrection. *See* sentiments, antigovern-
    ment
Internet, 12, 16, 193, 201, 202, 206,
    260n37, 263nn110–12, 263n114,
    263n116, 264n139

Jacobs, Andrew, 250n14
Jacobs, Sunny, 215–17, 218
Jagger, Bianca, 193, 199
James, Barry, 267n84
James, William, 69, 235–36n10
Jefferson, Thomas, 13, 21–23, 76, 128,
    227n3, 227nn7–9

Jensen, Erik. *See The Exonerated*
Jentz, John B., 238n89
Jesus, 87, 195, 253–54n109
Jews, 108, 110–11, 113–15, 118, 121,
    125–28, 129, 136–37, 158
Johnson, Stephen, 261n51, 262n84
Jones, Curtis, 250n16
journalists. *See* newspapers
judicial system, 14, 15, 16, 17, 18, 25, 26,
    30, 31, 35, 37, 42, 43, 48, 50, 51,
    57–65, 68, 70, 72, 73, 79, 80, 81, 85,
    89, 95, 100–101, 108, 110–20, 123,
    127, 130–32, 136, 142, 151, 154–59,
    164, 172, 189, 193, 199, 203, 204, 209,
    210, 214, 216, 217, 218, 219–20, 221,
    223, 226n20, 243n220
juries. *See* judicial system
Justice for All, 193
Justice Project, 213

Kallaugher, Kevin, 208
Kant, Immanuel, 227n5
Kasserman, David, 40, 230n15, 230n30,
    230n32, 232n90
Keaton, David, 215, 216
Keil, Hartmut, 238n89
Kellman, Steven G., 258n75
Kempton, Murray, 249n3
Kengott, George F., 231n44
Kessenides, Dimitra, 264n7
Kimball, John C., 75, 78–79, 84, 87,
    237n56, 238n81, 238n87, 239n130,
    240n155
King David, 205
King, Florence, 199, 262n92
King, Larry, 190, 191, 203–204, 259–60n6,
    260nn9–10, 260nn13–14, 260nn24–25,
    261n41, 261n54, 261n56, 261n63,
    263n119, 263n121, 263n123, 263n125,
    263n129
Kirschke, David, 193
Kirschke, Melody, 201
Knights of Labor, 89, 90, 241n166
Knights of Mary Phagan. *See* Ku Klux Klan
Koestler, Arthur, 218
Kokoralies, Andrew, 211
Ku Klux Klan, 122, 158, 255n141

labor reform movement, 15, 17, 67–75,
79–89, 91, 93, 96, 98, 101–103,
105–106, 108, 109, 115, 121, 124, 126,
127–28, 129, 131, 139, 239n115
Larsson, Cloyte Murdock, 131, 250n8
law, 21, 24–26, 29–32, 34, 60, 65, 77–79,
84–86, 104, 105, 109, 116–17, 120,
123–24, 130–31, 133, 135, 152, 163,
168–69, 173, 178, 180, 183, 189, 200,
204, 205, 210, 218, 220, 222, 224,
226n20
law and order. See public order
Lawson, John D., 236n15, 238nn82–83,
238n94, 245n11, 245n13, 245n17,
246n24, 246nn28–29, 246n45, 247n46,
247n52
Lee, George, 133
Lee, Harper, 156–61, 254nn123–26,
254nn128–35, 254nn137–40,
255nn143–47, 255nn149–60
Lee, Newt, 107, 109, 111
legal authorities. See law
Leibrant, James, 192
Lennon, Michael, 256n7, 256n13
Lewis, David Levering, 126, 249n113,
249n119
Lewis, Leon, 86, 240n141
Lezin, Katya, 209, 264nn10–11
Lichtblau, Eric, 250n14
Lindemann, Albert S., 111, 126, 246n30,
246n33, 249nn115–17
Lines, Andy, 262nn95–96, 262n98,
262n100, 263n101
Lingg, Louis, 67, 68, 75, 77, 82, 86, 87,
236n18, 239n115, 240n147
Liptak, Adam, 266nn69–70, 267nn73–74
literary reputation. See artistic reputation
literature. See art
Lloyd, J. William, 243n223
Locke, John, 178
Lombroso, Cesare, 75, 236n33, 237n57
Lowry, Beverly, 190–94, 206, 260nn11–12,
260nn18–19, 260nn21–22, 260n26,
260n29, 260nn34–36, 260n39, 261n42,
261n45, 261n49, 261n52, 263n115,
263n128
Lum, Dyer, 73, 74, 81, 94, 236n25, 237n37,

237n39, 237n48, 237n54, 239n105,
242n191, 243n208, 243n215
lynching, 15, 16, 17, 65, 105–11, 116, 119–
24, 127, 129–30, 131–46, 149, 200,
207, 226n4, 248n102, 249n123,
255n153
Lyons, Alexander, 118, 247n67

MacLean, Nancy, 111, 121–22, 127, 244n2,
244n4, 246nn31–32, 247n49, 247n53,
247n55, 248n87, 248n93, 249n123
Mailer, Norman, The Executioner's Song, 16,
164–86, 256n4, 256nn7–8, 256nn16–27,
257nn28–35, 257nn37–41, 257n44,
257nn46–47, 257n50, 257nn53–55,
257nn57–58, 258n66, 258nn78–80,
258nn82–84, 259nn86–91, 259n93,
259nn98–103, 259nn105–106
Male, Roy R., 226n2
marketplace. See public sphere
Marovitz, Sanford E., 249n111
Marshall, David, 226nn2–3
Marshall, Edward, 120
Marshall, Louis, 116, 120, 127, 248n83,
249n120
martyrdom, 77, 86, 87, 91, 96, 97, 98–99,
104, 127, 173, 194–95, 239n115,
240n147, 241n170, 254n109
Marx, David, 248n80
Marx, Karl, 79
Marx-Aveling, Eleanor, 85, 86, 240n134,
240n142
Mason, Jeremiah, 58
mass meetings. See public sphere
Massachusetts Bay Colony, 12, 14, 23
Masters, Edgar Lee, 90, 241n168
Masur, Louis, 31, 226–27n3, 227n12,
228n43
Mather, Cotton, 27, 228nn25–26
Mauro, Lucia, 266n37, 266n46
McCarten, John, 153–54, 253n83, 253n108
McConnell, Samuel P., 239n115
McCormick, Cyrus, 70
McLean, George N., 235n7, 236n24
McLoughlin, William C., 44, 50,
230nn33–35, 232n73
McGill, Ralph E., 251n32

Melnick, Jeffrey, 111–12, 114, 125, 245n5, 246n34, 246nn39–40, 247nn49–50, 249n110, 249n121
melodrama. *See* theater
Meltsner, Michael, 255n1
Menand, Louis, 181, 258n85
mercy. *See* clemency
Meredith, James, 152
Merrill, Robert, 175, 257n55, 259n92
Methodist Church, 15, 17, 37–44, 46, 49–56, 58, 64, 65, 70, 83–84
Metress, Christopher, 136, 141, 250n3, 250n9, 250n17, 251n28, 251n30, 251n39, 254n122
Milam, J. W., 131–36, 142, 151–52, 156–59, 249n3, 254n134
Mill, John Stuart, 227n5
Millet, Martha, 138–39, 251n46
Mills, Steve, 264n13, 264n16
Mississippi, 16, 131–32, 134–41, 149, 150, 152
mob violence. *See* lynching
Molette, Carlton W., 252n75, 253n99
Monge, Louis, 164
Montag, Sig, 246n24
Moon, Henry Lee, 141
Moore, Thomas, 243n204
Morris, William, 85
Mount, Thomas, 229n46
Mullan, John, 226n2
Munson, Fayette, 93, 242n186, 242n190, 243n218

Nader, Ralph, 265n24
National Association for the Advancement of Colored People (NAACP), 129, 131–32, 133, 136, 141, 165, 258n82
National Coalition to Abolish the Death Penalty, 222
nativism, 71, 116, 126, 128
Neebe, Oscar, 68, 74, 76, 79, 236n18
Nelson, Bruce C., 76, 238n66
Nelson, Cary, 102, 103, 244n230, 244n233, 244n238
New York State Council for the Arts, 213
newspapers, 39–41, 43, 50, 56, 58, 59, 67–73, 75, 80–83, 87–90, 95, 97–101, 103, 107, 108, 110, 111, 113, 116–19, 121–27, 129, 131, 135, 141–42, 166, 174, 182–83, 187, 194, 196, 198, 201, 207, 209, 210–11, 222, 229n8, 245n13, 248n80, 248n90, 262n82, 264n12
Newsweek, 162, 174, 257n45
Noble, Frederick, 72, 82, 86, 235n1, 236n28, 239n113, 240n148
Northwestern University Law School, 217, 221
novels, 21, 22, 23, 27, 29, 35, 37, 50, 60, 90, 114–15, 164, 166, 169, 176, 178–79, 181–82, 185–86, 226n20, 227n6, 228n32
Noxom, P. S. 83

Ochs, Adolph, 116, 248n83
O'Connor, Sandra Day, 265n23
Odell, George C., 230nn25–26
O'Donnell, Edward, 243n197
Oglesby, Richard J., 85, 237n49
Oliver, L.S., 241n175, 242n187, 243n198, 243n205, 243n211
Oney, Steve, 245n7, 248n102
Open Society Institute, 218–19, 266n65
oral history. *See* theater

Paine, Thomas, 65, 76, 128, 235n171, 237n63
pamphlets. *See* ephemeral literature
Parks, Mary, 143–44, 252n55
Parrish, Timothy L., 68, 235n3
Parsons, Albert, 67, 68, 70, 72–77, 80–81, 85, 87, 94, 97–98, 236n18, 237n43, 237n49, 238n65, 242n192
Parsons, Lucy, 74, 81, 91, 237n43, 237nn45–46, 237nn52–53, 237nn61–62, 238nn67–68, 238n70, 238nn72–73, 238n77, 238n80, 238nn85–86, 238n88, 238n97, 239nn101–102, 239n104, 239n125, 240nn132–33, 240nn149–51
Payne, Ethel, 254n109
Pedersen, Daniel, 260n38, 261n57, 263n130
penitence. *See* repentance
Phagan, Mary, 105–17, 119, 122, 124–25, 128, 245n5, 247n51

philosophy, 11
Pinkerton Detective Agency, 69, 99, 110
Pinsky, Robert, 104
Plato, 11, 18, 225n1
plays. *See* theater
Plummer, Amanda, 265n34
Poe, Edgar Allan, 61
poetry, 11, 12, 21, 23, 32, 43, 57–58, 62–63,
    67, 79, 87–104, 137–44, 146–49
political action, activism 89–90, 93–94,
    96–99, 101–104, 106, 116–18, 120,
    122, 124–27, 129, 130, 134, 137,
    139–41, 193, 210, 213, 214, 218, 221
political consent, 14, 13, 22, 25, 28, 43,
    105, 123, 124, 126
politicians, 11, 15, 131, 210, 212, 218, 221,
    223, 250n23
Polunsky, Allan, 199
Pope John Paul II, 193, 200
popular literature. *See* populism
populism, 37, 42, 43, 51, 58, 59, 60, 62, 67,
    88, 90, 92, 98, 102, 105, 114, 116, 122,
    124, 125, 129, 199, 213, 240n157,
    244n237, 247n55
Porter, Anthony, 211
Powderly, Terence, 89
Powell, Adam Clayton, Jr., 139, 251n47
Powers, Ann, 264n6
Prescott, Abraham, 43, 230n31
presidential race 2000, 212, 215
propaganda, 14, 15, 17, 46, 67, 79, 81, 87,
    89, 92, 94, 102, 103, 118–20, 124–28,
    135, 137, 141, 151, 188, 194, 203, 218,
    266n37
protest. *See* sentiments, antigovernment
Proteus, 41, 42, 230n22
public debate, 14, 17, 24, 38–43, 50, 56,
    58–60, 64–65, 70, 72, 80–81, 83,
    87–90, 92, 100, 103, 106, 107, 115–16,
    118–19, 127, 132, 136, 142, 159,
    163–67, 170, 178, 180, 184–85, 189,
    192, 193, 196, 197–99, 201, 207, 209,
    210, 211, 212, 218, 219, 221–22, 223,
    246n18, 259n4
public opinion, 11, 12, 14, 84, 85, 87–90,
    98, 102, 105, 108, 113–15, 117, 119–
    23, 125, 127–28, 130–32, 135, 141,
        150–51, 163, 165–66, 196, 201, 202,
        210, 233n118, 235–36n10, 239n115
public order, 14, 18, 21–27, 29, 31, 33–35,
        65, 123, 173, 175, 176, 178, 185, 195,
        200, 211, 218, 226n20, 227n5,
        233n118, 235n9, 264n18
public performances. *See* theater
public sentiments. *See* public opinion
public sphere, 11, 13–18, 24, 26, 28, 31, 34,
        37, 43, 60, 63–64, 67, 79, 85, 87–90,
        97–104, 113–15, 118–19, 122, 124–27,
        131, 133, 136, 150, 178, 185, 189,
        195–97, 199, 201–203, 206, 207, 208,
        209, 213, 214, 215, 218, 221, 223,
        242n189
Pullman, George, 70
punishment. *See* vengeance

racism, 107–10, 121–23, 126–28, 129,
        133–34, 136–37, 139, 145, 150, 159,
        161, 198, 201, 220, 250n23, 255n158
Ramazani, Jahan, 92, 103, 241–42n176,
        242n177, 242nn181–82, 242n193
Rampersad, Arnold, 140, 251n49
Rampton, Calvin, 164
Randolph, A. Philip, 136
Rascoe, Burton, 111–12, 116–17, 244n1,
        244n3, 245n15, 246n25, 246n35, 246n38,
        246n41, 247n58, 248n90, 248n100
Ratcliffe, R. G., 263n136
Rauschenbusch, Walter, 83
Reade, Brian, 200, 262n75, 262n93, 263n107
readers, 11, 12, 14, 18, 21–24, 29, 33, 35,
        40–41, 43, 60, 63–65, 73, 75, 86, 88,
        90, 95, 97, 100, 102, 104, 109, 113,
        139, 159, 164, 166, 175, 180, 201, 206,
        226n20, 227n6, 228n32, 237n39,
        244n235
rebellion. *See* sentiments, antigovernment
redemption. *See* rehabilitation
Reed, Julia, 198, 262n80
reform. *See* rehabilitation
reform of death penalty. *See* death penalty,
        opposition
rehabilitation, 168–69, 180, 187, 190–93,
        199, 203–206, 222
Reitzel, Robert, 94, 242n194

religion, 23–28, 33, 83–84, 91, 93, 118, 187–95, 198–200, 201, 204–205, 217–18, 228n25, 260n6, 260n38
religious enthusiasm, 54–55
Renton, Alex, 262n94, 262n99
repentance, 13, 27, 28, 29, 30, 167–68, 173, 189, 191, 198, 202
retribution. *See* vengeance
revenge. *See* vengeance
Rhodes, Norman, 217
Richards, Ann, 211
Richards, Lydia Platt, 91, 241n172, 243n226
Rivenburgh, Eleanor, 249n121
Roan, Leonard S., 125
Robbins, Tim, 213
Robertson, Pat, 188, 189, 193, 194, 195, 259–60n6
Rodgers, Esther, 28, 29, 195
Rodriguez, Victor, 203–204, 263n122
Rogers, John, 28, 228nn29–30, 261n58
Rogers, William Curran, 117, 247n61
Rogoff, Gordon, 253n103
romance. *See* sentimentality
romanticism, 21, 32, 60, 62, 259n105
Rose, David, 197, 262n74, 263n104
Ross, Harold, 109, 246n19
Rosser, Luther, 110
Roth, Philip, 153, 253n83, 253n104
Rousseau, Jean-Jacques, 178, 227n5
Roy, Gregor, 253n84
Ruchames, Louis, 238n83
Rush, Benjamin,15, 16, 19, 21–24, 27, 29, 33, 34, 173, 179, 187, 202, 223, 226n1, 226n3, 227n10, 228n31, 228n42, 258n77, 267n88
Ryan, George, 211–12, 213, 214, 220–23, 264nn14–16, 266n72, 267nn78–85

Sabir, Wanda, 266n36, 266n64, 266n68, 266n71
Salamon, Julie, 264nn8–9
Salter, William, 77, 81, 82, 84, 235n5, 235n10, 238n71, 239n110, 239n112, 239n115
Sarah Maria Cornell; or, the Fall River Murder, 42
Sarandon, Susan, 213

Scheffler, Judith A., 176–77, 257n58, 258n62
Schiff, Jacob, 126
Schiller, Lawrence, 164, 166
Schmidt, Ernst, 85, 86, 240nn136–37, 240n143
Schneirov, Richard, 241n166
Schor, Esther, 103, 242n178, 244n241
Schwab, Michael, 68, 77, 79–80, 85, 236n18, 236n33
Scoresby, William, 45, 231nn47–51
Scott, Dred, 84
seduction novels. *See* sentimentality
segregation. *See* desegregation
sensational fiction. *See* sentimentality
sensibility. *See* sympathy
sentimental fiction. *See* sentimentality
sentimentality, 21, 50–51, 53–55, 58, 60–63, 93–94, 101, 113–14, 146–47, 174, 185, 201, 205, 226n2, 234n156
sentiments, antigovernment, 12, 14, 15, 16, 19, 23–26, 28, 30–34, 38–39, 41–43, 58–59, 73, 75–79, 83, 84, 86, 87, 89, 92–96, 98–102, 103–104, 114–15, 120, 123–24, 127, 129, 133, 134–35, 137–40, 143, 158, 172, 174, 176–77, 179, 181, 187, 189, 193, 197–202, 207, 209, 210–13, 218, 221, 222, 223, 224, 228n40, 228n42, 230n32, 235n171, 235n2, 235n8, 245n15, 248n103
Shakespeare, William, 60, 61, 88, 148
Shapiro, Yonathan, 249n114
Shaw, George Bernard, 85
Shaw, W. David, 242n176
Shay's Rebellion, 228n42
Sherrill, Robert, 255–56n1
Shurtleff, William, 24–26, 227n11, 227n14, 227nn17–20, 262n83, 266n59
Simon, John, 252n75
Skipwith, Robert, 22
Slaton, John M., 108, 112, 118–20, 122–23, 245n14, 246n36, 247n54, 248n79, 248n91
slavery, 74, 77–78, 121, 129, 146, 237n43
Smith, Adam, 21, 179, 227n3, 258n76
Smith, Carl, 70, 73, 75, 79, 84, 235n8, 236n16, 236n34, 237n55, 238n93, 238n95, 239n128

Smith, Lamar, 133
social control. *See* public order
social problems, social questions, 17, 44,
    53, 68–70, 72, 80–81, 84, 87–88, 92,
    95, 102–104, 106–108, 111–12, 116,
    122, 125–28, 129, 133, 145, 150, 167,
    180, 197–98, 200, 207, 212
social stability. *See* public order
socialism, 68, 70, 72–73, 76, 80–82, 84, 87,
    89, 102, 126–28, 252n79
Socrates, 87
Sommer, Elyse, 266n38
songs. *See* ephemeral literature
Sontag, Susan, 153, 253n100
Soros, George, 213
Southern Reconstruction, 112, 115–16,
    121–22, 124, 146
Spalding, J. L., 82, 239n114
Spearhead, *Stay Human* 212
Spies, August, 67, 68, 70, 71–77, 79–80,
    83–87, 97–98, 236n18, 237n49,
    237n64, 239n115
Springsteen, Bruce, 212
Stanton, Elizabeth Cady, 21, 120, 227n4,
    248n82
state. *See* government
Stevens, Earnest Wakefield, 138, 251n45
Stone, I. F., 136, 251n36
Stone, Melville, 237n38
Stowe, Harriett Beecher, 77–78
Strand, Mark, 146, 252n69
Strider, Clarence, 136
Strom, Linda, 194, 206, 260n23, 261n53
Sullivan, Andrew, 195, 261n65
Sullivan, Thomas P., 220
Sunday, Billy, 118, 247n71
Swango, Curtis, 156, 254n126
sympathy, 14–16, 19, 21–26, 28–35, 49,
    61–64, 69, 73–75, 80, 82, 89–90, 98,
    100–103, 139, 141–43, 159–61, 167,
    169–77, 179–83, 185–86,191, 193–95,
    197–98, 201, 202, 205–207, 114, 209,
    217, 218, 222, 223–24, 228n32,
    229n44, 229n48, 234n150, 239n115,
    241n166, 242n178, 255n153, 257n55,
    259n92, 262n82

Tafero, Jesse, 217
Taubman, Howard, 154, 252n75, 254n114
Tebbel, John, 23, 227n13
television, 16, 22, 131, 188, 195, 196, 201,
    202, 203, 204, 209, 259n2
Texas, 11, 187, 193, 196, 197, 199, 202,
    204, 207–208, 210, 211–12, 215, 217,
    223, 260n42,47, 265n22, 267n86
Texas Coalition to Abolish the Death
    Penalty, 194
theater, 42, 46–47, 49–50, 55–56, 61, 65,
    79, 88–89, 98–99, 102–103, 136–37,
    149–55, 178, 198, 205,–206, 213–20,
    230n25
Thew, Daniel, 30
Thomas, H. W., 69
Thomas, Marlo, 213
Thompson, W.E., 245n10
Thoreau, Henry David, 30, 77–78, 128, 139,
    228n40, 238n73, 238n75, 238nn78–79
Thulstrup, Thure, 235n8
Tibbs, Delbert, 215, 216, 219
Tifft, Susan E., and Alex S. Jones, 247n57
Till, Emmett, 16–17, 131–47, 149–58, 161
Tompkins, Jane, 18, 226n20, 226n2
Toqueville, Alexis, 227n5
Torn, Rip, 151
Trumbull, M. M., 81–82, 84, 239n109,
    239n118, 239n131
Tucker, Carolyn Moore, 192
Tucker, Karla Faye, 11–12, 16–17, 187–206,
    207–208, 211, 212, 259nn2–4, 259n6,
    260n9, 260n15, 260n23, 260n27,
    260nn31–33, 260n37, 263n132
Turner, Darwin, 152, 253n98
Turner, John, 237n50, 240n153
Turow, Scott, 264n17
Turpin, Waters E., 252n75, 254n116

United Nations, 200
United States, colonial, 12, 14–16, 23–24,
    27, 167, 177, 187–88, 195, 217–18
United States, early republic, 15, 19, 21, 30,
    33–34, 51, 187, 223
United States Supreme Court, 16, 74, 81,
    85, 118, 119, 129–30, 133–35, 163–65,
    188, 203, 204, 210, 255n1, 265n20

Brown v. Board of Education Supreme Court Decision, 16, 130, 133–35, 145–46, 158, 161
evolving standards of decency, 163, 165, 166, 173, 210
Furman v. Georgia, 163, 166, 178, 256n2, 256n5, 256n12, 263n124
Gregg v. Georgia, 163, 256n3, 256n6, 263n126
Ury, John, 27, 228n28
Utah, 165, 169, 172, 173

vengeance, 13, 17, 33, 63–65, 85, 95, 139, 168, 173, 194, 199, 200, 203, 222, 263n124
Verhovek, Sam Howe, 259n4, 260n20, 261nn43–44, 262n86, 263n109, 263n133, 264nn1–2

Wald, Alan M., 241nn159–60
Walt, Kathy, 260nn15–17, 260n27, 260n32, 261nn47–48, 261n50, 261n62, 261n68, 262nn69–70, 262n78, 262n81, 263n118, 263n131
Warren, Robert Penn, 145–46, 152, 252nn58–64, 252nn66–67, 253n95
Watson, Tom, 110, 114, 121–22, 124–25, 127–28, 246n23, 247n47, 248n92, 249n109, 249n123
Watt, Ian, 228n32
Weinhold, Dick, 198
Welch, Matt, 265n24
Wells, Ida B., 21, 227n4
Wheeler, Tom, 213, 265n25
Wheelock, Lewis, 83, 239n120, 239nn122–23, 239n126
Whitaker, Hugh Stephen, 133, 251n25
White, Hugh, 131
White Citizens' Councils, 134, 148, 158, 255n141
White, Mary Jo, 219, 220
Whitfield, Stephen J., 250n12, 250n15

Whittier, John Greenleaf, 240n135
Wiggins, Gene, 110, 246n22
Wilbur, Thomas, 38, 62, 63
Wilgoren, Jodi, 265n23, 267nn75–77, 267n83, 267n85
Wilkins, Roy, 132, 136
Williams, Catharine, 41, 43, 46–48, 51–56, 58–59, 61–64, 230n20, 230n29, 231n54, 231n60, 231n62, 231nn66–68, 232n69, 232nn75–95, 232n100, 232n104, 233nn107–10, 233n113, 233nn124–25, 233nn130–31, 233n136, 233–34n137, 234n138, 234nn142–43, 234nn146–50, 234n153, 234n162
Williams, Daniel E., 26, 187, 227n12, 227n23, 228–29n44, 229n46, 259n1, 263n117
Williams, Montel, 213, 219, 220, 266n36, 266n68, 266n71
Williams, Robin, 213, 265n34
Wills, Gary, 226n2, 227n3
Wilmer, C. B., 118, 247n68
Wilson, Robert S., 243n196, 243n202, 243n227
Winger, Debra, 213
Wise, Stephen Samuel, 118–19, 123, 247n66, 247n72, 248n95
Withington, Lathrop, 243n196
women, unmarried, 44–48, 106–107, 231n41
Wordsworth, William, 32–33, 60, 90, 229nn48–49
World Wide Web. *See* Internet
wrongful convictions, 211, 212, 213, 215, 216, 219, 220, 266n53

Young, John, 15, 29–34, 228nn33–39, 228n41
Young, S. Edward, 118

Zeiger, Melissa F., 241n176
Zeisler, Sigmund, 240n139